W9-ALU-161

HOLLYWOOD

ALSO BY GARSON KANIN

PLAYS
Born Yesterday • The Smile of the World • The Rat Race •
The Live Wire • Come On Strong

Musicals
Fledermaus • Do Re Mi

Adaptations
The Amazing Adele • The Good Soup • A Gift of Time

NOVELS
Blow Up a Storm • Do Re Mi • The Rat Race •
Where It's At • A Thousand Summers

SHORT FICTION
Cast of Characters

FILMS
With Ruth Gordon
A Double Life • Adam's Rib • Pat and Mike • The Marrying Kind

In Collaboration
From This Day Forward • The More the Merrier • The True Glory

Original Stories
High Time • The Right Approach • The Girl Can't Help It

Original Screenplays
It Should Happen to You • Where It's At • Some Kind of a Nut

NONFICTION
Remembering Mr. Maugham • Felix Frankfurter: A Tribute •
Tracy and Hepburn

HOLLYWOOD:

Stars and Starlets,
Tycoons and Flesh-Peddlers,
Moviemakers and Moneymakers,
Frauds and Geniuses,
Hopefuls and Has-Beens,
Great Lovers and Sex Symbols

GARSON KANIN

 Limelight Editions ● New York

First Limelight Edition, March 1984

ISBN 0–87910–010–9

Manufactured in the United States of America

Library of Congress Cataloging in Publication Data

Kanin, Garson, 1912-
    Hollywood; stars and starlets, tycoons and flesh-
peddlers, moviemakers and moneymakers, frauds and
geniuses, hopefuls and has-beens, great lovers and sex
symbols.

1. Kanin, Garson, 1912–   . 2. Moving-picture
producers and directors—United States—Biography.
I. Title.
[PN1998.A3K28   1984]   791.43′0233′0924 [B]   83-27547

Acknowledgment is made to Warner Bros. Music for the excerpt from
"Hooray for Captain Spaulding" by Bert Kalmar,
and Harry Ruby. © 1936 Harms, Inc. Copyright Renewed. All rights
reserved. Used by permission of Warner Bros. Music.

HOLLYWOOD

1

Mr. Samuel Goldwyn and I sat alone in his throne room, looking at each other.

We had met for the first time some five minutes earlier, and he had insisted, testily, that our interview be private. Abe Lastfogel of the William Morris Agency had brought me in, made the introduction, and now was gone.

It was a crucial moment for me. A nod of this formidable man's head could signal the beginning of my career in films. Was there anything I should be doing—could be saying—to elicit that movement? The pause stretched out.

Mr. Goldwyn, his right forefinger clamped firmly to the side of his nose, continued to study me through his small gray eyes. It was as though I were a mysterious, unopened box that had been delivered to him, and he was trying to guess the contents.

In the inflating silence I was taking him in. A large man. Why had I expected him to be small? Beautifully dressed and groomed and shod. A smooth, pink face under a finely shaped, bald dome. An impressive presence.

At last his finger came down from the side of his nose.

He clasped his hands under his chin and said, in a high, penetrating voice, "Sidney Howard tells me you're a very clever genius."

Could it be? Had I heard correctly? Did I own, so soon, a personal Goldwynism? Never mind. He had cued me neatly into a story that would at least give me a chance to show him I could talk. I had begun to feel doltish, sitting there mutely.

"Well, Mr. Goldwyn," I said, "that's certainly kind of Sidney Howard—and generous—but I have to tell you every time I hear that word I'm reminded of a letter Bernard Shaw once wrote to a young playwright."

"*What* word?" asked Goldwyn.

" 'Genius.' The playwright was a fellow named James Elroy Flecker and he'd written this play called *Hassan* and—" Oh, Christ. Goldwyn looked bored. I was flopping. My palms were moistening. Should I stop? Too late. I forged ahead. "—and he sent it to Shaw. And Shaw wrote back, 'My dear Mr. Flecker, *Hassan* is a work of genius, but do not take this as a compliment. Geniuses are tuppence ha'penny in London. What is difficult to find is a writer who is sober, industrious, honest, and has been for several years at his last situation.' "

Goldwyn digested the story and nodded, sagely. Had I done all right, after all? My spirits rose.

"Shaw," said Goldwyn, "is a real tough bastard. Hard to get along. To do business with. And say, listen—me, I can do business with *anybody*. But not with him. Still and all, anyhow —what he says there about geniuses and tuppence and working-men there—he's damn right."

He poured a glass of water from a silver carafe, and drank it slowly.

"Is it true," I asked, "the story that he ended a negotiation with you saying, 'The difficulty is, Mr. Goldwyn, that you are interested only in art, while I am interested only in money'?"

"Listen," he said, nettled. "Don't believe everything you read in the goddam papers. In the newspapers. F'Chrissake."

"Right."

He studied me again.

"Well, young man. What can I do for you? What do you want?"

"What do *you* want, Mr. Goldwyn?"

"What?"

"*You* sent for *me,* didn't you?"

"*I* sent for *you*?" he repeated, amazed.

"Certainly," I said, without breaking the rhythm. "You paid my fare out here, didn't you?"

The ping-pong of negotiation was under way. I could almost hear him say, "Good shot!"

Instead, he grinned and said, "Say, you're pretty good!" Suddenly, the grin disappeared. His piercing eyes grew smaller, intensifying the sharpness of their focus. "Well, young man, let me ask you. How would you like to learn the business?"

"I'd like it," I said.

"And get *paid* the same time."

"Sounds great."

"I'm not making a firm offer, y'understand," he added quickly. "I'm only asking."

"I understand."

"All right," he said. "Now. So tell me something about yourself."

He leaned back in his chair and waited. His finger was back on the side of his nose.

I told him something about myself, carefully, all the while reflecting upon the curious set of circumstances that had brought me to this time and place:

I had been for several years an assistant to George Abbott, working with him on *Three Men on a Horse, Boy Meets Girl, Brother Rat, Room Service,* and other plays. After a string of failures, Mr. Abbott was enjoying a meteoric streak of success. Gossipy Broadway had it that the change in his fortunes had a good deal to do with that kid in his office. Although I did or said nothing to encourage this nonsensical idea, I confess I did or said nothing to discourage it, either.

There existed, at that time, a Broadway rivalry between George Abbott and another George—George S. Kaufman. They both wrote, both directed, both (at times) acted, both specialized in comedy, although now and again each ventured into other fields as well.

Each of them had champions and detractors. I thought them *both* surpassing. When a new comedy came up, the agent or producer or author or star usually had to decide: Abbott or Kaufman?

Beatrice Kaufman—Mrs. George S.—was Samuel Goldwyn's

3

eastern representative. It was she who got the idea that I might be a valuable piece of manpower for Mr. Goldwyn in California.

That is why an odd-looking, twenty-four-year-old bundle of nerves who had been an early high-school dropout, a mediocre musician, a burlesque stooge, a stock clerk at Macy's, a drama student, a mildly successful minor New York actor, and the director of one Broadway failure, was sitting here reciting a bowdlerized version of his professional life to Samuel Goldwyn.

"That's enough," I heard him say. "I get the whole idea of you."

"You do?"

"Sure. You're an ambitious kid. Like *I* used to be."

"Some people say you still *are.*"

He wheezed a laugh, his face crinkling with delight, and said, "They're right! You know it? They're right."

He rose. So did I. We shook hands, firmly.

"I'll talk to Abe," he said. "We'll see what we can work out. On some reasonable basis. How's your health?"

"Fine."

"You sure?"

"Sure I'm sure."

"Take care of it. Your health. And it will take care of you. Listen. You haven't got your health, you haven't got a goddam thing. *Remember* that. You lose a hold of your health and not only you're not worth a goddam thing to yourself you're not worth a goddam thing to *me.* I get up every morning. What time do *you* get up? Me, always before seven. And no coffee. Hot milk and sugar. You should be careful not to eat. Too much, I mean. And walk. I walk four five miles every day at least. This night life, f'Chrissake. I've seen it *kill* 'em. Listen, you know what I love? Ice-cream sodas. That's why I never eat them. Because one is not enough. I need *two.* So I don't have *any.* Nobody can take care of you but you yourself, y'understand?"

"Yes, sir."

"I tell you I get more goddam sick people around me here all the time—they all got migraines and ulcers and f'Chrissake heart attacks. I seem to pick 'em. That's why I asked you your health."

"It's fine," I said. "So far."

He looked at his watch, said, "Jesus!" and propelled me out of the room.

Abe had left a message for me with Goldwyn's secretary. I was to get a taxi and meet him back at his office.

On the way, I reviewed the meeting and made notes. When I reached the end and recalled Goldwyn's complaint that he always seemed to pick men with migraines, ulcers, and f'Chrissake heart attacks, it gave me pause.

"How'd it go?" asked Abe.

"I don't know. I've never done anything like it before so I've got no basis of comparison. He said he'd talk to you."

"He did?"

"Yes."

"That's good. That's a good sign. Now. I'm having lunch with Pan Berman—he's the head of RKO now—so you better come along. And tonight you'll have dinner with Frances and me at Chasen's. And with Benny Thau. He's Metro. It'll all get back to Sam, see?"

"What will?"

"These meetings. These two meetings. With Pan and Benny. I don't want him to think—Sam—he's getting a free ride."

"*I* did."

"What?"

"Well, he paid for my trip out here, didn't he?"

"But you're not talking business with Benny or with Pan. They're not interested in you."

"Oh."

"Let me handle it, okay?"

"Okay."

The next morning, he handled it and got Goldwyn to offer me

a seven-year contract starting at $250 a week for the first year, $400 the second, then in yearly stages—$600, $750, $1000, $1250, $1500.

I would be paid fifty-two weeks a year. Holidays would be worked out. Duties? Learn the business and then we'll see. Like most signers of seven-year contracts, I concentrated on the far end, the promise it held, the opportunity, the $1500.

It was 1937 and along with the rest of my generation I was still groggy from the slugging we had taken during the desperate Depression years. Further, having spent years in the hit-or-miss theatre, which offered possibilities of glory, but no security, the idea of a weekly paycheck throughout the year was intoxicating. Still, I was troubled by the vagueness of the arrangement.

"Don't worry about it," Abe advised. "Part of your job will be to *make* yourself a job. The main thing is to get in there. Get to know the business. Get to know *him*. And him, you."

Actually, there was no alternative. I had no prospects back East. My job with George Abbott had dwindled to a routine, part-time dead end.

I accepted Goldwyn's offer and did not return to New York. Instead, I checked into the Goldwyn Studios on Monday morning and Alice in Wonderland was a piker.

My first month there was euphoric.

I had somewhere to go every morning, a pleasant office, and an efficient secretary to assist me. I had the fascinating studio world to play with; charming, witty, talented colleagues; and a library of films at my disposal.

I was indeed learning the business. Each day was a revelation. I was acquiring not only the language of films, but the lingo.

The second month was less happy since I began to see that my chances of becoming a director were remote. Each of the major studios was making some seventy or eighty films a year. They ran huge factories with contract players and writers and

6

directors constantly assigned, reassigned, and substituted. Goldwyn, however, made only two or three pictures a year. Each one was expensive and important and it was doubtful that he would ever entrust one to someone who had never before made a movie.

The subject was seldom absent from my mind. I discussed it with friends, with people at the studio, with my agent, and (by mail) with my family.

A strategy occurred to me, and later became a plan. I would continue to study and work and observe. When I thought I was ready, I would try to get a small picture somewhere to direct on a loan-out basis. When that and the next two or three proved to be smash hits, I would return triumphantly to the Goldwyn Studios and become one of Goldwyn's directors.

To this end, I tried to find work involving the camera. I attempted to become part of a second unit on the Goldwyn lot. No luck. Second-unit directors were often required to have even greater expertise than the director.

Tests! I thought. That's it. Why not? Tests were being made constantly for makeup, hairdressing, costumes, and often for acting. But I was unsuccessful in getting even a test to direct, although they were being made daily by assistants, second assistants, casting directors, and, once or twice, by a casting director's secretary.

One afternoon, I took the matter up with Mr. Goldwyn at his home. I thought it best to pursue it in an informal, casual way.

"There are so many tests to make next week," I said. "Would you want me to direct one or two—to help out?"

"No, no," he said, impatiently. "I can't spare you for that. That's silly, a waste of time. Most tests are nothing."

"Still," I said, "it would give you some idea about what I can do."

"I *know* what you can do," he said. "I would just like you to *do* it."

"I think a lot of the tests are poorly made," I persisted.

7

"Sometimes you don't even get a chance to judge the person fairly, because the tests aren't really directed, they're just photographed."

"Well, what the hell do you think, we're going to spend a lot of time and money producing tests? A test is a test, that's all, it's not a picture."

"But why wouldn't it be a good thing for me? You say you want me to learn the business. If I directed a few tests and cut them myself and showed them to you—"

"What's the matter with you?" he said irascibly. "Jesus Christ, here you are, a young nobody, and you're getting this great opportunity, and you want to be a *test* director, f'Chrissake."

"I don't want to be a test director," I said. "I want to be a director."

"How can you be a director?" he said. "You've never directed."

"Well," I argued, "there was a time when Willie Wyler and John Ford and Leo McCarey had never directed."

"Don't you believe it," he said gravely.

The conversation ended, but not my determination.

In the months to come, I was to bring up the subject over and over and over again, always with the same result.

One afternoon, I went too far, pressed too hard. Goldwyn exploded.

"God damn it!" he shouted. "I don't want to hear any more about it! I want you to, God damn it, develop the way I'm developing you. You can be very helpful to me, very valuable. Directors, f'Chrissake. Directors are a dime a dozen. You know how many directors are in Hollywood? Yes! And most of them looking for work. But executives, producers—real producers, not these jerks call themselves producers. Producers, men who can take charge. With authority. What's a matter with you? Don't you see that when you're a producer, you *hire* directors? Producers hire directors, and sometimes they *fire* directors. Did you ever hear of a director hiring a producer? Did you ever

8

hear of a director *firing* a producer? Did you? No. So what do you want to be, the fellow who can get fired or the fellow who can do the firing?"

"Neither," I said.

He looked at me, shook his head tragically. "I don't understand you. I wish I could understand you. But I don't. You take a lot of patience, but maybe someday you'll learn. And maybe not."

"Well, Tallboy, what do *you* think?"

The first time he called me that I did not get it. I thought that perhaps in calling me "Tallboy," he was twitting me about my short stature. It turned out later that he was saying "Talboig" or "Talberg," meaning Irving Thalberg, the brilliant young producer who had become the head of Universal at the age of twenty, and of M-G-M a few years later.

Someone had erroneously suggested to Goldwyn that I resembled Irving Thalberg, and it pleased him to accept this as fact. He derived a vicarious pleasure out of having someone in his employ whom he could call "Talboig," especially since he paid "Talboig" less then he paid his secretary.

For years, he addressed me thus. "Talboig"—always followed by one long, wheezy, exhaled laugh.

Sam Marx, a friendly, huge, football player type, was a member of Goldwyn's large production staff when I came to work at the Goldwyn Studios. He had been Irving Thalberg's associate and closest friend. They had known each other back in New York when they were still young and reaching for their respective moons. When Thalberg made good in California, he sent for his friend, who worked at his side until Thalberg's death in 1936.

Marx had been Thalberg's right-hand man. Now he felt ready to strike out on his own.

It happened that Goldwyn needed a story editor. He knew if he offered Marx this position, Marx would turn it down. Instead, he told him he was looking for an associate producer who would in time be made a full producer. Marx accepted at once.

9

When he had been at the studio for a month or so, Goldwyn sent for him and said, "Marx, I'm going to ask you to do me a personal favor and I want you to do it. In fact, you're *going* to do it. Because I'm asking you."

"What is it, Mr. Goldwyn?"

"You know, Marx, I'm very tired and one of the reasons I'm very tired is that all around me I've got people who don't know how to do their jobs so that's why I'm very tired. These people. I'm not talking about *you,* y'understand. *You're* very good. That's why I'm going to ask you to help me."

"Yes?"

Goldwyn sighed and continued. "My whole story department. It's terrible. I don't have to tell you. You've been around. You've been here. What's the use? I'm in bad trouble so I'm going to ask you, Marx, as a personal favor to me, to go in there and set up a story department and run it any way you want. *Your* way. It shouldn't take you long. And as soon as you've got that department organized, then *you* hire a story editor. Anybody you want and then we'll see."

Sam Marx reports that he demurred, feeling he was about to be trapped.

"Well, I don't know, Mr. Goldwyn. I don't want to run a story department. I came here to be a producer."

"Who said you didn't? I'm asking you to do me a favor."

Thrust, parry. Parry, thrust. In matters of psychological fencing, skill is often less important than will.

Goldwyn prevailed. Now, a year later, Marx found himself still the story editor at the Goldwyn Studios. The story department he had organized and was running was considered the best in the business, but Marx was restive, unhappy, and frustrated.

Goldwyn, too, began to be dissatisfied with the situation. The story department was fine, yes; but he was paying Marx far more than a story editor was worth. The subject came up often in their increasingly acrimonious meetings.

"I checked around," said Goldwyn gloomily one day. "You're getting twice what any story editor in town is getting."

"But I'm not *supposed* to be a story editor, Mr. Goldwyn.

the name of Christian charity, being unendingly submissive and respectful. When she began therapy my patient revered her father for his mildness and "lovingness." It was not very long, however, before she came to realize that his meekness was weakness, and that in his passivity he had deprived her of adequate parenting every bit as much as her mother had with her mean self-centeredness. She finally saw that he had done nothing to protect her from her mother's evil and nothing, in fact, to confront evil, leaving her no option but to incorporate her mother's bitter manipulativeness along with his pseudohumility as role models. To fail to confront when confrontation is required for the nurture of spiritual growth represents a failure to love equally as much as does thoughtless criticism or condemnation and other forms of active deprivation of caring. If they love their children parents must, sparingly and carefully perhaps but nonetheless actively, confront and criticize them from time to time, just as they must also allow their children to confront and criticize themselves in return. Similarly, loving spouses must repeatedly confront each other if the marriage relationship is to serve the function of promoting the spiritual growth of the partners. No marriage can be judged truly successful unless husband and wife are each other's best critics. The same holds true for friendship. There is a traditional concept that friendship should be a conflict-free relationship, a "you scratch my back, I'll scratch yours" arrangement, relying solely on a mutual exchange of favors and compliments as prescribed by good manners. Such relationships are superficial and intimacy-avoiding and do not deserve the name of friendship which is so commonly applied to them. Fortunately, there are signs that our concept of friendship is beginning to deepen. Mutual loving confrontation is a significant part of all successful and meaningful human relationships. Without it the relationship is either unsuccessful or shallow.

To confront or criticize is a form of exercising leadership or power. The exercise of power is nothing more and nothing less than an attempt to influence the course of events, human or otherwise, by one's actions in a consciously or unconsciously predetermined manner. When we confront or criticize someone it is because we want to change the course of the person's life. It is obvious that there are many other, often superior, ways to influence the course of events than by confrontation or criticism: by example, suggestion, parable, reward and punishment, questioning, prohibition or permission, creation of experiences, organizing with others, and so on. Volumes can be written about the art of exercising power. For our purposes, however, suffice it to say that loving individuals must concern themselves with this art, for if one desires to nurture another's spiritual growth, then one must concern oneself with the most effective way to accomplish this in any given instance. Loving parents, for example, must first examine themselves and their values stringently before determining accurately that they know what is best for their child. Then, having made this determination, they also have to give great thought to the child's character and capacities before deciding whether the child would be more likely to respond favorably to confrontation than to praise or increased attention or storytelling or some other form of influence. To confront someone with something he or she cannot handle will at best be a waste of time, and likely will have a deleterious effect. If we want to be heard we must speak in a language the listener can understand and on a level at which the listener is capable of operating. If we are to love we must extend ourselves to adjust our communication to the capacities of our beloved.

It is clear that exercising power with love requires a great deal of work, but what is this about the risk involved? The problem is that the more loving one is, the more humble one is; yet the more humble one is, the more one is awed by the potential for arrogance in exercising power. Who am I to influence the course of human events? By what authority am I entitled to decide what is best for my child, my spouse, my country or the human race? Who gives me the right to dare to believe in my own understanding and then to presume to

I'm just doing you a favor. Remember?"

"Don't do me no favors!" shouted Goldwyn. "*Godammit!*"

Marx had learned to contain himself in the face of these outbursts.

"I've suggested seven story editors to you, Mr. Goldwyn, and you've turned down every one."

"Who were they?" said Goldwyn. "Nobodies. *Friends* of yours."

"They weren't friends of mine."

"If they weren't friends of yours, how would you know them?" asked Goldwyn craftily.

Sam Marx would come out of these meetings and report to those of us who happened to be around.

"He wants me to quit," Marx explained. "I've got four years to go yet on my contract, with a raise every year. He's not going to let me produce. What he wanted was a story department and now he's got one so he wants to get rid of me. He forgets about my years at Metro. The studio politics. The infighting. I know all about these gambits. *This* time he's going to *lose*."

"If he does," said someone, "it'll be the first time."

The Marx-Goldwyn struggle became one of the more interesting tensions of our daily life at the studio. In conferences with the full production staff, Goldwyn took to insulting Marx or ridiculing him or humiliating him. Marx remained imperturbable, to Goldwyn's growing annoyance.

Hollywood story editors were in the habit of going to New York three or four times a year to see the current plays, investigate upcoming productions, meet with eastern agents and publishers and writers.

Sam Marx returned from one of these trips. A production meeting was called at which he made a careful and interesting report. He described the plays he had seen, discussed the important novels about to be published, and distributed galleys of some of them.

When he finished his report there was a smattering of applause in the room. It irritated Goldwyn. He leaned back in his chair and fixed Marx with a hard look.

"Let me tell you what happened around here while you were away," he said. "I bought a story. You know how long it is I bought a story? Six months. What am I saying, six. *Seven* months. You're around here getting three times as much as any story editor in town, f'Chrissake, and with your whole staff, all those dummies, all your friends you've got on my payroll and what happens? *Nothing* happens. We don't buy one God damn thing. All we do is waste our time with all that junk you keep sending us, but as soon as I get you out of here for a couple weeks, what happens? I buy a story."

Marx nodded gently and asked, "What story did you buy, Mr. Goldwyn?"

Goldwyn turned to us. "Did you hear that, gentlemen? What story did I buy. He's supposed to be the story editor and *he* asks *me* what story did I buy? Some story editor."

"There's no way I *could* know, Mr. Goldwyn. You haven't told me or anybody in my office and you haven't announced it."

"I'm announcing it right now," Goldwyn yelled. "*Graustark!* That's the story I bought. *Graustark*. And it's going to make one hell of a great picture. So why couldn't *you* come up with *Graustark?*"

Marx stayed in control. "Because, Mr. Goldwyn, you've told me over and over again and written me and I can show you your own memos, you've told me that the one thing you definitely would never buy is any story about a mythical kingdom."

"Is that so?" shouted Goldwyn.

"Yes, sir. That is absolutely so, and *Graustark* is certainly a story set in a mythical kingdom."

"You think I don't know that?" asked Goldwyn, flustered.

Marx sensed that he had, for a fleeting moment, the upper hand. He pressed his attack.

"Do you deny," he asked, "that you said definitely no mythical kingdoms?"

"Do I deny? What in the hell kind of talk is that? Who do you think you are? Some kind of a district attorney? Some kind of a cross-examiner?"

"Never mind that. Answer the question. Didn't you tell me no mythical kingdoms?"

"Sure I did, God damn it, but I didn't mean *classics!*"

Sam Marx laughed. The rest of us, unable to keep it in, followed suit. In the circumstances, what could Mr. Goldwyn do? *He* laughed, too.

Some months later, during a production meeting at which the atmosphere was remarkably relaxed, Marx made an aimless comment about the preview we had all seen the night before.

"You know *your* trouble, Marx?" Goldwyn demanded.

Marx took a deep breath, exhaled, and said meaningfully, "Yes, I do, Mr. Goldwyn."

"You're stupid. *That's* your trouble. I don't know why I didn't realize it all these years you've been taking my money—and for nothing. You're stupid. The only time I ever buy a goddam story is when you leave town." He paused, waiting for a reply. There was none. He went on. "You're not only stupid, you've also got a terrible *personality*. That's why nobody likes you. In fact, they all *hate* you. I'm talking about *everybody!*"

The atmosphere in the room had changed. Goldwyn was apparently out for the kill today. How much further would he go? How much more could Sam Marx take? How much *would* he take, and how much more could the rest of us bear? Apparently this was a relative matter because at this point Merritt Hulburt, the patrician Philadelphian who had been editor of the *Saturday Evening Post* before coming to work for Goldwyn, rose quietly and walked out of the room. Goldwyn did not see him leave, or perhaps pretended not to.

He moved a step closer to Marx and went on. "All the writers hate you and the agents hate you. That's why they don't give you their good stuff. And all the people on your *staff* hate you. You should hear what they say about you. Behind your back. It would make you ashamed." He paused. Sam Marx had gone pale but still did not reply. Marx's passiveness appeared to swell Goldwyn's growing fury. "And another thing," he said tightly. "You're a slob. Look at that suit you wear. A man earns your salary comes around here every day looking like a slob. With a cheap dirty suit like that suit. Not even *pressed,* f'Chrissake!" Marx looked Goldwyn straight in the eye but said nothing. At that moment I would have bet that Goldwyn was going to be struck within a matter of minutes. He went on, relentlessly. "Thalberg—supposed to be your such a friend— he only kept you around because he was *sorry* for you. He *told* me that."

Marx smiled faintly at this obvious untruth.

"What're you laughing at?" thundered Goldwyn. "You think it's funny, you fourflusher you? You deadbeat? You're not worth a goddam thing to me. Or to the business. Or to your *wife!* You want to know something? *She* hates you, too."

Was this at last the climax? I saw Marx's hands become fists. I saw his knuckles whiten, and his face redden. The pause was long, too long. Goldwyn appeared to be near exhaustion. Now to our surprise, he stepped close to Marx, put his hand on Marx's shoulder and said, gently, "And besides, Sam, I don't think you're *happy* here!"

There was a flabbergasted pause, then Marx exploded a laugh. We all laughed. Goldwyn laughed.

The situation continued. In time, it became intolerable to Goldwyn rather than to Marx. The torturer was bested by the tortured. Marx accepted a full settlement, with no concessions, and went off to Palm Springs to write a play.

The greater part of Goldwyn's professional relationships were stormy. Passionate lovers do not enter into relationships casually, nor do they bring them gently to a close. The movie business was the love of Sam Goldwyn's life and he never took it lightly. He was a skillful, ardent wooer of talent and as a rule got what he wanted. But, as in a love affair, when it was over it was over.

One morning, browsing sleepily through the trade papers over dollar-sized pancakes at Armstrong-Schroeder's, I saw a story

14

that woke me as though it were a thunderclap.

Warner Brothers announced it had bought the film rights to *Boy Meets Girl* by Sam and Bella Spewack, and were going to make it with James Cagney and their dumb blonde of the day, Marie Wilson.

Boy Meets Girl. What a film it would make! The film business making uproarious fun of itself. I could see that I was the man for the job.

In my naïve enthusiasm, I truly believed I could direct practically anything better than practically anyone. It is often so. When you watch an expert, what he does seems simple. It is only when you try to do it yourself that the difficulties begin to proliferate.

More and more, as I considered it, this planned film seemed like an ordained breakthrough for me. Here was a happy circumstance indeed. *Boy Meets Girl*. I had had a good deal to do with it. As George Abbott's assistant, I had read the play and brought it to Mr. Abbott with my enthusiastic recommendation. He had agreed, bought it, produced and directed it. It was a great success. I had been responsible for much of the casting, was finally in the play myself. I had directed all the road companies. I knew and liked the Spewacks.

Surely Warner Brothers would want me to work on the picture in *some* capacity. Of course, I would try to get to direct it. Who could arrange it for me? Cagney? Call Jack L. Warner? Mr. Abbott? If these ploys failed, perhaps I could work on the film as dialogue director, *something*.

I had reached a point where the word "executive" made me physically ill. I had no wish to be an executive. I wanted to be a director. I had said so to Goldwyn five or six hundred times— so many times, in fact, that he had stopped listening.

I phoned my office, told my secretary I would be delayed this morning.

"If Goldwyn wants me," I said, "say I had to go to the doctor."

"No," she said, "I don't want to do that."

"Why not?"

15

"Because," said Jean, an old Hollywood hand, "it's not a good idea. Don't ever get it around that you're sick or sickly."

"You're right. Say I had to go to the dentist."

"Well, even *that's* not so good, but it's a little better. I'll think of something. How late are you going to be?"

"Not much. Maybe half an hour."

"Okay," she said, "I'll think of something. Let's just hope he doesn't call."

I went to see Abe Lastfogel, told him my plan. He thought my chances of getting to direct the picture were infinitesimal, but worth a try.

"I could call Jack Warner," he said, "or Hal Wallis, but I know what they'd say. No, I think this ought to start somewhere else, not in the front office. Let me find out who's connected with the picture, the preparation of the picture. You know Cagney, don't you?"

"I've met him a few times, yes. In New York, with Phil Loeb."

"That would be a good bet," said Abe. "If Cagney would have you."

"Well, I don't mind asking. I mean, after all, I *do* know the material."

"Yes," said Abe, "you've got a point there. Let me see what I can do."

Later in the day, he phoned me to say that Steve Trilling was the first man to see. Trilling was then the principal assistant to Jack Warner, and greatly respected by him. Abe believed that if I could convince Trilling, Trilling could convince Warner.

Abe set up a date. He and I met Trilling for lunch at the Beverly Brown Derby. Abe thought it a more prudent move than going out to the studio, where we might be seen and where news of the meeting might get back to Goldwyn. At the Derby it might be strictly social.

Steve Trilling turned out to be an amiable and receptive young man. I made my pitch. He saw the advantages in my scheme, but candidly pointed out the disadvantages.

16

"Let me say this right now," said Trilling. "There's no question in my mind that you could make a contribution to this thing. I called George Abbott in New York yesterday, and he gave us a good report on you. He said you knew the property as well as anyone."

"You called Mr. Abbott?" I said, somehow encouraged by this information.

"Yes," said Trilling, "I'm very thorough. I'm sure I could get you onto the picture doing something. Would you like to play your original part? You weren't bad."

"Well, as they say," I said, "I wasn't *supposed* to be."

No laugh. Trilling was all business. "Would you? *That* I think I could swing."

"Jesus, no," I said, "I'm finished with all that."

"I can't really promise you dialogue director, because we've got so many contract ones of our own, and we'd run into a studio mess. Actually, it might be easier to get you the *picture* than *that* job."

"That's fine with me," I said.

"I'm going to think about this—I mean seriously," he said.

"I'll come over and direct some tests," I said. "For nothing. How would that be?"

"No, no," said Trilling. "We have test directors for that."

I could see I was being forced into the top spot.

There were further meetings, one with J. L. Warner himself. A rough-talking, vital man who loved to laugh.

When it began to appear that a deal of some kind might indeed be made, Abe decided to broach the subject to Mr. Goldwyn.

We went in to see him.

"I'm very busy today," said Goldwyn, as we came through the door.

"This won't take a minute, Sam," said Abe. "In fact, we won't even sit down, how's that?"

"That's good," said Goldwyn.

"What I want to ask you, Sam, is simply this. If anything came up somewhere for Gar, say like a chance to direct a picture, how would you feel about loaning him out? Naturally, I'd try to get you a good price, and Gar doesn't expect any part of it. It would just be a loan-out. The idea is that it would be a start for him, he'd get some experience. Then, of course, he'd be back here with you."

Even before Goldwyn responded, I could see it was no go.

"God damn it!" he shouted. "You think that's all I got to do is train people for other goddam studios? Let 'em train their *own* goddam people, not steal people from other studios. From me." He looked at me and pointed a finger. "You take *my* money and then you want to go and work for them!"

"That isn't it," I said. "I want to see if I can direct a picture."

"You want to see? You don't *have* to see. I'll tell you right now you *can't* direct a picture. How can you direct a picture? You never *directed* a picture."

"Don't get excited, Sam," said Abe.

"Don't tell me not to get excited!" Goldwyn shouted. "I'm in my own office, in my own studio, and if I want to get excited, I can get excited. Here's a kid comes out here, a nobody, takes my money, and then he wants to go someplace else."

"I'd still be under contract to you, Mr. Goldwyn, for another six and a half years."

"What makes you think I'm going to *want* you around here for another six and a half years if you're going to be such a pain in the ass?" he asked.

Abe and I looked at each other. It was not going well.

"I'm beginning to not to like you," said Goldwyn. "You've got something going somewhere, that's why you bring up the subject."

"Of course I have," I said. "I didn't mean to keep anything from you."

I told him what it was.

"That play is no damn good," he said.

"You're dead wrong. I know it line by line, and it's one of the best American comedies ever written."

"For the theatre!" yelled Goldwyn, and brought his fist down hard on his desk top. "For the *theatre*! But all that making fun of Hollywood in that play, how can that be a picture? Listen, I got the Spewacks working for me here, but when I have them, I have them write something that's good for pictures, not for the goddam theatre."

He was out of control now, completely unreasonable. There was no point in going on with it. We left.

Three more meetings on the same subject were filled with increasingly bitter exchanges.

In between, I had gone to see Cagney. To my surprise, he remembered me. I outlined my plan, practically acted the whole play, performed the routines, explained how each laugh was achieved. "Would it be all right with you if they put me on the picture as director?"

"Certainly," said Cagney, "just so long as you don't tell me what to do."

He laughed.

"I wouldn't even come *near* you," I said.

The *Boy Meets Girl* deal fell through, but by now I had begun to believe I was ready to direct. So virulent was my germ that Lastfogel became infected and actually got me an offer from RKO. I could scarcely believe it. I had, as yet, done nothing.

All that stood in the way was the Goldwyn contract.

"He *has* to let me out," I said. "Doesn't he? I mean, what good am I to him if I don't want to be there? I can just horse around and do nothing. I don't want to do it that way. I'd rather have it amicable."

We went in to see Goldwyn again. I expressed my feelings. He looked hurt, and said, "Well, you're not the first one who stole money from me."

Abe was outraged.

"That's a *hell* of a thing to say, Sam," he said. "So I'll tell you what. You give him his release, and we'll give you back all the money you've paid him this last year."

It was Goldwyn's turn to be outraged. "You think I need the money?" shouted Goldwyn. "*F'Chrissake!* It's the *principle*. Of

19

the thing. I wouldn't take a penny from you *or* from him. It would be from you anyway because what has *he* got? Nothing. And I'll tell you something else. He's *never* going to have anything. He's got a little talent, but he doesn't know how to use it. Bothering me, day in and day out—he wants to be a director, f'Chrissake, when I was giving him all this opportunity." He turned to me. "Listen, you don't want to be around here? Nobody's going to put you on a ball and a chain. You want a release? I'll *give* you a release."

"Thank you, Mr. Goldwyn," I said, and extended my hand before he could change his mind.

He looked at my hand, significantly, and did not take it. I shrugged and left quickly.

When Abe did not emerge for half an hour, I began to worry. When he did come out, he looked stony, and motioned to me with his head to follow him. We walked down the hall, down the stairs, and went outside.

"It's not good," he said. "This is what he wants us to sign."

He showed me the form of release, in which I agreed I would not accept employment from any other studio, without his permission, for the length of the contract. This meant that I could not work in films, in any capacity, for *six years*! My heart pounding, I strode back to Goldwyn's office with Abe following me all the way, imploring me not to go further with the subject today. But there are times when reason fails.

I burst into Goldwyn's office and began yelling. Goldwyn yelled back.

Neither of us was making sense.

When we were both exhausted, I said to him, "All right, *keep* your release!" I crumpled it and threw it at him. "I'll stay here. I'll report every morning, and I'll be here from nine to six, but you'll never hear a word out of me, and you'll regret you're putting anybody through this. Slavery. That's what it is."

"Slavery," said Goldwyn. "You're *some* slave. If you *were* a slave of mine, you know what I'd do? I'd *sell* you!"

I left. The next day Goldwyn gave me an unconditional release. That was on a Saturday. On Monday, I reported to work at RKO.

Seven months later, my first picture, *A Man to Remember,* was having a success. It was a small, inexpensive film, but, unlike the usual run of B pictures, did not insult the intelligence.

I was at last an accepted member of the Hollywood film community.

When Willie Wyler, whom I had known at Goldwyn's, took a new wife—a girl named Margaret Tallichet—he invited me to the wedding. Talli was a Southern beauty who had been one of the discoveries of the highly publicized nationwide search for a Scarlett O'Hara. She came out and made a test. She did not get the part but she did get Willie Wyler.

At the reception, I was standing at the bar with a glass of champagne in my hand when I saw Samuel Goldwyn coming toward me.

I had neither seen him nor spoken to him for almost a year. He seemed to be smiling, although with him, it was not always easy to tell. He stopped and stood looking at me.

"Hello, Mr. Goldwyn," I said. "How are you?"

"You dirty little bastard," he replied. "You dirty, double-crossing little son of a bitch."

He smiled. I did not.

"Why do you say that, Mr. Goldwyn?"

He laughed. "Because that's what you are. A little double-crossing bastard." He put his hand on my shoulder in the most avuncular way and said gently, "Why didn't you ever *tell* me you wanted to be a director?"

He clapped me on the back, too hard, spilling some of my champagne and said, "Call me up. Come over to lunch. I want to talk to you."

He was gone.

I sought out Willie Wyler and told him what had happened. "How do you explain it?" I asked.

21

"Well, I'll tell you," said Willie. "He believes with all his heart that you spent a year at his studio and never mentioned the subject of directing. He believes it because he *has* to. He's convinced himself that's the truth, because—don't you see?—if he admits to anybody or to himself that there you were, under contract to him, begging him every minute for a chance to direct, with him turning you down, then you go out and become a successful director for another studio, he's made a blunder. He's used bad judgment, so rather than admit this, he convinces himself you never mentioned it. That's his mentality. I think it may be one of the main reasons for his success. To himself, he's never wrong. He's a god. Not a bad thing to be, especially if you live on earth."

"What makes you think he lives on earth?" I asked.

2

In his long day, John Barrymore was considered by many to be the greatest American actor ever.

If, indeed, heredity is a factor in the mysterious art of acting, his credentials were impeccable. The Barrymores were the Royal Family of the American theatre.

John, usually called Jack, was the spoiled baby of the Barrymore family. His brother, Lionel, and his sister, Ethel, were more or less in charge of him after the death of their mother at an early age.

In addition to his talent, he was blessed with rare good looks. The word "beautiful" describes him better than the word "handsome." He was known as The Great Profile. He was magnetic, hypnotic.

He was one of the few Barrymores who at first firmly resisted the theatre. It might have been out of fear that he would not be able to live up to expectations, or perhaps he did not relish being compared with his illustrious relatives. Whatever the reason, he flatly refused, early on, to pursue a theatrical career. Instead, he turned to drawing and sketching and cartooning and for a time was thus employed by various metropolitan newspapers.

He wanted to be a journalist and did all he could to further this plan. Alas for his aspirations, the blood in his veins was actor's blood and in time he was drawn, however reluctantly, to the boards.

It had to be. Members of his family and cronies soon became

aware that he was giving better performances in saloons and drawing rooms than were to be seen generally on the stages of New York theatres.

He began to act professionally, but not in New York. He still objected to that, settling for touring companies or stock companies in various parts of the country.

He made friends easily and young Edward Sheldon became one of his closest. For a time they shared an apartment in Gramercy Park. Sheldon was a brilliant, wealthy, attractive, and talented Chicagoan who had written a play while still a Harvard undergraduate. It had been produced on Broadway with great success. Minnie Maddern Fiske in *Salvation Nell* by Edward Sheldon. Imagine it. A New York theatrical triumph starring America's outstanding actress, written by a college boy of twenty-two.

Sheldon was different from his chum in almost every respect. Interested in education, he was sober, industrious, honest, respectable, and, above all, wildly ambitious, not for material gain but for artistic achievement.

It was Edward Sheldon who was responsible for the change in the direction of John Barrymore's career.

Barrymore was not easy to influence. He enjoyed the perverse pleasures of being the black sheep of a great family. He drank and caroused and womanized. When he worked, he worked superficially, using no more than the tip of his talent with that historic enemy of artistic progress—facility.

But despite his lack of drive, he was soon building a reputation as a charming, expert, sure-fire *farceur* who connected magically with audiences from the moment of every entrance. All great actors possess a sixth, perhaps even a seventh, sense. They are able to convey to an audience what they are thinking and feeling no matter what words they happen to be speaking. Conversely, they are able to judge accurately the temper and the reactive power of the audience from moment to moment. It is as though they can tell what the *audience* is thinking and feeling, and then adapt their performance to match it.

This quality makes great actors sensitive, often oversensitive, in real life as well. (If an actor can be said to have a real life.)

For example: John Barrymore, while at the peak of his motion-picture career, was married to the equally successful Dolores Costello. They lived beautifully and extravagantly in their hilltop home, or abroad, or on Barrymore's famous yacht, *The Infanta*.

Dolores Costello became pregnant. The event took on exaggerated importance, as in all royal families.

Barrymore had a young daughter, Diana, by his second wife —the poet Michael Strange (Blanche Oelrichs). In aristocracies, however, sons matter more.

Anxiously, Barrymore kept changing obstetricians for fear that he did not have the best, the very best man available to usher his first son into the world. Finally, he settled on Dr. John Vruwink, who was, by general agreement, the outstanding man in his field.

Barrymore was content at last. He was able to relax. Still, he insisted that Dr. Vruwink pay a daily call on Mrs. Barrymore to make certain that all was progressing as it should. The doctor objected, pointing out that a daily visit was hardly necessary, but Barrymore insisted with such passion that the doctor acquiesced. After all—John Barrymore. The relaxed situation was not to last long.

Barrymore returned from the studio one afternoon, went directly to his wife and found her chatting with Dr. Vruwink.

After a few pleasantries and a good report, Barrymore said, "Well, that's capital. Simply capital. Were you just leaving, doctor?"

"Yes, I was."

"Let me show you to the door."

"No, no. That's not necessary. Goodnight, Mrs. Barrymore. Don't forget about that extra pint of buttermilk. Potassium."

"I won't," she replied. "Thank you, doctor."

At the front door, Barrymore and Dr. Vruwink shook hands.

"Well," said the doctor, "everything's fine."

"Everything's *too* fine," said Barrymore, fixing him with a hard look.

"I beg your pardon?"

"Goodnight," said Barrymore. "And *good-by,* you son of a bitch. Don't come back. If I ever find you in this house again I'll break your goddam jaw."

The doctor regarded him quizzically. (A madman or simply a Barrymore?) He left quietly.

Back in the bedroom Barrymore stretched out on the bed beside his wife, lit a cigarette, and said, "I fired the bastard. We'll get someone else. Someone better."

Dolores was understandably stunned.

"What are you saying?" she asked. "There *isn't* anyone better. You told me yourself. After all that investigation and all that—" She rose and began to move about nervously. "Look here, Jack, I don't understand this. Any of it. What happened?"

"I don't want him around here," said Barrymore calmly, "because he's stuck on you and I don't want anybody stuck on you touching you, especially the way this guy has to touch you. It's over. He's out."

"I think *I* ought to have something to say about it," Dolores insisted. "After all, I'm the one who—"

"Wait a minute," Barrymore interrupted. "Let's just wait one damned minute here." He rolled off the bed and moved toward his wife. Close to her, he looked deeply into her eyes and asked, "You don't want him out?"

"No, I don't."

"Why not?"

"Because, Jack—look—be reasonable, for God's sake. The baby's due in seven or eight weeks. He's the sixth man we've had. It's very difficult. More difficult than you can imagine. All this change and readjustment. It's nerve-racking. This isn't easy, this experience. Please try to be understanding. And anyway, how can you think—imagine! For heaven's sake, look at me! All puffed out and revolting, really. What could make you think—"

"Jesus Christ," said Barrymore, awestruck.

"What?"

"Jesus Christ!" he repeated. "Not only is *he* stuck on *you* but *you're* stuck on *him*. The two of you. You're stuck on each *other!*"

"Oh, Jack, for God's sake, will you—"

She might have said more, much more, had not Barrymore slapped her, hard. She staggered away and instinctively picked up the telephone.

"Who are you going to call?" he said scornfully. "Him? Or the police? Or that goo-goo mother of yours?"

"I don't know," she said, and put down the phone.

Barrymore left. She went back to bed. He was in and out of the bedroom all through the rest of the evening and all through the night. He questioned her relentlessly, screamed at her. She screamed back. Later, they discussed the matter quietly. Later still, another row.

Toward dawn, both exhausted, they slept.

For the next few days, Barrymore avoided all contact with her. In fact, he spent several nights at the studio. Dr. Vruwink, a thoroughgoing professional, continued to make his calls. The subject of John Barrymore's obsession did not come up again.

The baby was born. A girl. Dolores Ethel Mae.

It was not until two years later, on June 4, 1932, that John Barrymore's dream of a son was realized. Dr. John Vruwink supervised the birth of John Barrymore, Jr., this time without incident. Before another two years passed, the marriage of John Barrymore and Dolores Costello exploded in violence and bitterness.

Immediately following the divorce, Dolores Costello married Dr. John Vruwink.

Barrymore told me the story late one night on location.

"How do you explain it?" I asked.

"Explain what? There's nothing to it."

"I mean to say, how did you know? When you first knew."

"There was nothing to know," he said. "There was nothing going on between them back then. Nothing at all."

"But you said they were—I think the phrase you used was 'stuck on each other.' "

"That's right," he said. "They were. Only *they* didn't know it. *I* knew it. *I* knew it before *they* did."

"That's what I'm talking about," I insisted. "How *did* you know?"

He took a long, long puff on his cigarette, inhaled the smoke, exhaled it, and said, "I knew it because I am John Barrymore."

My relationship with this remarkable man began near the beginning of my own career as a film director. I had made one small film called *A Man to Remember.*

I was immediately assigned to a run-of-the-mill nonsense, objected, was told to do it or else, chose to do it, and suffered through it.

As I was finishing the second picture, the first one opened and was a surprise critical success, gaining much attention. At this point the front office executives looked at it for the first time. They too pronounced themselves impressed. Thus, about a month after *A Man to Remember* had been in national release, a preview was held, following which the film was re-booked into larger and more important theatres.

Pandro S. Berman, then the head of RKO, sent for me. I took the opportunity to blast my resentment of having been so cavalierly assigned to a nothing job.

Berman was entirely sympathetic and said, "Listen, I'm sorry but we'll make it up to you."

"How?" I asked. "How can you?"

"We'll let you do any picture you want next. Anything on the lot that you can put together."

As it happened there was a picture on the lot that interested me greatly. It was a shelved project called *The Great Man Votes.*

A *Saturday Evening Post* short story by Gordon Malherbe Hillman had been adapted for the screen by John Twist, one of the best writers at the studio. John Ford had, for a time, been interested in this piquant story of American politics and his touch was apparent throughout the final screenplay.

The reason for its abandonment was unclear. Explanations varied greatly. Ford claimed they would not come up with a workable budget. Pandro Berman said that it was satire and quoted George S. Kaufman's definition: "Satire is what closes Saturday night." Cliff Reid who, with John Ford, had made *The Informer,* said that it had been a question of casting. Whatever the reason, the script had been put away, along with hundreds of others, and seemed destined for oblivion.

John Twist was a studio pal, and one afternoon he dropped a copy of the manuscript off at my office. I read it and was instantly captivated by its whimsical, yet powerful premise: a once-promising, cultivated scholar, now a widower with two small children, lives and works as a night watchman in a forgotten precinct in lower Manhattan. Gerrymandering has reduced the voting population of this precinct to one and that one is the night watchman, Gregory Vance. In a hotly fought mayoralty election, the outcome depends upon this particular precinct and thus on this one man. Life has kicked him into obscurity, but he is all at once being wooed by both parties and is elevated to momentary greatness but then—a surprise ending.

One way to judge a script is to see if it comes to life as one reads. A script, after all, is not a play, nor is it a film. It is a set of directions for the acting out of a play or of a film, which, in time, will take place on a stage or a screen, or, more accurately, in the collective mind of the audience.

As I read *The Great Man Votes,* shots came into focus, sights and sounds, and shortly, visualizations of the various characters. To my eye, Gregory Vance was John Barrymore and John Barrymore was Gregory Vance. It was a piece of casting so obvious and yet so inspired that there was no second choice.

Taking Berman at his word, I went to him with the suggestion that he let me make *The Great Man Votes.* Of course, he refused, attempting to warn me off the subject, but I reminded him of his promise, and after a time he agreed, saying, "Okay. If—and it's a big 'if'—if you can cast it."

29

"It's all cast," I said.

"Go ahead."

"John Barrymore."

"Nothing doing," said Pan, in a way that made me fear it was final.

"Why not?" I asked.

"We don't want him here."

"You don't want him here," I repeated. "The greatest actor in America?"

"Was."

"Could be again. In this part."

"He's not going to work on this lot," said Pan. "He's unreliable and irresponsible and impossible."

"That's all changed."

"What makes you think so?"

"That's all over, Pan. This new marriage of his. He's all settled down. He wants to work. Let me do it, Pan. Trust me."

"I couldn't let you take the chance, kid. You'd be sticking your neck out. You might start it but you'd never finish it. Not with him."

"I would, Pan. I'll take the responsibility."

"You'll take the responsibility! Who the hell are *you* to take the responsibility? This picture could cost three, four hundred thousand dollars!" (A sizable budget for those days.) "What if it goes down the drain? Will you send me your check for the amount?"

"I'll send you my check," I said, deflated and miserable. "Just don't try to cash it."

I had lost Round One.

I conferred with Cliff Reid and John Twist, who were on my side. I talked to Barrymore's agent, who seemed eager yet hesitant. I tried to gain support from the production department but got nowhere.

Another shot at Pandro Berman. He listened to my marshaled arguments courteously, then said, "Listen. The last time we let that bastard on the lot—we didn't want him then but this big director from New York had come out, Worthington Miner, and he had the same bee in his bonnet you've got. Naturally, being from the theatre he would have. Barrymore in the theatre. Nobody ever greater. I know that. But we'd had bad experiences with Barrymore around here."

"Good ones, too," I said. "He was great in *A Bill of Divorcement*—and what about *Topaz*? And *Long Lost Father*? All terrific and all right here at RKO."

"Let me finish about Worthington Miner," said Berman, impatiently. "What was the name of the picture? Oh, yeah. *Hat, Coat, and Glove*. That was the name of it, I remember. I wish I could forget it. So Miner insisted on Barrymore, just like you and when I tried to warn him, he kept giving me the same kind of malarkey you're giving me. 'Leave him to me,' he kept saying. 'I can handle him.' So one thing and another we got talked into it. And they started shooting. And he was handling him just fine—just fine until one afternoon Barrymore took a whole gang of the crew over to Lucey's for lunch. He always gets very pally with the crew and they call him Jack and he calls them whatever, and they all have a lot of highjinks and nothing but fun and the picture goes in the crapper. So he took the crew to lunch and the crew came back. What the hell. They *had* to. They've got a union. But *he* didn't come back. Not that day or the next or the next. In fact, never. We had to stop it. The insurance covered some of it, sure, but not all and that's another thing. We can't get any insurance on the guy. So forget it."

I had one final trump to play and this seemed the moment to play it.

I rose and said solemnly, "All right, Pan. If that's your decision, I accept it, but I must say I'm surprised. You've got a great reputation in this business as a picturemaker but more important, everyone who knows you, who's dealt with you, says that you're a man of your word. A man of honor and I'm really surprised to see you betray that idea."

A look into his widening eyes told me I had struck home.

"*What* idea?" he blurted out.

"Well, after the rough time you people gave me about that second assignment, you promised you were going to make it up to me. You said I could do anything on the lot—"

"If you could set it up, I said!" he shouted.

I shouted back. "What the hell kind of promise is that? Anything I set up you can knock over you—you—"

"You *what?*" he challenged, demanding me to finish my thought.

"—you big—little *tycoon!*"

All at once, I could no longer see him. I saw only his finger, pointing directly between my eyes.

"All right, you dumb jerk," he said. "I'm going to give you enough rope and let's see what happens."

The Great Man Votes was under way. All I had to do now was to persuade John Barrymore to do it. He could be extremely erratic, I was told.

"Leave it to me," I said.

I got Barrymore's home telephone number from his agent, remembering Mr. Goldwyn's advice to deal with principals whenever possible. I phoned John Barrymore, identified myself, and began telling him about the script.

"No, no," I heard that great voice say. My heart sank. "No, no," he continued. "Let's not do this on the phone—a diabolical instrument, in any case. Come on over. Bring the manuscript. Although, to be perfectly candid, I prefer to have you *tell* me the story and describe the role. A movie script is so boring to read. It's like a plumber's manual, isn't it? Furthermore, I have no idea who you are but when you've told me the story, I'll have some idea as to your competence to convey it to an audience."

"When?" I asked.

"When what?"

"When can I come over?"

"Why not right now?"

I was on my way in a matter of minutes.

I had difficulty finding his hideaway house and it was precisely noon when I drove up to the front door.

I rang the bell. I heard it sound loudly inside and waited for a minute, for two, for three. I rang again. Five minutes later, I rang for a third and what I had decided would be a final time. The front door was flung open and there stood John Barrymore, the greatest actor in America, stark naked.

He squinted at me and asked, "What's this? Who are you?"

"RKO," I heard myself say.

"Oh, yes," he said. "Of course. Come in, RKO. Come in." He slapped me on the back as I entered and added, "Mind if I call you R?"

He laughed at his joke until I joined him.

"Were you out there long?" he asked. "I'm sorry. My apologies. We don't have any servants here. They keep leaving." He did his famous eyebrow trick, one up, the other down, and said, "More of them leave than we ever hire. I've never been able to figure that out. Can it be that they leave before they get here?" He looked around. "My wife should be here but she isn't. Would you like some coffee?"

"Yes, I would."

"All right, then. Why don't you go out into the kitchen and make it? It's out there somewhere. The kitchen. And there should be some coffee in it." He looked down at his nakedness and suddenly became a coy ingenue. "Would you excuse me while I slip into something more comfortable?" He minced off and up the stairs.

I found the kitchen. It was a mess, but I managed to prepare coffee. I put everything onto a tray and carried it out to the sitting room.

Barrymore sat there, beautifully dressed in slacks, slippers, a smoking jacket, and an ascot, smoking and reading the morning newspaper. He seemed surprised to see me, but said, "Oh, coffee. Fine. Put it right down there."

I felt as though I were about to be tipped.

I poured coffee for both of us and began. "This is a great honor, Mr. Barrymore."

"I should think it would be. Are you the director of this thing we're supposed to talk about?"

"Yes, sir, I am."

"Oh, I thought you might be his grandson working for him as his messenger boy."

"No," I said. "I'd like to direct this picture. That is, if you'll star in it. If you'll play the lead."

"The *lead*?" he asked, sharply. I could almost see his ears prick up. "May I ask how many *other* leads there are in this opera?"

"None," I said.

"None?" he echoed, except that in his pronunciation, the word had three syllables.

"No, Mr. Barrymore. This picture is about Gregory Vance— that's your part—it's the starring role and there are no other starring roles."

He looked at me long and hard and did not speak again until he had finished his cup of coffee. Then he lit a fresh cigarette, regarded me once more, and ordered, "Tell me the story."

I did so.

I was, by that time, beginning to be fairly experienced in the business of telling (selling) stories to various players. Sometimes I told them well; more often, poorly. On this afternoon with Barrymore, I surpassed myself and realized about one third of the way through that what it takes to tell a story well is a sympathetic listener. There has never been a listener to equal John Barrymore. He took it all in moment by moment and somehow I felt him helping me.

I reached the penultimate point. Gregory Vance leaving the polling place, being greeted by the crowd, and making his speech on the meaning of democracy, ending with the lines by John Greenleaf Whittier:

—Today, of all the weary year,
A king of men am I.
Today alike are great and small,
The nameless and the known,

34

My palace is the people's hall,
The ballot-box my throne!

Following this, I delivered the electrifying surprise finish. Barrymore roared with laughter and approval.

"When do we start?" he said.

The next few days were spent in the excitement of confident preparation. Everything seemed to be falling into place. I thought it time to invite Barrymore to dinner. I phoned him. Would he and Mrs. Barrymore have dinner with me on Friday at Chasen's at eight?

"I'll be there," he said. "Let's leave her out of it, unless you'd like to buy her from me."

I pretended I had not heard this last.

"By the way," I said, "we think we have a final script now. Shall I send a copy along?"

"Only if you're sure it is final," he said.

"Well, in that case, maybe we'd better wait a few days."

That Friday night, as I walked into Chasen's, at ten minutes to eight, I was simultaneously delighted and dismayed.

Sitting at the bar waiting for me was John Barrymore, not only punctual but more than punctual. What did they mean, unreliable? Irresponsible. There he was, beautifully gotten up and waving to me affably.

At the same moment, I saw Pandro S. Berman sitting with a party of friends in one of the booths. I would have preferred my first public meeting with Barrymore to have gone unscrutinized, but there it was.

I joined Barrymore at the bar. We shook hands.

"Good evening, Mr. Barrymore. I hope I'm not late."

"No, no," he said. "I'm early. I'm always early. I find it affords an opportunity for an extra ration of giggle water."

I shuddered. I hoped he did not notice.

He finished his martini, put it down on the bar, and tapped the rim of the glass with a long, graceful finger. The bartender made him a second martini. I ordered Scotch. By the time I had finished my drink, Barrymore had had another. That made three, I calculated. Three that I knew of. I prayed that Pan Berman would soon leave. I looked over to his table. He was just starting his soup.

"Well," I said, "shall we order, Mr. Barrymore?"

"In a minute," he said.

I signaled the headwaiter, who recognized my desperation and brought menus at once.

"What is this?" asked Barrymore. "A quick-lunch counter? I thought it was a restaurant." He waved the menus away and tapped the rim of his glass again. "You order for me. Anything out of season."

I ordered swiftly and unimaginatively. Shrimp cocktail. Sirloin steak, baked potato, string beans. Salad. Ice cream. The headwaiter left.

Barrymore drank slowly and steadily but it seemed to have no effect on him. He began to discuss the picture, not so much in terms of the story but in terms of his own role. He was brilliant—deep, thorough, and entirely original. The headwaiter came over to inform us that our first course was on the table. I slid off the bar stool and started off.

"No, no," said Barrymore. "Not yet. Let's have a drink." He looked at the headwaiter and added, "Want to join us?"

The headwaiter went off again.

Pandro Berman was looking at us. I hoped he could not hear.

"Let's eat," I said. "I'm starving."

"Not yet," he said and tapped that damned glass again.

I appealed to him. "Please, Mr. Barrymore?"

"I'm sorry," he said to me with the greatest dignity, "but I simply cannot eat on an *empty stomach*!"

I sat by while he consumed yet another set of martinis.

At dinner he ate, discussed the food, talked of other dinners in different places and times.

Then for a time, he was silent and conveyed somehow that he preferred no conversation.

I looked at that great, expressive face with its actor's skin, bearing the patina of thousands of applications of makeup. I thought about the life and work of this larger-than-life personality. His father, the brilliant British player, Maurice Blythe, who upon emigrating "out to the States" decided to give himself a name more likely to impress the natives and chose Maurice Barrymore. In time, he married the daughter of a great American acting family, Georgiana Drew, whose mother was the celebrated Mrs. Drew of the Arch Street Theatre, Philadelphia. Their children were Lionel, Ethel, and John, in that order. The outstanding American leading man of his day, John Drew was, of course, their uncle.

Could this weary man, slowly chomping on his steak, be the same one who, as a dashing young blade, played *Are You a Mason?, An American Citizen, The Man from Mexico,* and *The Dictator*?

He had made hit after hit in farce after farce. Then, through the encouragement of Edward Sheldon and later Arthur Hopkins, he began to take himself more seriously. He played in John Galsworthy's *Justice,* and, with his brother Lionel, in *Peter Ibbetson* and the memorable production of *The Jest.* He made history with his *Hamlet,* playing it for a hundred and one performances on Broadway.

John Barrymore looked up from his food and winked at me. The same wink he had used in the hilarious *Here Comes the Bride.* I began to think of his early silent films. *Raffles, Sherlock Holmes, Dr. Jekyll and Mr. Hyde, Beau Brummell, The Sea Beast* (a version of *Moby Dick*), *Don Juan.* His first talkie was *Show of Shows,* a revue in which he appeared in a scene from Shakespeare's *Richard III.* Then, in dazzling succession, *The Man from Blankley's* (the funniest picture I had ever seen), *Moby Dick, Svengali, A Bill of Divorcement, Arsene Lupin, Grand Hotel, Rasputin and the Empress* (with Ethel and Lionel), *Dinner at Eight, Reunion in Vienna,* and so on and so on. Four marriages and perhaps four thousand affairs. No wonder he looked weary. In his fifty-seven years he had lived several lives.

He ordered brandy. My worries burgeoned but now, well fed

and happily oiled, he began to talk about our project again and captivated me completely.

As we parted, he said, "Thanks. It was a splendid repast. I've enjoyed it."

"Thank you, Mr. Barrymore," I said.

"Mr. Barrymore!" he snorted, giving that well-known single syllable laugh of his, and was driven off by his chauffeur.

I wondered why he had reacted so oddly to being called by that name. He was more than thirty years my senior, a distinguished star. Why *shouldn't* I call him Mr. Barrymore? It struck me that because he had lost a certain amount of respect for himself, it embarrassed him to sense even the suggestion of it from someone else, especially a stranger. Could this be the key, I wondered, to the solution of the problem? I remembered what Pan Berman had told me about Barrymore's camaraderie with the crew.

I decided upon a stratagem.

Three days before shooting was to begin, I assembled the crew and that part of the cast which was available. I explained our mutual problem.

"Our star is John Barrymore and it's no secret to any of you, especially those of you who know him, who've worked with him, that he presents certain problems. I happen to think he's a great actor. I call him Mr. Barrymore, and I'd appreciate it very much if all of you would do the same. Now, it may seem like a small thing but I believe that one of the principal functions of a director is to create an atmosphere in which creative work can take place, and what worries me is that if we get into one of those loose work situations full of highjinks, horsing-around, laughing-it-up, everybody-topping-everybody-else, calling him Jack, and remembering all the peccadilloes, I'm not going to be able to do that. So I need your help. Let's keep it businesslike. We've got a long picture and a short schedule. Rule number one. He's Mr. Barrymore." I turned to my assistant. "And, Nate, anyone who isn't here, like the gateman and the people in wardrobe and makeup, please tell them to do the same."

A grizzled old grip raised his hand. "Can I say something?" he asked.

"You bet."

"Balls," he said.

It got the expected laugh, but not from me.

"What do you mean by that?" I asked.

"Look," he said. "The front office may think you're hot stuff but as far as I'm concerned you're just a lucky punk and a Johnny-come-lately."

"Okay," I said.

He went on. "Jack Barrymore's a friend of mine. I been out on the town with him many's the time. And he calls me Chuck and I call him Jack and nobody's gonna tell me what to call my pals. And if you want me off the crew I'll get off the crew. Get yourself another boy."

"That suits me," I said. "In fact, that's the way it's going to have to be. Anybody else?"

There were two more. They were replaced.

On the first day of shooting, as John Barrymore was driven onto the lot, the gateman greeted him.

"Good morning, Mr. Barrymore. Nice to have you back. Good luck with the picture."

He was driven directly to makeup where the head of the department, Mel Berns, awaited him along with his own makeup man, Jim Barker.

"Good morning, Mr. Barrymore."

"Morning, Mr. Barrymore."

He arrived on the set.

The doorman: "Good morning, Mr. Barrymore."

The script girl, Adele Cannon: "Good morning, Mr. Barrymore."

Russ Metty, the cameraman, who had been the camera operator on an earlier Barrymore picture, came over and offered his hand.

"Hello, Russ," said Barrymore.

39

"Good morning, Mr. Barrymore," said Russ.

Barrymore snorted again. "What the hell is all this Barrymore shit?" he said. "Who's Mr. Barrymore, for Christ's sweet sake? You must think I'm *Lionel.*"

A laugh, but my loyal cast and crew persisted.

Russ Metty said, "Okay, Mr. Barrymore, no shit."

Throughout the twenty-four days of shooting, no one called him or referred to him as anything but "Mr. Barrymore." In a matter of days, I believe he began to think of *himself* as Mr. Barrymore.

Never before had I worked with a more thorough professional. He was never late, never objected to overtime, gave everything on every take, and was totally prepared, although he insisted upon using his notorious blackboards.

This was the one thing about his work I could not understand. I am sure he knew his part perfectly, yet he insisted upon having his man somewhere in the line of sight, holding up that blackboard.

There were, in fact, many blackboards, in varying sizes and shapes. Large ones for the long speeches; small ones for the shorter speeches; oblong ones to fit between the lights if necessary; tiny ones for single lines.

In these days of Teleprompters and cue cards, the blackboards would not seem unusual, but I had never seen them used.

Barrymore's technique for using the blackboard was ingenious. He would position himself for reading the board. Often, this occasioned spectacular turns and twists and bends; a favorite trick was to turn his head sharply as though to scratch the back of his head, thus turning his eyes to the blackboard.

I discussed the matter with him.

"It seems to me, Mr. Barrymore, that what you do to get the words off those boards is a hell of a lot harder than learning them."

He looked at me balefully and said, "I've learned enough words in my time. Let somebody else do it now."

"Shall I tell you what I think, Mr. Barrymore?" I pressed on. "I think you really know your lines perfectly, and that this is just a habit you've fallen into."

He fixed me with his hard look again, and said, "Of course I know my lines. I always do."

"Then why the—?"

"Because," he interrupted. "Have you ever been to a circus? Seen the blokes on the high wire? Even doing back flips? On the tight rope. Have you ever seen one of them fall?"

"Of course not."

"Then why do you suppose they always have a net underneath them? Those blackboards are my net, that's all."

One morning, as we were about to begin, my cutter came onto the set and asked if, for his convenience, I would make one small additional shot. It was simply an entrance to tie in two scenes. The whole shot would consist of a medium angle on an empty door. A woman comes in and knocks. The door is opened by Barrymore. She asks, "Are you Gregory Vance?" He replies, "Yes." Whereupon she enters. That would be all.

We set up the scene and I went off to get a cup of coffee. All at once I heard a furious row from the vicinity of the camera. As a rule, these flare-ups died out as swiftly as they began but this one continued. I went over to see what the trouble was.

Henry, Barrymore's blackboard man, was engaged in a violent shoving match with the principal gaffer. The assistant director was attempting to intercede, but was being threatened by the gaffer's assistant. A free-for-all was imminent. It was only a question of who was going to throw the first punch. I heard myself yelling.

"All right! That's enough! Hold it! Shut up *everybody*! Now *cut it out!*"

I succeeded in bringing about a temporary abatement.

"What *is* all this?" I asked.

The gaffer spoke. "Listen. I've put up with this goddam pest every day since we started, but enough is enough. He doesn't have to be in here with that goddam sliver. I need this spot for my key light and I want him the hell out of here."

Henry, a dignified old gentleman, said, "I know my job and I'm going to do it and no one's going to prevent me from doing it. My job."

I was confused. "What job? What do you mean 'sliver'?"

Henry held up a blackboard the size of a child's slate. On it was written the word "Yes."

"All right, Henry," I said. "Just relax."

I went over to Barrymore, who sat in his chair smoking and smiling.

"Could I have you in the scene, Mr. Barrymore, for just a moment?"

"Of course. Of course," he said, and joined me near the camera.

"We have a little problem," I explained. "You know the scene. We're outside here with the camera. Miss Alexander knocks on the door. You open it. She says, 'Are you Gregory Vance?' You say, 'Yes.' She walks in and that's it."

"Fine," said Barrymore. "What seems to be the trouble?"

"Well," I explained, "Henry here seems to feel that he has to be standing here with this little slate that says 'Yes.' "

"Oh, by all *means!*" said Barrymore.

I did not grasp his meaning at once. "You mean it's all right for him *not* to be here. Is that it?"

"No, no," said Barrymore. "I'd like to have him there. With his slate."

I was losing patience, struggling for control. "But let's be reasonable, Mr. Barrymore. All she asks is, 'Are you Gregory Vance?' And you *are,* so what else could you possibly say?"

Barrymore thought for a long moment, then looked at me and said, "Well, I could say 'No,' and *then* where would you be?"

We found a spot for Henry and his slate.

Moviemaking is full of long, dull waiting time. But on this picture, the waits were never dull. John Barrymore talked. He tried to interest me in a theatre production of *Macbeth.*

"I've got it all worked out," he said. "I designed it with Willie Pogany—a genius. Do you know his work?"

"Yes, I do. Some of it."

"*Macbeth* always fails. We'll do the first successful *Macbeth.* How would that be? We'll make history. It's going to be Scottish. The whole damned thing. Kilts, by God, and tam-o'shanters and scarves."

His gestures accompanying these words made one see him in the costume.

He continued, "All through it, bagpipes, by God!"

He began to play an imaginary bagpipe. His elbow flailing, his fingers dancing, and out of his nose or mouth or ears a perfect reproduction of the sound of bagpipes—not a bagpipe— but *bagpipes.*

"The trick here," he went on, "is the sex thing. Why is Shakespeare the greatest dramatist who ever lived? Because he wrote the greatest characters. And *how* was he able to write the greatest characters? Because he understood the human race. He understood that every human being, male or female, is a combination of both sexes. And that sometimes the weak ones or the sick ones allow the opposite sex in them to take charge. That's why he made his most powerful men as tender, and sometimes as soft as women. Othello. Antony. Richard III. And why he gave some of his most marvelous women certain masculine aspects. Portia. Rosalind. And, of course, Lady Macbeth. Now the *Macbeth* trick is that *she's* the *man* and *he's* the *woman.* Do you see it? *She's* the *husband* and *he's* the *wife.* God damn it! If you had any *real* guts, you know what you'd do? You'd let Katharine Cornell or Judith Anderson or one of those play Macbeth, and let *me* play *Lady* MacBeth. That would *really* be the way to do it."

Whereupon he suddenly began to move in the most graceful, feminine way. His voice became another voice as he said:

" '. . . I have given suck, and know
How tender 'tis to love the babe that milks me:

43

I would, while it was smiling in my face,
Have pluck'd my nipple from his boneless gums,
And dash'd the brains out, had I so sworn as you
Have done to this.' "

The effect was electrifying.

And this, I thought, is the man who insists upon having the word "Yes" written on a little slate.

A visitor turned up on the set one day. A short, chunky man with a lovely Irish–potato face. He wore an old-fashioned suit and hat. Barrymore greeted him royally. They embraced, pounded one another on the back. Who could it be? The face looked vaguely familiar but I could not place it.

Barrymore led his visitor over to me and said, "Boyo, I want you to meet one of the great ones. I have the honor to present Mr. Marshall Neilan."

My knees buckled. We shook hands.

"All right if he hangs around a while?" asked Barrymore. "He's trying to break into this business, and perhaps he could pick up a few pointers?"

"I'm honored, Mr. Neilan," I said.

"Mickey," he said.

Barrymore spoke. "No, no. You'll never get anywhere. This kid calls everybody 'Mister.' I often think he has the soul of a bellhop. He thinks if he says 'Mister' he'll get a bigger tip. It hasn't worked so far. Has it?"

They moved away. I could not take my eyes off Marshall Neilan. Mickey.

No American director had ever done more interesting work. I had heard of a movie of his made in 1921 called *Bits of Life* and spent years tracking it down. Finally, a print showed up in Washington, D.C. I went down, ran it, and was not disappointed. It was a masterpiece, absolutely original and unlike any other film ever made. It turned out that he had also written it.

I remembered his production of *Penrod,* and *Tess of the*

D'Ubervilles, also a marvelous film with Mabel Normand called *Mike.* He had not made a picture for nine years, his last being a minor prizefight number called *The Lemon Drop Kid.*

It was easy to see why he and Barrymore were attracted to each other. They had both squandered great talent, had both ditched tremendous careers, could both blame the same enemy. Alcohol.

The great Marshall Neilan was having a bad time. He was constantly being picked up for disorderly conduct or drunken driving, and because he was out of money, often had to spend time in jail.

At a Directors Guild meeting one evening, when I was its secretary, the council voted to award Marshall Neilan the Directors Guild Award for that particular year. The form of the award had not been decided. Someone suggested a watch. Some thought it should be a trophy. Others thought a plaque.

"No," said Frank Capra, our president. "Not a watch. It ought to be something a guy can hang up in his—you know—in his—"

"—in his cell," said Ernst Lubitsch.

The bitter joke got a bitter laugh, but then we were all silent. It could happen to any of us.

And there he was, that day, on our set. The great Marshall Neilan. I went over to talk to him.

"Tell him about that time in Florida, Mickey," Barrymore urged.

"No, no," said Neilan.

"Go on," said Barrymore. "Tell it, and I'll give you a double bourbon. Twice."

"Tell it yourself," said Neilan. "Why do you hambos think everybody likes to act? Personally, I hate it."

"That has not prevented you," said Barrymore, "from giving some perfectly spectacular performances."

"All right," said Neilan to me. "I'll tell you about this crazy coot. We had a movie company together, he and I. Can you imagine the poor suckers who put their money up on a couple of stew bums? But we were smart enough not to tell them, and

45

there we were, doing this thing down in Florida. And this nut thought it was very funny to call me up all the time. He knows I need sleep. I'm hopeless without it."

"You're hopeless *with* it," Barrymore interrupted.

"I need sleep. Some people don't." He indicated Barrymore. "He doesn't. I do. So we'd be doing the town and when I knew I'd had enough, I'd go back to the hotel and go to bed. And he'd wait just long enough to figure that maybe I was asleep, and then he'd call up. And it would always be somebody like Diamond Jim Brady calling. Or sometimes, he'd even go falsetto and say he was Lillian Russell. A few times it was the Secretary of State."

"Once I was Dr. Crippen."

"I think you *are* Dr. Crippen," said Neilan. "You got away and changed your goddam name and beat the rap."

"Major Bowes!" cried Barrymore. *"That* was his name. I've been trying to think of it, ever since you came in. Major Bowes. That same pudgy, pompous, stale old birthday cake. He was our business manager."

"That's right," said Neilan. "And from us he graduated to the *Amateur Hour.*"

"What the hell was the name of that picture, Mickey? Do you remember?"

"The Lotus Eater. Of course I remember. How could I not? A *beautiful* title."

"And what the hell were we doing in Miami Beach?" asked Barrymore. "Weren't we supposed to be shooting in Palm Beach among the upper crust?"

"We *started* in Palm Beach," said Neilan. "Then they found out you were Jewish, and threw us out."

"Whatever gave them *that* idea?" asked Barrymore.

"Your real name," said Neilan. "They found out your whole real name. Somebody spilled the beans. Probably an unpaid hooker."

"My real name?" intoned Barrymore.

"Yes," said Neilan. "John Sidney Blythe. It was the 'Sidney' that gave you away."

"Go on, you half-wit. Tell him about that phone call."

"Speaking of hookers," said Neilan, "sometimes he'd come on the phone like one, and proposition me. God, what language! Once he—I mean she—kept me on the phone dickering for half an hour, and finally, after we'd made the deal, he never turned up. She." He turned to Barrymore. "Why didn't you? Where were you?"

"I got a better offer," said Barrymore, in his expert falsetto. Then, "Will you please tell him about that phone call?"

"Jesus God," said Neilan. "I'd have been through it and half-way home if you weren't around here hectoring me."

"I am as silent as the night," said Barrymore.

Neilan went on. "The phone rang about six in the morning, and I heard this rotund voice saying, 'Mr. Marshall Neilan please.' And I said, 'You goddam cretin. Do you know what time it is? I've just gotten to sleep. Get the hell off the phone and stay off.' But the voice went on, and said, 'I beg your pardon. I wish to speak to Mr. Marshall Neilan. My name is William Jennings Bryan.' And I said, 'All right, Mr. William Jennings Bryan. Go fuck yourself.' And hung up. A couple of weeks later, we got invited to a party at the Flagler estate, and the host was introducing us all round, and there was one nice-looking woman there, and when he said, 'May I present Mr. Marshall Neilan?' she turned and walked away. So a little later, I said to the host, 'What the hell was that?' And he said, 'She says you insulted her father on the telephone.' And I said, 'I've never insulted anybody's father on any telephone. What the hell is she talking about? Who's her father?' 'William Jennings Bryan,' he said. 'That's Ruth Bryan.' Well, I swear I thought *he* was pulling a fast one, but then he told me that William Jennings Bryan had written a story and was trying to sell the movie rights, so that's why he was calling me up."

"*The Lotus Eater*," said Barrymore, chuckling. "Did we ever make any money on that bloody thing?"

"*You* probably did," said Neilan. "You and that other dead-beat partner of ours. Godsel. All I know is I worked my canetta off and never got a sausage."

"You had the opportunity of associating artistically with your betters," said Barrymore. "That should have been reward enough."

They looked at each other with love.

I had heard that Barrymore had been in San Francisco on the morning of the great earthquake. I asked him about it.

"Yes, I was," he said. "I was waiting there for a few days for a boat to take me to Australia, where I was going to play a nice little piece called *The Dictator* and that was when it happened. Now I'm going to tell you the truth. I've been telling the truth about it lately. I didn't at the time, but the truth is I don't remember one damned thing about it. I'd been out on the town, raising all sorts of hell, because I loathed the idea of going to Australia. It seemed like going to Siberia. So I had a few, and yes, I remember something about buildings caving in and fires raging, but it was no different from most of my nights in those days. I just kept looking for a place to sleep, and finally I found one, and by the time I woke, it was all over, and I'll tell you what I did. I got the hell out of there as fast as I could. First by boat to Oakland and then by wagon to the nearest railway station. And off to New York instead of giving myself to the Aussies. And that, I'm afraid, is all I remember as a witness to one of the most spectacular holocausts in the history of mankind."

Late one afternoon, running behind schedule, and looking at the glowering faces of the men from the production department, I was doing everything possible to hurry things along.

I approached Russ Metty, and asked, "How about it, Russ?"

"Real soon," he replied, preoccupied. "Real soon."

Two or three minutes later, I was back. "Now?" I asked.

Irritated, he said, "Will you please give me a little *time*?"

"Russ," I replied, "I'd give you the shirt off my back, but I *can't* give you any more *time*!"

We stood looking at each other. There was a tense, awkward silence which was suddenly broken by a burst of laughter from John Barrymore.

Work went on, and so did Barrymore's laugh. I went over and sat down beside him.

"What's so funny?" I asked. "If I fall too far behind schedule, they'll probably fire me."

"You'll survive," said Barrymore.

"But what made you laugh?"

"Well, I'll tell you," he said. "Your little colloquy over there, or was it a set-to?—well, whatever it was—reminded me of a time when I was living at the Algonquin—kindness of Frank Case. Do you know him?"

"I know of him," I said, "but I don't know him."

"I suppose," said Barrymore, "that he's eased more impecunious players over the rough spots than anyone in Gotham. Certainly *I* am one of his beneficiaries." He laughed. "Anyhow I was living at the Algonquin and—"

"Ready!" called Russ Metty.

I jumped up and started for the camera.

"A moment!" shouted Barrymore. I turned back to him. He did his eyebrow business, and asked, "Did you walk out on me?"

"I've got to make this shot. So do you."

"Do you mean to tell me that the shot is more important than listening to my vintage memoirs?"

"Yes, Mr. Barrymore. Right now, it is."

He rose with effort and declaimed, "How have the mighty fallen!"

We made the shot in a single take. I walked Barrymore back to his dressing room. On the way, he continued his story.

"So one day I was making the rounds, and I ran into Bill Mizner and we stood on the corner of Forty-fourth Street and Broadway chatting. He asked me where I was living and I told him.

" 'The Algonquin, eh?' he said. 'Aren't their rates a bit steep for the likes of us?'

49

" 'Their rates,' I said to him, 'are exemplary. I live there as a guest of the owner, Frank Case.'

" 'Yes,' said Bill. 'I've heard that he's a touch of the softer type. Just *how* soft, would you say?'

"And I said, 'Well, this is a man—who—who—' I couldn't think of a description good enough, and so fell back on a cliché and said, 'Why, he's the kind of man who'd give you the—give you the—' and then I looked down and had to say, 'Jesus Christ, this *is* his shirt!'

"That's what made me laugh a while ago," said Barrymore. "Remembering that. Sorry. Goodnight."

"Goodnight, Mr. Barrymore."

There was only one difficult day throughout the course of the shooting. The two players with whom Barrymore had most to do were the children. Virginia Weidler, aged ten, and Peter Holden, aged six.

Barrymore terrified the boy with his presence, practically immobilizing him. But Virginia Weidler was so skillful, experienced, and accomplished that Barrymore constantly referred to her as "Mrs. Thomas Whiffen," the celebrated American actress who had continued to act well into her eighties.

In one scene, Barrymore had a long and, we hoped, moving speech in which he tells the children about their dead mother. The little boy sat on the arm of the chair, Virginia in Barrymore's lap.

Take one. Barrymore began. All of us watching knew he was reaching deep down into himself. He was playing beautifully. Virginia, on his lap, was listening carefully and I found myself admiring the marvelously childish thing she was doing—twisting Barrymore's necktie around her finger, letting it go, twisting it around again.

I watched, enthralled. My reverie was broken abruptly, brutally, by a scream from Barrymore.

"God damn it! What the hell do you think you're doing, you hammy little bitch!" He stood up abruptly. Little Virginia would have fallen to the floor had he not picked her up and thrown her across the set. Fortunately, three stagehands caught the trembling child, but Barrymore was not finished. He bore down on her. "Who the hell do you think you're acting with, you silly little brute. Silly, hell!—crafty, God damn you, *crafty*! I ought to kick you right in the—"

"Mr. Barrymore, *please*!" I said. "I'm sure Virginia didn't mean to—"

"Don't tell *me*!" he shouted. "Virginia. I've messed it up with bitches like her before. They don't fool me."

"Okay," I said. "Wrap it up." It was only four in the afternoon but I knew that nothing more of value would be accomplished that day.

The weeping Virginia was led off. Peter Holden giggled with hysterical delight until his mother slapped him.

I walked around the lot with Barrymore until he had calmed down.

Later, alone, I reflected on the whole upsetting adventure. What troubled me most was my own error. Barrymore was right. His important speech was being damaged by a cute piece of business. The fact was that even I, watching the scene, had put my attention on Virginia, playing with his necktie. The audience doing so would certainly miss the impact and import of what he was saying.

We did the scene again the following morning, and it is a credit to the profession of acting that neither Virginia nor Barrymore seemed to have any recollection of the fireworks. A single take was all that was required to capture a lovely moment, and Virginia played the scene without moving a muscle.

Some stars insist upon seeing the rushes of the work they have done on the previous day, and in fact wish to be consulted as to the choice of takes. Others eschew the practice, feeling that it tends to make them self-conscious.

I asked Barrymore about his feelings in the matter.

"Oh, I *love* to see the stuff!" he said. "If I can do it at the end of the day. First thing in the morning it always looks like a bad dream."

It was arranged for him. Having viewed the rushes at eight o'clock every morning, I saw them again with him at six. His deportment in the projection room was a revelation. I had never seen anyone react as he did. He was able to see himself on the screen with complete objectivity. It was as though he were watching someone else, not another actor but the actual character.

I had watched rushes with many players. Their comments were, sometimes, self-critical: "Oh, my God, that's hammy!" Or: "Speak up, ya jerk. I can't hear." Or: "Why am I making such a horrible face?" Or: "Holy God, please don't use *that*." And so on. Then I frequently shared warm baths of narcissism with others: "Oh, that's *beautiful*! See how I catch the key light in my eyes!" . . . "Oh, please not that one. There's a little shadow on the side of my nose." . . . "Oh, that's good. Look at those *lips*."

John Barrymore reacted not to the problems of the actor but to the problems of the character: "God, he's funny. Look at him. Is he going to turn that bastard down? Do you think so? I think so. There! What did I tell you? He turned him down. . . . Oh, God, isn't that awful? He loves her. I can feel it but he just hasn't the courage to tell her. Go on! Tell her. No. It's no use. He won't do it. . . . Oh, hell! He's going to recite. Why doesn't he just talk? Well, that's not so bad. Actually very moving. Very moving. He did that very well, you know."

To understand the art of acting, it is necessary to understand a special sort of schizophrenia. On the stage or screen, we deal with the phenomenon of the split personality. The actor and the character sharing one body, one brain. Ideally, the actor—hidden—lives inside the body of the character, controlling thoughts, feelings, and actions.

Barrymore's behavior in the projection room signaled a complete separation of these personalities in a singular way.

His acting technique was flawless.

When, toward the end of the picture, his part called for him to recite the lines by John Greenleaf Whittier he did them perfectly on the first take, with the aid of a medium-sized black-board.

"That's it," I said. "Print it." He beckoned to me. I went over to him at once. "Yes, Mr. Barrymore?"

"Would you like one with a little juice?" he asked.

"Juice?" I repeated, confused.

"Juice," he said. "A little eye juice?"

"Oh," I said, "I wouldn't have thought so. I always think that when the actor cries the audience probably doesn't. It's when the actor seems to be holding back tears that the audience is more likely to supply them. They like to cry *for* him, in a way."

"Oh," he said. "Very well."

I could see he was disappointed. I went on. "Still, no harm in trying. Let's do one."

"Good," he said, brightly. "Then you can decide."

We rolled again. He recited once more. To take best ad-vantage of the effect, I had arranged for the camera to dolly in toward him very slowly. As the camera approached him, the tears began to flow, splashing off his cheekbones.

"Cut!" he shouted, waving his palm at the lens.

I thought for a moment that the camera mechanics had dis-turbed him. Not at all. He looked at me. "Too much juice," he said. "I'm sorry. I apologize for my excess. May we do one more, please?"

"Of course," I said.

Another take. This time there were tears but they were dis-creet tears, one small one falling out of the right eye and when that was halfway down his face, a large one from the other eye. I watched him, agape, and forgot to say "Cut." The scene ended somehow. Applause.

"What did you think?" he asked.

"It looked fine," I said. "Surprisingly fine."

He frowned. "Did you like that little one first and then the big one or would it be better with the big one first and then the little one?"

I was content with two satisfactory takes in the can but I confess that by then I was riveted by this display.

"Yes," I said. "That would be *much* better. First the big one and *then* the little one."

"All right," he said. "But for that, you better move in a little quicker."

The camera operator nodded and said, "Okay."

The next take. We all watched, no longer interested in the scene or in the shot, not even concerned about the face. We were concentrating on the trick of the tears.

"Roll 'em."

He did not disappoint us. First the big one, then almost at the end, when we had given up hope, the little one melted out of his other eye.

Later, I discussed it with him.

"Oh, Christ!" he said. "It's nothing. Don't confuse it with acting. It's a trick, like being able to blush." He blushed. "Or wiggling your ears. You can wiggle your ears, can't you?"

"No, I can't," I said.

"Funny," he said, "they look to me like the kind that wiggle." He wiggled his own. "The crying thing is nothing. All women can do it. *Can* do it? Hell, they *do* do it! And kids. Kids bring on tears to get what they want. And when they've got what they want, they stop. That's how I learned to do it. When I was about seven, I watched Ethel do it, and Lionel, and that gave me the idea. I went off into the bathroom for an hour or so every day and practiced. When you've been doing something for fifty years, you're bound to get pretty good at it. But it isn't acting. It's crying. Doesn't mean a damn thing. When I was in India, I saw some of those yogis do things involving physical and mental control that you wouldn't believe. I didn't believe what I saw. Staying under water for half an hour. Remaining absolutely motionless in dreamlike meditation for hours, and some people, you know, can fart at will." He looked troubled. "I've never been able to learn to do that. I'm very disappointed in myself." He laughed his booming laugh. "Did you ever hear of Le Pétomane? The great French cabaret performer? That was his act. Farting. He was a tremendous hit. I saw him once when

I was a kid. He'd come on and give a sort of dissertation on the subject and illustrate the different kinds. I remember that for a finish, he farted La Marseillaise. How could I forget it? But I mean to say, I wouldn't call that acting, would you?"

Actors, by and large, especially stars, do not often acknowledge their director's contribution. In my case at least, John Barrymore overdid it. From the time we finished our film, until his death, he remained kind and generous and helped to propel my career.

The truth is that I had directed him hardly at all. Most experienced directors learn finally that the best direction is the least direction. But I was not an experienced director at that time, and was given to overdirecting, except in the case of John Barrymore. My principal contribution was casting him. After that, I left him pretty much alone. I think it is fair to say that he directed me more than I directed him.

A year or so before his death in 1942, John Barrymore was clowning away the last of his days in some foolishness in Chicago when he collapsed on the stage shortly after a performance began.

The news reached Hollywood quickly. There were rumors of a stroke, a few claimed to have heard that he was dead. I tried to reach him by phone, first at the Hotel Blackstone, where I knew he was staying, next at the Passavant Hospital where he had been taken. Unable to do so, I sent a telegram of enquiry. The next morning, I had a message from him. It read: DON'T WORRY. FOR A MAN WHO HAS BEEN DEAD FOR FIFTEEN YEARS I AM IN REMARKABLE HEALTH. LOVE. MR. BARRYMORE.

3

Ever since I can remember, the girls of America have shared a dream: To be a movie star. To be in the movies.

"You ought to be in pictures."

"Anybody can be in the movies. It's how they photograph you."

"You think Bette Davis is better looking them me?"

"My legs are as good as Elizabeth Taylor's."

"All you need is one good break. Look at Lana. Just happened to be sitting at the right soda fountain, the right time. If not, where'd she be today?"

By what other means of magic can you be a nobody one day; but rich, admired, adored, famous, and having a good time the next? The only question is, does the slipper fit? If not the slipper, how about the sweater? Consider the Lana Turner story. There are various versions. Here is one.

Billy Wilkerson, publisher of the *Hollywood Reporter,* walked into Currie's Ice Cream Parlor one day. Sitting at the fountain was a seventeen-year-old blonde, wearing a sweater that outlined a miraculous bosom. Wilkerson walked up to her and said, "I'm Billy Wilkerson."

"Julia Jean Mildred Frances Turner," she said.

"How would you like to be a movie star?" he asked.

She sucked up the last of her soda, noisily, and looked up. "Okay."

"Come with me." He took her to see Mervyn LeRoy, who was looking for a certain sort of girl to play a part in *They*

Won't Forget. It was a tough picture, an indictment of prejudice in the South, based upon the notorious Leo Frank rape case that shook Atlanta in 1933. To make it effective and believable, LeRoy needed a girl to walk down the street and drive everyone crazy. Eventually she is raped and the crime is pinned on the wrong guy because he is from the North.

It is said that when Wilkerson brought her in, LeRoy looked at her in that tight-fitting sweater, and not only did he think she was good, he thought the sweater was good, too.

Thus began the era of the sweater girls of 1937 and 1938. It was never chic or elegant but it was sexy and show-business and inexpensive. Any high-school girl could afford a sweater and did. The trick was to go into a shop and buy a sweater at least two sizes too small.

Could this go back to Louisa May Alcott? She once wrote about girls with poor posture who were admonished by the new gym teacher, "You must do this exercise, girls—otherwise you won't fill out your jerseys."

It is doubtful that Lana got the idea from Louisa.

In any case, stories such as Lana's captured the imagination of girls everywhere.

They would read about Shirley MacLaine, a chorus girl in *The Pajama Game,* understudying Carol Haney. One afternoon Carol Haney was ill. Shirley MacLaine went on. It happened to be the afternoon that Hal Wallis, a movie producer, was in to see the show. He saw Shirley MacLaine, signed her, and—a movie star!

What the dreamy girls forget is that Shirley MacLaine is a gifted actress, singer, and dancer.

But the legend of You Too Can Be A Movie Star is one of the myths of our time. David O. Selznick understood it and so did the writers, Robert Carson, Alan Campbell, Dorothy Parker, and William Wellman, when they did *A Star Is Born.*

They took this myth and turned it into a glittering fiction. A little bumpkin, Esther Blodgett, comes to Hollywood from a small town, wants to get into the movies, goes to Central Casting. They refuse even to register her as an extra.

A kindly man there looks at her and says, "Honey, it's a tough thing you're trying to do because a thousand people a day try it and maybe only one out of a thousand can even get in."

Esther Blodgett looks up at him and says, "Maybe I'm that one."

She becomes a movie star. Vicki Lester.

The legend is not entirely spurious. Oddly enough, many outstanding American actresses—Ethel Barrymore, Laurette Taylor, Maude Adams, Lynn Fontanne, Katharine Cornell, Judith Anderson, Julie Harris, Kim Stanley—did not become "movie stars." Apparently, talent is a less important attribute than some special quality—and we all believe we possess *that*.

The power of the dream is largely generated by the fact that every now and then it comes true.

It came true for a slightly chubby, very peppy blonde from Indiana named Jane Peters, later known as Carol Lombard, and later still as Carole Lombard.

"I think that 'e' made the whole fuckin' difference," she said to me one day, during the time I was directing her in *They Knew What They Wanted*. (It should be noted that this was Carole's normal style of speech. She used the full, juicy Anglo-Saxon vocabulary; yet it never shocked, never offended because she was clearly using the language to express herself and not to shock or offend.)

She was the only star I have ever known who did not want a dressing room on the set. What little makeup she used, she put on herself. She preferred to look after her own hair. All she asked for was a chair and a small table. There she would be, twenty minutes or half an hour before she was due, ready and able. I never knew her to fluff a line. She liked everyone and everyone adored her. She was happy.

On days when she was not required, she would drive in anyway, all the way from the Valley. The first time she turned up on one of those days, I panicked, certain there had been a mistake.

"What're *you* doing here?" I asked. "You're not called today."

"Piss off!" she said. "I'm in this picture."

She wanted to be around, to stay with the feel of things. She did not want to lose the momentum of work. On these days, she would hang around the set, watching; come along and look at the rushes; talk to various members of the cast. She was valuable.

I thought her a fine actress, one of the finest I had ever encountered. She was completely untrained, had never appeared on the legitimate stage. She came to Hollywood from Fort Wayne, Indiana, became a child actress, and later went to work for Mack Sennett as one of his bathing beauties. But the movies were growing, the business was burgeoning, and there was room at the top for a beautiful, talented girl.

Tremendously versatile, one of her successes was *My Man Godfrey,* a so-called screwball comedy, in which she struck new and original comic notes. But she was equally comfortable in serious drama. I remember an early talkie called *Ned Mc-Cobb's Daughter,* from the play by Sidney Howard, who also wrote *They Knew What They Wanted.* Her performance in *Twentieth Century,* opposite John Barrymore, is one of the best ever seen on the American screen. I once complimented her on her admirable range.

"It's the guys. It's all those goddam, different studs I've knocked around with. You know how it is. You always try to get in solid with the son of a bitch by playing his game. So when I was around with Bob Riskin—the prick never wanted to marry me, can you feature it?—I started in reading books. I don't mean just bullshit. I mean book books. Aldous Huxley and Jane Austen. Charles Dickens. William Faulkner. Because Bob, he was an intellectual. My first. Brainy as a bastard. And I felt I had to keep up. You know how it is. And then with Russ Colombo, he—Jesus Christ, he was a handsome hunk—

59

with him, I got to know all about music and songs and song-writing and publishers. And about records and recordings and which was the best key and big bands and sidemen and drummers. I even started in writing songs. Sometimes with him. We'd be in the hay and in between we'd make up songs. Can you imagine it? Listen, there were a few times there we got so interested in the songs we forgot to get our ashes hauled!" She laughed.

Has there ever been such a laugh? It had the joyous sound of pealing bells. She would bend over, slap her perfect calf, or the floor, or a piece of furniture. She would sink into a chair or to the ground. She would throw her head back. And you would be riveted by that neck. That throat.

"And not only music. With Russ, I became just about the best goddam Italian cook there is. I can do anything in that line because I used to do it for him. Learned it. Chicken Cacciatora. Eggplant Parmigiano. Veal Marsala. Squid. Anything. You name it. Now, with Philo it was different. Because, after all, Philo. It was legitimate. We were married." (Philo was her name for William Powell because he had once played the detective Philo Vance.) "With him, it was wife stuff. That's when I learned how to put a house together, and have everything supplied. And how to take care of his clothes. And what had to be dry cleaned and what not. I mean, I was the best fuckin' wife you ever saw. I mean a ladylike wife. Because that's how Philo wanted it.

"And now with Clark it's the ranch and the horses and the fishing and shooting. The only trouble is—about the shooting I mean—I've gotten to be so much better than he is that I've got to hold back. I can shoot like a sonofabitch, y'know. Anything. So when you say 'versatile'—well, I owe it all to the boys. They made me what I am today."

"Isn't it crazy?" Carole said one day over coffee in my trailer. "I just think about that husband of mine all the time. I'm really stuck on the bastard. That's *something,* isn't it?"

"Not so remarkable," I said, "considering he's Clark Gable, and sixty million other women are stuck on him. Now if you happened to be stuck on *me,* that would be news."

"And what's ridiculous is that we made a picture together for Wesley Ruggles, over at Paramount. Pretty good picture, too. *No Man of Her Own.* And we worked together and did all kinds of hot love scenes and everything. And I never got any kind of a tremble out of him at all. You know, he was just the leading man. So what? A hunk of meat. Of course, it didn't help that I was on my ear about a different number at the time."

"Who?"

"None of your business."

"I know, anyway. I was only asking to be polite."

"Polite, my ass!"

"So then what?"

"Well, about three years ago, Jock Whitney gave this party, and it said you had to wear white. That was the idea. Y'had to wear white. Everybody. You know those society mucky-mucks. They think of all kinds of crazinesses. So what I did was I figured white? What's white? And the first thing struck me was a hospital. So I got my doctor to get me what somebody in a hospital would wear. One of those white things that ties in the back, you know, with your ass out and a white mask over my face and a bandaged head. Everything white. And I even got a white stretcher and a white ambulance and I drove up in the white ambulance and I had myself carried in to Jock's party on a white stretcher, by two dressed-in-white interns. I was a smash. And for some reason, this got to ol' Clark. He thought it was hot stuff. Who knows? Maybe with all that white he thought I was a virgin or something. Believe me. I wasn't. If you want the truth, I don't think I *ever* was! And he started coming on. Clark. And he called up and called up and we started seeing each other and the more I got to know him, the more I saw there was more there than M-G-M was letting us see, but the tough thing was, he couldn't get a divorce. So we managed the best we could till last March when we went legal.

61

I'm really stuck on the son of a bitch."

"You ought to make another picture together."

"Yeah. We talk about that sometimes. But I don't know. We also talk about chucking the whole thing. He's nuts about the ranch, the whole twenty acres. We bought it, you know, from Raoul Walsh. He did all the work on it. It's really terrific. And it turns out we like it. I mean we both like it. The horses and the animals. You ought to see Clark run a tractor. And we shoot. I think maybe we *could* give it up. Of course, I don't know if we've got enough dough. I know *I* haven't got much. I wonder if *he's* got any?"

"Why don't you ask him?"

"Yeah, I think I will. Tonight."

If Carole did six takes they were six *different* takes. Each one had some small development, some sense of growth. A nuance that had not appeared before. There was always something going on inside of Carole.

Technically, she was a phenomenon.

One of the most difficult things film actors and actresses have to do is hit their marks. The assistant cameraman puts marks on the floor, and the players must hit those marks accurately. Should they fail to do so, the assistant cameraman in charge of focus may run into difficulty. Stage actors complain about this, but there is no way out.

With Carole Lombard it was possible to stage a scene with three or four different sets of marks. She would look at them, hard, for a time, fix them in her mind, and never look down again. Yet, without fail, she would always be on her marks perfectly.

"How do you do that?" I once asked her.

"By breaking my balls, that's how," she replied.

Carole had a scar on her face that had to be taken into account when a shot, especially a close shot, was being planned or lighted.

"Shows you how things go, huh? Another inch, half an inch maybe, a turn of the head and my whole fuckin' career could've been over. There was this nice kid. A rich kid. Harry Cooper. His father owned a bank or something. And he had this sonofabitchin' Bugatti roadster. And I was out with him one night, and he was showing off his Goddamned car. You know how it is with some guys. They think a car is like a part of their body and they want to show you how hot it is. So all of a sudden, wham! And I remember how I thought it was just beautiful, like a fireworks explosion, glass in a terrific pattern, and I passed out. It took a while. They finally got all the glass out of my puss and the doctors were great. So I only got left with this. I could have got left with more. Or with no head. And if I had been, Jesus, who do you think would be playing my part now?"

Then there was the matter of the missing light.

Harry Stradling was the cameraman on *They Knew What They Wanted*. An admirable craftsman.

One day he was preparing an important close-up of Carole. She had a stand-in but for important shots she preferred to stand in for herself. A tedious business of standing or sitting under the lights for half an hour or more, directly before playing the scene—but Carole would have it no other way.

"It's easier for the bum who's doing the lighting," she said. "And what the hell? It's my puss. So it's better for me, too."

Harry finished lighting and signaled to me that he was ready.

Carole checked her makeup and we were about to begin.

"Harry," she said softly, "there's a light out on the right side."

"Hold it," he said.

Some sixty or seventy lamps were focused on her from all directions, so finding the one that had blown, or was out, was not easy. Harry and his assistants began to check.

"No," he finally reported. "Everything's on."

"Except one," said Carole.

63

They looked again. Everything was on.

"All right," said Carole. Just as the assistant called, "Roll 'em!" Carole muttered, "But there's a light missing."

"Hold it!" shouted Stradling. He went up to the catwalk himself. Sure enough, a small keylight was out. Two larger lamps had blocked it, making it invisible from the floor, and the man on the catwalk had been careless. Harry repaired the light and came down.

All of us were amazed.

After we made the shot, Harry and I sat around with Carole, talking it over.

"But how could you tell?" asked Harry.

"I could feel it. I could feel it wasn't there. Holy Jesus, Harry, when you've done as many close-ups as I have, you get to know what the right close-up lighting *feels* like on your skin. And there was this whole little patch, right over my cheekbone that felt cool. So I knew something was out."

Harry Stradling abhorred flat light. He did not like a picture that looked like a picture.

Much of the action of *They Knew What They Wanted* took place in and around the vineyards of the Napa Valley in northern California. Harry felt it important to retain a rural feeling. He ordered a truckful of branches of various sizes as well as twigs, flowers, and leaves. No matter what the shot was he would see that it had the suggestion of foliage. If there were no trees or vines in the background, he would drop one in at the top of the frame in the foreground. If that did not seem practical, he would add a shadow of a twig or a branch. Even in close-ups, there it would be, on the back wall—the shadow of a twig.

As a rule, stars are not photographed with shadows on their faces.

One day, making a close-up of Carole, Harry asked, "Carole, would you mind this?"

"Mind what?"

"This."

He was holding a twig in front of the key light so that its shadow fell across her face.

"I don't know," she said. "What does it look like?"

"It looks like your face," he replied, "with a shadow of a twig over it."

"Well, do it," she said, "if you think it looks okay. What the hell do I care?"

"Look," said Harry, "I'll make you a shot without it, but let me make this one with it."

The one with it is the one in the picture. Harry was right. The film never lost the look and feel of the outdoors, of the country.

During the final week of shooting, there came a moment when we were about to break for lunch.

Carole asked, "Harry, would you come with me for a minute? I've got something for you."

She led him to the door of Stage 8 on the RKO lot. Two stagehands, previously rehearsed, opened the great door, revealing a ten-ton truck. On the truck stood an enormous maple tree, with all its roots and with its branches in full bloom. From the tree there hung an outsized card that read:

FOR HARRY, SO YOU WILL NEVER BE WITHOUT. THANKS AND LOVE.   CAROLE.

"Don't be too hard on me," Carole said one day, when we were having difficulty achieving the necessary effect. "I'm pretty tired. I'm getting on, you know."

"Getting on, f'God's sake. You're what?" I asked. "Thirty-four? Thirty-five?"

"Why you son of a bitch no good dirty bastard," she said. "Thirty-*one*. I'm thirty-*one*."

"You're thirty-two," I said.

"Oh, you knew that, huh?"

"Certainly. I know *all* about you."

"So if you knew I was thirty-two, why did you say thirty-four?"

"I wonder that myself, Carole."

"I know why," she said. "It's because you're nothing but a goddam—*man.*"

"All right. So you're thirty-two. So you have no right to be tired. You can be a little fatigued, but not tired."

"Jesus, you sound just like Riskin. He used to horse around with words like that too. What do you mean, tired, fatigued?"

"Well, fatigued means fatigued, worn-out, temporarily. But tired means sort of bored, sick of it."

"You know what you're full of?" she asked.

"Yes, I do."

"What you don't realize is that I've been doing this—what we're doing today—since I was about twelve years old."

"I remember," I said. "That was before you changed your name from Shirley Temple to Carole Lombard."

"That's right," she said.

"How did it happen? You're not the screen-brat type."

"Like everything," she said. "Craziness. No sense to it. We had this neighbor, and he had a friend, Allan Dwan, who was some kind of a movie director."

"What do you mean 'some kind of a'? He was a very *fine* director."

"Yah, I guess so. Anyway, he was a friend of this neighbor of ours, and he was doing a picture, and the name of it was *A Perfect Crime* and he needed a kid. So one day, the neighbor said to him, 'There's a cute kid lives next door.' I was the cute kid. So he sent for me and talked to me, and I got the job. And from then on, I had a lot of jobs. I guess I was good. But I didn't get a contract till later. With Mack Sennett and all. Till I was about sixteen. And that I didn't get from acting. That I got from dancing. I was in this exhibition ballroom contest at the Coconut Grove? And some guy from Fox saw me and tested me, and I'm not going to tell you the rest of the story."

"Clark's a wonder," Carole said to me one day. "I'm really nuts about him. And it isn't all that great-lover crap because if you want to know the truth, I've had better."

"Shut up, Carole."

"What'd I say? Somethin' wrong? I'm just tellin' you a couple of facts. You're not interested in facts?"

"Go on," I said, embarrassed. "You were telling me how you're nuts about your husband."

"Yeah. What I was tryin' to tell you was that I'm nuts about *him*. Not just nuts about his *nuts.*"

"Carole!"

"What?"

"Take it easy."

"We didn't have too simple a time getting going—me and Clark—because when we first started messin' around, he was tied up elsewhere and so was I, sort of. So we used to go through the God-damnedest routine you ever heard of. He'd get somebody to go hire a room or a bungalow somewhere. Like on the outskirts. A couple of times the Beverly Hills Hotel but that could be only at night. Then the somebody would give him a key. Then he'd have another key made, and give it to me. Then we'd arrange a time and he'd get there. Then I'd get there. Or I'd get there, then he'd get there. Then all the shades down and all the doors and windows locked, and the phones shut off, and then we'd have a drink or sometimes not. He's not much of a bottle man. And we'd get going. And that's how it went on for quite a time. Finally, he got unglued and I did too, and we thought what the hell, we might as well get married. But would you believe it? After we were married, we couldn't ever make it unless we went somewhere and locked all the doors and put down all the window shades, and shut off all the phones? Even now, swear to God, we've been married all this time, he still goes around putting down window shades and locking doors. Don't you love it?"

"I love *you,*" I said.

Shortly before *They Knew What They Wanted* was to open at the Radio City Music Hall, Russell Birdwell called a luncheon meeting to be held in a private dining room at the RKO studios. Birdwell was Carole Lombard's personal press agent and she adored him. She always referred to him as Boz (for Boswell) and delighted in his highly imaginative publicity schemes.

Birdwell invited me to join him and Carole, along with Erich Pommer, the producer, and Perry Lieber, the head of studio publicity. The luncheon was scheduled for two-thirty, when there would surely be no one else around.

Birdwell outlined his scheme. Carole Lombard would fly to New York for the opening. However—"Now, get *this*!"—somewhere across the country, the plane would go down and would be reported missing. Birdwell assured us he could keep it missing successfully for at least twelve hours.

"And in those twelve hours, fellas, we're going to be on every goddam front page in the United States of America. Not only Carole Lombard's name, but the name of the picture and the name of the theatre it's going to open at and how would you like to foot the bill for *that* kind of advertising?"

"And then what?" I asked.

"And *then* what? Well, somewhere—she and her pilot and whoever else come straggling out of the woods, because, see, they had a motor konk out or something—I'll get Paul Mantz to figure out the technical stuff—and they were forced down and the radio went on the blink and that's why they couldn't —well, you know—I don't have to spell it out for you, do I? This is *great*!"

Carole began to slap her thigh, yelling, "I'll die! I'll die! Isn't that something? I'll die!"

She expressed herself as perfectly willing to go through with the mad scheme.

I objected.

"Now, look!" I said. "You're assuming the whole thing goes off like clockwork, but a lot of people, especially newspaper people, are going to be pretty suspicious. And what if something happens? And it *doesn't* come off? What if it comes out the whole thing was a hoax?"

"Well, you're not supposed to know about it," said Birdwell. "So what do *you* care?"

For a time it looked as though they were going to go through with it. Eventually, someone put the kibosh on the scheme, only because it was too costly.

Two years later when I saw the extra with its startling headline on a corner newsstand in Washington on that awful day of her death, I could hear Carole's voice and the sound of her hand slapping her thigh, her voice yelling delightedly, "I'll die! I'll die!" I remembered Russell Birdwell's notion of the fake crash for publicity. I stood there hoping against hope that perhaps this was a postponed version of his scheme. For a minute or two I convinced myself it was—it *must* be—it could not be otherwise. Carole Lombard, the lovely Carole, so vital, so imbued with the love of life, simply could not be dead at thirty-five. But she was.

The awful irony of the situation was that only a few weeks earlier, in December 1941, Clark Gable had been appointed chairman of the Hollywood Victory Committee. In this post, he had assigned Carole Lombard to go to Indiana and open a bond drive in Fort Wayne. She had had a great success and was returning to California with her mother. On January 16, 1942, at 7:23 P.M., the plane crashed into Table Rock Mountain, about thirty miles southwest of Las Vegas.

There were other cruel circumstances. When Carole's plane crashed, Gable was in the middle of filming *Somewhere I'll Find You,* which was being directed by Wesley Ruggles, the director who had done the only picture Gable had made with Carole Lombard.

The part he played was that of a war correspondent whose brother dies in action. Consequently there was much dialogue regarding heroism and death. Ruggles arranged for some of it to be cut.

Clark Gable and Carole Lombard had always given the im-

69

pression of being just another movie couple, married for the time being.

When the tragedy struck, something more became known. The depth of feeling in their relationship was revealed. Clark Gable risked his life trying to find the plane—in the slim hope that his wife had survived. He might easily have been killed himself, but Spencer Tracy, who was with him during the search, reported that he did not seem to care. It was almost as though he wanted to be killed, too.

Filming on *Somewhere I'll Find You* stopped for a time. There were rumors the picture would be shelved, but Gable came back and finished it. Then, although forty-one years old, he enlisted in the Air Force and stayed in the service until the end of the war.

The news of Carole's death hit me hard. She had been a rich part of my life. Had she been one of the reasons I had wanted to come to Hollywood when I did? Or was it in the hope of meeting, of coming to know, Barbara Stanwyck? Katharine Hepburn? All three?

The boys of America had wild dreams, too.

4

hrough Carole Lombard, I came to know Carl Laemmle, Jr., and through Junior, I met the legendary Carl Laemmle, Sr.

The elder Laemmle was seventy-five but seemed as venerable as the Grand Lama. He was to die the following year, but when I met him, he was bright and cheerful and funny and loved to talk about movies and the movie business.

"You know," he said, "somebody should write a book about me, someday."

"Somebody *did,*" his son reminded him.

"That Drinkwater thing? By John Drinkwater?" He waved a deprecating palm. "That was a press release. That was not a book. What kind of a book is a man going to write when you hire him to write it? We hired him to write it. For money. So he wrote it. But that's not what I'm talking about. I mean a real book. About how this whole thing started. And how it is now. And about what's going to happen to it. It's very interesting. It would be interesting."

His speech retained traces of a German accent. He was a tiny man. Now, in age, he had shrunk even more.

I had been anxious to meet him because he seemed to me, from the record, one of the most fascinating and imaginative of the motion-picture producers.

He had been responsible for *Show Boat, The Good Fairy, Back Street, My Man Godfrey,* and hundreds of others. Although he was primarily a businessman, he was among the few important executives who were equally interested in the technical and artistic growth of the medium.

He had a great deal to do with promoting the careers of Erich von Stroheim and Lewis Milestone and Gregory LaCava.

He had had a profound effect upon the development of Hollywood as the film capital of the world.

I sat looking at him with admiration.

"One of the reasons I wanted to meet you, Mr. Laemmle, is because of a curious coincidence."

"What coincidence is that?" he asked brightly.

"Well, when did you start Universal Pictures?"

"In nineteen-twelve," he said immediately.

"Well, there you are," I said. "Nineteen-twelve is the year I was born. So your company and I are the same age."

"I wish my company looked as young as you do," he said, and laughed. "You don't think that would be a good idea?"

"What idea?"

"That somebody should write a book about me? Not about me as a man but about me and the movie business."

"I think it would be a *great* idea," I said.

"Maybe one of the reasons I would like to see it is because I already have a good title for it. A good *name* for this book."

"What is it?"

"I think they should call it 'The Long Store.' "

"I'm sorry," I said. "But I don't see why that would be a good title."

He laughed merrily and said, "Read the book, then you'll see."

I noticed, in our time together that day, and two subsequent meetings, that Laemmle was a joyous little man.

He seemed to see humor in everything, including himself.

"Tell him, Pop," said Junior. "Tell him why you want to call it 'The Long Store.' "

"You think he'd like to hear it?"

"I'm sure of it," said Junior. "He's crazy about movies. He used to work for Goldwyn."

"Goldwyn," said Laemmle. "Sam Goldwyn is a great man. He has great courage. We are competitors. We've always been competitors, but I respect him."

" 'The Long Store,' " I prompted.

"Yes," said Laemmle, and took a deep breath. "Sometime, when I think back on the whole thing, I wonder what would have happened to my life, and to so many other lives, if I hadn't happened to rent that long store. I mean to say, what if I'd rented a *different* store? The one across the street. Or the one next door. Well, there never would have been a Universal Pictures—and listen, there never would have been a Carl Laemmle. I mean not *this* Carl Laemmle. . . . What happened was, I was then in dry goods. I was born in Laupheim. Have you ever heard of it? It's in Germany."

"No, I can't say that I have, Mr. Laemmle."

"It was a good little town, and my people there, they were always merchants, so when I came over here that's what I did, in Oshkosh. That's all I *knew* how to do and I had different kinds of stores, and finally, I heard there was a good spot in Chicago. A big dry-goods store there—*too* big, maybe—went broke, and it seemed a good chance to open a branch of *our* store. So I went there to look over available space. I looked at all kinds of places, on the main streets and on the side streets, and finally, it came down to about two or three places. And after thinking it over, I decided on this one store on Milwaukee Avenue because it was very long and it seemed to me it would be a good shape for a dry-goods store, because you know how in a dry-goods store, you like to have long counters where you can pile things up. So I took that one. The Long Store. . . .

"The whole thing to move to Chicago with the branch was good because for a while there we were the only dry-goods store in the neighborhood. You have to remember I'm talking to you now about maybe nineteen-oh-one or oh-two. And one day a fellow came in and he started in looking around, and finally he said to me, 'How would you like to make ten dollars tonight?' I said to him, 'I'd like to make ten dollars *any* night.' So he said to me, 'I would like to come in here tonight and show some moving pictures.' Well, I didn't know what he was talking about but then he explained it to me. How he had this

73

machine and would hang up a white sheet, and then show these pictures that moved. He charged a nickel admission. And people came in and watched the moving pictures. So I said to him, 'But how come you want to do it here? In my place?' And he said, 'Because for the best results you have to have a long store.' Well, I made the arrangement with him, and pretty soon he was coming down about once every two weeks and people would come in for a nickel and he would show these pictures that moved. And they got to be more and more popular and I got to know this fellow. And the more people that came, the worse it was because they had to stand. And sometimes they leaned on the merchandise. So I looked around, and I found *another* long store with nothing in it. We put in some benches, and then he started coming every week, and we began developing it into a nice little business. And by nineteen hundred and six, I formed a company, and we made up a name for it. It was—"

"The Nickelodeons," I said.

"You know that?" said Laemmle delightedly. He turned to his son. "Say, this fellow's all right." He turned back to me. "The Nickelodeons. Yes. And that was a real success. Well, then we started buying more and more pictures. Renting them, I mean. Pretty soon, I began to have trouble with the suppliers. So the next thing, I looked into it and I decided why have trouble with the suppliers? We'll make our own. And we started in making our own. So you probably know already, after a while that led to the Universal Film Manufacturing Company. Then when everybody started moving out here to the sunshine, we did, too. It's been—the whole thing—a very interesting business. A very interesting life. And I sometimes think that it must have been God who pushed me into that long store."

"Mr. Laemmle," I once asked, "what do you think is the most important element in the success or failure of a picture?"

The answer came back at once. "The right actors in the right parts or the wrong actors in the wrong parts."

It is sometimes said that a star makes a part, but by and large, the opposite is true. Further, audiences have demonstrated that they are interested in their favorite stars only if the stars play parts they want to see them in.

When Clark Gable was known as The King and was as powerful a box-office attraction as the American film business had ever known, his pictures were sold in advance simply as Gables.

"We've got three Gables this year," the salesmen would say to the exhibitors, and book almost the whole Metro program on the strength of this pitch.

Gable was a superstar. At the peak of his career, it was decided at Metro to make a film of the play titled *Parnell*. It had been a great success on the London stage, but had failed in New York. Still, the story of the Irish patriot attracted someone, and that someone proved to be persuasive. *Parnell* was under way. It was planned as an expensive prestige picture.

"Prestige pictures," so-called, were an element of Metro production left over from Irving Thalberg's regime. Thalberg believed it was incumbent upon the industry to make a certain number of pictures each year without thought of profit. They were to be class pictures that would appeal to the theatregoing public and the book-reading public, the academic world, the professionals, the upper middle class. Thalberg believed such films broadened the base of the audiences and dignified the industry.

Parnell was made, then launched with an outstanding campaign.

Years later, an executive in Metro's sales department told me, "I want to tell you, the picture went out, and when the gross reports started to come in, I swear to God we thought something'd gone wrong with the telegraph keys. You couldn't believe the grosses that were coming in on *Parnell*. We kept telegraphing back, asking for confirmation, because we figured these had to be typographical errors. I mean, you couldn't *have* grosses like that, not with a Gable. It would be like, say, you did a play on Broadway today, and the cast was Lunt and Fontanne and Al Jolson, and you're going to open them in a show by Kaufman and Hart with music by Irving Berlin. And you open the box office Monday morning and nobody comes over to buy a ticket. What would you say? You would say, 'Well, they didn't get it, they didn't see the ads.' So you take the ads again, and five people come up the next day to buy tickets. I'm trying to give you an idea of what it was like with *Parnell*. We took a terrible beating with that whole picture. Nobody at the studio could understand what happened. Me, I still don't understand. The only thing I could figure out is they didn't want to see Gable in that kind of a part in that kind of a story. That's it."

As long as I had him on the subject, I asked, "And what about *Crisis*? You remember that?"

"Do I *remember* it? I wish to Christ I could *forget* it. *Crisis*. Oh my God!"

"What happened?"

"Well, Cary Grant, you remember what hot stuff he was? I mean, in some ways, he was as hot as Gable. He'd had a string of hits you could hardly believe, *The Philadelphia Story, Suspicion, Once Upon a Honeymoon, Destination Tokyo, Mr. Lucky, None But the Lonely Heart, Arsenic and Old Lace, Night and Day, Notorious, The Bachelor and the Bobby-Soxer, Mr. Blandings Builds His Dream House*. I mean I'm talking about a string of hits. So this story comes up and it's a beaut. Everybody at the studio is jumpin' up and down. It's about a terrific brain surgeon, see? And about this South American dictator, a Fascist or a Communist or something, and he's threatening the peace of the world. And what happens? He develops a brain tumor. So they send up to the States and they kidnap the brain surgeon and they bring him down and they make him perform the brain operation on this son of a bitch. What a spot, huh? If he pulls it off, maybe he screws up the peace of the world. And if he doesn't do it, I mean the brain operation, they may think he's screwed up on purpose and they'll probably remove *his* head, right? A very strong story.

I forget how it came out. But we had José Ferrer around, who was also hot as a pot at the time, and, of course, perfect for the South American dictator, right? But he wasn't all that kind of a box-office attraction. So, for insurance, they started looking around for the brain surgeon and somebody came up with the idea of Cary Grant. So everybody thought, 'Oh, sure, Cary Grant. Great. But how do you get him?' Well, a lot of pressure, a lot of money, a lot of conditions. Next thing you know, we've got him. And everybody thought the whole quarter was saved, just with that one picture. So they made it. And what happened? It went out and e-g-g. I'm talking about capital E, capital G, capital G. And this was when Cary Grant couldn't make a wrong move. They didn't care who the other people were, or who the leading lady was, just give 'em Cary Grant. Except give 'em Cary Grant in *Crisis*. I want to tell you we could've made more money with that picture if we'd cut the film up and sold it for mandolin picks. It was a full disaster. So what does it prove? It proves that no matter how big a star is, the public is only going to accept him in certain kinds of parts. In the kind of parts they want to see that guy in. Cary Grant, they wanted to see him with a broad. They didn't care what broad, so long as it was a broad. I mean—now—looking back on it, when I tell you that Cary Grant played the part of the greatest brain surgeon in the world, I can hardly keep from laughing myself. And that's what the public did. They bust out laughing. They thought it was ludicrous. So here's another question: Why did we go with him? All right, here's the answer: If you can get Cary Grant to say, 'Yes, I'm going to come over to your studio and make a picture,' you don't say, 'No'; you say, 'Yes.' In fact, you say, '*Hooray, yes.*' And here's a last question: How come that public that's supposed to have the mentality of a twelve-year-old, how come they knew more than all these six-thousand-dollars-a-week executives at Metro? Can you answer me that?"

Once, in the middle of a Goldwyn casting conference, when any number of leading ladies had been suggested and rejected,

I suddenly jumped up and cried, "I've *got* it!"

"You have?" asked Goldwyn eagerly. "Who?"

"Anna Sten," I said.

The joke laid an egg, as it should have done.

In the early 1930s, Goldwyn was considering a production of *The Brothers Karamazov*. He heard about a German film, called *Der Mörder Dmitri Karamazov,* and arranged to screen it. Although he did not respond favorably, he was forcibly struck by its star, Anna Sten. He arranged to meet her, was further impressed, and soon had her under contract.

Discussing the Anna Sten saga, he said to me one evening, "Everybody thought she was German, some people still think so. Maybe because she made all those big hits in the German movies. But no. She was Russian. Ukrainian. That's right, she was born in Kiev. And she was on the stage in Russia. In Moscow, in fact. And she made movies there, too. But it wasn't till she went to Berlin—I don't know why, something with a husband—that she made her sensation. . . . I tell you, you never know. The day I signed her I thought it was the greatest day of my whole career. I thought, 'This is some star!' She had everything. She had looks and style and sex and class. She had tremendous life and she could act like a son of a bitch. . . . And we talked and talked for almost a year to try to figure out what we could make with her. She was a great actress, and a great actress has got to have a great part. And after a while we went to the classics. And somebody came up with *Nana* by Zola. A great story. A great part. I got two fine writers and I decided, for a woman's story like this, why not a woman director? There was only one woman director in those days—Dorothy Arzner—and she was good. And my God, what a cast I got to surround her! Sten, I mean. Phillips Holmes, remember him? What a good-looking boy! Lionel Atwill, one of the greatest actors. And Richard Bennett, maybe *the* greatest actor. And even in the small parts, I had Mae Clarke, Reggie Owen, people like that. We didn't spare a goddam thing. Rodgers and f'Chrissake Hart even to write a song for the picture. But it didn't go. I tell you, looking back on it, I think the original property was a mistake. We couldn't do the real story because the censors wouldn't let us. And when you tell a story, you've got to be true to the story. If you're not true to the story, then don't make it in the first place."

I said, "I read somewhere that you said she was—just a minute." I took a note out of my pocket and read, " 'An actress whose beauty seems to have sprung from the soil, and whose intelligence is that of the instinctive artist and the earnest student of life.' "

Goldwyn waved a hand at me in a deprecating way. "Some goddam press agent," he said. "Probably Pete Smith."

"Pete Smith, the comic? The one does those great one-reelers?"

"That's the fellow. He used to be my press agent. He was a good press agent. Listen, I *made* him into a good press agent. He made *himself* into a lousy comic. That's how people are. They don't know what to do with themselves."

"Well, *then* what happened with Anna Sten?"

"Who knows? Another goddam classic we had to go for, in fact another goddam *Russian* classic, how do you like *that*? I must've been *crazy* that year. We took the Tolstoy book *Resurrection*. We figured nobody would know what that means, that title. In fact, they wouldn't even know how to *pronounce* it. So we called it *We Live Again*. Amounts to the same thing. And you talk about writers. Did I have writers on *that* one! Preston Sturges. Maxwell Anderson. I can't even *remember* who else. I got her Fredric March, how do you like *that*? He was about the best actor around in the movies at that time. So what happened? Great reviews and no business. . . . Then Eddie Knopf did an original and I got her King Vidor and I gave her Gary Cooper. *The Wedding Night,* that was the name of it. So what happened? Again, nothing. In fact, more nothing than *before* even. . . . Well, I don't know much about baseball, but I know that three strikes is 'Out.' So we had a few meetings. Pleasant. They were nice people. Anna and her husband and me. And we all decided we should call it quits. . . . I look back now. That night I sat in that room and I saw that goddam Karamazov thing and she came on the screen. I tell you, everything in my heart told me she was going to be the biggest thing in the history of the motion pictures. And plenty of other people thought so too, believe me. They don't admit it like I do, but plenty of people. . . . So when I sit here, day in and day out, and people come in and tell me, 'I'm *sure* about this, I *know* that, I *guarantee* you this, there's no *question* about that,' I just look at them, and inside I'm smiling. To myself. Because I want to tell you something about this business. Nobody *knows* anything. You can think and you can feel and you can believe, but you can't *know*. . . . That's why I make the picture to please myself, and I hope everybody else will like it. I have to guess. I have to please myself, that's the main thing. *I* have to like it. Then sometime, when it's finished, even *I* don't like it, so what can you do?"

I asked, "Do you think the trouble might have been that these were talkies? If you'd brought her over in the silent days, do you think the result would have been different?"

"Who knows?" he replied wearily. "And are you starting in with me again about that talkie thing?"

"No, no, Mr. Goldwyn, really not."

"Because I want to show you something. I show this to lots of people. They're usually surprised. I think *you're* going to be surprised also."

He reached down into a desk drawer and handed me a photostatic copy of a letter.

"Read this," he said.

I took it, and asked, "Who's it from?"

"That's what I'll tell you later." I noticed that the signature had been obliterated. "It's from an actor," said Goldwyn. "From an actor I had under contract. He was under contract to me for a long time, and he was doing very well, a big star, and his pictures were hits. And the way things were going, somebody in my legal department told me they believed we should put an amendment in everybody's contract, everybody we had under contract, to cover sound pictures. They didn't even call them talkies yet. Sound pictures, they called them. So we sent out all these amendments to all these actors and actresses, or to their agents, and they all came back. Signed. It was nothing. Just routine. Then I got this letter, the one you've got in your hand. Read it."

I found it so interesting that later I asked Mr. Goldwyn to let me have a copy.

5th August, 1928.

My dear Sam,

With reference to the additional clause in the contract, I would rather not sign this, at any rate, just at present. Except as a scientific achievement, I am not sympathetic to this "sound business." I feel, as so many do, that this is a mechanical resource, that it is a retrogressive and temporary digression in so far as it affects the art of motion-picture acting—in short, that it does not properly belong in my particular work (of which, naturally, I must be the best judge).

That the public are, for the time being, demanding this novelty, is obvious, and that the producer is anxious to supply it, is natural, and for the actor to contend against it would be foolish. After four years of experience with myself, the firm should have no doubt as to my reasonable cooperation in this matter—as in others.

For me to function conscientiously before the microphone is one thing, but to sign a legally phrased document authorizing this is a very different matter, and would logically presuppose my approval of this mechanical accessory to my work.

I hope I have made this clear, Sam. May I ask that the company will respect these conditions and leave the matter where it is? Kind regards, always,

I looked up. "Who?"

"You'll never guess," said Goldwyn. "Ronnie Coleman. With that beautiful voice and that beautiful speech, he had plenty of stage experience and everything, but you see, *he* didn't believe in sound pictures either. Talkies. It was a funny time, only what—eighteen, nineteen years ago? And it's like it was a whole nother world. And how the whole revolution happened was just crazy. Business was bad. In the theatres, the big ones, they were putting in stage shows and vaudevilles. In the small houses, they were giving away dishes and presents and turkeys and business was bad. And nobody knew what to do. Sure, all these people were around with their ideas for sound and talkies, but it was going to cost a fortune and nobody had the money. And the ones who did have a little didn't want to risk it. But Jack Warner and Harry, they were in terrible shape. In fact, Jack told me they were getting ready to pack it in. Maybe even take a bath. So they took the flier. They had absolutely nothing to lose. They were broke anyway. So they took the flier and made the whole revolution. I'm not saying it wouldn't've happened anyway, but it wouldn't've happened *then,* maybe not for a long time, not for a *long* time."

I think of Samuel Goldwyn as an American Primitive, possessed of a superior instinct for the profession in which he finally found himself. This is not to say that he was not often duped or snowed or conned. Those who retain a part of their innocence are easy prey for those who have lost all theirs.

I remember the day when, along with the rest of his staff, I was called in to hear Leo McCarey tell a story.

Leo McCarey was a Hollywood meteor. He had begun in the business as a property man but soon was a property man making suggestions for gags and routines and bits of business. He was graduated to gagman. From there it was only a short step to directing one-reelers, then two-reelers and, finally, feature pictures.

McCarey possessed a rare comic intelligence. He could create hilarious situations, and imaginatively, almost inexhaustibly, develop those situations. He was not a writer, but he was a superlative talker, and in a time and place where there was a paucity of readers and a plethora of listeners, talkers were more effective (and more successful) than writers.

Goldwyn had under contract, among others, Gary Cooper

and Merle Oberon. We were told daily by him to f'Chrissake find something for Cooper. Also for Oberon. Nothing for either of them had turned up.

Hollywood had always been a small town. There were few secrets there and everything about every studio was generally known by those who made it their business to amass that most valuable of all commodities—accurate information.

We assembled in Goldwyn's office.

"Gentlemen," said Goldwyn, "Mr. McCarey here has a great idea for a great picture and he is going to do us the honor this afternoon of telling us. It's very nice of you, Leo, and I want you to know we all appreciate it. And I know right now if this is your story it must be a good story because you're good. At stories. In fact, you're one of the best. I've always said so, right from the beginning. 'Ruggle in Red Gaps' and so forth. All right, gentlemen, Mr. McCarey is going to tell us his story, so please, I want everybody to listen very carefully and keep quiet. If you want to make notes, make notes quietly. Go ahead, Leo."

He leaned back in his chair, put his long finger against his long nose and gave his full attention to Leo McCarey.

McCarey did an unprecedented thing. He stretched out on Goldwyn's office sofa, crossed his ankles, put his hands back of his head, closed his eyes for a moment, then opened them and began.

(This is the way to do it, I thought. By God, if *I* ever get a chance to tell a story, this is how *I'm* going to do it. Just stretch out, look relaxed as hell, and let everyone *else* in the room be tense. He had not yet begun and already I had made a few notes. Quietly.)

"Well," said Leo, smiling confidently, "the guy in my story is a cowboy. I'll introduce him around the ranch with about, maybe say three, four hundred feet of spectacular cowboy stuff. Damnedest stuff you ever saw. You know, just to get the audience hooked. Riding, roping, wrestling a steer, out on the roundup, different seasons, snow, heat. I want to do a quick portrait of the manliest, sexiest, bravest, ballsiest son of a bitch you could ever imagine. Right? Now, *wham*! Cut to Saturday night. In town. A little town. Arizona. Say Douglas. Okay? How do you like it so far?" He laughed and continued. "We're in the bar. It's a kind of a dance hall, too. But this is modern, you understand—this is *now*. Right *now*. And I'm in a full shot of the dance hall and the orchestra's playing some kind of Dixieland stuff." McCarey, a musician, sang a few merry bars:

> " 'Wah dah dah *dee* dee *dee*
> Wah dah dah *pah* pah *pah*
> Tah dah dah dah *dee dee dee*. . . .'

Like that, see? And it looks like a jolly evening and we move in with the camera and we begin to see there're hardly any women there, for cryin' out loud. Most of the couples are two cowboys. Get it? Cowboys dancing with cowboys. Now, this has *got* to be a terrific jolt after we've seen him in that cocksman introduction. Right? And there's nothing fairy about this, mind you. It's just that there aren't enough dames to go around. So cowboys dance with cowboys. That's what I used to do when *I* worked the ranch. And I don't think anybody's ever suspected *me*." (Laugh.) "Well, anyway. There's our cowboy dancing with another cowboy. And each one of them's kind of flirting with whatever dame happens to dance by. Right? Now. In the part of the cowboy, the *main* cowboy—our lead—I see somebody like, well, I don't know. I suppose there're several could handle it. Could play it. Maybe—well, I don't know. I suppose the *best* one—I mean as I think about the story, the image I get in *my* mind, is somebody like say—well, say— *Gary Cooper*." He paused. Goldwyn nodded gravely. McCarey went on. "Wham! We cut to *another* dance hall but this one's entirely different. There's a string trio playing some kind of a waltz." Again he sang, simulating the trio.

> " 'Doo *doo*-doo dee *doo*
> Doo *doo-dee-doo*!"

And you know where we are? I'll tell you. We're in the ballroom of the classiest damn girls' finishing school on the East coast. Virginia, someplace. And what have you got? A roomful of these beautiful, uppercrusty girls. Heiresses. All of them. And they're dancing with each other because this is their dance class, see? Girls with girls. You follow it so far? Arizona: men dancing with men. Virginia: girls dancing with girls. This is terrific, isn't it? I mean is this a never-forget-it opening?"

"You said it," someone piped up.

Goldwyn glowered in the direction of the voice.

"Shhhh!" he hissed.

"Okay," said McCarey. "We move in—slow and easy—on one couple. Two girls. You never *saw* such beauties. And one of them, the one who's leading, is *really* class. It ought to be somebody like, well—I'm not sure because you all know as well as I know that the one hard thing to find out here is real class. See, it isn't enough for her to be stunning. She has to be beautifully spoken. This is for the contrast we're going to need later on. Maybe somebody English? I don't know. Maybe there isn't *anybody*. Maybe this whole idea stinks. Wait a minute! I'll tell you who could do it. *Merle Oberon!* Yeah. She could do it. I don't know if she's available, or if you could get her. But *she* could do it." He sat up suddenly. "Hey, would that be bad? Gary Cooper and Merle Oberon? Oh, by the way, did I tell you the title? No? Get this. Gary Cooper and Merle Oberon in—" He paused significantly. "—*The Cowboy and the Lady.*"

I looked over at Goldwyn. His finger came down from his nose. He gulped. He blinked. He grinned suddenly then changed it into a scowl, fearful that the grin might cost him extra money.

Still, he could not keep himself from saying, ever so softly, "*The Cowboy and the Lady.* Mm-hm."

I could see him tasting it, and the taste was clearly delicious.

McCarey, an experienced fisherman, knew when his catch was well and truly hooked. He was on his feet now, overgesticulating and laughing it up. Full speed ahead. Throttle open.

His method was to recite routines, not necessarily in dramatic or chronological order. Some of them could be visualized and were, indeed, entertaining. Others were unclear. All were finally punctuated by McCarey shouting, "They'll piss! I tell you, they'll *piss!*"

Ten minutes into it, I was having trouble following the story. Ten minutes later, I began to see the reason for this: there *was* no story. There were jokes, double meanings, comic situations, and character descriptions. No more. But so infectious was McCarey's spellbinding and so entertaining his delivery that he was getting respectable laughs.

He knew the importance of rhythm in creating laughter. Most laughter is generated by surprise, usually arising from a break in rhythm.

No one in the room understood his verbal shorthand. He was making sounds, punctuating lines with a snap of his fingers, a punched palm, or a line garbled in laughter, followed by—"They'll *piss!*"

"Now!" he said tantalizingly. "Now comes the funniest scene in the picture. Where he takes her through the whole house, see? That isn't even *built* yet. There's *nothing* there. Just a few pegs in the ground with strings on them. Right? They go through it. And in the kitchen part they're behaving like they're in a kitchen. And then the hall, the living room—and all the time you know he's leading her, or trying to lead her, to the bedroom. And *she* does too, see? But remember, there's no bedroom. There's no bed. There's nothing. Grass. Pegs and string. But I tell you, now this is the most sensational scene in the picture, I mean of the comic ones—not the terrific romantic ones or the sex or the action—the comedy here is him trying to lead her across this one string where the bedroom is going to be, and of course finally he does and the *way* he does it, with the pieces of business and sight gags and one-liners and double meanings—even a few *triple* meanings—I mean is *hilarious!* They'll piss!"

He sat down and laughed. We joined him. He had told us virtually nothing but it seemed a *funny* nothing.

He continued. There were descriptions of a rodeo, of two people looking for each other and just missing several times.

86

The lady, awkward in the cowboy's world. The cowboy doing comic stuff back East in her world.

"So they're in this elegant restaurant—see?—like The Colony? And they've just ordered, and at the next table—see?—people are having, are about to have, crepes suzette." (What's this now?) "So the classy headwaiter is working on them and he pours all the brandy and gonk all over the stuff and of course he *lights* it." (Could I believe my ears? Was the great McCarey actually going to pull out that old chestnut of the country bumpkin extinguishing the crepes suzette? My God, I had seen it in a silent picture with Charles Ray when I was ten. No, of course not. He probably has a switch on it.)

McCarey went on. "So the flames shoot up and the head-waiter's working there at his little table. Gary gloms it, stands up, hollers, 'Don't panic, folks! Keep your seats!' And he picks up a big pitcher of ice water, pours it *all over* the crepes suzette and puts out the fire! They'll piss, I tell you!"

He went on. On and on, leading finally to an expected and conventional, but satisfactory, ending. Boy meets girl. Boy loses girl. Boy gets girl.

He was holding to the rules of the game. If you have Gary Cooper and Merle Oberon in a picture, the audience knows from the beginning they are going to wind up together. No surprise there. The surprise must be in *how* they wind up together.

"Well, that's about it," he said. "It's just the bare outline. I don't want to take up too much of your time. Actually, I left out most of the best stuff. Some of it's a little hard to tell and also the faces in this room today don't look too honest to me, so I don't mind giving away a few little samples. But I don't want to hand over the whole tutti-frutti." (Laugh.)

"Leo," said Goldwyn, grandly, "you've got a fine story there. Very good characters, good parts for stars. I'm going to tell you frankly I think it needs work—a little work, not much, in the construction."

"Don't worry about the construction, Sam," said McCarey. "I never made a picture yet that fell off the screen. Oh, hell. That's the trouble with telling an outline. Why I didn't want to do it. People forget it's an outline, and start to criticize it as though they've heard the whole thing. You haven't *heard* the whole thing. I was only trying to give you a feel of the kind of picture I think you ought to make. Maybe it was a mistake."

Goldwyn was cowed for a moment and said, "No, no, Leo, I realize that. Only a feel. I was just commenting on my impressions."

"Well," said McCarey confidently. "Let me know." He walked to the door, turned and added, "By Friday, huh?"

He left abruptly.

There was a long pause. No one seemed anxious to be the first to comment. Finally.

"Well, gentlemen," said Goldwyn. "What are your views?"

The mumbles began.

"Lots of funny stuff in there."

"Yes."

"Needs work."

"Yuh."

"Is it written yet? Could we see some of this in writing?"

"Yeah."

"Will he work with the writer?"

"The Cowboy and the Lady," said Goldwyn.

"Yuh."

"Would *The Lady and the Cowboy* be better?" asked an eager beaver.

"No, no," said Goldwyn. "F'Chrissake, *The Cowboy and the Lady*. Jesus Christ, what's a matter with you? In the first place if we get Gary Cooper and Merle Oberon in *The Cowboy and the Lady,* that's how it has to go. Because that's how the *billing* goes. You think Cooper's going to let us call a picture *The Lady and the Cowboy* with him second? I mean his character second in the title? What's a matter with you?"

"Just a thought," said the contrite blunderer.

Goldwyn found it difficult to calm down.

"The man *always* comes first. He's supposed to. In any title or anything. Like you get a letter. What does it say? It says 'Mr. and Mrs. Samuel Goldwyn.' Right?"

"Of course," I said. "And every speaker always begins a speech by saying 'Gentlemen and ladies.' Right?"

Goldwyn looked at me. "Didn't I tell you," he said, "I want you to spend more time in the cutting rooms? What the hell're you doing here, anyway?"

"You sent for me," I said.

"Well," said Goldwyn, "that only proves *I* can make a mistake, too. I want to tell you something, Talboig. Frankly. I'm getting goddam sick and tired of your wisecracks. If you want to make wisecracks go sit in the round table in New York in the Algonquin with all those other wisecracks, f'Chrissake. Don't bring them around here and waste my time."

We looked at each other through a fog of hostility.

"I think *The Cowboy and the Lady* is a terrific title," I said, "especially on a picture with Gary Cooper and Merle Oberon."

"I agree with you," he said. He turned to the others in the room. "Well, gentlemen," he said. "Now that Talboig likes it, we can go forward."

He was still laughing as the last member of the staff left the meeting.

The next morning Goldwyn called us in, one by one, and asked each of us to tell him the story of *The Cowboy and the Lady* as we understood it. By the time he had heard it nine times from nine different men, he had a firm notion of what was there.

Goldwyn bought the story from McCarey the following day for $50,000.

That night, I ran into McCarey at the Vendôme and congratulated him.

"Yeah," he said, "but now the trouble is, I've got to write it down, or get somebody to write it down, and I can't remember what the hell I said. Can *you?*"

"Some of it."

"How would *you* like to write it down? I'll give you five hundred."

"I'm not a writer."

"So what? Neither am I. And what's the difference if you're *not* a writer? Goldwyn isn't a *reader*. No kiddin'. I mean it. Would you want to tell me some of what you remember? Because swear to God I only remember a few flashes."

One afternoon, about two weeks later, a story meeting on *The Cowboy and the Lady* took place in Goldwyn's office in a somber atmosphere.

McCarey's agent had delivered a twenty-five-page outline that morning, and had picked up the check. The outline was disappointing and hardly worth the $2000 a page (double spaced) it had cost. Needs work, was the consensus. The meeting had been called to discuss possible screenwriters.

Goldwyn was the cheeriest one in the room.

"Listen," he said. "Nobody kill yourself. I've started in with f'Chrissake less than this and come up with some great pictures. Let's not forget we got here a great premise here. A fine springboard. McCarey's great, but he's lazy. This is just an outline— a treatment, that's all." He looked at me. *"You* like it, don't you, Talboig?"

"When he told it, yes. It was quite entertaining, but this treatment needs a treatment."

It was out before I could stop it.

Goldwyn looked at me. I feared that my career was over, that my life at the Goldwyn Studios had ended before it had actually begun. He was still looking at me and I could think of nothing to do but to look back. There must have been remorse in my eyes. His were flaming with anger, but all at once, tears welled up in them.

He shook his head, gently, and said, "I don't know what I'm going to do with you."

The first team of writers assigned to *The Cowboy and the Lady* was Anita Loos and John Emerson.

A few days after they had begun, the staff was hastily summoned to Goldwyn's office for the shortest staff meeting I can remember.

We assembled and Goldwyn said, "I want to report something to you, gentlemen. For the record. I just now had Leo

McCarey on the telephone. I asked him. If he would like to work with Loos and Emerson on the script. And then direct the picture. And do you know what he said to me? I'm going to *tell* you what he said to me. He said, 'What makes you think I would want to spend my valuable time on a piece of crap like *The Cowboy and the Lady*? That's all, gentlemen."

We filed out.

There was worse to come. Goldwyn, with considerable fanfare, announced his forthcoming production. He had Gary Cooper and Merle Oberon come in and make a set of portrait stills which were sent, with a well-written press release by Jock Lawrence, to motion-picture editors everywhere. His most important director, William Wyler, had tentatively agreed to accept the assignment, adding weight and importance to the announcement.

Two days later a registered letter from the Paramount Pictures legal department was delivered to Mr. Goldwyn. It informed him that Paramount owned the title, *The Cowboy and the Lady,* not merely by virtue of registration with the Motion Picture Producers Association, but because Paramount had acquired, long ago, from the estate of Charles Frohman, the rights to several Clyde Fitch plays, one of which was titled *The Cowboy and the Lady,* copyright 1915.

Goldwyn was shattered. It seemed increasingly clear that what he had mainly acquired from McCarey was the title. Now he found he did not even own that.

He phoned McCarey and had a row with him on the telephone. McCarey claimed he had never heard of the Clyde Fitch play, which was probably true. After all, none of us had.

Goldwyn yelled, "Now I'm going to have to *buy* the goddam title from *Paramount!* What if they try to stick me for the whole property? Maybe they *will."*

"What's wrong with that?" asked McCarey. "It's probably better than *mine."*

"I'm going to let you know what it costs me, Leo, and I expect you to reimburse me for the amount."

"Yeah," said McCarey. "Just don't hang by your left testicle till my check arrives."

Goldwyn called a staff meeting to announce this exchange as well.

The next day, another meeting. Another announcement. This one in the form of a question from Mr. Goldwyn.

"Gentlemen. I asked Paramount what they wanted for the title and what do you think those dirty bastards had the nerve to ask?"

"Ten thousand," guessed someone.

"Twenty," said someone else.

"Don't tell me twenty-five?" asked another.

Goldwyn remained impassive.

I took a chance, and said, "A hundred thousand dollars."

He turned to look at me so sharply that I could hear the sound of a crick in his neck.

"Who told you?" he asked, glaring.

"Just a guess,"I said.

"I don't believe you. You can be very sneaky at times, Talboig."

I lost my temper, rose, moved to his desk and shouted, "Look here, Mr. Goldwyn! The fact that you pay me a salary doesn't give you the right to insult me or impugn my integrity!"

"Impugn?" he echoed, quietly.

"What the hell do *I* care how much Paramount asked or how much you pay? It's no skin off mine, but you get us in here to play these silly goddam guessing games—"

"Watch your language," said Goldwyn.

"—and then you whack it to anybody who happens to say what you don't want to hear. What's so mysterious? I guessed a hundred thousand because you call Paramount 'dirty bastards,' and I figured that to earn that it had to be six figures. Anything lower they'd have been just plain 'bastards.' "

Goldwyn turned to the room. "This is a smart kid," he said. Then to me, "Sit down."

I sat down.

Goldwyn said, "I'm not going to pay a hundred thousand dollars for this title. I only paid McCarey fifty for the whole story, f'Chrissake. So why should I pay a hundred for a title to a story that cost me fifty? Now I tell you what we're going to do. We are going to come up with *another* title for this story. A different one. For this picture. And we're going to come up with a *great* title for this *great* picture and you want to know something? It's going to be *better* than *The Cowboy and the Lady*. *The Cowboy and the Lady*," he continued scornfully. "F'Chrissake, it's old-fashioned. It *stinks*! Look when it was copyright. Nineteen-*fifteen*. This is going to be a *modern* picture. This is not a period. So let's get going, gentlemen, and come up with a better title. Whoever comes up with it, believe me, it's going to be worth their whiles. Thank you, gentlemen."

"Worth their whiles" was hardly a powerful incentive, but at that point we were all sympathetic. Goldwyn had been unfairly treated. Everyone went to work on the problem.

Goldwyn enlisted the aid of every writer on the lot. Titles began to come in by the dozen, none satisfactory. Three or four days went by. The situation grew more grim by the hour.

One morning, I went into Sam Marx's office and said, "Sam, I've got an idea about a title for *The Cowboy and the Lady*. See, the thing is—that's the title Goldwyn likes and he's never going to like any other. The idea is to give him the same title but with different words. See what I mean? So here's my notion. Let's make a list of every possible word that suggests 'cowboy,' and every word for 'lady' and put them on cards and see if we can't come up with a combination."

Marx, a glum-looking man to begin with, looked even glummer. "This could take a long time," he said. "It took Dr. Ehrlich six hundred and six."

"Come on, Sam," I urged. "What the hell. We're getting paid."

We began: rancher, ranch hand, cowpoke (why not?), Westerner, Texan, farmer, cattleman, horseman, cowpuncher, broncobuster, cowman. We then moved into symbols: saddle, cactus, spurs, and so on. We moved on to "lady": debutante, heiress, co-ed, schoolgirl, princess, duchess, countess. Then to the symbols: perfume, diamonds, orchids.

"Orchids!"

It struck us together.

As Marx yelled "Orchids and Cactus!" I was yelling "Cactus and Orchids!"

He typed it out.

I took a large calendar from the wall, turned it over, and improvised a three-sheet. "Samuel Goldwyn presents," I scrawled, "Gary Cooper and Merle Oberon in *Cactus and Orchids* by Leo McCarey, directed by William Wyler."

"*Cactus and Orchids*." Of course. The man comes first.

Marx worked over my three sheet, making it more presentable. We were sure we were home free. We called his secretary in and tried it out on her. She was most enthusiastic (probably because she was sick of the whole damn thing and anxious to see it come to an end).

Marx got Mr. Goldwyn on the intercom and asked, "Can we see you for a minute, Mr. Goldwyn? Kanin and I."

"Who?" said Goldwyn.

"Garson," said Marx.

"I don't get you," said Goldwyn.

"Thalberg," said Marx. *"Thalboig."*

"Come on in," said Goldwyn.

We walked down the hall, flushed with the anticipation of victory. On the way we stopped in every single office and tried our title out. We were a smash wherever we went.

Goldwyn's office. We stood in front of his desk.

"It's about the title, Mr. Goldwyn," said Marx.

"For *The Cowboy and the Lady*," I added.

"We've got it," said Marx.

"It's *better* than *The Cowboy and the Lady*," I said.

"It's about time," said Goldwyn, crossly. "Go ahead."

"Say it, Sam," I said, hedging a bit. If it failed, I preferred that Marx take the blow.

"No," said Marx. "You."

I looked at Goldwyn, took a deep breath and said, " 'Samuel Goldwyn presents Gary Cooper and—' "

"I know all that, f'Chrissake," said Goldwyn. "Tell me the goddam title!"

" 'Cactus and Orchids!' " I shouted.

Goldwyn blinked and asked, "What?"

I leaned forward and said quietly but impressively, "Gary Cooper and Merle Oberon in 'Cactus and Orchids.' "

A long pause.

"I like it," said Goldwyn.

We unfurled our makeshift three sheet and held it up.

"I *love* it!" said Goldwyn, smiling broadly.

"And it'll look even better in print," I said. "It's sensational. It's got class. I mean it goes with 'Goldwyn.' "

Goldwyn buzzed for his secretary. Jack Hutchins came in.

"What do you think of 'Cactus and Orchids'?" asked Goldwyn.

Jack was understandably confused.

"The title," I said. "The new title for *The Cowboy and the Lady.* 'Cactus and Orchids'."

"Good," said Jack. "Very good."

Within fifteen minutes the staff had been assembled. The reaction was predominantly affirmative. Marx and I were the heroes of the hour and there was a champagne atmosphere in the room.

It ended abruptly.

On important matters, Goldwyn was always his own man.

While the subject was being discussed, Goldwyn stared at the three sheet mock-up which, by now, we had Scotch-taped to the wall.

All at once, Goldwyn said, "No. It's no good. No."

"You liked it, Mr. Goldwyn," I said. "Your first impression was good. Why don't you stick with your first impression?"

"First impressions," he said, "don't mean a goddam thing. This is something we're going to have to live with for a long time."

"Sleep on it?" asked Sam Marx.

95

"I don't have to sleep on it," said Goldwyn. "It's no good. 'Cactus and Orchids' is *no goddam good.*"

"But why not, Mr. Goldwyn?" I asked desperately.

"I'll tell you why not," he said, slowly and carefully. "It's because people who know what orchids are don't know what cactus is and people who know what cactus is don't know what orchids are. *That's* why. *That's* why not."

The meeting was over. Goldwyn bought the title, *The Cowboy and the Lady,* from Paramount for an undisclosed sum and the picture was made, finally, with a screenplay by S. N. Behrman and Sonya Levien, directed by H. C. Potter (Wyler having quit shortly before shooting began), and failed badly.

Traditionally, everyone connected with the picture blamed its failure on everyone else. When a film succeeds there is always sufficient credit to distribute and even the assistant location manager's wife takes her bows. In failure, however, there are never enough people to take the blame.

In the case of *The Cowboy and the Lady,* Goldwyn blamed the stars.

"The audience didn't take it serious," he complained to Cooper's agent, Bill Hawks, during a gin rummy game. "The way it came out, I didn't believe a goddam word of it. He didn't love her. She didn't love him. In fact, they didn't each love one another. That's why they went on their ass."

"Listen, Sam," said Hawks, "the script was lousy, that's why Willie walked away from it and you threw Potter in before he was ready so it had no concept and the technical side stunk. Those doubles fooled nobody and the process stuff was the worst I've ever seen. It was supposed to be funny but it wasn't. Gin."

"Four," said Goldwyn. "The audience didn't take it serious. The way it came out, I didn't believe a goddam word of it. He didn't love her. She didn't love him. In fact, they didn't each love one another. That's why they went on their ass."

I was to hear this set piece dozens of times. In fact, whenever the subject of *The Cowboy and the Lady* came up, it was Goldwyn's official explanation to Goldwyn.

5

G arbo.
No.
Garbo!
Better.

I saw her first in *Flesh and the Devil* with John Gilbert. She made an indelible impression on me and I saw her for countless days and nights afterward. I was fourteen, beginning to be aware of the place of the female in the scheme of things and of my possible relationship to this overwhelming phenomenon.

I saw her not long ago on Madison Avenue in New York, walking along under an umbrella, stopping from time to time to look aimlessly into a shop window.

Can it be that after almost fifty years she has lost not one jot of her magical beauty? As a figure, as a presence, as a screen personality, she was and is so arresting that it is hard to believe she has not made a film since 1941. Can it be? *Thirty-three years?*

She always worked with dedication: felt, thought, projected, communicated, listened, and talked.

Greta Garbo saved her personality for her work. She was never a scintillating dinner companion or an avid partygoer.

I recall a Sunday luncheon at George Cukor's in honor of an unmarried British couple, recently arrived in Hollywood. The girl was to play Scarlett in *Gone with the Wind*; the man to play Maxim de Winter in *Rebecca*. Vivien Leigh and Laurence

Olivier. Among the guests was Greta Garbo. I had never met her and disgraced myself by staring at her for three and a half hours.

Shortly after lunch, Greta Garbo and Laurence Olivier strolled away into Cukor's beautiful gardens. Up, up a long flight of stone stairs, around the esplanade, and down another flight. Aristocracy, I thought, true aristocracy. They were deep in serious conversation.

From afar we could see him talking and her listening. Then *she* talked and *he* listened. She laughed, soundlessly. They stopped. He gesticulated. She looked surprised, asked another question. He replied, underlining the reply with expansive gestures. In the fading light of the cloudy afternoon, it all began to seem like a scene from a silent film.

I found it entertaining but the beauty at my side had a distinctly different reaction. Vivien Leigh was smoldering in the flames of irritation, anger, and jealousy. She was hardly accustomed to being anything less than the most beautiful creature in any assemblage. Thus, the presence of Garbo unnerved her, and the idea of Garbo in deep, intimate conversation with her husband-to-be was a further annoyance.

"Look at him," she said tightly. "He's behaving like a ninny."

"What's a ninny?" I asked.

"Him," she replied logically. "Look at him. Stumbling all over himself."

"Well, I would be too, in his position," I said.

"Oh, *would* you?" she said, using five musical tones.

"You have to admit," I said, "she's a pretty spectacular number."

"I don't have to admit anything of the sort," said Vivien. "She's too large for a start. And why he's sucking up to her, I simply can't fathom. She once had him sacked."

"You mean out of *Queen Christina*?"

"Of course."

"But how do you know *she* was the one? I understand it was Thalberg, or the director, or—"

"It was her," said Vivien firmly.

Her tight little face suddenly changed expression. Her beautiful smile illuminated her visage as she said, "Ah, *there* you are! *Bonne promenade?*"

I turned and saw that Garbo and Olivier had returned.

Less than five minutes later, we were in my car, Vivien, Larry, and I, and I was driving them home. Our departure had been so swiftly and gracefully engineered by Vivien that I could remember none of its details. Had I said good-by to everyone? To Garbo? Had I thanked George, our host? I could not remember.

At my side, the most romantic couple in the world was having a spat.

"—the last time I *ever* go to lunch with *you!*" said Vivien. "Do you hear? The last. I'd rather *starve.*"

"Now be reasonable, Puss—"

"Why should I be? Are you?"

"Of course."

"Hah!" she said.

"What does that mean?"

"What does what mean?"

"What does 'hah' mean?"

"It means," said Vivien, "that I'm fed up with that David Copperfield performance."

"Oh my God," said Larry. "Will you give it a rest?"

"Floating around the garden like some moonstruck ninny."

"She asked me if I would like to walk a few steps," said Larry. "What was I to say?"

"Did you try 'no'?" asked Vivien.

"Of course not."

"Why not?"

"I was being polite. It's as simple as that."

"*Simple,* all right," she said.

I laughed, hoping it might prove to be contagious and that the whole small contretemps would dissolve in gaiety. I was wrong. They both turned on me.

"Shut up!" said Larry as Vivien said, "What's so funny?"

They turned to each other again and continued the set-to.

"What was so enthralling?" asked Vivien.

"Enthralling?"

"That conversation. What was it about?"

"All right!" Larry shouted. "If you insist. I'm about to *tell* you what it was about."

"Thank you," said Vivien. "And do not dissemble, if you please. You know what a rotten liar you are and how I always know when you're lying."

"I have no intention of lying this time," said Larry. "There's no need."

"Ah!" said Vivien. "Then you admit that sometimes you *do* lie?"

"Jesus, Puss!" he said, pained. "How many battles do you expect me to fight at once?"

"Go on about your enthralling little tête-à-tête with your new enthusiasm, Miss Greeta Garbo."

"One: it was *not* enthralling. Two: it was *not* a tête-à-tête. Three: she is *not* my new enthusiasm. And four: it is *not* Greeta. It's *Greta.*"

"It's *Greeta,*" said Vivien, "and I don't want to hear any more about it."

"Good," said Larry. "I'm glad *that's* over."

He lit a cigarette.

"I meant," said Vivien, "about the pronunciation of her name. Who cares? I *do* want to know about the subject or subjects of your *enthralling* little tête-à-tête."

"Here it is!" cried Larry, with the air of a man broken down by the third degree and about to confess all. "We began to walk and she said, 'This is a nice garden.' "

" 'Yes,' I said. 'It *is* a nice garden.' "

His imitation of her voice and accent was uncanny. Since I was keeping my eyes on the road, it was easy for me to get the impression that the account which followed was a replay of the conversation. It was almost as though Miss Garbo had joined us on the front seat. Now and then I had to turn my head to the right to convince myself that both parts of the conversation were emanating from a single being.

" 'We have gardens in Sweden.'

" 'Yes, you must have.'

" 'Do you have nice gardens in England?'

" 'Yes, we have *many* nice gardens in England.'

" 'In some of our Swedish gardens, we grow fruit. Apples.'

" 'We have apples in England, too.'

" 'And strawberries?'

" 'Yes. Very good strawberries.'

" 'Do you have oranges?'

" 'No. No oranges. But we have peaches.'

" 'We have peaches in Sweden.'

" 'Oh, I'm *so* glad! And do you have nectarines?'

" 'No. No nectarines. . . . Cabbages.'

" 'Yes. We have cabbages, too, but not in our gardens, unless, of course, you'd call a kitchen garden a garden.'

" 'Yes. I think I would.'

" 'Gooseberries?'

" 'What are gooseberries?'

" 'Gooseberries. You know. To make gooseberry jam with. Or a pie. Or a gooseberry fool.'

" 'What *is* a gooseberry fool?'

" 'Well, it's the same as a *raspberry* fool or a *damson* fool, except that it's made with gooseberries.'

" 'Do you have artichoke?'

" 'We have them but I don't think we grow them. We import them. However, we do have asparagus.'

" 'We have asparagus, too. But no Cranshaw melon.'

" 'Nor do we.'

" 'Cranshaw melon is good.'

" 'Watermelon is good.'

" 'And cantaloupe?'

" 'I don't like cantaloupe.'

" 'I like this garden. It's a nice garden.'

" 'Yes, it is. A very nice garden.'

"And that was it until *you* said, 'Ah, there you are. Let's go home.' "

Nothing more was said until I swung off into the driveway

of their house on Camden Drive.

We all sat quietly until Vivien said, "I don't believe one bloody word of all that."

"No," said Larry. "I didn't think you would."

It was not my place to say anything, but *I did* believe it. Every bloody word.

What it indicated to me was that inventing conversation, making charming small talk, and forming opinions was not generally her mode of expression. Greta Garbo's art was akin to music, in which the expression vented goes beyond words.

Once, quite by accident, I learned an astonishing thing about Garbo.

My wife, Ruth Gordon, had acted with her in that fateful, final picture, *Two-Faced Woman.* They met one morning on Fifth Avenue—Garbo was out walking with Cecil Beaton—and stopped to chat. The meeting culminated in a date for dinner at our house a few nights later. There were to be no other guests.

There was, however, a long series of phone calls during which the menu was discussed (Garbo is a food nut); what to wear (Garbo seldom goes out); what time (Garbo prefers 6:00 P.M.). And so on. The evening arrived and was passed beautifully. She seemed relaxed and content and the conversation ranged over a large number of subjects.

We had recently returned from Paris and, for a time, the talk was of the current Paris theatrical season. I described the remarkable scene in a play called *Sud,* written by Julien Green: A very young girl, played by Annie Fargue, is describing to her girl friend the adventure of receiving her first love letter, and says, in effect, "I read it and then read it again and read it again and again until I knew it by heart, then I went upstairs to my room and I took off all my clothes and I rubbed the letter all over myself—*all over*—and then—I *ate* it!"

I described the effect that this recital had had on the French audience. A gasp, a laugh, applause.

A moment passed, then Greta Garbo said, "Isn't it strange? I'm no longer young. I've had a long life. And in all my life I have *never* received a love letter."

"What?" I exclaimed. "But that's not possible."

"Oh, yes," she said. "I assure you that it is." A rueful smile came over her face as she added, "I suppose mine were not the sort who wrote love letters. It's very sad. I think it must be so *comforting* to have a love letter."

Garbo was one of the figures who brought to the screen an idealization of womanhood so overpowering that it captured the imagination of the moviegoing public the world over. At Metro, it was common knowledge that Garbo pictures were never significantly successful at the box office in the United States, but they did so well in Europe that they were worth making. Very few Garbo pictures lost money.

The story of *Camille* has always strained credibility, but when Garbo played it, it became believable.

After *Flesh and the Devil,* she made *Love, The Divine Woman,* and *The Kiss.* This was to be her last silent film. Sound came. The talkies. A revolution. Careers collapsed.

At Metro, someone came up with an inspired idea. Eugene O'Neill's *Anna Christie* for Garbo. "Garbo Talks!" read the streamer on the billboards and ads.

The effect of her first line, spoken in that husky, sensuous and thrilling voice—"Gif me a whisky!"—was immense. She became, with that film, a greater star than she had ever been in the silents.

The odd thing was that she had never had any stage experience. It did not seem to matter. Rules do not apply to Garbo.

Unlike many of her contemporaries, she did not become preoccupied with the mechanics of the new blimp-covered cameras, with the microphones hanging overhead and hidden in the furniture. Her concern, as it always had been, was with the character, the scene, the feeling, and the interrelationships with the other players.

103

There were times in the major studio days when even the most important players were handled carelessly. But Garbo inspired everyone, even the most crass businessman in the front office, to do his best for her.

In *Anna Christie,* she was given a remarkable supporting company. Charles Bickford as Matt Burke, George F. Marion (who had scored decisively in the stage production) as Chris Christopherson. And in the comparatively small, first act only, role of Marty, the incomparable Marie Dressler.

Garbo's career now moved from strength to strength. *Romance, Susan Lenox, Mata Hari,* Pirandello's *As You Desire Me, Grand Hotel, Queen Christina, The Painted Veil, Anna Karenina, Camille, Conquest, Ninotchka.* Then, in 1941, came a mechanical, incomprehensible film finally titled *Two-Faced Woman.*

There were many difficulties on this production. Shooting was stopped several times. Garbo thought, long before it was finished, that the film would be a disaster.

When her fears were realized, she took it badly and decided not to work for a time, perhaps to renew herself. The sabbatical lengthened and lengthened, projects came up but failed to materialize for one reason or another. After a long and difficult career she had lost the drive and energy necessary to sustain it and we have not seen her in a new film on the screen since. A tragedy.

In 1941, when Garbo ended her career, she was thirty-six years old. In a well-ordered professional life, her greatest triumphs would have lain before her.

I was among those who tried to lure her back to the screen. My idea was to do a production of *The Cherry Orchard,* with her as Madame Ranevskaya. During our first meetings, she surprised me with her wide knowledge of Chekhov and his work. We talked of it for months. I never got her beyond the "perhaps" point, and in time the idea melted away.

I once asked Ernst Lubitsch, who directed her in *Ninotchka,* how he came to put her into a comedy. It was something she had never done before.

"Because she was funny," said Ernst. "You couldn't see it? You didn't know it off the screen? How funny she was? How she would make certain remarks about some of the producers? Once she came to my house. Hauser brought her and we went all over the grounds. She wanted to see them. And for some reason, she started to tell me about her affair with Stokowski, about traveling with him in Mexico and New York and she was so *funny*! About how Stokowski would try to play the idea of wanting to hide from the crowd, and then becoming furious when no one recognized him, and then what he would do about that. She was funny. And I knew she could be funny on the screen. Even in some of the serious things she showed humor. You didn't notice how she always had such a light touch? Most of them are so heavy. *Heavy!* But she was light, light always, and for comedy, nothing matters more. When someone has a light touch, they can play comedy, and it doesn't hurt if they're beautiful. There was only one thing worried me a little. I wondered if she could laugh, because I didn't have a finish if she didn't have a laugh. She had the most beautiful smile. What am I saying? She had a whole *collection* of smiles. Every kind of smile. Warm, motherly, friendly, polite, amused, sexy, mysterious. Beautiful smiles. But a smile is not a laugh. And when I began to talk to her about *Ninotchka,* I said to her one day, 'Can you laugh?' and she said, 'I think so.' I said to her, 'Do you often laugh?' And she said, 'Not often.' And I said, 'Could you laugh right now?' And she said, 'Let me come back tomorrow.' And then next day she came back and she said, 'All right. I'm ready to laugh.' So I said, 'Go ahead.' And she laughed and it was beautiful. And she made *me* laugh, and there we sat in my office like two loonies, laughing for about ten minutes. From that moment on, I knew I had a picture with her."

Looking back, it is easy to see why she occupied a place of her own on the film scene. There was only one Garbo. And she, alas, gave up.

6

There is a show-business game called "Who Do You Think You Are?" In it the subjects reveal—or have revealed—the object of their inspiration or emulation. Almost everyone in the world of film or theatre has a hero or heroine, model or master. The pairings are frequently strange, often surprising.

About Samuel Goldwyn's there was no mystery. He felt a powerful affinity for Florenz Ziegfeld.

"That name," said Goldwyn, "Ziegfield—is like Tiffany stamped on a—you know—on an anything! It's like *Goldwyn* on a picture. You *know*?"

It is not difficult to see how this influence came about. Consider the young Goldwyn in 1907—working, scheming toward success with little to sustain him except his irrepressible confidence. There in New York—all about him—is the magic name, Ziegfeld. Florenz Ziegfeld, Jr., presents: . . . Or—The Sixty Club! Or Ziegfeld and Anna Held. The Midnight Frolic on the Ziegfeld Roof. Delmonico talk about Ziegfeld and Billie Burke. And Lillian Lorraine. Heady stuff, all this.

Finally, the apex, the most dazzling jewel in King Florenz's crown: *The Ziegfeld Follies*. The power of these five syllables is such that even now—more than forty years after Ziegfeld's death—they still command impressive fees and royalties for their use. Ziegfeld's designers and creators of stage effects: Joseph Urban, Ben Ali Haggin, Julian Mitchell. His songwriters: Victor Herbert, Harry Tierney, Raymond Hubbell, Irving Berlin.

His collections of stars approached the profligate: *The Ziegfeld Follies* of 1908 with Barney Bernard and Nora Bayes; of 1909 with Eva Tanguay, Lillian Lorraine, Sophie Tucker, Jack Norworth, and Nora Bayes. Year after year, bigger and bigger, better and better, until *The Ziegfeld Follies* of 1920 with Ray Dooley, Fannie Brice, W. C. Fields, Charles Winninger, Van and Schenck, John Steel. In 1922: Will Rogers, Gallagher and Shean, Andrew Tombes, Nervo and Knox, Gilda Gray, Mary Eaton, Lulu McConnell, and The Tiller Girls.

The extravagances burgeoned. Ziegfeld was a creative artist rather than a businessman. His attention was ever on quality, not cost. Moreover, he set a standard that he himself had to top year after year. Since this is neither theatrically nor practically possible, he ended his life in bankruptcy.

Goldwyn was greatly troubled by *this* aspect of his identification with Ziegfeld. When M-G-M's film *The Great Ziegfeld* was released, Goldwyn sent for it time and time again to run at his house. On one occasion, Goldwyn was blowing his nose and wiping his eyes as the lights came up after the end title.

"That's just how *I'll* finish," he said in a choked voice. "Broke. You'll see. I'll go broke. Just like him."

He could not be persuaded otherwise.

Although this condition never materialized, it is possible to speculate that Goldwyn might almost have welcomed it as a final embrace of the Ziegfeld/Goldwyn amalgam. A logical, inevitable outgrowth of this kinship was Goldwyn's production in 1937 of *The Goldwyn Follies*. Can this title have been influenced by one not dissimilar?

Earlier, Goldwyn had spent much time, money, and effort to establish and promote a group of beauties known as The Goldwyn Girls. (It may be supposed that he had heard of The Ziegfeld Girls.) Goldwyn's bevy included, at various times: Lucille Ball, Paulette Goddard, Virginia Bruce, Susan Fleming (later, Mrs. Harpo Marx), and Marian Marsh. Among the alumnae of Ziegfeld's group were Marion Davies, Joan Crawford, Gertie Vanderbilt, and Mae Murray.

107

It rankled Goldwyn that no one on his staff was able to come up with a gimmick to match Ziegfeld's felicitous slogan: "Glorifying the American Girl."

Goldwyn envisioned a yearly version of his extravaganza and, incomparable showman that he was, knew that the first one would have to be an overwhelming success. To this end, he spared nothing: not himself, not his fortune.

He engaged George and Ira Gershwin to write the score; Ben Hecht (finally, after many false starts) to do the book; George Balanchine (who brought out a company of sixty, including Vera Zorina) as choreographer.

George Balanchine and his troupe, The American Ballet of the Metropolitan Opera, arrived and made Hollywood history. The requirements and demands of his company were unheard of.

Balanchine and his various assistants had determined that the existing sound stages and their floors were not suitable for dance rehearsals. Goldwyn cheerfully ordered a new building— a dance studio—to be constructed on a faraway part of the lot.

The studio establishment was hostile and uncooperative, but Goldwyn seemed to revel in the proliferating difficulties. The more unreasonable Balanchine's request, the more he respected it. He sensed that he now owned a genuine group of first-class artists; that he was somehow entertaining royalty.

The American Ballet had brought out its own rehearsal musicians, wardrobe attendants, makeup artists, and assorted experts. Balanchine's studio began to operate with complete autonomy. No one except members of his company was allowed inside at any time, including Samuel Goldwyn.

A month went by. Another. Rumors abounded. One: Balanchine was creating the greatest ballet ever. Two: Balanchine seldom appeared. Only ballet classes were in progress. Three: Balanchine was about to pack up his company and leave, because George Gershwin's illness was delaying the completion of the ballet music. Four: Balanchine was not working on *The Goldwyn Follies* at all, but was preparing his program for the following season in New York.

Goldwyn's well-planted spies reported everything. Goldwyn received them impassively. He admired Balanchine. Never had he signed anyone who had made a greater impression on the press. The publicity that the company was generating was priceless.

"Free publicity!" Goldwyn exulted, looking through the press book Jock Lawrence had carefully prepared. "Look at this! And *this*! Free, you see what I mean? Anybody f'Chrissake can *buy* publicity—but to get it for *nothing,* that you got to have experience and guts and the main thing—ideas. Am I right, Jock?"

"You bet."

Anyone at the meeting could have pointed out that the free publicity was costing him about $15,000 a day, but no one did.

One afternoon, Goldwyn sent for Balanchine. Instead, an assistant appeared.

"Balanchine working," he said. "Very *sheddule.* Big discipline, yes? Also, he tell me come not he. Because. He has ashamed for his English. Make him full with nervosity. You have messages? You give *me.* I give *him.* Yes?"

"No," said Goldwyn.

We waited for the showdown blast.

"No?" echoed the messenger.

"You go back and you tell Mr. Balanchine I'm sorry I disturbed him. I know he's doing a great job. But tell him two weeks from today at ten o'clock—*sharp*—we're going to have a conference and I want him to come himself. To be here personally."

"Okay," chirped the messenger, eager to be gone.

"And tell him," said Goldwyn, "not to be ashamed of his English. Mine isn't so perfect either!" He laughed. We all laughed. "Also," Goldwyn added, "by two weeks from now it should be a lot better!" He laughed again.

Two weeks passed, during which further rumors spread

109

regarding the activities in the increasingly mysterious structure on the edge of the lot.

The day. 10:00 A.M. We assembled.

A receptionist opened the door and said, "Mr. Balanchine is here."

"Send him right in," said Mr. Goldwyn and, of all things, stood up.

The rest of us did, too.

In walked the same little sweaty assistant in his same turtleneck and beret. He was surprised to find the room on its feet.

"Sit, gentlemens," he said. "Sit."

We all followed his direction, all but Mr. Goldwyn, who remained standing.

"Balanchine say—" began the assistant.

Goldwyn interrupted.

"Tell Mr. Balanchine to come here. Right away. Like I said. Tell him to stop whatever he's doing. I don't care what he's doing. And to come here. Go tell him."

He pointed to the door with what looked like a two-foot-long finger. The gesture, like the tone of his order, had unmistakable, final authority. Only a fool would have questioned it and Balanchine's man was not a fool. He left with dispatch.

Goldwyn sat and calmly began a discussion of another crisis. Ira Gershwin had reported that his brother George was too ill to function. (George was to die of a brain tumor three weeks later—on July 11, 1937.) He had finished most of the score, but someone else would have to provide the incidental music, the ballet music, main and end titles, and so on. Any suggestions?

Al Newman, the musical director, said, "George mentioned Vernon Duke. He would be happy with Vernon Duke."

The door opened again and Balanchine's messenger came in again, followed by George Balanchine.

Goldwyn rose. Balanchine went around the room quickly and gracefully, providing a mechanical handshake for everyone in the room. He approached Goldwyn, they shook hands and sat down. They exchanged a grim look.

"Mr. Balanchine," said Goldwyn. "I think the time has come when we should have a nice talk and give each other our views."

Balanchine looked puzzled. Ashamed for his English, perhaps?

Goldwyn leaned forward, raised his voice, and slowed the rate of his speech.

"What I mean is," he said, "I want you to give me *your* views and I want to give you *my* views."

Balanchine turned to his assistant in confusion and asked, *"Vyoose?"*

The assistant shrugged.

"Never mind," said Goldwyn. "Mr. Balanchine. George."

"Yes. *George,*" said Balanchine, glad to be on friendlier footing.

"George," said Goldwyn. "You came here. I brought you. Your whole company. Everybody you wanted. Everything."

"Yes," said Balanchine. "Everything."

"I built you a studio."

"Good," said Balanchine.

"I left you alone. To work."

"Yes," said Balanchine. *"Merci.* All is good."

"Yes," said Goldwyn. "But what is *all?*"

"What?" asked Balanchine.

"Mr. Balanchine—"

"George?" asked Balanchine.

"Mr. Balanchine," said Goldwyn sticking to his guns. "What the hell are you *doing* in there? Over there?"

"Ballet," said Balanchine, giving the word a French-Russian pronunciation that made it all but incomprehensible. Bah-*lyay.*

"What did he say?" Goldwyn asked the assistant.

"Bah-*lyay,*" the assistant replied.

"What's *that?*"

When no one volunteered for a few seconds, I jumped in. "Ballet," I said.

"You speak Russian, f'Chrissake?"

"No, Mr. Goldwyn. But that's what they said."

"Jesus Christ!" said Goldwyn. "Mr. Balanchine. This ballet

you're doing for *The Goldwyn Follies*. . . . I know it's great, George." Balanchine shrugged, modestly. Goldwyn went on. "But what's it *about,* Mr. Balanchine?"

"About," said Balanchine.

His assistant sprang to his side and whispered something into his ear.

Balanchine nodded, gravely.

"About," said Balanchine frowning. "Is difficult."

"Never mind," said Goldwyn sternly. "We're all friends here."

Balanchine appeared to retire into himself for a long, troubled time. We all waited with varying degrees of impatience. My own instinct was that an interior earthquake was about to hit.

Balanchine rose, moved purposefully to Goldwyn's desk, and cleared it. (Would Goldwyn stand for *this*? I wondered. He did.) We all gathered around the desk. It seemed the thing to do.

Balanchine looked about for necessary props, found them. Goldwyn's silver carafe and a large onyx paperweight.

"Difficult," he said. "Because ahb-*strahct,* yes? Two group. Sixteen both. Eight of boy. Eight of girl. First group—positive." He held up the carafe. "Other group—negative." He held up the paperweight. "So. Is four movements of classical form. Suite or sonata. Gershwin knows. We have discuss. So. First movement. Positive." He slammed the carafe down onto the middle of the desk, denting it. Goldwyn, concentrated on the demonstration, took no heed of the damage. Balanchine, a wild look in his eyes, began to move the carafe about, intoning, "Positive. Positive. Positive. Pos-i-*tive!*" He slid the carafe off the desk and replaced it gently with the paperweight as he cried, "Second movement! Negative!" He moved the paperweight about in a hypnotic pattern. The carafe again. "Third! Positive positive positive." The paperweight. "Negative negative negative."

Fred Kohlmar whispered to me, "Sort of like the old shell game, huh?"

I prayed that Goldwyn had not overheard.

112

Balanchine went on, his face glistening. The carafe and the paperweight had become living things. The patterns were fascinating and imaginative and surprising.

"Fourth movement!" The action on the desk top went mad. The movements became wilder and wilder.

"Positive negative positive positive negative negative negative positive positive negative negative positive positive positive negative positive positive. Positive. *POS—I—TIVE!!*"

He sat, still holding the paperweight, but leaving the carafe in the middle of Goldwyn's desk. Goldwyn stared at it. The silence was profound. We all stood stock-still, waiting. Time stood still.

Goldwyn looked up. What did the unreadable expression on his face signify? Pain? Confusion?

"I *like* it!" he said, and completed the beaming smile.

He came round, slapped Balanchine on the back. Balanchine walked (danced?) out, followed by his assistant, who had turned haughty.

Goldwyn went around the room shaking hands with everyone.

Long before there was a script or even a concept for *The Goldwyn Follies,* Goldwyn began to sign players, one by one: Bobby Clark, Phil Baker, Kenny Baker, Adolphe Menjou, the Ritz Brothers, and others.

As the screenplay began to take shape, I was surprised to find it was a musical comedy rather than a revue. It had characters, a story, development, climaxes, and all the paraphernalia of drama. I wondered how it could be called *The Goldwyn Follies.*

At a production meeting one morning, I was rash enough to introduce the subject. Looking back, I find it difficult to understand how even so distantly related a creature as myself at twenty-five could have been so callow.

"Something worries me, Mr. Goldwyn."

"Go ahead," he said.

All eyes were suddenly upon me. Eight men whose salary averaged over $3,000 a week waited for me to go on. I hesi-

113

tated, wondering if I were on the verge of a major *gaffe*. I lit a cigarette, stalling. The pause cost Goldwyn a small fortune.

I exhaled, finally, and pressed on.

"Well," I said, "it's the title."

"The *title*?" echoed Goldwyn, amazed.

"Yes," I said, brazening it out.

What the hell, I reasoned doggedly, how am I going to get anywhere if I don't speak up? I had not yet learned that the secret of success in a bureaucratic setup is to be passionately and thoughtfully noncommittal. Those who have learned to say, "I . . . don't . . . know!" with conviction and the appearance of cerebration are the ones who survive and prosper.

"*The Goldwyn Follies*?" he asked, still not believing his ears. "That's your worry? That *title*?"

The concern on the faces of my colleagues told me I had entered the swirling rapids, but it was too late to turn back. I plunged ahead.

"That's right," I said. "It's wrong."

Goldwyn opened his mouth, but was literally speechless. He looked at everyone else in the room as though requesting reaction. A few meaningless head-shakes, and two or three indecisive nods were all he got. Those fellows were seasoned veterans and knew the score. It was apparent that I did not even know the *game*.

Finally, Goldwyn looked back at me and, in all kindness, asked, "Why?"

"Well," I said, "what you've got here—what Mr. Hecht has done so far—is a book show. Not a revue." Silence. "I mean it's like *Of Thee I Sing* or *Girl Crazy* or *Sunny.*" A longer silence. "Not like *The Bandwagon* or *As Thousands Cheer* or *The Ziegfeld Follies.*"

Goldwyn exploded. "What the hell is 'The Ziegfield Follies' f'Chrissake got to do with it?"

"It's a *revue*," I argued. "So the title is right. But for a book show it's wrong."

Goldwyn rose, took his attention from me and regarded his staff.

"What the hell's the matter with this kid?" he asked, accusingly. It was as though *they* and not *he* had made the mistake of hiring a half-wit. "Everybody ever *tried* a goddam revue, they went on their ass! Excuse me. F'Chrissake. Warner's with that—what was it—with Barrymore and the French fighter and everybody?"

"*The Show of Shows,*" said someone.

"Yeah," said Goldwyn. "Some show. They lost their balls. And Paramount with—"

"*The Big Broadcast,*" from the room.

"And Metro when they tried—what was it?"

"*The Broadway Melody,*" said the same know-it-all.

"F'Chrissake," said Goldwyn scornfully. (In point of fact, *The Broadway Melody* had been a great success—but not today, not in this room.) Goldwyn turned to me. Was I through? Not yet. His voice took on a warm, sympathetic tone as he asked, "What the hell's the matter with you?"

I had no reply, and retired in disgrace.

Mr. Goldwyn returned to his desk. The conference went on. The subject of the title never came up again.

One night Goldwyn listened to *The Rudy Vallee Show* on NBC. An obscure ventriloquist named Edgar Bergen and his dummy, Charlie McCarthy, scored a resounding success. Goldwyn lost no time in signing him (them) for *The Goldwyn Follies.*

Someone on the staff had the temerity to suggest that this may have been something less than an inspired idea.

"A ventriloquist on the screen?" was the objection. "What's *that*? *I* could be—in the movies—the greatest ventriloquist in the history of show business. My lips wouldn't move. I could smoke and drink a glass of water—listen, I could sing a bloody duet with myself! A ventriloquist on the screen—it's ridiculous."

Goldwyn listened impassively, his finger resting on the side of his nose.

"If that's the case," he said, "if what you say is the case—then let me ask you how come these fellows are such a sensation on the *radio,* f'Chrissake? Could you be a big ventriloquist on the radio, f'Chrissake? Then why *aren't* you? Why is *he?*"

No answers were forthcoming to any of the questions concerned in this barrage, and two days later the production staff contained one man less.

Goldwyn was right again. He had relied upon instinct rather than reason. Edgar Bergen and Charlie McCarthy captured the imagination of the country that spring in an astounding way. By the time the picture was ready to start, there were no bigger names on the roster of stars.

Bergen and his agents were understandably unhappy. They had committed themselves too soon, a matter of months before Edgar Bergen and Charlie McCarthy had become folk heroes. In the open market, they could now command ten times the fee specified in the Goldwyn contract. They sought an adjustment.

Goldwyn knew that the contract notwithstanding, he would have to revise its terms; a discontented player is not an effective one. Further, Goldwyn did possess a modified sense of fair play. As an inspired negotiator, however, he took the opening position that he stood pat on the original deal and expected Bergen to fulfill its terms and conditions.

Sitting on the periphery of strategy conferences in Goldwyn's office, I was beginning to lose my professional innocence. I learned that Goldwyn was prepared to double, even triple Bergen's fee and to improve his billing, build up his part and spot it well, and get Gershwin to write him a number—but. The "but" would involve further commitments, and Goldwyn's right to sell them to other studios in the event that he had no suitable picture ready on the specified date.

Bergen's agents and Goldwyn's carefully briefed representatives met every few days. No progress. The agents must have recognized the weakness of their position. A contract is, after all, a contract. Still, they persevered.

One morning, after listening for half an hour to sentences beginning, "Bergen says . . ." or "Bergen wants . . ." or "Bergen won't . . ." Goldwyn said, wistfully, "Bergen, Bergen, Bergen, f'Chrissake! All the trouble with him—but it's the other one— the little one—who's funny. The dummy. Isn't that silly?"

Fred Kohlmar dared a joke. "How about the hell with Bergen and just sign the dummy?"

Goldwyn's look said, "We are not amused."

One of the meetings on the subject had a truly surrealist atmosphere. Consider the background. The most popular attraction in the world of entertainment was about to make a motion picture debut and be paid $400 a week with an eight-week guarantee.

When the situation had reached its penultimate point, Samuel Goldwyn took over. He always preferred, he told me again and again, to deal with the principal, man-to-man, face-to-face. Even on so minuscule a matter as my own deal with him.

So it was in the Edgar Bergen crisis, except that Goldwyn decided to invite not only Bergen's agents, but the entire Goldwyn executive staff.

We assembled. Goldwyn sat behind his intimidating desk. Bergen was placed in an armchair facing Goldwyn. The rest of us were ranged about the room like an audience.

The meeting began with a long silence. It did not take much imagination to view the scene as a sort of prizefight or cockfight or chess match. There they were, the two adversaries, sizing each other up. Here we were, excited by the sense of battle in the air, wondering what the outcome would be. Any bets? What are the odds?

Goldwyn smiled. (A daring, new opening gambit?)

"Mr. Bergen," he said. "You are a great artist. You know it and I know it and the world knows it."

"Thank you," said Bergen, every inch a gentleman.

"And *I* knew it before *anybody* knew it," said Goldwyn meaningfully.

Bergen glanced at his agents. They conveyed, "Keep still."

"You know what a great artist needs?" A pause, mysterious. Goldwyn continued. "A great artist needs a great showcase. A great presentation. Like Flo Ziegfield made for Will Rogers and

Bert Williams and Ed Wynn and all the rest of them. And if you ask me—you want my opinion—you're better than all of them—that's what I think of you—of your talent—than all of them put together."

"Well," said Bergen, quietly. "I wouldn't know about that. But you're better than Ziegfeld."

Goldwyn blinked, then blushed, his pink face turning red, redder. He was truly nonplussed. He opened his mouth to speak but produced silence.

As spectators, we could scarcely refrain from applause. Here indeed were two masters. An intrepid opening play had been topped by an audacious response.

"We're going to make a great picture!" Goldwyn shouted. "All your life you'll be proud you were in it. I'll show you a showcase, f'Chrissake."

"I'll certainly do my best, Mr. Goldwyn," said Bergen. "And so will Charlie."

"Who?" asked Goldwyn.

"Charlie McCarthy," said someone foolish.

Goldwyn looked blank for a moment. The members of his staff recognized the momentary difficulty. Only yesterday Sam Marx had suggested that Ben Hecht bring in his erstwhile partner Charlie MacArthur.

Goldwyn recovered. "Oh," he said. "Charlie MacArthur. The little dummy."

Then he laughed—his wheezy, keep-it-in, face-crinkling laugh. We all laughed.

Goldwyn rose and moved around toward Bergen.

"It's great to have you, Mr. Bergen, in this great picture."

Bergen rose.

"I'm looking forward to it," he said.

Was the whole thing over, then? A sense of disappointment flooded the room. We wanted to see Grant vs. Lee at Richmond, not at Appomattox. F'Chrissake.

But wait. Bergen looked over at his agents (his seconds?) once more.

Now *he* smiled, and said, "Which is why I hope we can come to some arrangement, Mr. Goldwyn."

The temperature of the long look they exchanged dropped to zero. Goldwyn returned to his chair. Now. There was to be a joust, after all.

Bergen resumed his seat.

Goldwyn's blush had faded, and his pink complexion continued to fade toward the opposite end of the spectrum. He was pale.

"We came to an arrangement, Mr. Bergen, last May," he said.

"Yes," said Bergen, "but last May was last May. A long time ago. A whole career ago."

"What do you want?" asked Goldwyn suddenly.

The room trembled. No one had expected this question for an hour.

It was Bergen's turn to be thrown. He looked over to his team on the sidelines, helplessly appealing. His chief agent nodded.

Bergen looked at Goldwyn in the friendliest way and said, "I think it would be fair if you were to pay me—say—half of what I'm being offered elsewhere. That would seem fair to me and to you. Half."

Those of us who knew him saw that Goldwyn was deeply offended.

"Offered by who?" he asked.

"Several," replied the agent mysteriously.

When Goldwyn spoke again, it was in a new voice—even higher than his normally high key. He became an actor playing the role of a foolish, innocent, country plow-jockey up against the city boys.

"Several people are making *The Goldwyn Follies*?" he asked, all innocence. "My goodness, we'll have to look into that. Look into that, somebody."

"Just a minute, Sam," said the agent, unwilling to play this footless game. "You know what we're talking about. Not the assignment. The money. And as long as you've brought up the assignment—Edgar hasn't seen the script or heard a number—he's taking that on faith—so—"

"Listen," said Goldwyn. "He's got nothing on me. *I* haven't seen a script *either.*"

He laughed his mirthless laugh.

"We all trust you," said Bergen's lawyer.

"Good," said Goldwyn. "I trust me, too. So if you trust me so much, why don't you trust me all the way? Stand by your contract—by our deal—and let's see what happens—how everything comes out—if it comes out right—don't you trust me to make the proper adjustment at that time? At the proper time?"

A pause.

"No," said Bergen.

The game was over.

"What did you say?" Goldwyn demanded.

"I said 'No,'" answered Bergen. "No, I don't trust you to make the proper adjustment at that time."

Goldwyn was wounded and showed it.

"Very well," he muttered. "You want to deal arm's length? We'll deal arm's length."

"Fine," said Bergen.

"I'd like to ask you a question," said Goldwyn. "Suppose after we made our deal you went ahead and flopped and didn't go over so big. And suppose then I came to you and I said, 'Well, you fellows seem to have flopped and not go over so good. So I think you should not hold me to my contract and you should come to work for half what we agreed.' What would you say?"

"That's not the—" the agent began.

Bergen interrupted. "Just a moment. Let me answer that."

"Yes," said Goldwyn. "Let him answer that. So. What would you say?"

"I would say, 'No,'" said Bergen.

"Is that so?"

"Yes, that is so."

"Why?"

"Because, Mr. Goldwyn, when you signed me I was *not* a flop. I was already a hit."

"Call me Sam," said Goldwyn.

"I'll call you Sam when we've got a deal."

"We've *got* a deal!" yelled Goldwyn. "And don't you forget it. *None* of you!"

His finger was waving wildly.

Bergen rose and said to his entourage, "Let's go."

"Just a moment, Eddie," said Goldwyn. "Before you go, I want to say something to you."

He got up and moved around his desk to Bergen. Close to him, he spoke as though the rest of us were not meant to hear.

"I've been in this business a long time, my boy. Maybe before you were born. I seen them come and I seen them go. Up and down. All over the place. Right now—you're up there. You're on top. But let me tell you something, Mr. Bergen. . . ." He put his hand on Bergen's shoulder and continued. "It's a goddam sight easier to climb up a greased pole than to *stay* there!" He took Bergen's hand, shook it, and said, "Remember that." Then he added, "Send in your agent tomorrow morning, I'll work something out with him. It's a great picture! And you're great in it!"

The meeting was over. We all returned to our respective offices. I have no idea what the others did, but I began to dictate an account of the extraordinary event.

The buzzer on my intercom sounded. Sam Marx.

"Got a minute?" he asked.

"Sure."

"Come on in here."

In Marx's office, I found him with Fred Kohlmar and George Haight.

Fred said, "We just wanted to check something with you."

"Check what?"

"What was that thing about a greased pole Goldwyn said to Bergen? Did you hear it?"

"Certainly. And I just made a note of it. He said, 'It's a

goddam sight easier to climb up a greased pole than to *stay* there!' "

"Right," said George. "You got it right. Go to the head of the class."

"Not so fast," said Marx. "Not till you tell us what it means."

"It means he's trying to scare Bergen—reminding him that just because he's big stuff today, he may not be tomorrow."

"Great," said Fred. "And what's a greased pole got to do with it?"

"He probably meant greased pig," mused George.

"No, no," said Marx. "He meant pole. You don't climb up a greased pig."

"You might," said George. "If you were Goldwyn."

Merritt Hulburt joined us. He was asked for *his* recollection of Goldwyn's remark and responded accurately.

"What's extraordinary," said Merritt, "is that what he said makes no sense whatever and yet it made perfect sense when he said it—to all of us—and conveyed his meaning eloquently and actually it would be—the idea, not the words—a hell of a good thing for Bergen to keep in mind."

"Actually," said George, "it's a goddam sight *harder* to climb up a greased pole than to stay there."

The idea had not occurred to me. Of course.

"The man's a genius in the art of communication," said Merritt.

"He's got a big edge," said Marx. "His own language."

Years later, I read an interview with Sam Goldwyn in which he was quoted as saying: "When I was a kid back there in Gloversville, there used to be a fair come around and one of the barkers there said he would give a prize—ten dollars—to anybody could climb up this greased pole. Well, I thought, what have I got to lose? So I started in and I wrapped my arms around that pole and I inched up holding on as tight as I could and I won the ten dollars, but I won something more important —a very important lesson. And it was this. That even after I climbed the pole, it was harder to stay on top of it after I got there. And I have found that life is a lot like that."

Edgar Bergen and Charlie McCarthy did well enough in *The Goldwyn Follies,* certainly as well as anyone else—but where films were concerned, Goldwyn was right about the greased pole.

Bergen's success in radio and clubs and theatres continued for years, but movies did not prove to be his medium.

Perhaps if Charlie McCarthy *could* have gone off on his own, as Fred Kohlmar had suggested, things would have worked out differently.

The power of that amazing little dummy was astonishing.

I went onto the set the first day Bergen was to shoot his routine. There he was in a two-shot—he and Charlie—holding the dummy on a waist-high stool. Bergen had done this act a thousand times, so there was no need to rehearse it. It was simply a matter of setting the lights and the camera.

George Marshall was the director. A grizzled, no-nonsense veteran of the silent days.

The first take was soon under way. It did not get very far. First I broke up on the sidelines, then others, and soon everyone. The cause was the officious little boom man, charged with operating the overhead microphone for the sound department.

In two-shots, the live side of the mike would be twisted to pick up the player who was speaking. In this case, the dialogue exchange between Bergen and Charlie was swift and the boom man was desperately making every effort to get a good recording —twisting the mike back and forth from Bergen to Charlie, from Charlie to Bergen—forgetting momentarily, along with the rest of us, that the sound was coming out of Bergen alone.

The Goldwyn Follies, for all its strengths, a lovely Gershwin score (his last), and many thrilling moments, was not a success.

123

"It didn't have enough—I mean the right enough—enough of the right f'Chrissake glamour. That's what it didn't—glamour. That Zorina. Sure, she's all right, but she's no Garbo."

"Who is?" I asked.

He nodded sagely and said, "That's it. I should've had Garbo. But a fat chance to get her from those Metro bastards. They wouldn't give me *anything,* let alone Garbo." He was growing angry. "And you want to know something? I wouldn't give *them* anything neither. F'Chrissake, I wouldn't give them Garbo. If I had Garbo. Those bastards."

In an attempt to comfort him I said, "But Garbo's not a dancer, Mr. Goldwyn."

"So what?" he said. "She could've learned. F'Chrissake. That Balanchine had them there, locked up for how many months was it—three, four? She could've learned. Garbo. And if not, for the hard stuff, in the long shots, we could've doubled her. But at least we would've had the right glamour—enough glamour in the close shots."

Garbo was Goldwyn's ideal actress. For him, she had everything: beauty, sex, talent, mystery. Above all, she had made the rare transition from silents to sound.

He seemed always to be seeking another Garbo. He had had Vilma Banky, but the talkies wiped her out. Could he have seen Garbo in Anna Sten? He certainly tried to see her in Vera Zorina and, briefly, in a beautiful young Norwegian actress named Sigrid Gurie, who turned out to have been born in Brooklyn. The information had a traumatic effect upon Goldwyn.

7

"How would you like to see me and Sophia Loren in a picture together?" asked Spencer Tracy one evening. "I'd like it," I said. "In fact, if for any reason *you* can't make it, I'd just as soon see her in a picture *without* you. Just so long as I can see *her.*"

Sophia Loren had recently come upon the scene, bringing with her a sultry, volcanic, sexual quality that had long been missing from the screen. Even in her small part in *The Gold of Naples* she had made a distinct impression. It was reinforced in *Boy on a Dolphin. The Miller's Wife* was notable only for the shots of Sophia, as was *Scandal in Sorrento.*

Stanley Kramer put her into *The Pride and the Passion* with Cary Grant and Frank Sinatra. She appeared to be a potential star. The picture failed. She followed it with *Legend of the Lost.*

Five of her films were released in 1957. She was clearly somebody, but no one knew what to do with her.

At Paramount she was miscast in *Desire under the Elms.* Under the management of Carlo Ponti, she appeared in four films in 1958. Nine films in two years. The others in 1958 were *Attila, The Key,* made in London; *Houseboat,* back in America and again with Cary Grant. It was during this time that Spencer asked his question.

Sophia Loren had moved to Hollywood. Ponti and his partner, Marcello Girosi, were planning a program to build Sophia Loren's career. They owned a story by Cesare Zavattini which they believed could be adapted for American production. Spencer recommended me to them, and we had a series of meetings.

Carlo Ponti had just begun to study English. He did not yet dare sentences, and spoke only single words. One of them was the word "incredible" which he pronounced "een*cred*ble."

He dropped it into the conversation often, and I was amazed to note how many times it fitted perfectly.

With Girosi interpreting back and forth, some of the conversation went: "How much do you think this picture will cost to make in America?"

"Oh, I should think two million, two million two."

"Eencredble!"

"We would like you to write it. What would be your fee?"

I told him.

"Eencredble!"

"You will direct it, too?"

"Yes, if you want me to. If everyone wants me to."

"But for this you get paid more?"

"Of course."

"Eencredble."

And so on. Nevertheless, we all got on famously.

I wrote the screenplay, which was titled *Big Deal*. The film would have to be shot partly in Italy and partly in New York.

The reactions were affirmative. Production planning began. Ponti and Girosi now had a screenplay, a director, and two stars. What they needed was financing and distribution. The submissions began.

Bad news. No one wanted the project. The reason? Sophia Loren's recent pictures had not been successful at the box office, nor had Spencer's, nor had mine. I suggested that I withdraw from the directorial part of the package. Three other directors were tried, at least two of whom were riding high. Even they were not able to counterbalance the unbankable stars.

Big Deal became *no* deal.

It was suggested the budget be cut down. I went back to work on the script, simplifying it, devising ways to keep the cost at a minimum. We got it down to a million-three. By sheer persistence, Abe Lastfogel was finally able to get United Artists to finance the picture. However, they would only go for one million.

Spencer and I began to worry. We did not want to come up with anything less than first class. The budget was re-examined, combed. Spencer offered to take less, Sophia would take less, I would defer my director's fee. By doing all this, perhaps, the picture could be made after all. We put our attention on the work rather than on the humiliation and proceeded—until we were informed one day that United Artists had changed its corporate mind. The picture was off again.

Undaunted, Abe Lastfogel insisted that I go with him to Twentieth Century-Fox where he had learned that, because of a cancellation, a picture was needed to go into production at once. He had also found out that the studio owned impounded funds in Italy. We drove to Twentieth full of confidence.

The man in charge of negotiation there was Lou Schreiber. He listened attentively to our pitch and seemed to be responding. I kept describing the leading man until Schreiber said, "It sounds like Spencer Tracy to me. Could you get him?"

"We sure in hell could try," I said. "Great idea, Lou. I have a feeling he might go for this."

"He'd be good," said Schreiber. "He's a pain in the neck, and he's no box office, but he's great."

"In a good picture he'll be box office," I said. "And he's not a pain in the neck, I've worked with him."

"He'd have to be reasonable. I mean about money," said Schreiber. "Them days, them other days, y'know—they're *gone.*"

"Don't worry about it," said Abe, "We'll work something out."

I began to describe the leading lady. This time, my strategy failed. Schreiber listened but came up with no idea.

I took the plunge and said, "I'll tell you who I'd like to get for the girl."

"Who?" he asked.

"Somebody absolutely terrific—and with Spence, the chemistry would be fantastic. The whole thing would be original and interesting, sexy, box office, electrifying."

"Who?" said Schreiber.

"Loren," I said.

(I do not know why I could not bring myself to utter her full name. Was it that I thought it would be easier for him to digest if I gave it to him a piece at a time?)

Schreiber looked at me, bewildered, and said, "Lauren Bacall? She's not Italian."

"No, not Lauren Bacall," I said. "Sophia Loren."

Schreiber exploded. "Sophia Loren! Are you nuts? Loren? Do you think we—? *Sophia!*"

"Wait a second, Lou," said Abe.

"Sophia Loren!" Schreiber repeated incredulously.

We could not have done worse had we suggested Tokyo Rose.

"What's the matter with Sophia Loren?" I said. "She's beautiful, she's young, she's a tremendous screen presence. Spencer thinks so, too. This whole project has been tailored for them."

"I see," said Schreiber. "That was the casting all along, huh?"

"That's right," I said. "That was the casting all along."

"Sophia Loren!" he said. "We had 'er here in—what was it?—that goddam dolphin picture." He flipped a key on his Dictograph.

"Yes, sir?"

"Give me some gross sheets on that dolphin picture."

"What picture?"

"Loren, Loren."

"Lauren Bacall?"

"No, God damn it, Sophia Loren, the dolphin picture. Last year or two years ago. I'm trying to forget it."

"Yes, sir."

"You don't have to show me that stuff, Lou," I said. "I know the picture did nothing. But how come you guys always blame somebody else? She didn't pick the subject and she didn't write the picture. She didn't direct it or cut it or release it. So how come it's her fault?"

"You know why?" said Schreiber. "It's because that's the kind of personality she is. Women don't like her. She makes them nervous. She's too sexy."

"What's wrong with that?"

"Too sexy in the wrong way."

"I didn't know there *was* a wrong way."

"And men? Men are frightened of her. She's too big, she's too powerful, too ballsy."

"Only up against insipid leading men," I argued. "Not with Spencer Tracy."

Abe, ever the pragmatist, said, "And Lou, you can get a great deal with these two. They're both willing to play ball because they love the project."

The gross sheets arrived. Lou Schreiber put on his glasses and studied them in the manner of a Supreme Court Justice studying briefs. He opened the drawer and put them away. He took off his glasses.

"I'm not even gonna tell you," he said. "It's too embarrassing for everybody. We didn't even get our prints and advertising back."

"But this is another project entirely, Lou."

"A bargain," said Abe.

"You don't seem to get it," said Schreiber. "So let me tell you. If you came in here and told me you're gonna give me Sophia for a picture, and she'll take Screen Actors Guild scale, y'hear me? Minimum scale. You know what I'd say to you? I'd say, 'No. Keep 'er, we don't want 'er on the lot!' Have I made myself clear?"

I rose and started out. Schreiber continued.

"If you came in here and said, 'She'll make a picture and pay *you* twenty-five thousand dollars.' If that Ponti of hers brought all the financing even, we wouldn't want to release 'er."

Clearly, he was out of control.

"You've made your point, Lou," I said. "Don't beat it to death. You've not only made your point, but you've made a mistake."

"We'll see!" he shouted, "We'll *see* who's made the mistake."

I left. Abe followed a few minutes later. We drove back to Beverly Hills in silence. *Big Deal* was abandoned. Sophia and Spencer went on to other things.

Fifteen months passed. Abe Lastfogel received a call from Lou Schreiber at Twentieth Century-Fox. Schreiber wanted to know if Lastfogel still represented Sophia Loren.

"Yes."

Good. Would she possibly be available at such and such a time for an important film they were planning?

Lastfogel, astonished, continued the conversation. When Lou Schreiber finally made the firm offer, Lastfogel insisted he put it in writing and send it over by messenger.

Abe phoned me and said, "Come on over here. There's something I want to show you."

"You're not going to believe this," he said when I got there. "That's why I made him put it in writing. I'm going to show you this. Ordinarily I wouldn't, but in a way you're part of the whole thing and I don't want you to forget what I'm showing you. You remember that last meeting we had with Schreiber about Sophia Loren?"

"How could I forget it?" I said.

"All right, then," said Abe. "Now look at this."

I looked at it. Twentieth Century-Fox was offering Sophia Loren the leading role in *The Story of Ruth* and a guarantee of a million dollars. It was a lesson I have not forgotten.

Sophia Loren's spectacular success, including the classic *Two Women,* for which she won an Academy Award, the Best Actress award at the Cannes Festival, the New York Critics' Award, and the British Film Institute Best Foreign Actress Award—is not entirely the result of clever management and good fortune.

A great factor is her own determination, industry, and developed talent. This is the girl who, with her mother, hitchhiked from Pozzuoli, near Naples, to Rome when she was fourteen. She found work as a movie extra along with thousands; entered a beauty contest along with hundreds; signed up with a modeling agency along with dozens—but always believed in herself as singular.

A parallel career is that of Sophia's friend Silvana Mangano. They had been extras and small-part players together and caught the eye, respectively, of two dynamic producers, Carlo Ponti and Dino De Laurentiis.

It was Ponti who changed Sophia's name from Scicolone to Loren and gave her her first real part in *Africa under the Sea,* which he and De Laurentiis produced.

She and Ponti were married by proxy in Mexico in 1957.

De Laurentiis sponsored and managed and married Silvana Mangano. She became a star of sorts, but preferred home life and voluntarily ended her career.

Sophia, with Ponti, traveled another road. Ambitious and resourceful, she became not only a star, but a superstar, and what is even more rare, a lasting star.

The importance of the director is exemplified by her career. She began in 1948 and made dozens of pictures: dramas, comedies, musicals. This went on for six long years, but when Vittorio de Sica directed her for the first time in *The Gold of Naples* she became an actress.

More than any star I know, Sophia Loren has (or has learned) serenity and imperturbability. She understands the importance of these qualities.

When I heard that Marlon Brando and Anna Magnani were scheduled to co-star in a film (*The Fugitive Kind,* from Tennessee Williams' play *Orpheus Descending*) I was troubled by the imminent clash of temperaments. The producers were friends of mine and I worried for them.

"What do you suppose will happen?" I asked Sophia. "You know them both. Will they manage, do you think, or what?"

"It will be a battle," said Sophia. "Terrific. And Marlon will win."

"How do you know?" I asked. "How can you tell?"

"Because," said Sophia, confidently. "Marlon will stay relaxed."

When I first saw *Two Women* and watched Sophia—in the long sequences involving her and her young daughter trudging the roads, facing the terrors and the ugly vicissitudes of life— with only question marks at the end of the journey—I wondered if she was remembering herself and *her* mother and their similar pilgrimage from Pozzuoli to Naples to Rome.

The road eventually led to Hollywood, as it did across decades for film artists from every part of the world.

8

For most of the 69 million (or so) Americans who were alive on that day, September 14, 1895, was unexceptional.

Grover Cleveland was serving his second but nonconsecutive term as President of the United States.

His Administration seemed remarkably colorless after the fireworks of his candidacy. Accused during his first campaign of having fathered an illegitimate child, he had ordered his aides, "Tell the truth!" They did so. Soon, the whole nation was smirking over the ditty:

> Maw, Maw,
> Where's my Paw?
> Gone to the White House!
> Haw! Haw! Haw!

The push to the West, an historic population shift, was continuing. Horace Greeley exhorted, "Go West, young man!"— and many did.

The wounds of the Civil War were healing slowly. Children of six and seven worked in fields and factories. The rich were extremely so; the poor, desperate. The financial panic that was soon to overwhelm the country gave no signs of its imminent arrival.

Ellis Island was processing thousands of immigrants daily.

The new century was just around the corner.

It was at this time and place that Sammy Goldfish, a thirteen-year-old orphan, arrived. He had come from Warsaw, Poland, by way of Hamburg, Germany; Birmingham, Manchester, and London, England. He had entered the United States through Canada because of quota restrictions.

On that day, although America had countless theatres, music halls, cabarets, and tent shows everywhere, there did not exist, anywhere in the country, a single motion-picture theatre.

Forty-five years later there were 19,032 motion-picture theatres and an industry that produced some 700 feature films each year to supply them, and no individual in this industry was more important or more powerful than Samuel Goldwyn, who had metamorphosed out of young Sammy Goldfish.

His story bears careful consideration on two counts. First, it is the epic of the American film industry from cradle to almost grave. Second, it proves the United States of America. In Goldwyn's case, at least, the promised land provided the opportunity it had promised, and he responded with energy, enterprise, imagination, and unflagging effort.

The thirteen-year-old proceeded without delay to Gloversville, New York, because the people who had befriended him in England chanced to be glovemakers. They had given him the $50 required for immigration entry, and a recommendation for apprenticeship.

In Gloversville he set to work, learning the trade and acquiring a working knowledge of the English language. According to Goldwyn, he did not become a craftsman.

"I never got the hang," he explained. "Maybe because I wasn't too interested. In life, you got to be too interested. I mean, interested. If not, nothing. Even so, I got to be pretty good—not bad—on setting a thumb, though."

He was possessed of a restless nature and envied the natty salesmen he saw coming to the Kingsborough Hotel and going out into the great world beyond.

He resolved that *he* would become a salesman and wear those highly polished, pointed shoes, fancy cravats, fashionable derbies, and would smell of Lilac Végétal, the way they did.

By the time he was eighteen, he had become an English-speaking glove salesman covering the New England territory.

"I had it on my mind to be a salesman," he recalled. "I wanted to go around and see people, meet people. Listen, I love people. Why not? Look what people did for *me*. I asked him and asked him—Mr. Lehr the boss—and at first he laughed at me, at my English. But listen—it got better fast—better than *his*, even. I was going to night school every single day. So— sixteen and a half years old, I said to him one time, to Mr. Lehr the boss—I said, 'Listen. Give me the worst territory. Give me a place you can't sell and let *me* try to sell.' Hanging around, you understand, I picked up from the salesmen that there were such places. So finally—maybe to get rid of me, he gave me a territory. The worst. In New England. The Berkshires. Pittsfield, Mass. They had a big store there never bought a thing from Lehr. I went there. They looked. Nothing. I went back a few days later and you know what I did? I told the buyer in that store there my story. I told him this was my chance and if I failed I was finished. You know what he did? He gave me an order—for three hundred dollars—and I don't think he even liked the merchandise. I hear them talk sometimes—in a story conference—about Yankees—those tight, mean, hard Yankees and I always get mad. I tell them they don't know what the hell they're talking, f'Chrissake. I think of that fellow in Pittsfield. How he took pity on me and helped me out. So that started me."

Out in the new world at last, he was discovering America.

"I built up that territory from the worst to maybe the best," he boasted. "So when New York City opened up—Mr. Lehr the boss—gave it to me. A few years later, you know what I was? A sales manager. But for a different company. Not for Lehr the boss. I had an office—Fifth Avenue and Nineteenth Street and I lived on Sixty-first. And I walked home every night. They all thought I was crazy. And you know where they all are? They're all *dead*! Time went by and the next thing, I was a partner in the business. I had a drawing: fifteen thousand a year.

135

That would be like today maybe seventy-five. You could go f'Chrissake in those days to Delmonico's and get the best steak for maybe a dollar and a quarter."

As he recalled those days, his small eyes grew larger, his age fell away, his energy increased.

"The glove business was all right, sure. Fine. But I began to find out about *other* businesses—better ones. But I saw—I was a smart kid, y'know—I saw that my chance would be better in some *new* business—because in the established ones it was first of all hard to get in with no connections—and what connections did I have? *No* connections. And to go in business for yourself in one of those businesses you would be in competition right away with the ones who were already in and way ahead of you. No, I could see my best chance was in some *new* business where I could start out even and have some kind of a fighting chance."

"And was that when you met Lasky?"

"No, Jesse came later. First I mostly would hang around with business friends. You know, customers and buyers and other sales managers. And also Abe Lehr, my old boss's son— we were friends—we liked each other. And we used to go out. To the theatre, sometimes. I always loved it, the theatre. I couldn't get enough of it. And what theatre then! In those days. Great actors and actresses—real ones, not these plastic, careful kind we got mostly now. Big people who did big acting. Like Nazimova. The first time I saw her, I saw her downtown—The Irving Place Theatre—and she was doing it in Russian—I don't understand Russian—but I understood talent—and she had it. Wonderful. And Modjeska—well, Polish I understood—she was great. There's nobody like her now, is there? Who? Why, the way she used to come out and take the curtain call—the bow— I wish I could show you—imitate it for you—but I can't. She had this way of putting her eyes all over the house so that each and every person thought she was bowing to him alone, or to her. Those were some days—nights. I used to fall in love every night, practically. And the men. My God! David Warfield. *The Music Master*. I cried my eyes out, f'Chrissake. *The Return of*

Peter Grimm. And William Gillette. Talk about a gentleman. And what about Holbrook Blinn? Richard Mansfield—a little guy, but great. Ambitious. All of them. Not for money, like now—but to achieve something. Like Belasco. He didn't give a good God damn for money or expenses—so long as it was great up there on the stage."

"You sound as though you were really stage-struck. How come you didn't get into the theatre business somehow?"

"I just told you. You didn't hear me? You don't listen. You should learn to *listen*, f'Chrissake."

"What did I miss?"

"I told you. I was looking for a *new* business. Against Belasco and Frohman and Klaw and Erlanger what the hell kind of a chance did a poor greenhorn kid like me have? Frohman. There was a giant. He had Maude Adams. My God. You would never forget her. So *lively*."

"So it was then you met Lasky?"

"No. His sister. Jesse Lasky's sister. Blanche. She was once an entertainer. In the vaudeville. Then in the costume business. We started going around together. A good person. She always was. We got married later—after I met Jesse. Her brother. He was then in the vaudeville, too. A booker. And I was the one explained him how a new business was our best bet." He chortled happily, remembering. "You should have seen the things he came up with! All kinds of mining propositions. And tamales. He said they were very big in California and we should introduce them to New York. Can you imagine it? Me in the tamale business? And once he was sure we should go in the pectin business. I bet you don't even know what that is."

"No, I don't."

"It's to make jellies and jam. Can you see me in that business? And then around Union Square, Herald Square—a few places—like stores—started in to show moving pictures. And everybody went. A novelty. Have you noticed how people like novelties? Miniature golf. A novelty. The gramophone when it first came out. Brownie cameras. People like novelties. Moving pictures. To tell you the truth, I wasn't too interested. Then

137

somebody—I think Blanche, maybe—told me it was an invention by Thomas Alva Edison and then I wanted to see it. Because to me—he was one of my idols—Edison. What a brain! What a mind! The things he thought up. When I heard he only slept four hours, *I* started in only sleeping four hours—but I didn't do too good. I became a wreck." He laughed heartily. "I went to five, then six. But I never went back to eight, I tell you. On account of Thomas Alva Edison. So I went to see these moving pictures. No stories, y'understand. No situations even. Just trains going. And people jumping. Horses. I liked it right away."

"And went into it? The business?"

"No, no. Not so fast. It wasn't even a *business* yet. It was just a—you know—a novelty. A sideshow. Not a business. No theatres. A few little companies—one of the first ones I can remember was the Universal Film Manufacturing Company— still going, only they changed the name several times—and no more 'Manufacturing,' but still Universal. And they made these little movies—two, three minutes. Then Jesse lost his job—the people he was working for went broke—and he started in to sell these little movie strips. That's how we got to know about it from the ground up—from the beginning. The very beginning."

"And then did *you* go into it, too?"

"A little later. After I left the gloves. And it didn't take me long—one, two, three—I said to Jesse, 'This is nothing, this peddling. What the hell's the difference if it's gloves or vaudeville acts? Or moving pictures? Peddling is peddling. We should *make* the product. Let somebody *else* do the peddling.' "

I often heard Samuel Goldwyn tell the story of their first production. He never changed it for effect; never embellished it, as most raconteurs do; never deviated from the facts as he remembered them. It was almost a set-piece, and I believed every word of it.

"All of a sudden," he said, "it *was* a business. There was this one came out, *The Great Train Robbery*. This must've been nineteen-oh-three, or maybe four. A fellow named Porter made it. Not a story, but a situation. A drama. And the *big* thing was— I pointed out to Jesse—there was something you couldn't do on the stage! In a way it made me mad, because I loved the theatre and I don't like to see anybody taking advantage of it. Still and all, we saw we had a chance. I put in some money. Jesse some, and Blanche, too, and another fellow—a backer— Arthur S. Friend. And even then I knew the important thing was—the story. Nobody could tell me different *then*. Nobody can tell me different *now*! F'Chrissake. So the first thing we did with our money was we bought a story. A play. It was not a terrific success. A terrific success we couldn't afford, but it was good. The name of it was *The Squaw Man*. The next thing we started in looking for a director and there was this fellow, Bill DeMille—William C. DeMille—and Jesse knew him from the vaudeville. He used to put on a lot of vaudeville acts. Also, he was connected with Belasco. So we went to him with the property and we asked him would he direct it. Well, you should have heard the man. It was like we would have insulted him in the worst way. He *hated* the movies and he thought any actor did it was a disgrace to his profession and that the movies were going to hurt the theatre or kill it and he practically threw us out. Then a couple days later, he called us up and recommended his brother, Cecil. That's right. Cecil B. DeMille. C. B. DeMille, and he came around and we made the deal with him—one hundred dollars a week—and the next thing we started going around trying to raise the money. We had to raise about thirty thousand dollars to make the picture, and you can laugh if you want, but in those days to raise the thirty was harder than today to raise thirty *million*. But we did it and we made it. In Flagstaff, Arizona. It took eleven days. That was the shooting schedule. Eleven days. I'd like to see Willie Wyler with an eleven-day schedule someday. It takes him sometimes eleven days to decide where to put the camera for the first shot of the day. So anyway, we shot the picture in Flagstaff, Arizona, on account of Indians and in Hollywood, California, on account of cameramen. And cameras. And then it was put together and we

139

took it to Philadelphia to show it to this man who had a little distribution chain. It was one of the first. And this man said all right, he'd look at it, but with an audience—so he could tell the reaction. So in one of his little theatres down there, we put it on one night—and, so help me God, even to this day when I tell about it, when I think about it I feel sometimes like I'm having a heart attack because the picture started and—look, what did I tell you? Look at my hands. Sweating. From just *remembering*. The picture started and it started in jumping all over the screen. Just jumping and blurring and once in a while for three or four seconds it would stand still and then it would start jumping again, and the people started in whistling and stamping their feet and laughing. And I was running to find the projection booth to stop it, but I couldn't find it. And after a while he stopped it himself—the projectionist—and we went up to the booth to see what happened and the projectionist started in explaining everything, but I didn't understand. It was too technical. It was something with the sprocket holes. Something was wrong with the sprocket holes. They were all different and not the same like they were supposed to be. And this was it. The theatre man, he didn't even want to talk to us. A couple of amateurs, he figured. And you should have seen us on that train home from Philadelphia, with the tin cans of film on our laps. I don't think we said—Jesse or me—three words the whole way home. . . .

"There it was. All our money, and all our investors' money, shot. Listen, I'm not ashamed to say it. I cried—and Jesse cried, too, but what good was that gonna do? Well, the next day, we started in to try to see what could be done and everybody was putting the blame on everybody else. You know how it is in the movie business. They *still* do it. Everybody blames everybody else. The cameraman, the lab, the actor. What it was, was DeMille had to use different cameramen with different cameras. Pathé, Edison, Lumière. And they didn't match. And he didn't know it. Or *we*. Finally, by luck, we found this film technician. In Philadelphia. By the name of Sig Lubin. So we're on the train again. Again with the cans of film on our laps. And Sig

Lubin said he could fix it. He was a technician. Remember, there weren't many in those days. But we had to raise some more money and you can imagine how easy *that* was. It was like getting people to invest in a sunken ship! But some way or another we made it. We sold everything. Hocked everything. Gave up most of our interest but we had to save that picture. Our first picture. And Sig Lubin, he came through for us. He saved us—and when that picture went on and didn't jump around, it was damn good. In fact a hit. We were in business. . . .

"We put together this company. Cecil—Jesse and me—B. DeMille. We called it 'The Jesse L. Lasky Feature Play Company.' Jesse was the president. I was the treasurer and the general manager, and Cecil was the something. I can't remember. And we signed up Geraldine Farrar, from the Metropolitan Opera. We gave her twenty thousand dollars. To make three pictures. In eight weeks. Everybody thought we were crazy. Not the three-pictures-in-eight-weeks part, but the twenty-thousand-dollars part."

"But why Geraldine Farrar? She was an opera singer. The main thing she could do was sing, and you weren't going to use *that* on the screen."

"I'll tell you. This was an idea Cecil B. DeMille had. He was very smart—young and smart—and he noticed something. What he noticed was he noticed how most of the stage actors didn't act *big* enough. Now you got to remember the movies then were not too clear, sometimes they would be grainy and sometimes the focus would not be in focus. In certain places, sometimes the screen would go dim, and sometimes because there weren't enough regular theatres, they couldn't get it dark enough, so on the screen it was sometimes hard to see. So Cecil figured out that one way to get around this was for everybody who acted for the camera, they should act pretty big. But there were some of them, these stage actors, who they didn't want to do that. They thought they would look foolish, or hammy maybe. So Cecil said, 'In the opera, everybody acts big, with big gestures and big expressions on their faces.' So that's how he got the idea that opera people would be good. For on the screen. Dim or dark or whatever. Big enough would be the answer. And that Geraldine Farrar! My God, she was beautiful anyway. So it was a good idea. And we went on like this for two, three years."

"Excuse me," I said, "but how come it was called 'The Jesse L. Lasky Feature Play Company'?"

"Well, he got together—Jesse—most of the financing," said Goldwyn. "And that's how he wanted it. So we let him have it. Listen, I didn't care. In those days, I didn't realize how important it is to make your name. Anyhow, for me in that time, the main thing was to get into the business. But then, well, what can I tell you? Partners. That's why I've never had partners. If you have one partner, that's already trouble. When you have *two* partners, you might as well go kill yourself. And Jesse started to get very ambitious. We had a lot of competitors, and one of the worst ones—I mean, *best* ones—was Zukor. Adolph Zukor. He had a company. The name of it was 'Famous Players.' And Jesse got the idea that if we would merge our two companies, we would really have some power. And wouldn't spend too much time and energy and time fighting each other, or one another. So the merger went through and that's how it became Famous Players-Lasky Corporation. Jesse and Cecil, they were going to make the pictures, and Adolph and me were going to take care of the business. But you remember what I said about two partners? So now I had *three* partners and I couldn't stand it. So I got out. I sold out my stock. And I tried to put something together myself, but I wasn't ready. So there were these two men I loved and I respected very much. They were no doubt the finest theatrical producers in New York. Brothers. Edgar Selwyn and his brother Archie. Archibald Selwyn. That's a funny name, Archibald. People used to make fun of it, so finally he just used to call himself Arch Selwyn. But his real name was Archibald. Don't let him kid you. And we formed our company and for the name of it, we decided to take half of each name. Half of my name, Goldfish, and half of their name, Selwyn, and so we called it the Goldwyn Pictures Corporation. It came out Goldwyn because we wanted to put our names together—and listen, it was the only way to do it. Archie—he was the jolly brother—I remember he said, 'Another way to do it is to call it *Selfish Pictures, Incorporated.*'

"You mean the president of the Goldwyn company was Samuel Goldfish?"

"That's right. What's wrong?"

"Nothing."

"Certainly it was Goldfish. In fact, I didn't become Goldwyn for a couple of years yet. After that . . . well, we started signing up people, mostly theatre people that the Selwyns knew. Wonderful people. There was this fellow Bayard Veiller. He wrote a play *The Trial of Mary Dugan* and then this fellow Hopwood, who had a big hit every year, and there was Edgar's wife, Margaret Mayo. What a fine writer! And the Selwyns brought in Maxine Elliott and Jane Cowl and we signed up Robert Edmond Jones—the designer—because all the pictures up to then *looked* lousy. And I remembered what Cecil said about opera people. So we signed up Mary Garden. She was the greatest of them all. With Geraldine Farrar with Cecil, we did *Carmen* because that was one of her big parts at the Met. And it was all right. We gave her a leading man, Wallace Reid—he was a fine, handsome man and a great actor and he died a dope fiend. So then with the Goldwyn company with Mary Garden we decided to do another one of her big opera parts. It was *Thaïs.* To tell you the truth, it didn't turn out too good. But we got a lot of publicity out of it. It was a religious subject, you know. And they showed it in the Vatican. Right inside of it. The first movie in history to be shown at the Vatican. . . . Then, in Europe—I used to go to Europe—I saw this wonderful picture, *The Cabinet of Dr. Caligari.* And we bought it to release in America. And we showed it at the Capitol Theatre. And what a flop *that* was! People asked for their money back, but it used to get great reviews, and today they call it a classic. Then we signed up Will Rogers. I knew him from the Ziegfeld Follies. But it didn't turn out too good. It wasn't till the talkies he got to be a success. We had him in quite a few pictures. . . . I put in four years with that company. With that sonofabitchin' company. I was with it longer, but for four years I was the president. And I nearly killed myself. And then I got out of it. It was too hard. Partners. Partners. Not only the Selwyns, but we even had a board of directors. And it was no good. And I made up my mind, never again partners. No more partners. And, say, listen. I later on made all those *Potash and Perlmutter* pictures. And I said *that's* the place to be partners. Up on the screen, but not in real life. And I made up my mind. No more. And that's the way it's been. I've never had any partners."

"Was that when all that trouble about you using your own name came up?"

"Sure. By then, I'd gone to court and changed my name to Goldwyn. Legally to Goldwyn. It was more dignified. More American. A man with a name like Goldfish, people make fun of it. And that's one thing I didn't need. So everybody knew me—I mean, I was to them Samuel Goldwyn. Why not? And then when I left the Goldwyn company, I sold out, and I decided I'm going to form my own company. That's when they said I couldn't use my name. My own name. Legal name. It took a year in court. And that great, great judge, Judge Learned Hand, he handed down the decision where it said I could use 'Samuel Goldwyn Presents,' except under it, it had to say, 'Not now connected with the Goldwyn Pictures Corporation' in the same size type. He was a great judge, like I said, but that was a God damn foolish decision. Because it looked ridiculous on the billing. But then, the next year came *another* merger and the Goldwyn company merged with the Metropolitan and L. B. Mayer and they formed the Metro-Goldwyn-Mayer. M-G-M. And that's when I made the deal with them that I could say 'Samuel Goldwyn Presents' and not have anything under. On the billing."

Many years later, there was Hollywood talk that a merger was being considered involving M-G-M and Samuel Goldwyn. It was rumored that Goldwyn insisted that if the merger went through, the company be known as Metro-Goldwyn-Mayer and Goldwyn.

It would not have worked out in any case. Goldwyn was

clearly a loner. Had he not been, the story of United Artists would have been different.

The original formation of United Artists, dedicated to the freedom of film expression, involved D. W. Griffith, Douglas Fairbanks and Mary Pickford, Charles Chaplin, and Samuel Goldwyn. What should have been a perfect partnership disintegrated because each member of the combine was a loner, and none more than the incomparable Chaplin.

9

Artists create art forms. In exceptional cases, the form creates the artist.

Charles Spencer Chaplin is the outstanding exemplar of the latter case.

Charlie Chaplin (both the creator and the creation) is the most important single figure in films till now.

I have never known life without Chaplin. His name, I am told, was part of my earliest vocabulary. I learned to identify that derbied, mustached, baggy-pants image along with "horse," "tree," and "trolley car."

For a long time, it was "chollychaplum." Anything and everything funny in my budding life was a chollychaplum. If my father played the clown, if my brother walked funny, if my cousin Davie threw a rock through a window, I would scream delightedly, "Chollychaplum!"

Later on, childhood games were similarly involved with this folk hero.

> Eight times eight
> Is sixty-four,
> Cholly Chaplin
> Went to war.
> When the war
> Began to play,
> Cholly Chaplin
> Ran away!

Was this used for rope-skipping? Ball-bouncing? What? Memory fails, but I have always known how much eight times eight is.

Charlie Chaplin invited imitation. At children's dress-up parties there would be more Charlies than Indians. Little girls especially were attracted to the idea of the trousers, mustache, and derby.

Growing up, we identified with him on a more serious, social plane. He was all of us: downtrodden, kicked-around, treated unfairly by life and by fate. His enemies, like ours, were the bosses of the world, the bigger-than-us guys, the cops, and all other forms of authority. Charlie could outsmart them, he could charm them. Small wonder that he lived in our blood.

His impact was not confined to the United States. Silent films were as universal an art form as music or sculpture or painting. Thus, he was known and loved in France (Charlot), in Italy (Carlo), in Spain (Carlos), in Germany (Scharlie). Charles de Gaulle, at the height of his popularity in France, was known affectionately as "Le Grand Charlot."

When Samuel Goldwyn brought me to Hollywood "to learn the business," I took immediate advantage of my good fortune. I returned to the studio nightly to run pictures. I began with the Goldwyn library, running one film each night, sometimes two. Once in a while, three (at twenty-four, sleep matters less). On weekends I would continue. The projectionists on overtime adored me and I heard no objection from the front office. I was, after all, following Mr. Goldwyn's orders—"learning the business."

I singled out a few superior pictures and began to study them in earnest, ordering from the files the original material, the early treatments, the first draft screenplay, the revisions, the final shooting script, the cutting continuity. I would then run the film, often reel by reel, rerunning intricate or especially interesting sections. I must have seen John Ford's *Arrowsmith* twenty or thirty times. I ran William Wyler's *Dodsworth*, the original *Stella Dallas* with Belle Bennett. Also failures such as *Roman Scandals, The Dark Angel,* and *Nana* to see if I could figure out what was wrong with them. In a few months, I qualified as an expert on the oeuvre of Samuel Goldwyn.

I turned now to important films from other studios, many of which I had never seen. In time I felt I was ready to begin my study of the work of Charles Chaplin. I had heard that Chaplin still maintained his own studio, although he used it infrequently, and that he kept a skeleton staff on the payroll mainly to look after the prints and negatives of all his films in the vaults.

I asked John MacIntyre, Goldwyn's production executive, if I could arrange to screen the Chaplin films.

"I don't see why not," he said. "Most of them were released by us, by United Artists."

I ordered *Shoulder Arms*.

"Not available," came the reply.

"How about *The Kid*?"

"Not available."

"*City Lights*?"

"No."

I discussed the matter with someone in charge at Chaplin's studio and was told that Mr. Chaplin's pictures were not loaned out.

"Could I come over there and screen them?"

"No. Sorry."

My frustration turned into a challenge. I was determined to have my way. There seemed to be something sick about the attitude. What if Picasso were to lock up his paintings? Or Stravinsky his music?

I picked up the phone and said to my secretary, "Get me Charles Chaplin."

"Who?" she enquired.

"Mr. Chaplin," I said.

"Do we have his number?"

"Get it from somewhere. Goldwyn's office. Somebody must have it."

"Chaplin, did you say?"

"Chollychaplum!" I heard myself say.

"Oh," she said. "Charlie Chaplin. Of course."

In less than a minute, the buzzer sounded. I picked up the phone. "Hello? Mr. Chaplin?"

"Who is this?" asked a high, fractious voice.

I identified myself as one of Mr. Goldwyn's assistants, which seemed to melt but not break the ice. I described my long efforts to get to see his films, explained why I wanted to do so, and did not forget to include about a minute and a half of shamelessly fulsome flattery.

When I finished, there was a long pause, then he asked, "Do you play tennis?"

"No, sir, I'm afraid I don't."

"Well, come on over here anyway some day and we'll talk about it."

Could I believe my ears? Was I being invited over by Charlie Chaplin?

"When?" I asked.

"Any time," he said. "Any afternoon."

"How about right now?" I asked.

He laughed, and said, "All right. I'll tell you where I am."

"No, no," I said. "Don't bother. I'll find you!" I hung up, stepped into the outer office, and said grandly to Jean, "I'm going over to see Charlie Chaplin. I don't know when I'll be back."

My neighbor was Lillian Hellman. I stuck my head through the door of her office and said, "I'm going over to see Charlie Chaplin."

Lillian looked at me, blankly. "What about it?"

"Nothing. I just thought I'd tell you."

"Is it about anything?" she asked, bemused.

"Yes," I said. "I'm going over to not play tennis."

"Well," said Lillian. "That should be enjoyable. Send me a postcard."

Mr. Goldwyn always wanted to know where each member of his staff was at any given time. We were all hooked up to the Dictograph on his desk. Frequently, there would be a buzz. I would press my button and hear his voice say, "Come on in

149

here." If he ever buzzed me and I was not there, I would certainly have to explain where I had been. I thought it best to check in.

I buzzed him and asked, "Is it all right if I skip the staff meeting this afternoon, Mr. Goldwyn? I'm going over to Charlie Chaplin's house."

"What the hell are you going to do *that* for?"

"He invited me."

Immediately suspicious, he asked, "What's it about? What does he want you for? What do you want *him* for? Come on in here."

I did.

"What's all this about?" said Goldwyn, as I walked into his office. "All this Chaplin business. You don't work for him. You work for me."

"I know that, Mr. Goldwyn. It's just that I'm interested in screening some of his pictures and he doesn't want to make them available, so I'm going to try to change his mind."

"What the hell do you want to look at *his* for, f'Chrissake? They're so goddam old-fashioned. He's old-fashioned, that man. Nobody can tell him a goddam thing. That man."

"Well, that may be, Mr. Goldwyn, but Chaplin is the greatest man in films and I certainly wouldn't want to miss an opportunity to meet him."

"Oh, f'Chrissake," said Goldwyn. "You haven't learned a goddam thing around here. I pay you every week for nothing and you don't even want to come to the staff meeting."

"I'll be here," I said.

"No, no," said Goldwyn. "Go on. Go to Chaplin." It was a bad moment. I started out and heard Goldwyn's voice. "By the way, come back after and tell me what he said about me."

I stopped in Mr. Goldwyn's outer office and got Chaplin's address and instructions on how to get there.

As I approached the high wall surrounding Chaplin's house on Summit Drive, I could still scarcely believe what was happening to me. I drove through the gate, parked my car, and was about to ring the front doorbell when I heard a tennis game in progress.

I made my way around to the tennis court. A tall, handsome man, whom I would later know as Tim Durant, was playing against Bill Tilden. Actually, he was taking a lesson from Bill Tilden. Bill Tilden! The greatest tennis player in the world and Charlie Chaplin in the same day. It was too much. Chaplin rose and came to greet me at once.

"Why, you're just a kid," he said.

"Call me Jackie Coogan," I said.

Chaplin smiled and led me to a table. He was even smaller than I had imagined but vital and bursting with energy.

"Iced tea?" he asked.

"Fine," I said.

He picked up a pitcher full of iced tea with one hand, and a glass with the other, and did something extraordinary. He put the spout of the pitcher onto the rim of the glass, then spread his arms, one high and one low, creating a long stream of tea from pitcher to glass. He brought his hands together again, put the pitcher down, and handed me the glass.

It is not possible, I reflected, for this great, great clown to do anything in the ordinary way. I wondered if he took his comic sense along when he went to bed with a girl. He told me later, much later, that he often did. In fact, he considered it larkish to fix his sights on the least likely, least attractive female he could find and play Don Juan to the end. Often, he told me, with astonishing results.

It turned out to be the most pleasant of afternoons. Following a short discussion of my situation, he agreed to let me screen any of his films I wanted to see. He preferred that I run them at his studio and made it clear he would expect Goldwyn to assume the expense. Before I left, he invited me to dinner the following week. He became a warm and generous friend.

I spent the next three months running Chaplin pictures. The scripts were hard to come by, but now and then I was able to find a treatment or a sketch. Discussing the work with some of

151

the players, I learned that there was a great deal of improvisation during each shooting day. Whenever possible, I met with Chaplin himself to ask questions about his pictures.

"What did you think—what went through your mind when people like George Jean Nathan and Gilbert Seldes and T. S. Eliot began to discuss your work in terms of great art? After all, you were a music-hall comic, the son of a music-hall comic, doing the job you'd done for years on end, and all of a sudden, sort of—just because you were now doing it in front of a camera, you were being hailed as a great figure in the arts."

"What's your question?" asked Chaplin.

"Well, I mean—what did you think of all this? How did it affect you? You must have been pleased, but were you surprised?"

"Not at all," said Chaplin. "I always knew I was a poet."

Charles Chaplin employed a unique and personal method. An idea for a film would strike him. He would then tell it to someone, acting it out, improvising as he went along.

The next day or night he would tell it to someone else, changing, developing, building. A week later he might have friends in for lunch or dinner and again, he would present it. His new creation. He might do this fifty or sixty or a hundred times, and finally he would have it, fully developed, in his head. Then it was only a matter of capturing the concept on film, building the complicated props (the feeding machine in *Modern Times*), finding the right actors (Jackie Coogan for *The Kid*), settling on the best location (Alaska for *The Gold Rush*), and, finally, improvising, creating, and inventing as each day progressed.

I must have seen him perform *The Great Dictator* a dozen times or more and never have I learned more about the creative process. The dance with the globe of the world began, in an early recital, as a funny little piece of business. Alone in his quarters, Hynkel picks up the globe, holds it possessively for a moment, then twirls it about on his finger. In subsequent performances the action developed as his audience responded. Charlie gave more. It turned into a routine and finally into a spectacular ballet. The globe became, as he described it, larger and larger still. The dance became more graceful, more audacious.

I never dared ask but I felt certain that between performances he was rehearsing and practicing details by himself.

It was no small part of his genius that he could do or learn to do virtually anything. Consider his roller skating expertise (*The Rink*), his juggling (*The Circus*), his falls and trips and dives throughout the overflowing cornucopia of his work.

As is the case with all original creators, Charles Chaplin's working life was an amalgam of arrogant self-confidence and deflating self-doubt. With *The Great Dictator,* his worries proliferated along with his ideas. In 1938 to joke about Adolf Hitler was no joke. It was a nervous world in which anything might happen at any given moment. There might come a sudden time when Hitler might prove to be an impossible subject for comedy. A film takes a long time to make, especially when it is being made by a perfectionist. *The Great Dictator* would take perhaps a year and a half. What if Hitler were to die in the interim? What if he were assassinated? What if the United States went to war against him? (An unlikely thought but one that had to be considered.) These questions and many more were constantly under discussion.

Yet, there was something magnetic and irresistible about the subject and Chaplin's creative juices were flowing. Several times he abandoned the project completely. Each time he returned to it.

Someone suggested that he arrange to go to Washington and do the whole damn thing for President Roosevelt and let *him* decide. Chaplin considered this plan for a week or so, decided against it.

153

"What if he said, 'No' ?" he asked.

His closest collaborators, his friends, and the rest of us who were casual acquaintances, rode with him up and down the roller coaster of vacillation. One night, I was at dinner with him and Paulette Goddard, his wife, who was urging him to go forward with his project. He stared at his uneaten food, bit his lip, and said, "I don't know. I just don't know. It's such a risk. Such a *risk*."

"Everything's a risk," said the beautiful Paulette.

His agitation had communicated itself to me. To calm myself, I had another glass of wine. Instead, it made me bold.

"I don't know what the hell you're talking about. I hear you up and I hear you down and you're like that guy in vaudeville. What was his name? The single—who used to wrestle with himself?"

"Charlie McGuire," said Chaplin, morosely.

"Charlie McGuire, that's you. But I don't see that you've anything to decide. You know you're going to make the picture. Paulette knows you're going to. So do I, and so does everyone else. Why waste all this energy talking yourself out of it again? That energy ought to be going into the picture."

"Go away," said Chaplin.

"No, no, don't go away," said Paulette. "I'm paying for dinner tonight, so sit still."

Chaplin began to eat, unhappily. Paulette winked at me, egging me on. I took another swig. "Look," I said, "I'm not a believer and anything even suggesting the supernatural gives me a pain, but once in a while there's something in circumstance or in fate that's absolutely shattering, and this is one of those cases."

"What do you mean?" asked Paulette.

"I mean that here is a time in the history of man when the greatest villain civilization has ever known and the greatest comedian civilization has ever known bear a physical resemblance to each other. Think of it. It's—well, unbelievable, but we have to believe it because it's there." I took a deep breath and continued in an awesome tone, "Who but God himself could be capable of such an idea?"

Chaplin, a man not easily impressed, was impressed. Drama is frequently based upon a triangular structure, and one consisting of Hitler, Chaplin, and God was not bad.

"Well," said Chaplin, modestly, putting down his fork. "I don't know—"

"Of course you do," I said. "You don't have to decide about this picture. It's all been decided for you. It's inevitable. A foregone conclusion."

There was a long pause. We finished dinner.

"You may be right," said Chaplin.

The following day, he called the picture off for good. The subject became taboo for several weeks.

Then one night, at his house, the evening was growing duller by the minute. Political pontification by swimming-pool intellectuals filled the air.

Suddenly Chaplin was into it.

"We open," he said, "in a little barbershop in the ghetto. Outside, storm troopers are patrolling." He became two storm troopers patrolling. "Inside the shop . . ."

This time the performance was spellbinding. He transferred each image, each sound from inside his brain to the collective mind of his listeners. Everyone there that night saw the film, complete.

The Great Dictator went into production and I did not see my friend for almost two years. When he worked, he worked, and had no time, no interest in such nonsense as friends.

When *The Great Dictator* was to open in New York, I contrived to be there and told Charlie so. He got me a ticket for the opening at the Capitol Theatre and invited me to the various festivities.

It was a tremendous success, but one small detail in the film troubled me.

155

After the opening, after the party, after the move of a dozen or more stragglers to the Oak Room of the Plaza Hotel, it was getting late. But Chaplin, excited and stimulated by the events of the opening, was hardly ready for bed. He wanted to talk. He and Tim Durant and I left the Plaza and began to walk down Fifth Avenue.

Charlie reminisced movingly about his early days in New York, working in an act called "A Night in an English Music Hall." He described the Fifth Avenue he remembered, began to contrast it with the Fifth Avenue of now, and became increasingly annoyed by it. The buildings were too tall. The shops were too grand. It was all oppressive to the human spirit.

"Let's get the hell away from here," he said. "I hate it. All this ostentatious show of wealth and power. Let's go down to the East Side, to the pushcart market. That's where real life is."

"It's two-thirty in the morning, Charlie," I reminded him. "The pushcart peddlers are all asleep."

We were standing in front of St. Patrick's Cathedral. This structure, too, offended him. We turned left and walked toward Third Avenue.

We entered P. J. Clarke's, crossed into the back room, and sat down at a table. It was after hours but insiders or Chaplins could still get a drink. We ordered. Chaplin looked at me seriously.

"What didn't you like about it?" he asked.

I laughed loudly. Too loudly.

"Never mind the stage laugh," he said. "Yours stinks. You're no actor. What don't you like about it?"

"Charlie," I said, "I know you're not entirely reasonable tonight. Why should you be? You've just had the triumph of your life and I'm sure it's hard to take it all in, but for the past three hours or more, along with everybody else, I've been telling you that it's your greatest picture, your greatest performance— greatest *two* performances—that it's sure to be a world-wide smash . . . Didn't you hear me?"

"I heard you," he said, "and there was something about it you didn't like."

156

"No," I said. "You're wrong. I liked it all. Every foot. Every frame. But it reminds me of the time Noël Coward opened in a play and everybody crushed backstage to see him afterward, dripping praise. All his friends were trying to outdo one another, the encomiums were blowing around like a snowstorm. Finally, one drunken chum spoke up and said, 'Well, *I* loathed it. What a revolting evening. And *you* were simply inept!' Whereupon Noël threw his arms around her and said, 'Oh, thank you, darling. Thank you *so* much. How *sweet* of you!' "

Charlie smiled and said, "I'm not Noël Coward. So why don't you tell me?"

"Tell you what?"

"What troubled you."

I could see it was no use, so I said, "All right. If you insist. I wish you'd let me think about it for a day or two. I'd probably come up with the answer myself."

"What's the question?" asked Chaplin.

"Well, just this. In the picture you do the most fantastic imitation of Hitler—no. Imitation's the wrong word. Caricature—maybe even caricature is wrong. It's a portrait beyond a portrait, like a Goya, where you can see the soul of the subject coming through the canvas. Your impression of Hitler makes it possible for us to understand Hitler and what he's about. You certainly had the look of him and the sound of him and all his gestures and facial expressions and posturing and attitudes. The uniforms, the mustache. Everything."

"Yes, yes," said Charlie, impatiently.

"Everything but the hair," I said. "That's what I couldn't quite understand. You kept your own curly hair and didn't bring that forelock brushed down against the forehead. That would have completed the reflection. Wait a minute! Even as I talk I'm getting it. Was it because you wanted a kind of blending of the Hitler image with the Chaplin image? Is that why you left out that one detail?"

"No," he said, crossly. "Of course not."

"Oh. Then why? Why didn't you provide that one last touch?"

Chaplin was tense with anger. "Well, God damn it!" he said

righteously. "Why should I? I was using that makeup before *he* was."

The coming of sound was disastrous to the art of Charlie Chaplin. He had brought the silent film to its highest point of personal creativity. He had trained an audience to understand every subtle nuance of his pantomime, and had given more joy than any other figure in the arts of his time. Suddenly, the medium changed, and the greatest pantomimist in the world would be called upon to talk.

The problem was not his alone. Other great figures of the silent screen were similarly affected. John Gilbert, the most attractive and magnetic leading man of the day, proved to have a high, squeaky voice that ended his career almost overnight. Certain suave sophisticates sounded like Brooklyn truck drivers. Beautiful women had ugly voices or faulty speech. It was a hard time.

Chaplin, after due consideration, decided to ride out the storm by ignoring it. There were many who thought the talkies were a temporary novelty that would soon pass and that the art of the film would return to its true form—moving pictures.

Chaplin considered that his world was his own, that fashions and trends might affect others but not him.

In the midst of the talkie revolution, he made *City Lights,* one of his finest films. Daringly, audaciously thumbing his nose at progress, he made it as a silent film. Even now it seems perfect.

The soaring wonder of Charlie Chaplin is that working in a complex communal art form, filled with problems of dependence and interdependence, he was able, by the force of his genius, to use it as a means of personal expression.

Every work of art represents a single point of view. No great symphony was ever composed in collaboration. No important painting was ever achieved by a committee, no great novel ever done by two.

American films have been mainly committee-made. This explains why so few have true individuality. Some have more than others. The force of men such as Ernst Lubitsch, Preston Sturges, or John Ford frequently came through, but even these giants were, in the end, subservient to the front office, the sales department, the board of directors, the bankers.

I once prepared, as a birthday gift for Charlie Chaplin, a series of interoffice memos I had carefully typed up on purloined Universal interoffice communication stationery. As a final stroke, my secretary suggested that instead of sending him the original, we send him the carbon, or even the second carbon. This was done. The following set of memoranda was mounted on the pages of a leather-bound folio and delivered to Charlie Chaplin's home at 8:00 P.M., April 16, 1939, commemorating the precise hour and date of his birth.

UNIVERSAL PICTURES CORPORATION
Inter-Office Communication

To: NY; MS; BL; HD; ST

From: Coast; BG; LD; CL

Subject: Casting: Charles Caplin   Date: 9/10   1913

Current VARIETY (weekly), reviewing Keith-Albee bill,
singles out comedian named Charles Caplin, now appearing
with Carn troupe, as outstanding. Please cover and report.

UNIVERSAL PICTURES CORPORATION
Inter-Office Communication

To: Coast; BG; EM; SF; CL

From: NY; MS

Subject: Casting: Carno troupe   Date: 9/20   1913

Re your memo dated 9.10.13, sorry but no Caplan in Carno
troupe; Could you have meant Carl Chaplin?

159

UNIVERSAL PICTURES CORPORATION
Inter-Office Communication

To: NY;   BL;   HD;   ST;   MS

From: Coast;   CL

Subject: Casting   Date: 9/27   1913

Re your memo dated 9.20.13

Yes.

UNIVERSAL PICTURES CORPORATION
Inter-Office Communication

To: Coast;   C ;   MS

From: NY;   LD,   MS,   DS

Subject: Casting: Charles Chaplin   Date: 10/5   1913

Re your memo 9.27.13 see Chaplin.   Interesting eccentric
comedian.   Better in sketches with dialogue than sight
gags.   However, not outstanding enough to warrant either
testing or sending to coast.

UNIVERSAL PICTURES CORPORATION
Inter-Office Communication

To: NY: BL;   HD;   ST;   MS

From: Coast: BG;   LD;   CL

Subject: Casting: C. Chaplin   Date: 10/11   1913
           (comedian)

Believe Chaplin should be tested, as Keaton's demands for various
controls and rights becoming difficult.

Interested finding substitute for Keaton.   Could this be man?

160

UNIVERSAL PICTURES CORPORATION
Inter-Office Communication

To: Coast: BG;   CL

From: NY: LD;   RO;   MS

Subject: Casting: C. Chaplin   Date: 10/21   1913

Re your memo 10/11/13 do not think Chaplin can sub Keaton.
Refer you to earlier memo re his weakness in pantomime
but strength with spoken gags.

However, can make test here if you insist.

UNIVERSAL PICTURES CORPORATION
Inter-Office Communication

To: NY: BG;   LD;   RO

From: Coast: CL

Subject: Charles Chaplin   Date: 10/28   1913

Please go forward with short Chaplin test but do not
exceed $350.00.

UNIVERSAL PICTURES CORPORATION
Inter-Office Communication

To: Coast: CL

From: NY: SS;   WL;   TD;   MS

Subject: Chaplin test   Date: 11/7   1913

Chaplin test made and shipped today. Result not
bad. Crew and editor and projectionist all laughed.

161

UNIVERSAL PICTURES CORPORATION
Inter-Office Communication

To: NY: MS

From: Coast: CL

Subject: C. Chaplin test   Date: 11/16   1913

Chaplin test very disappointing, but LBM wishes to
pursue matter because of first instinct or hunch or
whatever. Please arrange send Chaplin here for
further testing. Will pay his rail fare (coach)
and $5.00 daily expenses, and will provide room
while on coast.

UNIVERSAL PICTURES CORPORATION
Inter-Office Communication

To: Coast;   CL;   BG

From: NY: SS;   WL;   TD;   MS

Subject: Charles Chaplin test   Date: 11/25   1913

Chaplin will arrive L.A. 12.1.13 and will phone RO
as per instructions.

UNIVERSAL PICTURES CORPORATION
Inter-Office Communication

To: SS;   WL;   TD;   BN

From: CL

Subject: C. Chaplin test   Date: 11/30   1913

Before proceeding with Chaplin test, wish all concerned would
run New York test several times! Many objections have been
raised to the use of the derby, which is fast becoming stale
because used by too many current comics. Try other hats
and caps, possibly even beret or tam o'shanter.

Also mustache must go. This type of mustache now being
used by Charlie Chase.

Speaking of Charlie Chase, Chaplin will have to change
name. Too easily confused with Charlie Chase if his
name remains Charlie Chaplin. Also Chaplin sounds Jewish.
Please send in ideas for new name in case test is successful.

Do not allow Chaplin to walk comically. This may look
all right on English music hall stages but for mass
audience we must try to avoid offending people who are
bow-legged, or crippled.

Do not let him overact.

162

UNIVERSAL PICTURES CORPORATION
Inter-Office Communication

To: CL

From: SS; WL; TF; ZZ; AB

Subject: Chaplin image   Date: 12/ 6   1913

Chaplin strongly objects changing make-up and style
and even more adamant about name change.

UNIVERSAL PICTURES CORPORATION
Inter-Office Communication

To: SS; WL; TF; BN; ZZ; AB

From: CL

Subject: C. Chaplin test   Date: 12/14   1913

Cancel Chaplin test and tell him return East.

UNIVERSAL PICTURES CORPORATION
Inter-Office Communication

To: CL

From: SS; WL; BN; ZZ; AB

Subject: Chaplin test   Date: 12/20   1913

Chaplin will make test as directed, without derby,
without mustache, funny walk or overacting.

163

UNIVERSAL PICTURES CORPORATION
Inter-Office Communication

To: NY: SS; WL; BN; MS

From: Coast: CL; BG

Subject: C. Chaplin   Date: 12 /28   1913

Chaplin returning today. Test unsatisfactory. Very bland style,
no personality, and too short.

Please keep looking for comics. Keaton becoming impossible.

UNIVERSAL PICTURES CORPORATION
Inter-Office Communication

To: Coast: CL

From: NY: MS ; LD ; DS

Subject: Chaplin test   Date: 1/8   1914

Sorry Chaplin fiasco, but wish refer you to my original
memo reading 'Interesting eccentric comedian.
Better in sketches with dialogue than sight gags. However,
not outstanding enough to warrant either testing or
sending to the coast.

Fortunately for us all, Chaplin's art and its destiny remained
in his own hands. No one made him a star. He made himself a
star. The front office had nothing to do with it.

10

Black-and-white images projected on a screen are among my earliest memories.

During World War I, my father, through a complicated real-estate deal, found himself the owner of a movie theatre in Rochester, New York. It was called the Panama because it stood near a small local canal.

I was five and became a fixture of the establishment. I remember many films that I saw five and six times. Annette Kellermann in *Queen of the Sea*. Alla Nazimova in *War Brides*. A movie called *Enlighten Thy Daughter* (which I was forbidden to see, and saw at least *ten* times). The comedy shorts with Chaplin, Harry Langdon, Charlie Chase, Buster Keaton. The serials: Pearl White in *The Black Hand, The Purple Mask*; Elmo C. Lincoln in *Elmo the Mighty*. The Gish Sisters in *Romola, Broken Blossoms*; Richard Barthelmess in *Tol'able David. The Big Parade*.

These films, among others, formed the behavior patterns of my generation, continuing on through the Rudolph Valentino days when we all doused our heads in brilliantine and hoped to be called "Sheik" by someone.

The influence of films upon manners and morals can hardly be overestimated. Clark Gable wore no undershirt in *It Happened One Night* and put a crimp in the undershirt industry. Hat manufacturers were irritated if a leading player wore no hat.

Lobbyists were constantly at work in Hollywood attempting to get stars, male and female, to smoke; sometimes to get men to smoke cigars instead of cigarettes. I was offered a handsome gift if I could induce Ginger Rogers to smoke a cigar in a scene.

I once objected to the idea that Ginger had to have a change of wardrobe for every scene.

"She's a telephone operator f'cryin' out loud," I said. "And all right, girls have a lot of dresses, but does she have to have a different one in every scene?"

"Yes, she does," said the producer.

"But why?"

"Because the front office wants it and they want it for a damn good reason."

"I'd like to know what that reason is."

"The reason is that girls and women go to the movies just as much to see what the stars are wearing as for any other reason, and if you bring somebody on in the same dress all the time, they're going to be disappointed. They want to see dresses. In a way, it's a kind of a fashion show. Sure, rich dames go to Paris to see the collections. Or to New York. But the women all over the country don't have this opportunity and they want to see what Joan Crawford is wearing, and Jean Harlow and Ginger Rogers. So shut up."

I shut up. Ginger Rogers changed for practically every scene.

During the run of the Brackett and Wilder film about alcoholism, *The Lost Weekend*, Joe E. Lewis walked out on the floor of the Copacabana in New York and said, "Anybody here except me see that picture, that picture *The Lost Weekend*? I want to tell you something, ladies and gentlemen, it sure got to me, that picture. And I want to tell you, after seeing that picture, I have sworn off. I am *through*! I will never go see another picture again as long as I live!"

When I was first getting regularly drunk on movies, one of my favorite players was Charles Ray. His name is scarcely known today and the films in which he starred are yellowing or cracked.

But I need nothing more than the projection of memory to summon up the image he created. *The Old Swimming Hole, The Barnstormer, Sweet Adeline,* and *The Courtship of Miles Standish* (the latter produced largely with his own money, and bankrupting him) were outstanding by any standards. Another of his films, *The Clodhopper,* was about a country boy who comes to the big city and makes good as a dancer. It gave us all hope.

He was a distinctly American type, and specialized in an American folk myth: Small Town Boy in the Big City.

In 1938 I was directing Ginger Rogers and David Niven in *Bachelor Mother* for RKO. Shooting a nightclub scene, I happened to glance over at a table of four and saw a familiar face. I stepped closer. The familiar face smiled and I was almost certain. Could it be true? I sent for the assistant director and asked the identity of the round-faced man at the third table over.

"Charlie Ray," he said. "You know Charlie Ray, don't you?"

"No, I don't," I replied, "but I'd like to."

We were introduced. I invited him to lunch.

He talked easily and charmingly of his beginnings in films in 1919, remembered the great successes with pleasure, and told almost humorously the story of his ruinous enterprise—*The Courtship of Miles Standish.*

What surprised me was the tone of his account. Here was a man who had been one of the most successful, affluent stars in Hollywood. Now he was working as an extra, but there was not a single note of bitterness in any of his recitals.

"All a question of the hazards of the profession," he said. "Every profession has its pitfalls. It was grand, though, while it was going on."

"But why an extra?" I asked. "You're an actor. Why not parts?"

He laughed. "No, no, no. They're too much trouble. Strain. I've had my share of strain. All I ask of this business now is to provide a living and and it does that."

"But what if a part came up?" I asked. "What if I offered you a good part?"

He looked at me evenly and said, "I wouldn't play it."

Over coffee, we talked of his contemporaries: Wallace Reid, Mabel Normand, Betty Bronson, May McAvoy.

A few minutes later I felt close enough to him to ask, "I heard an unbelievable story about you. I wonder if you'd verify it for me."

"If I can."

"Well, I heard—from Anita Loos, I think—that when you were a star you used to go to a dentist every day and have your teeth polished."

"That's perfectly true," he said. "Why is that unbelievable?"

"Well, holy smoke!" I said. "I should think it would wear your teeth out."

"Oh, no. It only took a few minutes each day."

"But what was the point?"

"Well," he said, "in those days the camera used to come in close quite a lot and a stock in trade of mine was my smile. One day, I was watching the rushes and I smiled one of those wide smiles and my teeth didn't look right. And I thought, what could it be? Then I figured out that they just weren't sparkling. So the next day I went over to the dentist and he polished them up and then I watched the rushes again, and the teeth were fine. So after that—yes, it's true—I *did* stop at the dentist's every day to have my teeth cleaned and polished. Anita's got it a little wrong, though. It wasn't *every* day—not three hundred and sixty-five days a year—just on those days when I was *shooting*."

We returned to the set. I saw Charlie Ray often after that. He was always an extra in any film I had anything to do with.

What shakes me now is the realization that I thought him then a charming old has-been. Actually, when I met him, he was *forty-seven years old!*

His case was by no means singular. Many former stars worked as extras or bit players. Mae Marsh, Mae Clarke, Maurice Costello.

Almost without exception, they took it well, did their work, and did not complain.

Needless to say not all stars or important players ended at Central Casting. Corinne Griffith became a Beverly Hills real-estate tycoon. William Haines, a notable interior decorator. Others were content to make room for the new and live out pleasant lives.

In the early 1930s, Hollywood became a haven for Mrs. Patrick Campbell. The redoubtable Stella had used up her resources and possibilities in London, whereupon she traveled to New York. Although she was respectfully received there she was not able to stage a comeback.

Mrs. Campbell added greatly to the gaiety of New York as she did wherever she went. But money was running out. She accepted a gift of a certain amount from Gerald Murphy, saying, "Thank you, Gerald. I accept this because I have always believed that money is for those who *need* it!"

She moved to smaller and smaller hotels, and finally across the river to New Jersey because it was cheaper.

Mrs. Patrick Campbell decided to try Hollywood.

It proved to be a revelation. She found a number of old friends and admirers. She was as entertained as she was entertaining, and for a time, was much in evidence on the Hollywood scene.

Acting in a movie at M-G-M with Norma Shearer, who was then married to Irving Thalberg, the head of the studio, she noticed that in almost every shot Miss Shearer was brightly lighted while the other actors or actresses in the scene were dim or dark or in shadow.

When someone asked Mrs. Campbell what she was doing, she replied, "I'm over at Metro-Goldwyn-Mayer. I'm one of Norma Shearer's Nubian slaves."

A Warner Brothers unit publicity man handed her the customary mimeographed form to fill out. She dutifully wrote out her name, the color of her hair and eyes, her height. Her debut,

169

her hobbies, her favorite roles, and so on. Then, turning to a sheet headed "Experience," she wrote, "Edward VII."

George Cukor gave a dinner party for her. Thornton Wilder was her escort.

Wilder called for her at her apartment. She invited him in for sherry. They exchanged talk about mutual friends. She showed him some of her letters from George Bernard Shaw, which Shaw had forbidden her to sell or publish.

"No, Stella," he had said, in the famous turndown. "I will not play the horse to your Lady Godiva."

Mrs. Pat and Wilder proceeded to George Cukor's new home. There they were shown about. Special attention was called to the formal garden that had been planned and built by George Hoyningen-Huené. Pressing a button, Cukor showed them how the lighting effect in the garden could be changed from amber to purple to white.

On the way home, Wilder made a deprecatory remark about Hollywood's efforts to improve upon nature.

"Stop it!" said Mrs. Campbell. "Stop it at once. I won't hear a word against this place, do you hear? Not a word against Hollywood. I have spent years in London, subsisting on a sandwich and a cup of tea a day, and no one would give me a job. Around the corner sat Ellen Terry, subsisting on a sandwich and a cup of tea a day, and no one would give *her* a job. I go to New York, they make much of me, but no one gives me a job. I come here, I am given work, and am paid well for it—and my self-respect is restored. So I won't hear a word against Hollywood. Hollywood to me means cash, courage, and climate."

It was magnanimous of her. She had learned to settle for less. Surely, in the course of her years in Hollywood, better use of her remarkable talents could have been made. She appeared unimportantly and fleetingly in *The Dancers, Riptide, One More River, Outcast Lady, Crime and Punishment.*

It was through Charles Ray that I met a number of other old-timers.

170

Some of them had been in on virtually the beginnings of film-making in America.

Eddie Sutherland (A. Edward Sutherland) arrived in Hollywood in 1913. He loved films and the life of the movie community. He went from silent shorts to silent features, into the talkies, through color and the coming of the wide screen, and ended his days in television.

The transitions were not always clear. I recall visiting his set one afternoon. There were a number of animals in the scene, a full-stage exterior.

I reflected upon the curious circumstance. Movie-makers had originally come to southern California mainly because sunlight was needed to achieve effective photography. Every set was an exterior interior. The early Chaplin shorts were shot out-of-doors in ceilingless rooms. As time went by, lighting improved. The powerful klieg lights were invented, and artificially lighted sets could be used independently of the vagaries of the sun.

Here, on Eddie Sutherland's set, an enormous exterior was being shot indoors. The animals were restless and noisy. The chickens and horses and pigs and dogs did not respond to the assistant director's, "Quiet!"

I could barely hear the dialogue, and wondered how the players were able to hear their cues.

When the scene ended, I said, "You know, Eddie, I'm trying to learn, so don't get mad if I ask you a question."

"Shoot," he said.

"Well, with all that ungodly noise going on, what kind of sound recording are you getting?"

"Oh, I never worry about that," he replied. "We put the titles in later."

To Eddie, the titles of the silents and the spoken dialogue of the talkies were interchangeable.

Among other things, Eddie was known for his prowess with women. He was a diminutive man, not particularly handsome, yet had developed a considerable reputation around town as a ladies' man.

171

"How do you explain it?" I asked him one dawn at the weary end of a pub crawl.

"How?" he echoed, and winked a broad wink. "I'm going to tell you—because you're a beginner, see—and I'm an old master. I don't usually give away my trade secrets, but you've gotten me pretty plastered tonight. I guess that was your scheme, huh? To get me plastered and to get all my secrets, huh?"

"That's right," I said.

"Okay, it worked. You're gonna get 'em. Get us another double and I'll spill everything."

Another double was ordered, served, and shortly thereafter, Eddie began.

"It's taken me years," he said. "A lotta years. But I built up this reputation. Like you say. And the way I did it—now don't go around tellin' everybody around. This is for *your* pearly ears alone. The way I did it was—I worked on it, see?"

"No, I don't."

"I mean I *talked* about it. Myself. For years. I keep tellin' everybody how terrific I am and so naturally it gets around. In fact, when it started gettin' around too much I started denyin' it and that's even better, see? The more you deny something, the more everybody believes it. Like once I started tellin' everybody how I never had any affair with Jean Harlow. I would say, 'How did all that talk get started about me and Jean Harlow? I never had anything to do with Jean Harlow. I knew her, sure. She was a good pal of mine but that's all.' I just kept sayin' that, see? And the more I said it, the more they believed I *did* have. But I never did. See how it works?"

"Eddie," I said. "You're sensational."

He laughed. "See, even *you* believe it! But listen, there was some I *did* have, no foolin'. Like for instance—listen, you want a laugh? I'll give you a laugh. Let's go somewhere and get a drink and I'll tell you a bedtime story."

"It's pretty late," I said. "I think every place is closed."

"*This* place isn't. This place is *open.*"

"That's right."

"Okay then," he said. "Let's stay here. In *this* place."

172

"They're putting the chairs on the tables, though."

"Let 'em. But if they want me to sit in one—they've got to give me a stunt check!"

Another drink.

"Clara Bow," he said. "Did you ever know Clara?"

"No," I said. "But for a good long while there she was my all-out favorite."

"Mine too," he said. "Well, hell, just about everybody's."

"The 'It' girl," I mused. "What about *Dancing Mothers* and *Roughhouse Rosie? The Saturday Night Kid.*"

"And *It*," said Eddie.

"She was a dazzler, all right," I said.

There were tears in Eddie's eyes as he said, "Oh God! Oh God, help us. They've got her put away now, y'know. She cracked."

He blew his nose, took a hefty gulp of his drink, and continued.

"We had a great thing goin' there for a while. She wasn't married, I wasn't married, and we were crazy stuck on each other. The best way. Even Stephen."

"Why didn't you get married, then?" I asked.

"Well, you know how it is. This'll be hard for you to believe —but, you know, she *wanted* to. *I* was the one held back. The trouble was—see?—she was such a big star, maybe the biggest. And me, I was just, you know, gettin' along. I guess if I'd have made it big even with one picture, we'd have gotten hitched. And I kept thinkin' any day I might come through with that TNT one. But the way it was, her so big and me so not, I couldn't see it. So we went along the way we were and everything was hunky-dory till I began to notice—y'know how sometimes you begin to notice?—that I wasn't gettin' with her as much as before. There would always be a reason, a good reason, like she had an early call or a costume fitting or a cold, or it was, you know, her time—or a business meeting. But the point was when it all added up, I just wasn't seein' as much of her as I was used to. . . . Then it started in that she had to go out of town for a few days—somebody in her family sick or something like that. And I began to get a little suspicious. Or a lot. On top of everything I began to notice that even when we *were* together, it wasn't the same. It was—I don't know how to describe it—wasn't like a fella and a girl any more. It was gettin' to be more like a guy and his wife. So I began to get more suspicious and I did something about it. What I did was I told her I had to go to New York to see a play. Now, don't forget, in those days going to New York was a production. You had to go by train. Three and a half days there and then back three and a half days. And a couple days in New York. So that meant like ten days at least. I told her I had to go to New York. The night before, we went out. The Coconut Grove. And then we went home and we had one of our *big nights*. It was almost like before. And in the middle of it I got to thinkin', Jesus maybe I'm wrong about all this. Maybe I shouldn't be going through this whole nasty routine. But it was too late to get out of it. So the next day, off we went. She took me down to Union Station in L.A. and on the platform she cried and I cried and I got on the train. And her driver took her home and I got off at Pasadena. That night, I got in my car and I kept drivin' around her block. Around and around and about nine o'clock I see this terrific car pull up into her driveway—a Stutz—I'd never seen it before. I couldn't stop so I went around again and by the time I came back, the lights on the car were out and I was shakin' like a leaf. I drove a few more blocks and parked my car and waited about a half an hour. Then I walked back to the house. I let myself in with my key and I went upstairs real quiet and when I got to the bedroom door I got myself set for action and started in, but the door was locked. This was a real tip-off, because the one thing she never did, she never locked the door. So I knocked— good and sharp—and I heard all kinds of scuffling in there and then I heard her holler out, 'Who is it?' and I said, 'It's me, baby. Who do you think?' And she said, 'You? My God, what are *you* doing *here*?' And I said, 'Open up. I'll tell you all about it.' Well, what could she do? So she let me in, in a robe with nothing on under. And I said, 'The damndest thing. When I got to Pasadena there was this guy from Universal paging me and

174

he said Laemmle wants to see me right away.' And she looked at me and she said, 'Eddie, I don't believe you.' And I said, 'Well, that makes us even, because I don't believe *you* either.' And she said, 'What do you mean you don't believe me? I haven't *said* anything yet.' And I said, 'I know, but I don't believe what you're gonna tell me when I ask you who's in here with you.' 'Nobody,' she said. And I said, 'That's *it*. That's what I don't believe you. Who is it? And how long's this been goin' on?' And she was hollerin', 'Nobody, never.' And I said, 'Don't tell me. I can practically *smell* a man in here.' And she said, 'What are you, a bloodhound or something? Leave me alone. Go 'way, Eddie.' And she started shoving me. I mean *tryin'* to shove me out of the room. And I said, 'What's that Stutz doin' in your driveway?' And she said, 'How should *I* know? What Stutz?' I took off my jacket and loosened my tie. And she was startin' to yell 'Get away from here or I'll call the police.' And I said, 'Okay, baby, you call the police, but while you're waitin' for 'em to get here you're gonna see a bloodhound in *action.'* And I opened the closet doors, first one and then the other one. She had these big closets full of clothes, big as a big room. Both of them. But nothing. So I started for the bathroom door and by now she was screamin' and grabbin' my shirt and yellin', 'Please, Eddie! Please *don't*. I'm *begging* you. Please go 'way. Tomorrow I'll tell you everything. Tomorrow.' But by now I was bangin' on the bathroom door and *I* was yellin', too, 'Open up! Come on out of there you son of a bitch. Open up or I'll break it down. Come on out of there you yellow son of a bitch!' And I banged on the door again and it opened and out came—he was so big I had to look up, and when I did, I saw it was —— I mention no names—the greatest prize fighter in the world at that time. Got it? Right.

"So that was the end of my thing with Clara Bow."

11

Hollywood and the Hollywood system have not ' produced a finer picturemaker than Billy Wilder of
Vienna, Austria. When I address him as 'Cher Maître' it is only
partly facetious. I do, indeed, think of him as a master. Even
his failures are the failures of a master.

Wilder began as a journalist, was a cub reporter at an early
age, and worked for several Viennese publications.

"I worked on *Die Stunde* for a while. It wasn't such a bad
job. One day I did some interviews for a Christmas number—
Arthur Schnitzler, Alfred Adler, Richard Strauss, and Freud.
All in one day. Not a bad job. Later on, when I left Vienna and
went to Berlin like a schmuck, I worked on the *B.Z. am Mittag*
for a while. But everybody wanted to be in the movies in those
days. We were known as the film generation. This bunch now
stole the title from *us,* that's how they are. My way was to write
scripts. I wrote thirty or forty. In those days my schedule was
about one a day. It's a little slower now."

"Well, at least one of them turned out not too badly," I
said. *"People on Sunday.* I saw it not long ago at the Museum
of Modern Art. It stands up beautifully."

"Still stands up, huh?" Billy commented. "I thought by now
it would be lying down."

"It's a fascinating little picture."

Billy laughed. "Little, you say. We thought it was very big.
It cost five thousand reichsmarks and don't ask me to figure
out how much that would be in present-day dollars. Maybe five
hundred bucks. And we shot it on Sundays only, out in the

streets. That's why you see that horrible expression on my face when they begin to talk about the new *cinéma vérité.*"

"And when did you go to Paris?"

"In 1933," says Billy. "It wasn't my idea, it was Hitler's. I hated Paris at first. I couldn't seem to get laid. So instead, I worked. And eventually sold a script. And then kept writing. I was only there about a year, and kept dreaming about Hollywood. Finally, I took off. What did I have to lose? By the way, I *had* gotten laid by that time. For some reason, I went from Paris to Hollywood via *Mexico!* Nobody's ever explained why this route. And there I was. The next thing I knew I was living with Peter Lorre and dreaming every night about how can I get back to Paris. And all of a sudden, there I am at Paramount, writing. There was one small handicap. I didn't have any English, so I kept writing in German, and some of my pals who were a little ahead of me would translate my stuff into English. I had a look at one of those translations a couple of years ago and I almost had a massive coronary. Then came Brackett and that changed everything."

Brackett means Charles Brackett, then one of Paramount's best writers. Brackett and Wilder became the most successful writing team in Hollywood. Their first collaboration was on *Bluebeard's Eighth Wife.* The director was Ernst Lubitsch. Gary Cooper and Claudette Colbert starred and the picture was memorable.

The following year, Brackett and Wilder had three credits, *What a Life, Midnight,* and, finally, *Ninotchka,* again with Lubitsch.

Then *Arise, My Love* and *Hold Back the Dawn,* after which they left Paramount and went to Goldwyn's for *Ball of Fire.*

In 1942 Billy Wilder felt ready to take on the responsibility of direction, and did a Ginger Rogers picture called *The Major and the Minor.* He and Brackett collaborated on the screenplay.

"Nineteen forty-four," says Wilder, "was 'The Year of Infidelities.' Charlie produced *The Uninvited.* I had nothing to do with it. Instead, I wrote *Double Indemnity* with Raymond Chandler. Because he asked me. Terrific book, and what a writer! It was quite an experience, the whole thing. Then Charlie and I got together again for *The Lost Weekend*—but I don't think he ever forgave me. He always thought I cheated on him with Raymond Chandler. He got very possessive after that."

Elsewhere, Charles Brackett is quoted as saying, "Billy got so despondent at being without me that we did *The Lost Weekend*." (The *Rashomon* syndrome?)

In the next development, Charles Brackett became their producer and Wilder continued to direct. From this producing-directing-writing team came *Five Graves to Cairo, The Emperor Waltz, A Foreign Affair,* and, finally, *Sunset Boulevard.* With this film, perhaps their most notable, the partnership came to an abrupt end.

Some years later, on a rainy Sunday in Bel Air, the dying Charlie Brackett talked about it.

"I never knew what happened, never understood it, we were doing so well. I always thought we brought out the best in each other, didn't you? But we met one morning, as we always did, and Billy smiled that sweet smile of his at me and said, 'You know, Charlie, after this, I don't think we should work together any more. I think it would be better for both of us if we just split up.' I could say nothing. It was shattering. And Billy—you know how he is, bright and volatile—got right into the business of the day, and we said no more about it. But it was such a blow, such an unexpected blow, I thought I'd never recover from it. And, in fact, I don't think I ever have. Of course, Billy's done wonderfully well, so it probably proved that he didn't need me at all. And I have no complaints, I've done well enough—not as well as he has—but then, it never meant as much to me. It was just that I loved working with him. It was so stimulating and pleasant. And such fun, you know. I never gave a thought to working with anyone else ever. Don't you think it was odd? What he did? There was no reason. We liked each other, even our wives liked each other. We had our disagreements, of course, but they were always professional, never personal. And I don't think in all our years together, in all those pictures we made, I don't think we ever had a serious quarrel."

Brackett sat for a long time, thinking hard, as though still trying to puzzle it out. Behind him on the table were, in a row, six Academy Awards, all tarnished and faded. (Why the hell can't someone shine them up? I thought.)

"Well, it happens, Charlie," I said. "I remember Kaufman and Hart. They worked together wonderfully well, and one day Moss told George he thought he ought to try one on his own."

"Ah, no, that was different," said Charlie. "I know about that. People have told me about that, and I've talked with them, both Moss and George. No, that was different. Moss, you see, was in psychoanalysis, and it was the analyst who urged him to get on his own. A matter of identity, I believe. But that was never Billy's problem. . . . No, if he wanted to write alone and direct, I'd have been pleased to be his producer. Or even work together now and again. Maybe not every picture. But he was firm and didn't want to work with me again ever at all. I suppose it was foolish of me to think it was going to go on forever. After all, it wasn't a marriage. 'Till death do us part.' "

"Well, you made some terrific pictures together, Charlie, and, in the end, that's what counts, isn't it?"

"Oh, I suppose so," he said, and laughed. "We got off some stinkers, too, didn't we? That *Emperor Waltz*. I don't suppose I ever understood it very well. I was sure Billy would know. After all, Vienna. And we *did* have Bing Crosby. I can't imagine *what* went wrong. The final result was quite boring, wasn't it?"

"I liked it," I said.

"No, you didn't, old pal, and you don't need to dissemble. Look at me. It's really too late for lies."

"Curious, wasn't it?" I said, changing the subject, "that Billy's first picture on his own—*Ace in the Hole*—didn't work either, did it?"

"No, no," said Charlie, "not at all. I think it was too cynical. Too critical of the audience, don't you know. It was the kind of picture in which the audience doesn't identify with the hero, but with the crowd, and, naturally, the crowd was the public, and behaved like the public in that situation. Talk about holding the mirror up to nature! If you're going to hold the mirror up to an audience and say, 'Look, this is how you are, what you are,' it better be a bit flattering, don't you think? Billy used to say he thought it failed because it was too tough. I don't think he's right about that. Tough is all right. I admire toughness. I don't admire hardness. That picture wasn't tough. It was hard. But then, Billy's hard, isn't he?"

"I've never found him so, Charlie, but then I haven't been as close to him as you."

"But the way he did it. Split us up."

"I think Billy was being pragmatic, that's all. He'd obviously been thinking about the situation for a long time and thought something ought to be done about it, decided this was the day, walked in, and said it."

"Yes, I suppose," said Brackett. "God, I'm sick, I'm so sick."

"You'll get better, Charlie. You're a hell of a lot better this Sunday than you were last. You'll get better."

He never did.

After the breakup, Brackett went to Twentieth Century-Fox as a writer-producer and did *Titanic, The King And I, Ten North Frederick, Journey to the Center of the Earth, State Fair,* and many others.

During a studio upheaval and reorganization the new administration canceled Brackett's contract on a technicality, saying, "Sue us." He had been at the studio for thirteen years and still had about two years left on his contract.

Billy Wilder, without previous announcement, called a press conference and made a statement in which he said, "In view of the treatment accorded Charles Brackett at Twentieth Century-Fox—" He then spelled out the details. "Therefore, I cannot imagine any self-respecting artist, whether director, writer, actor, producer, or musician, going to work for Twentieth Century-Fox under its present administration."

The statement was widely circulated and Twentieth Century-Fox was greatly upset. They contacted Wilder and gave him their side, but he was unregenerate. Brackett was paid off in full. Wilder remained loyal to his friend to the end. It was simply a question of a man deciding he wanted to be on his own, that being part of a team—no matter how successful—was not fulfilling.

Billy Wilder was taking a long time between pictures, longer than usual. I observed that the time between lengthened with each interval.

During one of our quiet, late-afternoon talks, I asked, "What is it, do you suppose, Billy, that slows us down so? There was a time around here when top directors made two pictures a year, sometimes three. Now we can't even count on one a year from guys like you. What is it? Have you slowed down? Or is it the whole business?" He was silent, seemed to be thinking. I went on. "Is it success that makes people too careful? Troubled? Worried about their next move? Is it as simple as rich and fat and lazy? What? There was a time—when you were still a writer—that *you* had two or three a year. Then, when you began to direct, you certainly did *one* a year. Every year."

"I should have skipped a few," he said morosely.

"Nonsense. Action's the thing. This whole damned business is a morass of imponderables."

"Maybe that's what it needs," said Billy.

"What?"

"More ass."

"Billy, please. We're having a serious discussion."

"*You're* having a serious discussion. *I'm* having a mild coronary."

"Why?"

"I lie in bed thinking my trouble is that I work too much. I come in here and you start beating on me because you think I don't work *enough*."

"I don't think any of us do. We get involved in deals and schemes and all sorts of distractions—like you and your damn football."

"I only watched three games yesterday," said Billy, pained.

"You call that distraction?"

I quoted. " 'Work strengthens us, pleasure consumes us. Let us choose.' You know who said that?"

"Hitler."

"No. Goethe."

"Same thing," said Billy.

"There's something in it, all the same. I think it's possible to get *too* smart about movies. Too experienced. Too—as the French say—*raffiné*."

"A lot *they* know."

"Better if we can retain at least a bit of our innocence. You don't agree?"

"I agree," said Billy. "But I don't know how." He laughed and muttered, " *'Il manque d'inexpérience.'* "

"What?"

"What Gounod said about Saint-Saëns—or was it Saint-Saëns about Gounod? What's the difference? Whoever it was—what he said was, 'He lacks inexperience.' See, you're not the only fancy quoter around here."

"Let me point something out," I said. "I've noticed it in many whiz-bangs—René Clair, you, George S. Kaufman, Carol Reed."

"Noticed what?"

"How you begin to work on a story and enjoy it—at first. And you're full of invention and ideas and the sparks fly—and then, slowly, a kind of poison sets in and you turn into fault-finders and begin to look for the weaknesses in the story instead of the strengths—and you use all your experience and background and knowledgeability to prove it's no good. And finally, you abandon it."

"Not me," said Billy. "I always come back to it—so I can tear it down and abandon it *again*."

"You know who did *not* work like that?"

"Who?"

"Our hero. Ernst Lubitsch. He always concentrated on the affirmative aspects—and kept looking for what was good and sort of ignoring the bad, sweeping it under the carpet—and finally he'd built so much strength that the weaknesses didn't seem to matter."

"We can't all be Lubitsch," said Billy.

"We can try."

"He was amazing," said Billy. "Wasn't he? That sense of fun, joy of life, that slant. You're right. He never lost it."

"And you think we have?"

"I don't know about you—but let me tell you about me. Did you ever—when you were a kid—get a Brownie camera for a present? Your first Brownie camera? Do you remember it?"

"Of course. I was born in Rochester, New York. Where the Brownie was born."

"Okay. Then you remember how you got the wonderful little magic black box and the roll of film and the book of instructions. And you loaded the camera and began to turn the roll—yes?—and there came first that hand pointing, and then dots, and finally—Number One! And you started. Focus, click. Turn the knob. Number Two. Focus, click. You could hardly wait to turn it to Three. And do you remember how when you got to Four or Five, you began to realize that there were only eight on the roll—so you got more careful, selective—and you waited for something really worth photographing. And sometimes you kept that roll in the Brownie for a week before you finally clicked your last picture on the roll."

"I remember," I said.

"Well, that's how it is with me. In the beginning, sure. One picture after another. But now—I feel I'm getting to the end of the roll. What is it?—three more, two more, *one* maybe?

That's why I'm so careful before I click it."

We had another drink and said no more on the subject that day.

Billy Wilder's first picture following the breakup, *Ace in the Hole,* must have given him pause. It was a failure. The word around town was he had blundered in splitting with Brackett. There was talk they were on the verge of being reunited.

Billy had other ideas. He bought a Broadway success, *Stalag 17,* about adventures in a World War II prison camp. Those of us who saw in him an original creative force were disappointed. No matter how well he did *Stalag 17,* it would not be a Billy Wilder picture.

This did not concern him. He was interested in success. He followed this with another Broadway hit, *Sabrina.* The picture did well. Next, he made *The Seven-Year Itch* with Marilyn Monroe. Another success, but not a Billy Wilder picture.

On the crest now, he inexplicably made *The Spirit of St. Louis.* It was costly and unsuccessful.

To shake off the dust of failure, he went to Paris and began work on *Love in the Afternoon.* It had been both a novel and an earlier film, but it became a Billy Wilder movie. The reception for it was mild. He reached for something sure-fire again, and made *Witness for the Prosecution.* His friends wondered why.

Then came *Some Like It Hot,* which many consider his best film. This, too, had been done earlier, but Wilder made it his own.

The following year came *The Apartment.* This was an original story by Wilder, with a screenplay by himself and I. A. L. Diamond.

Billy says, "I'll tell you where it came from. It came from Noël Coward. When I saw that beautiful picture of his, *Brief Encounter,* my God, it hit me hard. And what a job David Lean did! Well, they all did. I couldn't get over it. And I thought about that picture endlessly, the way you do about a picture that has an emotional impact on you. And I thought about it straight, and I thought about it sideways, and there were many times in the night when I would just put that whole picture down, that whole story, right in the middle of my head, and walk around it, around and around, examining it, and looking underneath, looking up on top. I finally had that story completely digested. Then I began to brood about one of the undeveloped characters, the guy who owns the apartment. And I thought, Now there's a really interesting character. A guy owns an apartment, or lives in an apartment, and he loans it out to somebody for the purposes of love. And, feeling as I do about business and about the competitive system, I thought, What if there's this little schnook, this eager beaver in a big company, trying to get ahead and he can't do it, until it comes out that he lives in this little apartment, and all the executives start to want to borrow it for their little *cinq-à-septs* and, what the hell? I don't have to tell you, that was enough, I was off and running. I wonder if I ever remembered to thank Noël Coward?"

The next year, Wilder made *One, Two, Three*. He and Diamond did the screenplay from a play by Ferenc Molnár.

"Don't ask me why," he says, "but I just got the feeling I wanted to make a picture again in Germany. I hadn't done it since 1948, when I did *A Foreign Affair*. And there's something else about it, I don't know what. Well, when you want to do something, you can always find plenty of reasons. And when I got Cagney interested, that was good enough for me. For me, there's never been anybody better on the screen. Also, I happen to think Coca-Cola is funny. A lot of people didn't. Maybe that's why the picture bombed out. I still think it's funny. And when I drink it, it seems even funnier."

Irma La Douce, his next picture, had begun as a small musical in Paris. Wilder bought it, and changes began.

"I have nothing against music," he says, "but the more I went into that story, the better I thought it was. And for me, the numbers got in the way. So, first, one of them went, then another one went, then we started talking that idiocy you hear

185

yourself go on about—you know, an intimate musical, or play with music—but, more and more, I could see that if I really wanted to explore all the avenues of this story, there wasn't going to be room for *any* numbers. And, one day, I made the decision, and we threw the whole score out and made it a straight picture. We used some of the music for underscoring, but that was all. I think it worked out very well. The truth is, I personally earned more out of that picture than any other picture I ever made. That doesn't mean it was the best. It just means I made the most money. And I enjoyed making it, too."

Billy Wilder's recent output has been uneven, but interesting, and he remains as able a film-maker as there is. His admirers are waiting for him to choose a stimulating subject, get excited, and provide once again a Billy Wilder picture.

12

On the complex subject of Samuel Goldwyn, his friend Lillian Hellman once put it best.

"To understand Sam," she said, "you must realize that he regards himself as a *nation!*"

The depth of this perception was demonstrated to me not long afterward.

1950. Spring. Mr. Goldwyn came to New York, ensconced himself in a sprawling suite at the Sherry-Netherland, and began a series of summonings.

My phone rang. I answered it.

"Hello?"

"How's Ruth?" asked the unmistakable voice of my old boss.

"Fine," I replied.

"Good," he said. "Come on over here a quarter after four. I'm at the—" his voice faded as he asked someone, "What's this place?" Another voice, far away. Then, "What?" To me: "The Cherry-Netherland. Come right up. It's room—" he leaves me again. "What's my number? What?" To me: "Nineteen eighty-four, eighty-eight. A quarter after four. Don't be late. I'm very busy and tied up."

"Fine," I said reflexively.

"How's Ruth?" he asked.

"Fine," I replied as he hung up.

I looked at the phone in my hand and reflected upon the extraordinary exchange it had just carried. I had said "Hello" and then "Fine" three times. Not much of a part, I thought, and hung up. I comforted myself with the reminder that no one ever has much of a part in a scene with a superstar.

Goldwyn had dealt with me as though I were an employee on his payroll, although I had not been a member of his staff for over ten years. Then it struck me. He thinks I still work for him! I had been warned to look out for this curious phenomenon.

"Once under contract, always under contract," Willie Wyler had said. "You'll see."

I arrived at the Sherry-Netherland five minutes early. Mrs. Goldwyn's maid admitted me. A secretary (female, middle-aged, efficient) showed me into the sitting room of the suite and left. I looked out at the view over Central Park. Impressive, but not half so impressive as the reverse shot. The room. It was fully three times as large as any hotel sitting room I had ever seen.

Another secretary (male, young, harassed) came in and asked if I wanted a drink.

"No, thank you."

"Tea, coffee?"

"Nothing, thank you."

"Coke, ginger ale?"

"No."

As this idiot exchange dragged on, we both pretended not to hear the angry voices overlapping in furious argument from a nearby room.

"Could I offer you some Vichy?" he asked.

He seemed determined to break me down. I would have welcomed a glass of Vichy at that moment but I replied stubbornly, "No, thank you."

He poured a glass of ice water from a silver pitcher, served it to me. He had won.

"Mr. Goldwyn will be right with you," he said victoriously.

"Thank you."

"You *are* four-fifteen, aren't you?"

"Yes."

He looked at his wrist watch and said, "Yes. Well, you *are* a bit early."

He left. As he opened and closed the door a blast of the ongoing vocal battle swept through the room like a high wind.

I drank the ice water.

A third secretary (female, young, temporary?) came through the room. We exchanged nods. A door clicked. She turned her head sharply in its direction and scurried out, successfully evading the entrance of Samuel Goldwyn. I looked at my watch as he came in. 4:15.

He moved to me, smiling warmly. Could he have been one of the fierce debaters I had been listening to only a moment ago? Impossible but true, I thought, like so many things about this remarkable man.

His hands were on my shoulders, his eyes were scrutinizing me.

"How's Ruth?" he asked.

"I'm fine," I replied.

"You're looking very well. Not too much weight. I'm glad to see you."

"Me, too," I said and wondered at once what the hell I meant.

"Let's sit down," he said, and added testily, "why don't we sit *down*, f'Chrissakes?!"

Taking orders, I sat down so swiftly that I jarred my spine. I winced, but he did not seem to notice.

"I hear at Columbia, they're making *Born Yesterday,*" he said. "You know, *your* play."

"Yes."

He looked at me gravely.

"And I want to tell you something very frankly. . . ."

Oh Christ, I thought as the pause stretched out. How am I going to handle *this*?

He spoke again. "I *like* that play. Your play. I saw it. I am very, very proud of you. It's a fine piece of work. Very strong. And very *American,* that's another thing. Yes, you turned out

189

to be some kid. Everything I believed about you." There were tears in his eyes. "I'm really proud of you. I mean it."

And I knew that he did.

"Who directed it?" he asked. "The play?"

"Why, *I* did," I said.

"You directed it *yourself?*" he asked again, astonished.

"Yes."

"I don't think you should do that."

"Why not?"

"It's not a good idea. Writer-director. It doesn't work out. Every director needs a writer and every writer needs a director. And they *both* need a *producer!*"

"Well," I said, huffily, "it worked out pretty well this time."

"This time," he said, scornfully. "Never mind this time—I'm talking about a *life*time."

"Okay," I said, remembering that argument with this man was fruitless.

"I *love* the theatre," he said. "If there's one thing I love in New York it's the theatre in New York. I *always* loved the theatre. Even as a kid I would go. The peanut gallery. Sarah Bernhardt, once. And Richard Mansfield. What a star. Modjeska. She was Polish. And Nazimova. She *wasn't* Polish. The theatre is great when it's good. Bob Sherwood. I love Bob Sherwood. Now about your play. About *Born Yesterday.* I want to tell you something."

I could hear it coming. How foolish I was to turn down his low bid in favor of Columbia's high bid.

Instead, he said, "I'm sorry to say this, but I don't think it will ever make a picture."

"You don't?" I blurted.

"No," he said, shaking his head. He seemed genuinely distressed. "I'm sorry for Columbia. In the first place, it's dirty. I mean censorable. This man living with this girl not married. And you can't have a crooked senator in a movie, f'Chrissake! Your ending is no good, either. Not for a movie. You've got your two stars and in the end you split them up. Audiences *hate* that. No, I know I'm right. It's no picture."

By now I was irritated. "Is that why you sent for me? To tell me that?"

"Are you sore?" he asked. "Because I express my views? Why is it people can't stand the truth?"

"The fact that it's your opinion, Mr. Goldwyn, doesn't make it the truth."

"You're sore," he said, truly surprised.

I was on the verge of a blast when he rose and said, "I have a very important project for you, my boy."

"Is that so?"

"I want you to write it and direct it. It will be a big thing in your life."

"All right. I could use a big thing in my life."

"This will be the *biggest.*"

"What is it?" I asked.

He paused impressively and said, "I considered a lot of people before I decided on you."

"What is it?"

"Different writers. Different directors. I considered them all. The ones who are available."

"What's the story?" I asked.

"I don't like writer-directors, but I'm willing to try an exception in your case. Or, if you'd rather only direct, I can get Moss Hart to write. Or you want to write only—what would you think of Willie? You like Willie, don't you?"

"Sure."

"So any way you'd like to work this out with me, let me know. But I'll tell you one thing—don't drag it out. This has got to go as soon as possible. Because it's topical, God damn it!"

Holy smoke, I thought. He's on my back already, and I don't even know what it is.

"What is it?" I asked.

"It's the greatest story of the year. The most important. With great characters. I know how you like great characters. I remember how you once said that was the most important thing —the characters—more important than the story. And you want to know something? You're right!"

191

By this time I was ready to sign, but as a matter of form, I asked, "What is it? A novel? Play?"

He walked out of the room. I got up and began to make plans for my imminent move to the coast. He returned, carrying a gray envelope that obviously contained a book.

"Take this home," he said, "and read it. Have Ruth read it, too. She's very bright. Then we'll talk. And then you can send Abe in and I'll work out something with him—don't worry about it. Your deal will be the best you ever had."

I got up, walked over to him and took the envelope from him.

"Call me later," he said.

I opened the envelope.

"Don't read it here," he said.

I took the book out of the envelope and looked at it. The bubble burst. It was a copy of a short-story collection by Edward Newhouse, with one of the stories carefully indicated. A week earlier Moss Hart had asked me to read it.

"Goldwyn wants me to do a screenplay," Moss had said. "But I don't know. I'm this way and that way about it. I guess it could be good, but I'm thinking of those endless phone calls —mostly in the middle of the night."

I had read it and talked it out with Moss, inconclusively. It was a straightforward story of family conflict with regard to the Korean War. A reluctant draftee. An overage volunteer. A patriotic finish. Apparently, Moss had decided against it.

"I've read this," I said to Goldwyn.

"I figured you would have," he said. "You're like Frances. My wife. She reads *everything.*"

"Well, I don't read everything," I said, "but I've read this."

"So?" he demanded.

I considered a number of replies. The first one that came to mind was, of course, 'I don't think it will make a picture.' I put it aside in favor of, 'Moss Hart asked me to read it for him' —then discarded that and said, stalling, "Let me ask *you* something, Mr. Goldwyn."

"Go ahead."

"Why do *you* want to make this?"

"Me?" he said. "I've *got* to make it. It's no question of do I want or why— I've *got* to!"

He had changed color. The rosy tan of his complexion had turned reddish-blue.

"Why?" I persisted.

"Did you see *The Best Years of Our Lives*?"

"Of course."

"Bob Sherwood and Willie. Seven Academy Awards? The greatest picture I ever made."

"It was fine," I said.

He walked to the window and looked out over the city—not the park—the city.

Then he said, in a charged voice, "Well, with that picture, I brought the boys home. And now—" His voice caught. He paused, recovered, turned to me and continued, "Now I've got to send them away again!"

I heard myself say, "Lillian's right."

"Lillian?" he said. "Lillian Hellman? Of course she's right. You want her to write it and you direct? Is that it? Well, let me see if I can work it out."

"Wait," I said. "Let me read it again."

"Very well," he said. "What time in the morning? Come for breakfast. Tell Jack what you eat. Eight-thirty? I'm going to the theatre tonight to see—something. I'm looking forward to it. I love the theatre. Since I was a kid."

We were at the door. Through another open door, I saw three men and an excessively pretty girl waiting in a smaller sitting room.

Mr. Goldwyn and I were shaking hands. His left hand clutched my shoulder.

"How's Ruth?" he asked, and went off before I could reply.

Men of size are full of surprises. One of Samuel Goldwyn's greatest charms was his unpredictability.

He once arrived in New York and phoned me.

193

"Say," he said. "I've just been reading *The New York Times,* about this wonderful English ballet company."

"Yes," I said. "The Sadler's Wells. They're at the Met."

"I have to see that," he said. "Get tickets and we'll go. I'll pay for them."

"All right," I said. "When would you like to go?"

"When? What do you mean, 'when'? Tonight."

"Well, I'm not sure I can get tickets for *tonight.*"

"Why not?" he said. "You just told me you could get tickets."

"Let me see what I can do."

Fortunately, I was able to acquire seats and was not at all surprised when I found myself canceling the plans I had made for that evening.

We took Goldwyn to dinner, but he was too excited to eat. As we entered the Metropolitan Opera House, he kept looking around and shaking his head in wonder.

"Hasn't changed," he said. "It never changes. Isn't it wonderful to have some things that don't change? I remember coming here and sitting way up high. Caruso and Mary Garden and Geraldine Farrar. What artists they were! But even *they* needed a producer," he added, fixing me with a hard and meaningful look. "They had this fellow in those days, Gatti-Casazza—Italian I think he must have been. What a producer."

We found our seats.

It was one of the great nights. Margot Fonteyn in *Giselle.* I could not help but observe Goldwyn and his reaction to what was taking place on stage. He was leaning forward in his seat, his hands clasped tightly. His lips were parted, and his small eyes had grown large.

During intermission, Goldwyn sat perfectly still, not wanting to talk or to step out to the lobby. He seemed to be digesting what he had seen and heard.

The *pas de deux* with Fonteyn and Robert Helpmann brought tears to Goldwyn's eyes. When it was over, he applauded and cheered. He got out his handkerchief, wiped his eyes, and blew his nose. At the end, he was the first one on his feet applauding and shouting "Bravo!"

"It was great," said Goldwyn at supper. "It was just great. I have to send that girl flowers. Remind me."

"Could I ask you something, Mr. Goldwyn?"

"Certainly," he said.

"Why did you want to see this tonight? Are you thinking of her for something in a picture? Or the company? Or what?"

I had hurt his feelings. "I wanted to see it," he said, "because I wanted to see it. Everything in my life isn't connected with my business. Do you think that? Is that what you think of me?"

"No, but I just wondered."

"The ballet," he said, "is something I've always loved. Maybe because when I first ran away from Poland—wherever I was, in Hamburg, in London, in America, I would love to go to the theatre. But mostly I had trouble with the language. So I started in to love the ballet wherever I was. Now, of course, I understand the language, but I still love the ballet, especially when it's great. Like tonight. She was wonderful—that Lynn Fontanne. The best I ever saw. Call me up tomorrow and remind me to send her some flowers. Some beautiful flowers."

I had reason to recall the evening a year or so later, in Hollywood. The American Ballet Theatre arrived to play an engagement. I was working at Columbia at the time and invited Harry Cohn to the opening.

"The opening of what?" he asked.

"The American Ballet Theatre," I replied. "Oliver Smith is a friend of mine and I have four good seats."

"Ballet," said Cohn. "Keep it."

"But this is a great company, Harry."

"Yeah, yeah, I know. But I can't stand ballet."

"Why not?"

"Because I don't like it where everybody chases everybody and nobody catches nobody."

A marked contrast, I reflected, between Cohn and Goldwyn, outwardly alike in many respects. The differences between them were small, yet vital.

"Harry," I said. "You've got no class."

"Who needs class? I've got money. That's *better* than class."

"I'm not so sure," I said.

"You think *you've* got class?" he demanded. "Your *wife's* got class. Not you."

"Who needs class?" I said. "I've got money."

"You haven't got that either," he said. "Don't kid me."

"How do you know?" I asked.

"Because," he said, craftily, "if you had money, would you be working for a bum like me—with no class? I'll tell you who had class. Aly Khan. He had class."

"Come on, Harry," I said. "Let's talk seriously. I don't think I can define class, neither can you, neither can anybody."

"You're wrong again," he said. "I'll tell you about class. It was in the South of France and Aly was married to Rita Hayworth, and he'd bought the most beautiful château down there. I think he bought it from Lady Mendl. And he gave a party. A big dinner dance down there. Black tie and everything. Rita was pregnant. And out on this kind of terrace, they put down a dance floor. Right on the water. You know, overlooking. And it was really unbelievable, but the whole evening went on and Aly—you know how he loved to dance—and of course Rita Hayworth was about the best dancer there was—listen, for all I know, that's why he married her—and he danced with everybody. First this one and then that one and he danced with everybody but Rita. Who was his wife. I remember I said to Joan, 'It's like that song John Golden once wrote, "I Can Dance with Anybody but My Wife." ' So Joan said to me, 'Maybe Rita's not *supposed* to dance. After all, she's six months' pregnant.' But finally—now you talk about class— finally, when Aly, the host, had danced with every woman there, there were about eight, he called the butler over and said something to him and the butler went out and in a few minutes all the lights on the terrace started to get dim. Because

196

the butler was dimming them. And they got dimmer and dimmer until there was just a kind of a glow. And then Aly nodded to the little orchestra and they started to play a slow foxtrot. It was 'Night and Day,' and then he went over and got Rita. And he danced with her for the rest of the evening. And with nobody else. And if you don't think that's class, then you don't know what the hell you're talking about."

It is easy to understand why this event would appeal to Harry Cohn. For one thing, he admired its showmanship. For another, like most roughnecks, he admired gentlemen. Above all, he wanted to be one but had no notion of how to go about it.

This was a quality he shared with Sam Goldwyn. The difference was that Goldwyn made it.

In 1932, Goldwyn produced a film version of Zoë Akins' Broadway success *The Greeks Had a Word for It*. Since it dealt with a group of modern-day courtesans, the title was on the Hays Office banned list. This meant that if the property were to be filmed, it could not bear its original title, which is why the picture was called *The Greeks Had a Word for Them*.

Even with the help of Lowell Sherman's sophisticated direction and sparkling performances from Ina Claire, Madge Evans, and Joan Blondell, the picture failed. Goldwyn withdrew it and rereleased it as *Three Broadway Girls*. Even that did not help.

It was for this picture that Goldwyn had secured the services of Coco Chanel. She came to Hollywood from Paris and did a stellar job. Goldwyn offered her another picture and a term contract but Chanel had had enough. Clearly, she was too individual an artist for factory work, even in a high-class factory.

"She was a great little woman," Goldwyn recalled. "She didn't take anything from anybody. And nothing from nobody. Not even from me. Those actresses. You know how they are with designers. They all think they know better. F'Chrissake. I hire the best, the most expensive dress designers and then some star—Miriam Hopkins or Oberon or whoever—starts telling the designer how to design. I used to say to them, 'When you go for an operation, do you tell the doctor—the surgeon—how to take out your appendix? Because it's *your* appendix?' That's why I liked that Chanel woman. She had power. She knew what she was doing and she took nothing from anybody. Not even me. Usually, I don't like that type, but I liked her. I don't know why."

René Clair recalls that shortly after the release of *The Ghost Goes West,* his brilliant collaboration with Robert Sherwood, Samuel Goldwyn turned up in London and invited him to lunch.

"He offered to me *The Adventures of Marco Polo* and I was sure from the title that it was not for me, but in any case he was Goldwyn—Hollywood. I was impressed and I took home the material to read. I was right. Not for me. So I met with him and that is what I have told him. Very good but not for me. 'What do you mean not for you?' he said to me. I said, 'It's not my kind of a picture. It's not my subject or my style.' Goldwyn said, 'You've only got *one* subject, *one* style?' I said to him, 'No, not one subject, but yes, one style, and if I changed that I'm worried they will not accept it.' 'They,' he said. 'Who is they?' 'Well,' I said, 'the public.' And he said, 'The public will accept anything if it's good.' And I said, 'But the critics.' He was very surprised and said to me, 'You care about *critics*? You worry about *critics*?' And I said, 'Of course.' He said, 'Do you know how much a critic makes?' 'In France, yes,' I said. 'I used to be one myself. In America, I don't know.' 'You don't know,' he said. 'Well, I'll tell you. The critic of *The New York Times* makes maybe two hundred and fifty dollars a week.' 'Is that so?' I said. 'Yes,' he said, 'and you know what I propose to pay you? Twenty times that.' I said, 'My God.' Then he looked at me and said, 'You're going to sit there and tell me you care what somebody thinks that you make twenty times

198

more than?' And when I said, 'Yes,' he was so disgusted he didn't want to talk to me any more."

Laurence Olivier has memories of Sam Goldwyn that stem from the time he played Heathcliff in the Goldwyn production of *Wuthering Heights*. This is the picture Goldwyn always referred to as "Woodering Height."

Olivier remembers: "Shortly after we began, they sent me over to the Western Costume Company or some such place, to get my Heathcliff suit and one of the items proved to be an old pair of boots. They seemed right enough to me, the very thing for tramping the moors, you know, and I wore them. I must say, they were rather uncomfortable and a bit smelly but, after all, Heathcliff was not Beau Brummell.

"Well, God knows where those boots had *been*! Within three or four days, my foot began to swell. Clearly it was an infection of some sort. I very nearly panicked. I'd heard that poisonings of this sort could be fatal.

"I rushed round to the doctor's, and was both delighted and dismayed when he told me I was suffering from a severe case of athlete's foot. I say 'delighted' because I had begun to think it was something far worse, and 'dismayed' because, good Lord, if you're going to be incapacitated and in pain, and put to the bother of dealing with an ailment, you do want it to be something slightly more glamorous than athlete's foot, don't you? In any case, for some days, my work was limited to medium shots and close shots. I simply could not walk into a room or anywhere else. Goldwyn heard about it, of course, and came down onto the set one day, and said, 'I hear you're having trouble. I've had it too. The same trouble. And it's no joke. It's a very, very serious thing. I want you to be very careful. That's no joke, that athletic feet.'

"And so we went on. I was in great pain, actually. Suffering and limping. Moreover, I was shot full of medication of all sorts. A few more days went by and Goldwyn came down onto the set again. I stood up to greet him—I suppose to show him how much better I was. He came over, looked at me, and put his arm across my shoulders, and I thought, Oh dear, this is going to be embarrassing, all this commiseration, and praise for being a trouper and continuing to work. I hope it's over soon!

"Then he beckoned to Willie Wyler. Willie came over, and Goldwyn, with his free hand, pointed to me and said, 'Willie, if you don't do something about this actor's *ugly, ugly* face, I stop the picture!' Well, you can imagine. I was stunned. So was Willie, I think. After all, it was the only face I'd brought with me and what was I to do?

"In the end, it turned out it wasn't so much my face that troubled him as some of the low-key photography, but that was his way. He went right to the point. Perhaps in the end, that's the best way." He looked off into the past and continued, "I wish he'd been running M-G-M when I came out to do the Garbo picture.

"I imagine he'd have sent for me and said, 'Olivier, you're no good. Here's your ticket back to London.' Instead, they kept telling me how good I was, but— And then endless obfuscation about my height vis-à-vis Garbo and my youth and my accent and all at once, it seems, I was back in London, realizing what had happened. There were letters later on, and a settlement and somewhere along the line, they put it onto Garbo. I suppose they thought that was the safe thing to do because they might— just might, some day—need me for something. In fact, as it turned out, they did. I never believed them about Garbo."

13

For a while there, Ingrid Bergman was just about everyone's fantasy friend. She turned up in Hollywood in 1938, a beauty of twenty-three, and made a film for David O. Selznick called *Intermezzo* opposite Leslie Howard. It was a touching, ephemeral story in which she had scored a great success in the original Swedish version.

The unique loveliness of the leading lady captivated us all. Ingrid Bergman was a new personality, however, and difficult to cast.

Selznick admitted he did not know exactly what to do with her. This may have been the reason he did nothing with her for almost three years, and then loaned her out to Metro to make *Rage in Heaven*. A dud. Next, to Columbia for *Adam Had Four Sons*. This, too, failed, but Spencer Tracy asked for her in his remake of *Dr. Jekyll and Mr. Hyde,* in which she made a considerable impression.

The following year, 1942, she appeared opposite Humphrey Bogart in *Casablanca* and was, overnight, the biggest star in pictures. There followed *For Whom the Bell Tolls, Gaslight, The Bells of St. Mary, Spellbound, Saratoga Trunk, Notorious,* and so on. It was not until 1950, after an astonishing and productive decade, that scandal struck and almost ruined not only her career, but her life.

One of her misfortunes was that her success came when David O. Selznick was preparing *Gone with the Wind,* working an eighteen-hour-a-day schedule on that monumental project, and finding it difficult to fix his attention on anything else.

He thought something would come up. Things did, but, for one reason or another, were not considered suitable, or the deal could not be made, or a decision was postponed until it was too late. Meanwhile, Ingrid Bergman sat.

The Selznicks invited her constantly to their home. She met many people. But no work. There were no parts. At the age of twenty-four this can be tragic.

She told me once that she had spent whole days walking up and down the beach at Malibu, crying. All she wanted to do was to act. Instead, here she was in a great beach house, getting up every morning with nothing to do, except on those rare occasions when a script would be sent from the studio for her to read or when she had a luncheon invitation. She recalls that the indignity she hated most was the gifts the Selznicks would always send her on birthdays or holidays: flowers, gold compacts, a Capehart record player.

"But all I wanted was a part," she says.

When she complained, it was pointed out to her that she was, after all, Swedish, that she was a star, and that she could not just play any old thing.

Somewhere in this time she came to know Burgess Meredith, who was going to do a stage revival of *Liliom*. He invited her to play opposite him. She implored Selznick to let her do it. To get her out of his hair, Selznick agreed. She went East, played it, and returned. Again nothing happened.

After *Adam Had Four Sons,* she went back East and did *Anna Christie*. I went to see it and thought she was tremendous. She returned to Hollywood. Still nothing.

The most important film in the making of a star is the one that follows the first big hit. If the second picture disappoints, the star-building process is aborted, the star-to-be becomes a flash-in-the-pan and has to start virtually from scratch. But if it is possible to follow one great success with another, the career is well and truly launched.

Ingrid Bergman's crucial time came after *Casablanca*. In her case, a fortunate set of circumstances fell into place to provide her with that second smash hit. It was Ernest Hemingway's *For Whom the Bell Tolls.*

I had just had a success and was asked by Paramount if I would be interested in taking on the direction. Since I was under contact to RKO, a loan-out would have to be arranged. Before approaching RKO, however, I wanted to make certain I was up to the formidable job and asked for a few days to consider. I took a copy of the book and went off to Santa Barbara. I checked into the hotel, went to bed, and rose at five the following morning. I went into town, had breakfast at an all-night diner, returned to the hotel, and began to read. I read until lunchtime, stopped for an hour; read until dinner, stopped; read again until late bedtime.

The next day I went through the same routine and finished the book. I walked around for a day—thinking, digesting what I had read. I spent two more days rereading the book and making notes. By the end of the second reading, I had convinced myself that I had at least the beginning of a concept.

I returned to the studio and told Pandro Berman I would like to undertake the job, if the right cast could be engaged.

"Okay," said Pan, "let me see what kind of trade I can make."

I spent a nervous week waiting for the outcome of negotiations. One morning I was dismayed to read in the trade papers that Sam Wood had been signed by Paramount to direct *For Whom the Bell Tolls.* I confess I was also relieved, since I had begun to have misgivings about bringing the difficult, complex story to the screen. Ernest Hemingway had created the device of using the word "obscenity" in place of the real thing. Clearly, this was not going to work on the screen—what would? Well out of it, I thought.

Casting began to be announced. Gary Cooper. Certainly the right choice. Vera Zorina for Maria. Excellent, I thought. She was a remarkable player with unique gifts. I began to wish that I *had* been given the plum.

While all this was going on, Burgess Meredith introduced

203

Ingrid Bergman to Ernest Hemingway. Hemingway was a man who responded to women. One of the types he particularly admired was the mysterious, exotic, foreign beauty—Marlene Dietrich, for example. It can easily be imagined what effect Ingrid Bergman had on him. He wanted to do something for her, but what could he do? The part of Maria had been cast. In any case, Maria was Spanish and not at all Bergman's sort of role. Still, he tried to get it for her, arguing that Zorina was Norwegian.

"Yes," said the studio, "but she's dark."

It was a losing battle and he knew it, but he was trying to impress Bergman. He kept bombarding the studio with objections to Zorina. He had no rights of approval, but behaved as though he did have.

Shooting started, and after three or four days, Paramount executives began to be troubled about Zorina's rushes. It might have been that Hemingway had shaken their confidence. They decided that Zorina did not look sexy. The rumor spread that they were thinking of replacing her.

The agents went to work, all sorts of replacements were suggested. Some were not available, others did not want to do it. Ernest Hemingway charged into this vacuum, beat on doors, worked on Sam Wood, the director, and despite the obvious obstacles, Vera Zorina was out and Ingrid Bergman was in.

She was not ideal casting, but the film was made in such a superficial way, with a combination of accents and types of all kinds, that it did not seem to matter. The picture was shot in California, not in Spain. The end result was mediocre, but Ingrid Bergman was electrifying. She worked beautifully with Gary Cooper, and revealed powerful sex appeal, unsuspected by those who did not know her.

In *Intermezzo* she had been polite and cool. *Rage in Heaven* was straight, *Adam Had Four Sons* corny. But when Gary Cooper grabbed her in *For Whom the Bell Tolls,* when they went into that sleeping bag together, something powerful happened in darkened auditoriums the world over.

The picture was not the over-the-moon success Paramount

had hoped it would be but it was important, and Ingrid Bergman scored a personal triumph. Then came the great succession of hits and, within two or three years, she was the most sought-after star in Hollywood.

Back in New City, New York, Maxwell Anderson was finishing a play called *Joan of Lorraine.* He showed it to his colleagues in the Playwrights' Company and they all responded favorably.

Maxwell Anderson lived his life remote from the Broadway razzle-dazzle, so it was not surprising to hear him say, at a casting conference, "I tell you who I'm going to have for Joan— that tall Swedish actress—I can't remember her name, but I saw her in a movie not long ago. It wasn't very good, but she's fine. I think her name is Berman. Something like that."

"Ingrid Bergman?" said someone.

"I believe you're right," said Max. "Ingrid Bergman, that sounds right. Yes. I think I'll have her to play Joan."

His friends could hardly bring themselves to tell Max that Ingrid Bergman was a great film star, that the chances of her going into a Broadway play for a run were minimal.

But Max Anderson, the innocent, persisted. He flew to Hollywood, went to the Beverly Hills Hotel, somehow got hold of Ingrid Bergman's telephone number, and called her. He told her he had written a play about Joan of Arc and would like her to read it without delay because he could only stay in Hollywood for a limited time.

Ingrid Bergman told me later she was so impressed by the audacity of this contact that she agreed to everything. She confessed she had only vaguely heard of Maxwell Anderson and was not sure exactly who he was or what he had previously written.

Max delivered the play personally and went back to the hotel to wait for her reaction. It arrived overnight. Ingrid Bergman read the play and was wildly enthusiastic.

"I've always wanted to play Joan of Arc," she told him on the telephone. "I feel an affinity for that character."

"Yes," said Max, "you'll be very good."

"The only trouble is, Mr. Anderson, that I have two pictures I am committed to do as soon as I finish the one I'm on now."

"Oh," said Max, disappointed, "can't they be called off, or postponed? Or one of them?"

"I'm afraid not."

"Well, then, what are we going to do?"

"I'd love to play this part in your play, Mr. Anderson, but I wouldn't be able to do it for a year."

There was a short pause, after which Max said, "All right, I'll wait."

Within a month, arrangements had been made for the following year's production of *Joan of Lorraine,* to the complete astonishment of the other members of the Playwrights' Company.

Max was not at all surprised.

Joan of Lorraine was constructed in the form of a play within a play, the story of the production of a play about Joan of Arc. It involved the offstage as well as the onstage interrelationships of the players and of the director, who was played by the vital young Sam Wanamaker.

Difficulties arose involving the actual director of the play, and what could be more natural than that this chore be assumed by the man who was playing the part of the director? Sam Wanamaker took over the direction of the play and all proceeded smoothly.

He and Ingrid Bergman became close friends. After the play had opened and succeeded, they were close enough to speak candidly to each other.

"Hollywood's ruining you," said Sam one night. "They're just using you. You're doing a lot for *them,* but what are they doing for *you?*"

"They pay me well."

"But what's that?" Sam argued. "You're a wonderful young

actress, you shouldn't be stuck in that Hollywood factory. You should be out in the world, making pictures in Europe with marvelous, creative directors. And then every few years you should do a play."

"Perhaps you're right," she said.

"Like Rossellini. Roberto Rossellini. Now there's a *director*, not a Hollywood hack. He's a creator. Have you seen *Open City*?"

"No," said Ingrid.

"You haven't seen *Open City*? We'll have to arrange it."

Wanamaker arranged a private screening of Rossellini's masterpiece. Ingrid Bergman was impressed.

"It would be wonderful," she said, "to work with a director like that, but how do you make it come about?"

"You call him up," said Wanamaker, "or you write him a letter." She laughed. "No, I mean it. What's wrong with that? He'd be flattered to hear from you. Write him. Who knows what could happen?"

Ingrid Bergman wrote a letter to Roberto Rossellini. ("Who knows what could happen?") Rossellini responded. They arranged to meet. They met. ("Who knows what could happen?") They planned to make a film together, *Stromboli*, to be shot on the island of the same name. The island's celebrated volcano did not erupt while they were there making the film, but life did.

Bergman and Rossellini fell in love and, in due course, there were rumors that the great star was pregnant by a man not her husband. Could it be true? It was.

Ingrid Bergman and her advisers decided to brazen it out, believing that her position was secure enough to withstand this situation. They were wrong. The bluenoses and the organized moralists raised a protest so loud and potent that Ingrid Bergman was banished from the American screen for six years. In the meantime, she had divorced her husband, Dr. Peter Lindstrom, and married Rossellini. This did not return her to respectability in the eyes of the great public.

In 1955, Fine Arts, a small independent company took a chance and cast her in a low-budget film called *Strangers*. It went almost unnoticed.

The following year, Twentieth Century-Fox was preparing a film of *Anastasia* and wanted to use Ingrid Bergman in the title role. Strategy meetings were held, officers of the Legion of Decency, the Daughters of the American Revolution, and the Motion Picture Producers Association were consulted. In time it was resolved that since the picture was going to be made abroad, Ingrid Bergman might be acceptable. Further, someone came up with the idea of casting Helen Hayes as the old Empress. Miss Hayes, the outstanding Catholic star in America, would help to ease the way.

It worked. *Anastasia* turned out to be a great success. Before this, Ingrid Bergman had made five Italian pictures which were not shown in the United States. Shortly after *Anastasia* she was teamed with Cary Grant in *Indiscreet*. Again, following the tradition of the power of two hits in a row, it propelled her into a second career.

14

The making of a motion picture is an enterprise that requires at least a million decisions—great and small —to see it from conception to completion. A successful film is one on which most of the decisions have been correct; an unsuccessful film is the opposite. It comes down to the question: Who makes the decisions?

Professor Albert Einstein and his wife were being interviewed by the world press on the occasion of their golden wedding anniversary. They were asked the routine question: "To what do you attribute the success of your marriage?"

Professor Einstein took his wife's hand in his and replied, "Well, when we were first married fifty years ago—*Gott im Himmel!*—fifty years—we made a pact. It was this. That in our life together I would make all the *big* decisions and she would make all the *little* decisions. And we have kept to it for fifty years. That, I think, is the reason for the success of our marriage." Then he looked up and added, "The strange thing is that in fifty years there hasn't yet been one big decision."

Things have changed, but in Hollywood until the 1950s, the final decisions, great and small, were made by the front offices, or by surrogates of those exalted founts of wisdom.

The head of the studio or the vice president in charge of production had his way. No writer, no star, no director of that period had the final say. Important directors were often replaced in mid-picture. Worse, they sometimes completed their work, only to have it taken out of their hands, recut, reshaped, and even reshot by the front office.

From the executives' point of view, they were behaving correctly. They had a responsibility to the banks and, as they often reminded you, to their stockholders. They had no responsibility to anything as abstract as the creative spirit, an artistic concept, or an instinctive feeling.

They were in business. A picture that did good business was a good picture. A picture that did poor business was a poor picture. Never mind what the critics thought, or the experts, or the scholars. If the mass audience did not turn up, willing to buy tickets in abundance, the work was a failure.

So it can be seen that the trouble with motion-picture art was (and is) that it is too much an industry; and the trouble with the motion-picture industry is that it is too much an art. It is out of this basic contradiction that most of the ills of the form arise.

I have known many Hollywood producers and studio heads. Some are literate, sensitive, intelligent men. Others are two-fisted, business-oriented politicians. Still others are lucky idiots.

Harry Cohn was the founder and, until his death, head of Columbia Pictures. If it were necessary to describe him in a word, that word would be "tough." He was also courageous, stubborn, energetic, ruthless, amiable, comical, attractive, gregarious—but above all, tough.

He had fought his way out of the hopelessness of poverty and had moved on to the periphery of show business. Because his innate talent lay in the area of salesmanship, he became a song plugger. Song pluggers were one of the principal means by which songs were promoted in the days before television, radio, and an extensive recording industry. They worked for the music publishers, and it was their job to get the publishers' songs performed in vaudeville, music halls, cabarets, restaurants, saloons, and stores. Most of them were performers of a sort. They would go around town, stand up, and sing the song.

Harry Cohn built a $400-million motion-picture empire but he was not as proud of it as he was of the fact that he alone had made a hit out of "Ragtime Cowboy Joe." He could not recount this adventure without growing misty-eyed.

"Everybody said it was nothin'. They said it was too fast and then somebody else said too hard, and mostly, right there at that time it was ballads, but I don't know. Somethin' about that goddam little song got me. Y'know what I mean? It got me right here. And I started in peddlin' it. *Jesus,* did I peddle it!"

Snapping his fingers on the afterbeat, he would begin to sing the catchy, bouncy words.

In mid-chorus he paused. "Well, listen, I see what they meant about hard. Even now, I see it, but I didn't care. I liked that song. Liked! I *loved* it. Would you believe it? I would sometimes sing it fifty, sixty times a night. I'm talking about all over New York. Rector's, Shanley's, Reisenweber's, in dressing rooms, in agents' offices. I knew it was catchy and I knew if I plugged it enough, it would have to catch on. Because it was catchy. I was right. It did. Do you realize people still play it? And sing it? Even now? And you know how long ago I'm talking? Forty-five years. He taught me somethin', that 'Ragtime Cowboy Joe.' He taught me if you believe in somethin' and you stick with it and with what you believe in, no son of a bitch around is going to get ahead of you."

He picked up from precisely where he had left off and continued, this time punching his right fist into his left palm on the afterbeat and beating time with his foot. The finish was triumphant.

Harry would sit there flushed and pleased.

He did not often go to parties, but when he did, he would always manage to find a spot in the course of the evening to get on and plug "Ragtime Cowboy Joe" with all the desperate energy of his younger self.

Harry Cohn was given to expressing himself with great vehemence. As he railed at his staff one morning about an unavoidable

211

accident, an associate sitting close to him said, "Take it easy Harry—you'll get an ulcer."

"I don't get ulcers," shouted Cohn. "I *give* 'em!"

There are many who worked with him across the years who would testify to the accuracy of this statement.

Norman Krasna was an early adversary. Young Krasna had written a play called *Louder Please* which was produced on Broadway and was something of a success. He returned to the studio in minor triumph, hoping for a great promotion, a plum assignment, or a raise. None of these was forthcoming. In an effort to break his contract, Krasna took to hectoring Cohn on every occasion.

Once, in the dining room, Cohn announced to the table, "I'm going to London next week."

"Take me with you, Mr. Cohn?" asked Krasna.

"You? What the hell do I need *you* for?"

"Interpreter?" suggested Krasna.

On another occasion, Cohn told his staff he was leaving for New York. In those days such trips were made by train. Krasna spoke up. "This time, Mr. Cohn, you've *got* to take me with you because on trains you have to write out your order for your meals."

"So what?"

"So what?" screamed Krasna in his high voice. *"You* can't write. You'll starve to death!"

Harry Cohn seemed to thrive on friction. He believed instinctively that it was only out of hostility, conflict, and abrasiveness that superior work could be created.

Considering all this, my own contacts with him were comparatively cordial, although we did have disagreements, battles, and long periods of nonspeaking.

Shortly after the end of World War II, he made me a remarkable offer.

"Tell you what I want you to do," he said. "I want you to take this check, this certified check for a hundred thousand bucks, and I want you to go 'way and I want you to bring me back a screenplay. And it better be good, you bastard, because you're takin' my money in advance. Who gives writers money in advance? Nobody. Only schmucks like me. But you've heard me say it before and you'll hear me say it again. I kiss the feet of talent."

"Harry," I said, "thank you. I suppose it's the most generous offer I've ever had in my life and I'm flattered and honored that you should make it, but I really can't accept it."

"Why not? Here's the check."

"I'd like to take it, Harry. Who wouldn't? But I don't think I can work that way. I mean, under the kind of pressure of having to come up with something that'll be worth what you've already paid me."

"Take it," he said, seductively.

"I'll tell you what I *will* do, Harry. Just to show my appreciation of your gesture."

"What *gesture*? I mean it."

"I know you do, but what I'd rather do is write something and then give it to you, and to no one else, and then if you like it and want it, you can give me the hundred thousand."

"Oh, yeah?" he said. "If you do it that way and if I like it and if I want it, I'll *tell* you what it's worth. Maybe it won't be *worth* a hundred thousand."

"No," I said, stubbornly, "it goes both ways. If you want it, that'll be the price. Maybe it'll be worth *more* on the open market but you're going to get it for that."

"If I want it," he said, quickly.

"That's right."

He studied me for a time, then said, "You know what I think you are?"

"What?"

"Nuts. You're nuts. I'm offerin' you here a check. A certified check. And you're turnin' it down and gonna go and beat your brains out and speculate. You don't think that's nuts?"

"Not really, Harry. I have to work my own way. I just couldn't take the responsibility."

"What *responsibility*? I *trust* you. Doesn't this prove I trust you? Listen, I know if you take my hundred thousand, you're going to write me somethin' good, somethin' I can use and nothin' controversial—like *niggers* or *God!*"

It was one of the few times in our relationship that I had my way.

It is often difficult to distinguish between courage, stubbornness, and principle—particularly as Harry Cohn exemplified these qualities.

When the notorious witch hunt was on, the House Committee on Un-American Activities was combing the film industry for signs of subversion. It was an ugly period and brought out the worst in many: cowardice, fear, greed, vindictiveness, deception, informing, and lying.

A solemn group of Cohn's executive assistants came in to see him late one afternoon on urgent business.

"What's a matter?" said Cohn, lighting a cigar. "You guys look like a funeral."

The group exchanged a look. The spokesman began.

"Listen, Harry. Those Washington guys from the Committee? You know. They're around."

"The hell with 'em," said Cohn.

"Take it easy, Harry. It's not so simple. They're moving, studio to studio, and they're going through the list of every single person on the payroll in every single department."

"So what about it?"

"Thank God we got tipped off. It cost something but we got tipped off."

"Cost what?" demanded Harry. "How much?"

"Never mind that for now. That's not important."

"It's important to *me*. It's my *money!*"

"Will you shut up, Harry, and listen for a minute?"

This sort of outburst from an associate—rare, unbelievable—conveyed to Cohn the gravity of the situation and he did indeed fall silent. The spokesman went on.

"The way they work it is this way. They've got their own list. Not just the *Red Channels* thing but their own list and that's what they use to compare it with our list and anybody they find makes us look bad, because we're not supposed to employ Communists."

"We don't," shouted Cohn.

"Wait a minute, Harry."

"Name me one!"

"Take it easy."

"Name me one," shouted Cohn. "I dare you!"

"All right. John Howard Lawson."

Cohn jumped up and struck his desk top with his open palm. A characteristic act. He had learned that it made a more startling noise than the conventional fist thumping.

"Who says so?" he demanded.

"He does."

"Who does?"

"*He* does."

"Who's *he* for Christ's sake?"

"John Howard Lawson."

Cohn sat down again and stared at his staff, incredulously.

"John Howard Lawson *says* he's a Communist?" he asked. "He says so *himself?*"

"He doesn't make any bones about it, Harry. It's his political affiliation. He doesn't hide it. He admits it freely. He takes the position that there's no law against it and that he has a right to be a member of any legal party there is."

"The Communist party is legal?" asked Cohn.

"It is so far."

Cohn shook his head. "Well, I'll be a son of a bitch," he said.

"So there you are."

"Where?"

"We've got to get John Howard Lawson off the lot right now. Today. Off our payroll, off our list. Off our property. But right away, Harry. It can't wait."

Cohn stared at the faces in the room, one by one. Everyone

215

knew what he was thinking. They were thinking the same thing: John Howard Lawson had written the screenplay for *Sahara,* one of the studio's few profitable films of the previous season. In fact, the *most* profitable. Without it, the company report would have made depressing reading for the stockholders.

John Howard Lawson had done a brilliant adaptation of a Russian film. Zoltan Korda had reproduced the original picture with great fidelity, and Humphrey Bogart had given one of his superlative performances. In the way of the Hollywood world, the next move was obvious. Put the same team together—Lawson, Korda, Bogart—and go again. Lawson had suggested another war subject, a Russian play titled *Counterattack.* Korda and Bogart agreed and all were convinced that it would top *Sahara.* John Howard Lawson was the man of the hour at Columbia, and as they say in the business, "Hot." The idea of removing him from the scene was equivalent to the notion of removing the star pitcher from the line-up just before the crucial game. No wonder the atmosphere in the room was grim.

Cohn sat and thought. His associates seemed to disintegrate before his eyes. The room fell away. Time stood still. He was alone with his problem. Now, characteristically, he made his decision. He rose. The conference was suddenly reconstituted.

"I ain't gonna do it," said Cohn.

"But Harry—"

"I ain't gonna do it, I don't care what. I ain't gonna louse up that picture that's gonna do three million two domestic. I need Lawson and he stays right here. They can't make me."

"But you can't do it, Harry. This is one time you're not going to have it your way. You've got to get rid of him. He's a Communist."

Cohn, who had been staring glumly out of the window, whirled suddenly and roared down from the top of his voice, "So what? I've got the greatest songwriter in the world on the lot working for me—what's his name?—and he's a *fairy!*"

On this note of frenzied logic, the meeting came to a close. Harry Cohn again prevailed. He defied the Committee and its attempts at extralegal enforcement. *Counterattack* was made and succeeded, and although it took years and left scars, the bad time passed.

Like a great many toughs, Harry Cohn had a powerful sense of morality, especially where the behavior of others was concerned.

George Cukor once gave a dinner dance in honor of the René Clairs, who were visiting Hollywood for the first time since their wartime residence. Since Cukor was working at Columbia, he engaged a small orchestra through the music department.

The party was a great success. Harry Cohn clearly enjoyed himself and got to sing "Ragtime Cowboy Joe" twice. At two in the morning only a handful of die-hards remained. The orchestra was playing soft, dreamy, slow music. The event was fading to a charming diminuendo.

As Cohn and I were leaving, we stopped and looked back at the beautiful house. Through a large bay window we could see into the sitting-room-cum-ballroom. There, in the dim light, the little orchestra was playing "As Time Goes By." A couple was dancing. The girl was a beautiful young English actress who, because her husband was on location in Mexico, had come to the party escorted by the man she was now dancing with, a beautiful young English director. It was a romantic sight indeed, and became more so as the couple kissed and continued to dance beautifully.

We watched for a moment. Suddenly Cohn grasped my arm.

"Wait a second," he said. "Isn't that What's'ername? I mean the one who's married to What's'isname?"

"That's right."

"Well, wait a second," he said with growing concern, "that guy she's dancing with—dancing, some dancing—that ain't him, is it? Her husband?"

"No. Just a friend."

"Some friend!" said Cohn, righteously. "Son of a bitch."

"Harry," I said, "you want some good advice? Mind your own business."

Harry turned to me with the air of a man who has no interest in taking advice.

"Listen, you dope," he said. "In this business everybody's business is everybody's else's business. Things like that," he pointed with his chin, "they give the whole business a bad name."

"Okay," I said, "but let's go. There's nothing *you* can do about it."

"There ain't, huh?" He pulled the cigar from his mouth, threw it into the beautifully tended hydrangea bed, and strode back to the house. I followed, since I could sense action in the air.

He clomped through the hall into the little ballroom, past the dancers, and up to the orchestra. "Okay, you guys. Knock it off! That's it."

The musicians looked at him blankly.

"That's it," said Cohn, waving with his arms in a criss-cross fashion. "Stop playing. Play 'Goodnight Sweetheart' for Chrissake." When the band failed to respond, Cohn moved a step closer to them and shouted, "I'm Harry Cohn! Cut!"

The music stopped in mid-note. "As Time Goes By" went by no longer. Cohn marched out of the room in triumph.

The dancers, finally aware of the absence of music, stopped, and floated out of the room hand in hand. The musicians began to pack up. For Harry Cohn the splendid evening had come to a most satisfactory close. He had exercised, in a fashion, his *droit de seigneur*. He had inhibited immorality. He felt a renewed sense of power as he settled back into his limousine and lit another cigar.

Although he was inclined to be close-fisted in his business dealings, I found Harry Cohn to be, as a rule, warmly generous

218

in private life. I once mentioned this curious discrepancy to him.

"What's hard to understand, you dummy? When I'm making a deal, it ain't only *my* money. It's the *company's* money and the company's money means other people's money, but if I want to send some broad some flowers or give you some kind of a cigarette case, that's out of my own pocket."

At one time the fashionable gift of the year was the deep freeze. It became a symbol of petty graft and corruption, and a number of government careers were wrecked as a result of giving or taking a deep freeze. It was the newest of American common luxuries, a status symbol, a much wanted creature comfort.

My wife and I had bought a house in New York City. When Cohn heard about it, he phoned us.

"I hear you bought a house," he said. "That's great. Everybody should have a house. I'm gonna buy you a deep freeze to put in it."

"Fine," said my wife, and, knowing Cohn, added, "not too big though, Harry."

Time passed. We made room for the deep freeze in our kitchen but it did not arrive. There were a number of conferences with Cohn but the subject of the deep freeze was not mentioned.

A year or so later, we were in Hollywood and went over to Columbia to sell Cohn a story. On that particular occasion, we failed. Still, the meeting ended amiably enough. Cohn saw us to the door of his office and as we were leaving, he decided to cap the hour gaily by telling a joke.

"Say, listen," he said. "Did you hear this one? Jessel told it to me. You'll get a belly out of it. Listen. These two little Jews get into a rowboat, see—"

That was as far as he got. My wife turned away abruptly and disappeared.

"What's a matter with *her*?" asked Cohn.

"Nothing," I said. "She just doesn't like that kind of comedy."

"What kind of comedy? Jew comedy?"

"That's right."

"I don't get it," said Cohn. "She's not even Jewish."

"That's right."

"So why should she care?"

"I don't know, Harry. That's how it is."

"Well, Jesus," he said, "you think she's sore?"

"Probably."

He turned back into his office and ran over to one of the windows. Looking out, he saw my wife crossing Gower Street to the parking lot. He flung open the window and shouted down.

"Ruthie! Hey, *Ruthie!*" She continued toward the parking lot. "Hey, Ruthie, listen!" She turned back for an instant. Harry cupped his hands around his mouth and shouted, "How big a deep freeze do you want?"

Although she did not reply then or ever, a few weeks later the best and biggest deep freeze on the market was delivered and installed in our New York house, gift of Harry Cohn.

Harry Cohn enjoyed nothing more than he did a feud, a battle or a fight. He thrived on friction, generated energy in combat. Since he was not given to compromise, he achieved his share of hostilities. There was the celebrated breakup involving his best director, Frank Capra; his long-continued swordspoint relationship with Rita Hayworth; his bitter lawsuit with Charles Vidor; and many others. Perhaps the most intense and lengthy of his wrangles was the one that involved Jean Arthur.

Jean Arthur was unique and irreplaceable. She hardly needed a part written for her since she always brought along her own enchanting personality. She was one of Columbia Pictures' greatest assets and starred for Cohn in a brilliant series of films, including *Mr. Deeds Goes to Town, You Can't Take It with You,* and *Mr. Smith Goes to Washington.*

But she and Cohn did not often see eye to eye on material. Therefore, she was frequently on suspension and relations between them deteriorated as the years passed. Early in 1941, after Jean had turned down four of the pictures Cohn had offered her, he placed her on suspension and it appeared they were permanently deadlocked.

I was in the Army at the time, having recently been drafted, and stationed in the East at Fort Monmouth, New Jersey. Jean and her husband, Frank Ross, were in New York for an extended stay. They were close friends, and I saw them every time I got a leave and came to New York.

From time to time, in order to strengthen his case, Harry Cohn would send Jean a script or a story or a book. She asked me to read some of this material for her. It seemed clear from the quality of the submissions that Cohn was simply going through the motions, that he would be horrified if by any chance Jean were to accept one of these scripts. Were this to occur, I believed he would find a way of pulling out.

I suggested to Jean and Frank that one way out of the dilemma would be for them to find a piece of suitable material and offer it to Cohn.

"He'd turn it down," said Jean.

"Not if it was good," I argued.

"But he'd never find out," said Frank. "Because he probably wouldn't read it."

"But what *if*?" I insisted. "What if you offered him a shooting script for nothing? Now that's something he couldn't resist. He'd have to look a gift script in the mouth, just out of curiosity."

"Maybe," Frank agreed.

"Sure," said Jean, "but where do we get one of those?"

"That's the next step," I said. "Let me think."

We had another drink.

At Fort Monmouth, I had made a friend—a gangly charmer from California, named Robert Wallace Russell. He occupied the bunk next to mine in the Company D barracks, but for the first week or so of our proximity, we exchanged no more than a morose grunt now and again. Morale was low.

At 3:15 one morning, I awoke from a nightmare in which I had become a paratrooper who knew that when his turn came, he would not be able to jump. I did jump, however—or was pushed—and floated down in soft terror until I landed on my cot in the Company D barracks. As I opened my eyes, I saw my bunkmate sitting on the edge of his cot, fully dressed, pressed, and carefully groomed. He simply sat, apparently thinking. It was a rare sight.

I raised myself on an elbow, squinted at him, and asked, "What's the matter, buddy? Can't you sleep?"

He looked back at me through his always-droopy eyes and replied, seriously, "It's my dreams. They *bore* me."

I knew at once we were going to be friends.

Bob had been trained in architecture; had gone to work for Walt Disney; had written fiction, plays, and screenplays; was an accomplished documentarian; and had written an impressive monograph on the subject of the dynamic screen, offering imaginative ideas for changing the size and shape of the conventional screen.

Some time later, when we were both placed on detached service to the New York headquarters of the film division of the Office for Emergency Management, we rented a small but ridiculously expensive house in New York from Miriam Hopkins—a reaction against our ghastly months in the barracks.

It occurred to me that Bob might assist in the Jean Arthur situation. I asked Frank Ross if he and Jean would be prepared to pay, say, $25,000 for that screenplay we were looking for. I was delighted when Frank agreed, since a solution of Jean's problems might also be a solution to ours. Ours was that we were flat broke, drawing Army pay—"Twenty-one dollars a day, once a month"—and borrowing heavily.

At dinner that night, I said to Bob, "Listen, how would you like to make twenty-five thousand dollars?"

Bob chewed his lamb chop slowly and did not reply. Wool-gathering, I diagnosed, and achieved his attention with a snap of my fingers in front of his nose.

"Bob!" I repeated with increased projection.

"Yuh?"

"How would you like to make twenty-five thousand dollars?"

There was another long pause during which he regarded me fretfully. Then he asked, "Would it be hard work?"

We began to root around for possible ideas. Most of his were wild and splendid, but I could not see Harry Cohn responding.

We spent many hours on this project and eventually developed something out of an idea for a play Bob had once had: a girl in an overcrowded city rents half of her apartment, for economic reasons, to an elderly gentleman. The elderly gentleman, in turn, rents half of his half to an attractive young man. Now all three are sharing a single apartment. Take it from there.

A weekend trip to Washington, D.C., proved to be the catalyst for the completion of the story. Wartime Washington was the ideal city for the situation. We returned to New York and wrote, with youthful speed and laughing all the way, a screenplay that Bob titled *Two's a Crowd*. This was delivered in due course to Jean Arthur and Frank Ross, who responded as we had hoped they would.

We could not imagine Harry Cohn turning it down, especially since he was going to get it free of charge. On the other hand, we could not imagine him, hostile as he was toward Jean, sitting down to read a script she had submitted. He would probably toss it routinely to a reader for a swift report, and who knew where that might lead?

When I learned accidentally from a film editor at Columbia that Harry Cohn was coming to New York, an idea struck me. After discussing it with Frank and Jean and Bob, it was carried out.

Although we had never met, I phoned Harry Cohn. He took my call and could not have been more cordial—until I mentioned Jean Arthur.

"Jean Arthur!" he shouted. "Don't talk to me about any goddam Jean Arthurs. If they were all like her there wouldn't be any *pictures*. She don't want to work, she only wants to aggravate *me*. You know how many scripts she's turned down? In a row?"

"Seven," I said.

"How the hell do you know that?" he asked.

"She told me."

"She did, huh? *Nine!* She's a liar on top of everything else. Not seven. Nine."

"All right," I said. "Nine. I'll tell her."

"Don't tell her. Stay out of this. Why don't you mind your own business?"

"Well, look, Mr. Cohn. I'm just trying to—"

"Harry," he said, firmly. "Not Mr. Cohn. Harry. Call me Harry. You're not that young and I'm not that old."

"All right, Harry. Listen. A friend of mine—terrific writer—and I have written a screenplay, and we've sold it to Jean."

"Are you nuts?" he shouted. "Sold it to *Jean!* Who's Jean? What *is* she? A studio? A producer? What's she going to do with it? Sit on it? She can't work for anybody, any place—except for me. What the hell is *she* going to do with a screenplay?"

"Well, I'll tell you, if you'll calm down," I said.

"I'm calm. Go ahead."

"She's going to give it to you."

"What?"

"She's going to give it to you."

"What do you mean 'give'?" he asked suspiciously. "What does she mean?"

"For nothing. Free. If you like it, it's yours."

He was thoroughly rattled by this unexpected strategy.

I went on. "And you're wrong about her not wanting to work. She does. More than anything."

"A script for *nothing*?" asked Cohn, in all disbelief.

"There's only one condition—" I began.

"I knew it!" he shouted exultantly. "I *knew* there was some kind of a gimmick—some wienie."

"Not much of a wienie," I said.

"Go ahead. What is it?"

Even over the telephone I could sense his resistance stiffening.

"Very simple," I said quietly. "I want to come over and read it to you. I think it's great and so does Jean and so does Frank. It's a comedy. Hilarious. And romantic. It's about wartime Washington and it's got three terrific parts and—"

"What do you mean, 'read it to me,' you stupid bastard? What do you think? I can't read? What am I? Some kindergarten you have to read it to me?"

"All right, Mr. Cohn," I said. "Never mind."

"Wait a second," he said.

I hung up.

It was a calculated risk, but in the circumstance I thought it worth taking. In five minutes my phone rang.

"I have Mr. Cohn for you," said a breathless operator.

"Fine," I said. "Put him on."

His voice was icy as he said, "I think we got cut off."

"No," I said. "I hung up."

"You hung up on me?" he asked. "Is that what you're trying to tell me? That you hung up on me?"

"I thought our conversation was over, Harry. I thought we both hung up."

"I did," he said. "What do you think? I'm gonna sit there holding an empty phone like a schmuck? I hung up."

"That's what I said. We both hung up."

This seemed to satisfy him.

"Okay," he said. "So when do you want to come over and read that crap out loud?"

"How about tomorrow morning?" I asked.

"All right," he said. "Come on up to my office. You know where it is?"

"Yes."

"That's where we'll do it. In my office. I don't want you up here. I don't even *know* you. This is strictly business. Not social. Business. Tell 'er I said so."

"Tell who?"

"That crazy broad you're workin' for."

"Ten o'clock," I said.

"Don't be late. And we'll see."

I rehearsed the reading with my cohorts and at ten o'clock the following morning presented myself at the offices of Columbia Pictures.

I was shown into Mr. Cohn's office. He had gathered a small group of his executive assistants. We shook hands. Having met only his voice, so to speak, the rest of him surprised me. I found him attractive, magnetic, and charming. He was beautifully dressed and every detail of his appearance showed care.

After a few empty amenities and casual introductions, Cohn said, "Okay, go ahead. They all know what it's all about, these guys."

I took the script out of my briefcase and said, "It's called *Two's a Crowd*."

"Don't worry about it," said Cohn. "We can change it."

Again I recognized a crucial moment.

"Before I begin," I said, "there's just one thing I insist on and that is—"

"Don't *ever* use that word around *me*," said Cohn, tightly. " 'Insist.' Nobody does." He looked around the room. "Tell him," he added.

"How about 'request'?" I asked.

"Request all you want," said Cohn.

"I'd just like the opportunity of reading this to you from beginning to end without interruption. I mean I don't want to get into a story conference here. Give me a chance to read it and then you can say 'yes' or 'no' or 'we can discuss it.' "

"What if I hate it right away?" asked Cohn.

This thought had not occurred to me. I replied, "Any time you hate it, say so and I'll stop."

"Go ahead," said Cohn.

I began to read.

The screenplay had an arresting opening, written by Bob. It was in the form of a Washington travelogue in which the juxtaposition of frantic film of current Washington life and the standard quiet recital of its beauties made for a comic effect.

Almost at once, I noticed a few smiles. At one point there was a little laugh, then a big laugh led by Cohn. I reached the end of the opening and was about to begin on the body of the script when Cohn held up a hand and said, "Hold it."

I was annoyed, looked at him and said, "I thought we agreed—"

"I'll take it," said Cohn.

"What?"

"You heard me. I'll take it. I'm no dummy. I know pictures. Any picture starts like that I'll take it."

"But you don't even know the story."

"Sure I do."

"How?"

"You told it to me on the telephone."

"I did?"

"You told me all I got to know."

He rose. "This is great. Tell Ross to come in here and we'll fix it up. And I'll tell you another thing. I don't take nothin' for nothin'. I'll make a deal with him. Some kind of a deal. It's going to be a swell picture."

We shook hands again and I was out on Seventh Avenue before I knew it, without the script, looking for a telephone to convey the news to Jean.

The picture was beautifully made by George Stevens not long afterward. Starring Jean, Joel McCrea, and Charles Coburn, it proved to be Columbia's greatest success that year.

True to his word, Cohn changed the title to *The More the Merrier*. Untrue to his word, he never reimbursed Jean Arthur for any part of the twenty-five thousand she paid to Russell. My own part in it remained anonymous because I was still under contract to RKO. No matter. It was a joyous affair all around.

Moreover, it taught me the trick of selling Harry Cohn screenplays. From that day forward I made it a point to read scripts to Cohn, a move he accepted cheerfully. He did not always buy what I read him, but always gave me a fair chance.

One of the scripts I read aloud to Harry and his wife, Joan, during an evening at his home was *The Marrying Kind,* which I had written in collaboration with my wife. After dinner, the reading went extremely well with both Mr. and Mrs. Cohn offering congratulatory punctuation from time to time. Less welcome was another sort of punctuation the evening offered. This came in the form of telephone calls from Cohn's broker, his bookie, two or three agents, and several mystery guests.

It made for a rocky evening but at the end Cohn accepted the material.

Interruption and distraction are the two principal enemies of creativity. The monstrous telephone is a symbol of both.

For Harry Cohn, the telephone was an indispensable organ. He could not have lived through a day without the telephone; it was a part of his anatomy. Seeing him in frenetic telephonic action one afternoon, the truth of the matter came clear. *He* was the interrupter. *He* was the distractor.

I scarcely ever saw him without a telephone at his side. In his office, in the dining room. He had telephones in his bathrooms, at the pool, in the steam room. Telephones in automobiles came after Cohn's day, otherwise he would have had two or three in every car.

The Columbia switchboard at the studio on Gower Street stayed open twenty-four hours a day, as did the switchboard in the New York office. Thus Cohn needed only to lift the instrument in order to be connected by direct wire to the nerve center of his life and work. If he needed suddenly to know the name of a picture, a writer, an actor, a theatre, all he had to do was pick up the phone.

How was a picture of his doing in Dayton? How was someone else's doing in Detroit? How did that play open last night out of town? Is it true that Twentieth is bidding for that musical?

For those who worked with him or for him or under him it

was a nuisance. He would suddenly reach for the telephone and call New York or Denver, London or Mexico City, and spend five minutes talking about something totally unrelated to the subject at hand. By the time he had finished his telephone call and said, "Go ahead, what were you saying?" you had usually forgotten.

It spoiled most luncheons. I never had a one-hour meal with him that did not contain at least half a dozen telephone calls, incoming and outgoing.

The practice continued in his home in Beverly Hills. You would be asked to dinner and there on the table in the formal dining room would be the telephone. During dinner Cohn would take only important calls, but would make outgoing calls at whim.

Cole Porter arrived in Hollywood and Cohn asked if he could give a formal dinner party for him. Cole accepted.

The evening arrived. When dinner was announced, we trouped into the dining room, beautifully candlelit, the silver reflecting the light, a gold service on the table, flowers, china, and glass I had never seen before. An impressive sight.

I looked over at Cohn's place at the head of the table and was pleased to see that there was no telephone. When I found my place, however, I looked again. There it was. I had not seen it at first because for this occasion, a formal dinner, the black telephone had been replaced by a white one.

Under the influence of Somerset Maugham and the accounts of his Spartan working discipline, my wife and I were attempting to follow his good example.

Despite the fact that we were theatre-oriented people, accustomed to late nights and late risings, we changed all that—rose at seven, got to work by eight, worked until noon, and then got ready for lunch. After lunch we would drive down to our offices, then located in the St. James Theatre building on West Forty-fourth Street.

One evening, as we were driving down, I noticed that Ruth

was uncharacteristically depressed. I tried to cheer her up using a few proven methods, but on this day they all failed. Was it that her morning's work had not gone well? Or could it be that she was not looking forward to the rest of the day? Or was it something more important? As we traversed Columbus Circle I noticed an enormous sign which was blank except for a square of rental information in its center.

"You know what I'm going to do?" I said brightly. "I'm going to rent that sign and have 'RUTH GORDON' painted on it in the biggest letters it will hold. How would you like that?"

Not a sound. Apparently she had not even heard. We continued down to the office. An hour later, Ruth told me she was going out to walk.

I was still thinking of that sign on Columbus Circle and began to wonder what it actually would cost. I had no idea, and phoned the rental agency to inquire.

To my surprise it turned out to be about $200 a month. I had thought it was going to be ten times that. I then found out what it would cost to have it painted. This, too, was within practical limits. I became giddy as I felt myself moving toward the fruition of this nutty idea. By evening, I thought better of it.

The look on my wife's face when I described what I had been planning to do as a surprise told me I had made the correct decision in abandoning it. But the notion stayed in my head and without meaning to do so, I began to plot a fiction involving such an act.

What if there were an attractive, but discouraged young man who has been beaten down by the city? He had come to New York a year earlier, confident he would make good somehow, that he would make a name for himself, that he would get there. It has all gone wrong and he has just about decided to take what is left of his savings and go back home. He walks around in Central Park, dejected. At Columbus Circle he looks up and sees that empty sign. He decides upon one final satisfying gesture. He rents the sign and has his name emblazoned upon it. One thing leads to another, and in the way of our world he becomes a celebrity, one of those who is famous for being a

230

celebrity. *Now* where? Perhaps he runs for office. Maybe gets elected and so on and so on. I played with the idea for a few weeks and finally had, in my head, what I thought was a solid story.

We were asked to come up to Boston to see a friend's play. On the way up I told Ruth my story. She listened carefully, intently, then said, "It's good but it's wrong."

"What do you mean, wrong?"

"Wrong sex," she said. "Think how much better that story would be if a *girl* did it. A girl makes it whimsical and special and audacious. If a man does it, he's just being pushy or dumb."

"I don't agree with you," I said.

"All right. But it feels like Judy Holliday to me."

"Fine," I said, "but it's going to be Danny Kaye."

A few days after we returned from Boston, I decided I was ready to turn my story into a screenplay. I began to write and even now I cannot explain how it was that my young man turned into a young woman, that Danny Kaye changed his name to Judy Holliday, and *A Name for Himself* became *A Name for Herself*.

When it was finished, I handed it to Ruth and said, "I've done that movie about the fellow who puts his name up on the sign in Columbus Circle."

"Good," she said.

When she had read it, she said, "I like it very much. Who do you see as the fellow?"

"Judy Holliday," I replied.

"Yes," she said. "He'd be good."

We went to Hollywood to present it to Harry Cohn. We assembled in the library of his home on Crescent Drive: Harry with his cigar, Joan with her knitting, my wife with her confidence, and me with my nerves.

I began with a speech. "Now, listen, Harry. We've been doing this for a long time and it's all been working fine. But the last time—on *The Marrying Kind*—you gave me a hard time."

"What hard time? It was a hell of a picture," he said.

231

"I don't mean that," I said. "I mean that while I was reading—trying to read—that phone kept going."

Cohn looked at me, all injured innocence.

"If the phone rings, that's my fault? Did I make it ring? If somebody calls me, that's my crime?"

"No," I said, "but this is important to me and maybe to you so why can't you shut the phone off and have somebody—"

"Shut the phone *off?*" he said, aghast. It was as though I had suggested he shut off the left ventricle of his heart.

"Just for an hour or so," I persisted. "Just till I finish reading."

"That's *more* than an hour," he said.

"I'll read fast."

Reluctantly, he made arrangements for messages to be taken.

Flushed by this small victory, I went on. "Another thing, Harry. Don't interrupt me and don't ask a lot of questions until it's over. And don't get up and walk around the way you sometimes do. It's very distracting."

"Jesus!" he said. "You're a real scoutmaster, you know it? I know you're a director, but don't direct *me,* d'you mind?"

"All right, Harry," I said. "I'll begin. But I swear if you do any of those things, I'm going to stop and leave and that's it."

"You're also a pain in the ass," he said. He sat down, planted his feet firmly before him as though he were an emperor on a throne, lit his cigar, and motioned me with his head to begin.

I read badly that night and sensed that the material was not getting over. I noticed that Cohn shifted in his chair uncomfortably from time to time. Compounding my seeming failure, I mistakenly began an attempt to compensate by speed, by volume, and by generally overacting.

I began to dislike the script myself. Cohn was increasingly restless and crossed his legs several times, left over right, right over left. About halfway through, I regained equilibrium and began to make contact. For fifteen minutes or so it went well. Feeling better about the whole thing I began to perform rhythmically, not so much turning the page at the end of each one but slapping it. Finally, I slapped one too hard and the whole sheaf of loose pages from which I was reading went flying all over the room. I was on my hands and knees immediately picking up the pages and trying to get them back in order. I felt something, someone brush behind me, looked around, and saw Cohn dashing out of the room.

It took me no more than a couple of minutes to reassemble my script. As I took my position again, Cohn came rushing back in and leaped back into his spot.

Irritated, I gave him a hard look. He looked back at me innocently, pretending, in a way, that he had not left the room at all. Before I could begin again, he leaned over, took the cigar out of his mouth and said petulantly, "I hadda go to the can. Did I *miss* anything?"

I went on and finished. Harry responded with special enthusiasm because he needed a picture for Judy Holliday.

I had not directed a commercial film since *Tom, Dick, and Harry* just before the war but I was anxious to do this one on several accounts. First, I enjoyed working with Judy Holliday. Second, the film could probably be made in New York. Also, it would be the first time I had ever directed anything of my own for the screen, and I was eager to learn if such an undertaking was practical.

Cohn agreed and negotiations began simultaneously with production plans. I told my agents to make the best deal they could but to insist on one point only, and that was that I would have the final cut.

Cohn made a fair offer for the screenplay and an overgenerous offer, I thought, for the direction. However, he dismissed my major condition out of hand.

The agents argued with him for several days and reported to me that it was no use. Cohn would not yield on this point. I decided to confer with him myself.

"You're a jerk," said Cohn, looking at me and shaking his head sympathetically. "Here I'm turning over my whole studio to you to help you make your picture and all you're worried about is the final cut. You haven't even got a *picture* yet so what are you worryin' about the final cut? Make the picture, then we'll see."

"No, Harry, then it'll be too late."

"Too late for what?"

"Look," I said. "This is how it seems to me. Try to see it from my point of view. This is my story. My characters. My dialogue. And I think I know how the picture should look and sound."

"Who said no? If I didn't think so I'd throw you the hell off the lot."

"But my point is that if I direct a picture from my own screenplay and my own story, I don't think it's right for anybody then to take it away from me and mess around with it."

"Who's goin' to do that?" said Cohn.

"I'm not saying you *would* do it. I'm just saying you *could* do it."

"I *could* bust you in the mouth," said Cohn, "but *would* I?"

"Who knows?"

"Listen," he said, "it's your story, it's your picture. I give you my word you'll have it your way."

I said nothing.

"You don't take my word, huh?" he guessed.

"It's more complicated than that, Harry. *You* know that. It has to be in writing. It has to be in the contract."

"I'll *die* first!" he shouted.

"That's another thing," I said.

"What other thing?"

"What if you die?"

He looked at me as though I were the Dark Angel in person.

"No, seriously," I went on. "Suppose you gave me your word and suppose I took it. And then suppose you died? *Then* where am I?"

"Where are *you*, you dirty son of a bitch? If I die, where am *I*?"

"I don't know, Harry. That's not up to me," I said.

For once Cohn was completely flummoxed. He looked at me

scornfully. "You know," he said, "you're really no good. You're supposed to be some kind of a gentleman and you got the nerve to come in here and tell me, a man with a wife and two small children, that I'm gonna die. Would you say that in front of my children?"

"You're way off the mark. I didn't say you were going to die. I just said 'What if?' from a business point of view."

Cohn began to yell in his habitual way. "That's it! I'm *finished*! I'm sick of the whole thing. I gave you my best shot. You don't want it, don't take it. The hell with it. Don't make the picture."

It was all off.

I was disappointed. Preproduction work had been going smoothly and imaginatively. Judy Holliday was built into this movie and since she was under exclusive contract to Cohn, all other avenues were closed. I decided to abandon the plan and to offer the script to Cohn on an outright-sale basis.

We planned to leave Hollywood on a Monday. On the preceding Saturday, during a long Beverly Hills walk, my wife urged me to try once again to reach a compromise with Harry Cohn.

"Maybe working in the theatre has spoiled me," I said. "That Dramatists Guild contract of ours is a masterpiece. The playwright has the final say. I don't see why that shouldn't be the same here."

"Except that here," Ruth pointed out, "you're well paid in advance for your work. In the theatre it's all speculation. You might work a year on a play, then it runs two nights and you've earned nothing."

I stopped walking and said, "Hey, wait a second! Maybe that's it. Let's get back to the hotel. I've got an idea."

I phoned Cohn and asked if I could see him.

"Tomorrow morning," he said, brusquely. "Today I'm busy. I'm very busy doing nothing. So tomorrow morning. That's the best I can do for you."

"What time?"

"Any time in the morning. I'll be out by the pool."

At ten o'clock on Sunday morning, I went to Cohn's house, was shown out to the pool. He assumed I had come to surrender and so was surprised at what he heard.

"Harry, I've been thinking, and here's a new proposal. You like the script. Your guys like it. Judy likes it."

"Get to the point," said Cohn.

"The point is, I'll give you the script for nothing. And I'll direct the picture for nothing. And I promise to make no major changes without permission. And I'll get it in on schedule. And on budget. And by the censors."

"Go ahead," he said.

"If the picture's profitable, we split fifty-fifty. If it makes nothing, I get nothing. And, by the way, I know all about cockeyed movie bookkeeping so you're way ahead there."

"Go ahead," said Cohn evenly.

"All I ask is that you let me make the picture my way. I'll discuss anything with anybody reasonably—"

"But the final cut, huh?" said Cohn.

"That's right."

"You see that water there in the pool? If you drank up that whole pool right now standing here, I wouldn't give you final cut. *Nobody!*"

"I'm not thirsty," I said.

"You're not thirsty. You're *crazy*," he said. "Here I'm offerin' you a fortune for the script and I'm willin' to pay you more than you're worth to direct the goddam thing and give you a piece of the action, what's more, and you're willing to gamble so that you could wind up with nothing. You don't think that's crazy?"

I explained slowly and carefully the work methodology of the theatre to which I had become accustomed.

"That's a different business!" he roared. Birds fluttered away. "God damn it! Can't you understand *anything*? I give you the final cut and the next thing Stevens wants it and then Wyler wants it and then Welles wants it and when all you bastards finally get it, what about *me*? The board of directors in New

York says to me, 'All those guys get the final say. What the hell do we need *you* for?' "

The argument went on for an hour serving only, as do most arguments, to make each adversary cling more firmly to his own view. The following day, I sold the script to Harry Cohn and went to Europe for three years. I realized, sadly, that for the moment, there was no place in Hollywood for me.

Harry Cohn, not much of a partygoer, was a considerable party giver. He was especially proud of his annual New Year's Eve celebrations, for which he and his wife traditionally provided superb food and drink, a stellar cast, and outstanding parlor entertainment.

In December 1943, *Cover Girl* was shooting on the Columbia lot. In the cast were two of the town's most accomplished parlor entertainers, Gene Kelly and Phil Silvers. Kelly was invited to the Cohn party welcoming 1944, and accepted. Phil Silvers went to see Cohn.

"The only thing, Harry—is like this. I know the reason you're asking me is you want me to get on and do some of my stuff. Right?"

"Right," said Cohn.

"But for what you want I've got to have my piano player. Like for instance when I do my Jerry Kern auditioning 'Ol' Man River' for Paul Robeson—"

"Kern's gonna *be* there," said Cohn.

"Great. But I can't do that number without Saul. Or when I do my singing lesson bit, not either."

"Yeah, that's a good one," said Cohn laughing. "Hey! You could do it with Sinatra. *Sinatra's* gonna be there."

"Fine," said Phil. "But—"

"Who's Saul?" asked Cohn.

"Saul Chaplin."

"Who's *he*?"

"Saul Chaplin, Harry. The songwriter. Cahn and Chaplin. I

thought you knew about songwriters."

"I know about songwriters," said Cohn. "More than anybody."

"Well, Saul's one of the best. He's never off the Hit Parade. And he's my friend. And he always plays for me."

"So where *is* he?" asked Cohn.

"Whaddya mean where *is* he?"

"I mean can we get *ahold* of him. That's what I mean."

"Why, he's right here," said Phil with some surprise.

"Right here in California?"

"Right here at *Columbia.*"

"Columbia?"

"Well, sure, Harry. He's working with us on *Cover Girl.*"

Cohn beamed as he said, "You mean he's workin' for *me*?"

"Sure. Don't you know that?"

"Of course I know it," said Cohn. "What the hell do you think?"

"So anyway, Harry, I'll be glad to come. I accept your invitation with pleasure. But if you want me to get on and do anything, you'll have to ask him, too."

"Don't worry about it," said Cohn. "He'll *be* there. That's all," he added, waving Phil out.

He flipped the key of his Dictograph.

"Yes, sir?"

"Get me—what's this guy's name?" he called out to the departing Phil Silvers.

"Victor Herbert," said Phil.

"Get me Victor—hey!"

"What?" asked Phil at the door.

"Don't kid around with me. I don't need you to be funny in here. I need you to be funny on the set. In the picture."

"Oh," said Phil. "And *not* New Year's Eve?"

"Get outa here!" said Cohn.

"Saul Chaplin," said Phil, and left.

Ten minutes later, Chaplin, a tall, thin, talented, and diffident man, stood nervously before Cohn.

"The trouble is, Mr. Cohn—I wish I'd known earlier."

"He didn't *tell* me earlier," said Cohn.

"But my wife and I, we're giving a party too and—"

"Okay, okay," said Cohn. "You can bring your wife along. Okay?"

"But what about *our* party?"

"Call it off," said Cohn.

"We've asked a lot of people."

"What's the difference?" said Cohn, irritated. "What kind of people could be coming to *your* party? Not *important* people."

"They're important to us, Mr. Cohn."

"Jesus Christ!" said Cohn. "What's a matter with you? I'm tryin' to put you over and you're fightin' me. What's your wife's number? I'll call her."

"No, Mr. Cohn," said Saul. "We just can't do it. It's too late. I'm sorry."

Cohn continued for another ten minutes, determined to have his own way. He pleaded and begged and charmed and cajoled and threatened. He hinted at improved billing, further assignments, and important opportunities. Saul Chaplin remained adamant.

Finally, exhausted, Cohn said, "All right, the hell with it. You don't want to come—and bring your wife? So all right. So *don't* come."

Saul started out, regretting the meeting's sticky ending. At the door he turned back and said, "I'm really sorry, Mr. Cohn. Maybe some other time?"

"Some other time," said Cohn without looking up, "I can't *use* you!"

Ben Hecht and Charles MacArthur had written a screenplay entitled *Gunga Din.* Their agent, Leland Hayward, was offering it for sale to the various studios. The accepted method at that time was to submit a property to the head of the story department of each of the studios on the same day, then wait for the offers, if any. In this way agencies could not be accused of favoritism.

The Hecht-MacArthur script of *Gunga Din* was delivered. They were excellent screenwriters, perhaps the best of their day, and *Gunga Din* was an impressive achievement. Rudyard Kipling's poem is only eighty-five lines long and has in it no story, no dramatic structure. It is, at most, a character sketch. But Hecht and MacArthur, realizing that the title itself had exploitation value, had invented a story and written an exciting adventure drama involving the British Army in India in the late nineteenth century.

It seemed strange to Hayward that every studio with the exception of Columbia had made an offer. Could there have been some mistake? Had the script been delivered to Columbia? He decided to investigate, and called on Harry Cohn.

"I thought I ought to check out about *Gunga Din,*" he said.

"Why?" asked Cohn.

"Well," said Hayward, "just that every studio but you is interested."

"I can understand that," said Cohn. "They're interested because they don't own it. I don't need to buy it because I already own it."

"What do you mean you own it?" asked Hayward.

"I've owned it for seven years," said Cohn.

Hayward was stunned. "Who did you buy it from?" he asked.

"I bought it from Hecht and MacArthur," said Cohn, smugly.

"That's impossible, Harry. Seven years? They only finished writing it three weeks ago."

"Under this title," said Cohn. "When *I* bought it from them, they called it *The Front Page.*"

Hayward, relieved, began to laugh.

"What's so funny?" asked Cohn.

"Gunga Din," said Hayward, patiently, "has absolutely nothing to do with *The Front Page.*"

"Have you read it?" asked Cohn.

"Of course I've read it."

"And you don't see it's the same picture?"

"Harry," said Hayward. "Thank you very much. You've

given me a great Harry Cohn story. I'll be dining out on this for weeks."

"Go to it," said Cohn. "Just don't try to sell me what I already own."

It took no more than three or four days for the story to be widely disseminated. The town was, once again, laughing at Harry Cohn.

Then I read the script of *Gunga Din* and stopped laughing. Cohn was absolutely right: Hecht and MacArthur had taken not only the story, but the characters of *The Front Page,* changed the period, the locale, and the occupations. It was daring and ingenious, but it did not fool Cohn.

The picture was eventually made by George Stevens for RKO. When the hidden *Front Page* structure went unnoticed by a majority of the critics and practically all of the public, I admired Harry Cohn's perception more than ever.

"Listen," Cohn said to me one Sunday afternoon, "anybody tells you they're a starmaker, tell 'em they're a knucklehead. I broke my ass tryin' to make a star out of Kim Novak. So what happens? She turned out to be Kim Novak. I tell y', I gave 'er the best scripts, the top directors, I brought in Jean Louis, and not only him—*other* terrific designers, hairdressers, makeup people, coaches. And if she had to sing, we dubbed her. And if she had to dance, we tricked it. She was a beautiful girl, she was willing, too. We put her in one picture after another. Nothing, nothing, nothing. She had talent, mind y'. In fact, she was good. But, God damn it, she didn't have that one thing, that plain one thing makes a star. Kim Novak. Jesus. Her name was Marilyn Novack, but everybody would've thought we were trying to make it sound like Monroe. So we picked 'Kim.' And we did a big campaign on 'er, and then we started 'er out in a movie with the name *Pushover.* Is that bad? Beautiful little blonde. How old could she have been at the time? Twenty-three, twenty-four? Kim Novak in *Pushover.* Sound good? Nothing. Then we stuck her with Judy Holliday and Jack Lemmon in

Phffft by George Axelrod. Is *that* bad? I figured workin' along-side of Judy some of the talent, some of the magic might rub off, right? Nothing. So then we put 'er with Sinatra yet in *The Man with the Golden Arm*. Preminger. The picture was sensational, Sinatra came through like Gangbusters—but her? Novak? Nothing. Then the biggest hit in the world, *Picnic*. She struck out in that one, too. *Jeanne Eagels*. Well, maybe that was a mistake. Then we gave her *Pal Joey, again* with Sinatra. *Bell, Book and Candle*. And I tell y' about now I began to give up because I began to see that she was okay, this kid, but no star. No. The public just didn't grab onto her. . . . Look, I've tried it before. Sometimes it works, so you get the idea you're doing it. But that's the bunk. It's always the *public* who's doing it. You need a better example than Goldwyn with that Anna Sten? I remember him telling me she was the biggest thing ever happened in his whole life. He sank millions into her. Made these tremendous, high-class pictures with her, gave her all kinds of leading men and directors. It didn't work. He never made a quarter with her."

"I'm inclined to agree with you, Harry," I said. "I remember an evening some time ago when L. B. Mayer—considered quite a starmaker, huh?—came over to Ruth and me in a restaurant in New York. And he sat down and said to us, 'Why don't you people write a picture for Howard Keel? I'll buy it from you sight unseen if you design it for Howard Keel. We're building him, so we can use material. He's going to make Bogart and Tracy and Gable and all those other bums look sick in a couple of years. They're old men, they're on the way down, but Keel, he's going up like a rocket. So, if you listen to me, take my advice, you'll write something for Howard Keel.'

"Well, nobody can deny that Keel is a gifted fellow—handsome, tall, good actor, splendid singer, and Metro certainly tried with him. But that big breakthrough never happened."

"Listen," said Cohn. "L. B. was good—as good as the best—as me or Goldwyn or J. L.—anybody. But we none of us are God. And only God can make a tree."

"A tree?" I asked.

"That's right," he said. "You gonna argue with me on that? What is it with you you always like to argue? All you intellectuals. What were you—captain of the debating team in college?"

"I never went to college."

"You're tellin' *me!*"

"I thought we were discussing stars. So what's a tree got to do with it?"

"You didn't let me finish. That's another thing with you. Always buttin' in, interrupting. What I was sayin' was, 'Only God can make a tree, and only the public can make a star! Satisfied?"

"Yes."

"Yes? Well, you're *still* wrong. My property department can make the best goddam tree you ever saw!"

"But not a star."

"But not a star."

Joseph and His Brethren was an odd subject for Harry Cohn to have approved.

It may have been that he was following the trend toward Biblical subjects that year, and that it was pointed out to him that there was a lot you could get away with as long as you stayed within the Biblical frame of reference.

Still, he was concerned about the production since it dealt with subject matter foreign to him. He decided to do an unprecedented thing and read the script himself.

He told his secretary, Donna, to get him a copy of the final shooting script of *Joseph and His Brethren,* told her to hold all his calls, and began to read. He had read no more than twelve pages when the intercom buzzers began to sound on desks in offices all over the building. The panic button, the alarm system, the S.O.S.

Members of his staff came hurrying through the halls, some of them sloshing coffee as they ran.

As each one entered the room, he could tell from Cohn's expression that a crisis was at hand.

When they were all there—Sidney Buchman, the producer; Otto Preminger, the director; Clifford Odets, the writer; the head of the story department; the research man; and assorted assistants—Cohn looked at them and said gently, too gently, "Do I have to do everything around here?" Then came the explosion. "God damn it! All you guys supposed to be doing whatever the hell you do. All you goddam college men with your diplomas and all that intellectual crap you throw around here all day, and I have to do everything and check up everything and watch the scripts. You guys'll kill me. Nobody can do everything."

"Harry," said Odets, quietly. "What is it? What's the trouble?"

Cohn's fury was unabated. "The trouble is, God damn it," he shouted, "I may not be a college man and I'm not supposed to be an intellectual, but there's one thing I know and nobody is going to tell me different. I know God damn well that in Biblical times people did not go around saying 'Yes, siree' and 'No, siree.' "

"Of course not, Harry," said Odets.

"Well, then, God damn it!" shouted Cohn. "What's it doing in the script?"

"Where?" asked Odets.

Cohn slapped the open script down on the desk and pointed to a page. Odets looked at it and nodded as he read, "Yes, sire" and at another point, "No, sire."

The others moved over to the desk and peered at the page.

No one had the nerve or the courage or whatever was required to straighten Cohn out.

After a time, Buchman mumbled, "We'll fix it, Harry."

The staff filed out quietly.

1957 was something less than a banner year for Columbia Pictures. *Full of Life, Beyond Mombasa, Jeanne Eagels, Aban-*

don Ship, Pal Joey, The Story of Esther Costello, Don't Knock the Rock, The Garment Jungle, Three-Ten to Yuma, and *Operation Mad Ball* represented, by and large, a disappointment.

What made things even more uncomfortable for Harry Cohn was the fact that prospects for 1958 and 1959 were not much better. Pressure was building up in this pressured man. He had the ability to transfer some of the strain to others but always took the final responsibility himself.

Television, too, was beginning to be an irritating thorn. His company had formed a television-producing subsidiary, Screen Gems, but like the others of his generation, Harry Cohn never quite understood television, especially as it related to motion-picture production.

Moreover, his health was failing. Four years earlier, he had undergone surgery for a throat malignancy. It had been successful, but left a scar of apprehension and insecurity. Further, it reinforced a premonition Cohn held: he would die at sixty-seven.

I told him it was a silly idea—on a par with tea-leaf reading and astrology.

"You'll see," he said darkly.

"Of course," I said. "If you work hard on an idea like that, you'll *make* it happen. Because you hate to be wrong."

In mid-February 1958, his wife, Joan, observed that tension had reached the breaking point. She insisted they go off to Phoenix for a holiday. Cohn agreed. After all, there were plenty of telephones at the Arizona-Biltmore.

The first two or three days passed off successfully. Cohn walked and rested, read, played cards, played golf, and talked to a few strangers.

On the evening of February 27, 1958, while dressing for a dinner party he was giving, and whistling happily (in the dark?), he felt suddenly ill. A friend who was with him urged him to call off the party and go to bed.

"Bullshit!" said Cohn. "I ain't gonna be sixty-seven till the twenty-third of July!"

During the party, his discomfort increased noticeably. His

wife took charge, got him to their bungalow, and sent for medical assistance.

By morning, his condition had worsened. An ambulance was summoned. Joan insisted upon staying at her husband's side throughout the journey. She and the doctor and Cohn were sped toward the hospital.

Harry Cohn, according to his wife, was game and courageous.

"You'll be all right, darling," she said. "Don't worry, it's all right."

She held his hand tightly.

Cohn, using the dregs of his fading energy, shook his head almost imperceptibly.

"Too tough," he whispered. "It's *too tough!*"

And died.

15

I n the spring of 1947, Samuel Goldwyn phoned me.
"I'm sending you this book," he said, "and I want you to
read it. Right away. It's the most beautiful story. A love story.
You'll love it."

"What's it called?"

There was a pause as he tried to remember.

"What the hell's the difference?" he asked, in a sudden
temper. "F'Chrissake! I tell you I'm sending you a great story
will make a great picture and you don't ask me about it or the
subject matter or who could play it—you're only worried about
the *title,* f'Chrissake—like you're the *sales* department. I'll send
it to you. 'The Highest Heaven,' that's the title. You satisfied?"

He hung up.

A few days later, the book arrived—*Earth and High Heaven*
by Gwethalyn Graham. I read it at once, expecting the phone
to ring at any moment.

The novel—a Canadian work—turned out to be a beautifully
written story but of no interest to me. A young Canadian man
(Jewish), meets a young Canadian girl (gentile). They fall in
love and what with her family's objection to him and his
family's objection to her and the concerns of their friends and
their inability to achieve reservations at a resort hotel in the
Laurentians, they have a hard time getting to a happy ending.

A curious subject for Goldwyn, I thought, until I remembered that this was the year of *Gentleman's Agreement.* Laura
Z. Hobson's best-selling novel about contemporary anti-Semitism had been made into a successful movie by Twentieth

Century-Fox. Darryl F. Zanuck had produced it. Screenplay by Moss Hart. Directed by Elia Kazan. Starring Gregory Peck. Academy Awards.

Clearly, anti-Semitism was *in*. A salable commodity. Fashionable. Discussed at the best dinner tables over the best dinners.

The phone rang. I picked it up.

"Isn't that the most *beautiful* love story you've ever read?" asked Sam Goldwyn.

"How do you know I've read it?" I asked.

"Why not?" he asked.

"I *have* read it, Mr. Goldwyn. Of course."

"Of course."

"It's beautifully written and—"

"*Why* don't you want to do it? Give me one reason. You should. You *owe* it!"

"Mr. Goldwyn,"—I still called him that—"listen. . . ."

"Go ahead, God damn it."

"How long have you and Mrs. Goldwyn been married?"

"Frances?"

"Yes."

"Twenty-two years. What are you *talking* about?"

"Wait. Ruth and I have been married for four and a half."

"Congratulations. I don't see—"

"Would you say your marriage has been a success?"

"Of course. Certainly."

"Fine. So has mine. Now. Frances is gentile and so is Ruth. And you and I are Jewish."

"Why do you take up my time with all this kind of—?"

"You don't see it?"

"See what?"

"Why I can't get interested in the drama of this subject—and why I don't see how *you* can?"

"You know what that book cost me? A fortune! Everybody wanted it, but I got it. It's a *great book* and it's going to make a *great picture*! I want to tell you something. You've lost something in your talent. I used to have hopes for you. Now I'm not

248

so sure. You can't seem to discuss stories seriously. You want to make jokes all the time. Jokes are nothing. A dime a dozen. Gags. Gagmen. The best gagmen in the world—they work for Jack Benny and Bob Hope and Eddie Cantor. You know what they make? They make two hundred dollars a week. The *best* ones! So you want to be a gagman? *Be* a gagman."

There was a long pause. Finally I said, "I'm sorry, Mr. Goldwyn. I didn't mean to upset you and I don't know what you mean about gags. I was simply trying to explain why this subject is not for me."

"You said for *anybody.*"

"No, I didn't."

"That's what you meant. If you were smart, you'd trust *my* judgment. I've made more hits than you, f'Chrissake."

Another pause.

"How's Ruth?" he asked. "Your wife."

"She's fine," I said.

"Give her my love," he said gently.

"All right."

"Call me up when you change your mind," he added, and hung up.

Earth and High Heaven was never made by Goldwyn, or by anyone.

We met soon afterward, and hundreds of times subsequently, but he never mentioned the subject again.

There were many such projects in Goldwyn's life—stillborn or aborted. He clung to some of them for years before abandoning them. Even then, he considered the abandonment only temporary.

He had arranged to pick up Mrs. Goldwyn late one afternoon at Elizabeth Arden's beauty salon in Beverly Hills. From there, they were to proceed to a reception at the Beverly Hills Hotel.

He waited outside in the car for five minutes—a long wait for him—then jumped out of the car, went through the famous red door, and strode into the teeming establishment.

"May I help you, sir?"

"Where's Mrs. Goldwyn?" he shouted, as though he were a knight come to rescue a maiden held against her will.

Before the receptionist could reply, he was on his way into the main room. What he saw there galvanized him. He stood, gaping. He could not believe his eyes. Rows and rows of women under dryers or hairdressers' hands. Manicurists. Pedicurists. Setters. Wavers. Tools. Machines. Lotions. Creams. Cosmetics. A conglomerate of glittering action. A new world.

Mrs. Goldwyn, on the verge of leaving, was tipping her manicurist, and was astonished to see her husband. She approached him.

"What is it, Sam? Is something the matter?"

"Look at this!" he exclaimed, pointing into the establishment. "All this."

"Yes," she said gently.

"This is some *business!*"

She led him out, reflecting that if forty years earlier he had chanced to see a beauty parlor in operation, he might now be the head of the coast to coast Goldwyn Salons, Inc., rather than of the Goldwyn Studios.

The Goldwyns went on to the reception, but Mr. Goldwyn kept thinking of the extraordinary sight he had just seen. He talked about it, told about it, inquired about it.

A seed had been implanted. Hundreds of people, hundreds of thousands of dollars were to be involved before the matter could be put to rest. Endless man-hours and woman-hours would be expended. Personal upheavals would take place. Careers would move forward or backward. Friends and enemies would be made. And all because Mrs. Samuel Goldwyn was five minutes late emerging from Elizabeth Arden's.

"Do you know how much women spend in the beauty parlors and for hair and cosmetics and treatments and facials and all like that?" Mr. Goldwyn asked us all at a conference one day. "Go ahead. Take a guess," he added, smiling secretly. Clearly, he knew the answer.

The guesses were slow in coming. To win the game here, it

was necessary to get a *wrong* answer, not a right one. Whoever got the right one would offer a personal affront to the boss, would reveal himself as a know-it-all.

"A hundred million," said someone.

"Ha!" cried Goldwyn. "Did you hear that?" He added a scornful echo, "A hundred million. F'Chrissake."

"Two hundred million," said Fred Kohlmar.

Goldwyn's pink face crinkled and he giggled, delightedly.

The guesses continued up and down the scale, to Mr. Goldwyn's immense delight.

Most of them had been on the low side. I decided, in the considerable time I had to think, to go in the opposite direction. Be outlandish. Think big. The sky's the limit. They love big numbers out here.

A pause. Everyone seemed to be looking at me. I shrugged modestly and said, "Two and a half *billion!*"

It got a titter from everyone, with the notable exception of Mr. Goldwyn. In contrast to the merry, smiling faces in the room, his own sudden, dark frown seemed even more forbidding than it was.

He looked at me, petulantly. The color of the room changed. I had blundered. Again, damn it. Would I never learn? I had spoiled the boss's day.

"Who told you?" he asked.

"Nothing," I said. "Just a guess."

"Who *told* you?" he repeated, firmly.

"I must've heard it somewhere. Read it?"

"Where the hell would *you* read a thing like that? You read women's magazines and something? What're *you*? A fairy?"

No laugh. It was worse than we thought.

"I guess someone told me," I said softly.

"Who?" he demanded.

"I don't remember."

"Well, God damn it, see that you *do* remember. Later—or the latest tomorrow. Don't forget."

"All right."

"I don't like this sneaky stuff around here."

A long pause. Mr. Goldwyn's secretary, Jack Hutchins, came in and handed him a note. As Goldwyn read it, Hutchins looked about the room. He sensed, correctly, that we were living through a minute of tension. He glanced at Goldwyn, poured a glass of water from the silver carafe, and placed the glass in front of Goldwyn.

"Call him back in twenty minutes," said Goldwyn, handing back the note. "Did *you* tell him?"

"I beg your pardon?"

"Him," said Goldwyn, pointing at me.

"Tell him what, Mr. Goldwyn?"

"The figure," said Goldwyn, testily. "The beauty figure."

"No, sir."

"No," said Goldwyn. "I didn't think so."

Hutchins left quietly. Goldwyn drained the glass of water, slowly. He set down the glass and looked around the room. He smiled, creating the air of the beginning of a meeting.

"Gentlemen," he said. "Do you know how much women in the United States spend each year in the beauty parlors? Not only Elizabeth Arden's and Rubinstein and those—but small ones—in small towns, even—the smallest." He put on his glasses, picked up a typed report, and read impressively, "Two billion six hundred and forty million dollars!"

Whistles of amazement.

"My God."

"I can't believe it."

"Holy mackerel."

And I said, "Whew!"

"So don't tell *me,*" said Goldwyn, "that we haven't got a subject here. A *big* subject."

No one *had* told him that, but he needed pretended objection to give power to his positive thought.

"It stands to reason," said Merritt Hulburt. "It all comes down to what one is selling. Is there a demand for it or must a demand be created?"

"Listen to this!" Goldwyn commanded the rest of us. He

leaned back, comfortably, delighted to hear one of his bought brains in action. Hulburt went on.

"There's an old bucolic saw on the subject. 'The best business is selling something that everybody needs every day.' Now in this case it isn't *everyone*—but say half. And what they're selling, you see, is not only things, objects—but a kind of hope. An abstract. They're proclaiming to all women, everywhere— 'You can be beautiful!' "

If Merritt Hulburt had pulled the plug of a hand grenade and tossed it into the middle of the room, he could not have caused a more startling detonation.

Goldwyn leaped to his feet and yelled, "That's *it!*"

Someone applauded.

"You can be beautiful," said Goldwyn. He came out from behind his desk and said it again, this time as if it were a title, " 'You Can Be Beautiful.' "

He went to Hulburt and shook his hand, warmly.

"I want to tell you something, my boy. That is *some title* you just came up with. That is the greatest title I ever heard and this picture needs a great title because it's a great picture. I want to tell you something, my boy. You just earned your whole goddam salary for a whole goddam *year!*" He turned to the rest of us, asking, "And you all know what he gets, don't you?"

"Sure," said Fred Kohlmar. "Two billion six hundred and forty million dollars."

A big laugh, at last. We were all on our feet. The meeting was over. Nothing could top this. Merritt Hulburt was blushing. The day was saved.

You Can Be Beautiful became a part of the daily life of the studio and remained so for the whole year I was there. Lillian Hellman worked for a time on the story and screenplay, so did Anita Loos and John Emerson. So did Dorothy Parker and Alan Campbell, and so did Cecelia Ager, who had been spirited away from *Variety,* where she had made a reputation specializing in feminine slants.

Frequently the assignments overlapped and writers or teams

of writers would find out only by accident that they were all working, confidentially, on the same subject. Embarrassing? Of course. Humiliating? A bit. But $2000 a week pays for a lot of humiliation or embarrassment.

Goldwyn's plan in this instance, since he was starting from scratch, was to get as many ideas, notions, slants, openings, finishes, routines as he could. In time he would engage one writer—a constructionist—to put it all together. It was a method that failed more often than it succeeded but Goldwyn liked it because it gave him a feeling of activity and effort going on all about him.

He often used this method in other ways. A novel would be submitted. He would acquire several copies, then call us in, one by one, and say, "I want you to read this. It's very important. Read it tonight. Tomorrow morning come in—Jack will fix a time for you—and give me your views."

For most of us it meant canceling everything and staying up half the night with coffee and Benzedrine. The following morning, or afternoon, perhaps even a day later or a week later if Goldwyn forgot or became involved in more pressing matters, we would be summoned, one by one, and ordered to recite.

"Don't give me a synopsisis," Goldwyn would say, sternly, pointing his finger. "If there's one thing I can't stand it's a synopsisis. Just tell me the story. Tell me the story in your own words. Don't give me an opinion. Just give me the story."

"I thought you said you wanted my views," I said one bleary-eyed morning.

"Later," he said, impatiently. "I'll get your views later. Right now, just tell me the story."

I did so as best I could and was dismissed. Throughout the day he called in the others who had performed the same chore and gave the same instructions.

The result was that without having read a page of the book, Goldwyn knew it far better than any one of us did. He would then ask for each one's opinion, after which, tempering it with his own, he would make one of three decisions. Yes. No. Or maybe.

You Can Be Beautiful was, for a time, the story of Elizabeth Arden, the story of Helena Rubinstein, the story of a small-town girl who comes to New York and conquers it by way of the beauty business, the story of an unhappy Plain Jane transformed into a happy-ending stunner, or (Dorothy Parker's twist) a happy Plain Jane turned into a miserable knockout. Goldwyn hated this one.

"God *damn* it, Dottie!" he thundered. "You and your God damn sophisticated jokes. You're a great writer. You're a great poet." He paused, frowning in an effort to recall something. He quoted, " 'Men never make a pass at girls wearing eyeglasses.' That's a great poem and you wrote it. You're a great wit. You're a great woman, but you haven't got a great audience and you know why? Because you don't want to give people what they want."

Dorothy's wide, innocent face looked up at him. "But Mr. Goldwyn," she said softly, "people don't *know* what they want until you *give* it to them."

"You see that?" said Goldwyn to the world. "You just did it *again*. Wisecracks. I told you there's no money in wisecracks. People want a happy ending."

Dottie rose. "I know this will come as a shock to you, Mr. Goldwyn," she said, "but in all history, which has held billions and billions of human beings, not a single one ever had a happy ending."

She left the room.

Goldwyn surveyed those of us who remained. "Does anybody in here know what the hell that woman was talking about?"

Months went by. Goldwyn held fast to the subject. Writers came. Writers went. Conferences abounded. Nothing came of any of it.

At his home one Sunday afternoon, he discussed it with me, dejectedly. "It needs the spark," he said. "It's all there but we haven't found the spark yet. You know, my boy, you can have a big bonfire with plenty of paper and straw and logs and even put kerosene on it but until you touch it with a spark you've got nothing and that's what we've got right now. Just a lot of logs with no spark."

I felt for him and wished I could have come up with the spark.

In my year with Mr. Goldwyn I frequently felt as though I were his son. This feeling was doubtless caused by the fact that he frequently dealt with me as though I were. He was the sort of man who somehow needed a son. His own was then about twelve and hardly the right casting for a confidant. He also had a daughter, I learned to my surprise, but she was the daughter of Blanche Lasky Goldwyn and they had long been estranged.

When it did not interfere with the thrust of his professional aspiration, Goldwyn could be warm and kind, gentle and considerate. I often felt the cloak of his friendship.

His relationship to Sammy, Junior, was complicated. Goldwyn seemed impatient for Sammy to grow up. He loved him but would love him more when he reached man-to-man age.

I remember a tense evening in the projection room at Goldwyn's house toward the end of the editing of *Dead End*. Willie Wyler, who had directed it brilliantly, was there. Danny Mandel, Goldwyn's chief editor, was there. The production secretary. Goldwyn's secretary. And, for some mysterious reason, I was there.

The film was run reel by reel, scene by scene, with many conflicts growing out of the circumstance that Wyler's sense of rhythm was different from Goldwyn's. Goldwyn seemed impatient to get on with it, especially in the earlier part of the film. Wyler, on the other hand, felt the exposition had great importance. Goldwyn wanted to cut every foot he considered irrelevant. Wyler had to give in every now and then but was reluctant to remove what he considered important detail. From time to time Goldwyn would acquiesce. It was akin to a complex game of chess.

Then came a breaking point. The scene was a barroom. Baby Face Martin, played by Humphrey Bogart, comes in with his sidekick, played by Allen Jenkins. They order whisky. The bartender puts down two shot glasses and sets the bottle down in front of them at the bar. He is about to step away when he looks appraisingly at Bogart and Jenkins. He picks up the bottle, takes a pencil from behind his ear, makes a mark at the level of the liquor, and retreats. A take from Bogart.

"Stop it!" yelled Goldwyn. "Stop it!" He pressed the signal button to the projection booth, furiously. The film stopped, the sound grinding down to silence. The lights came up in the room.

"*Now* what?" asked Wyler.

"That's out," said Goldwyn. "Take it out."

"Take what out?"

"The whole thing. The bottle business. It doesn't mean a goddam thing!"

Wyler was on his feet. "What the hell are you talking about, Sam? That's one of the most important things in the whole reel. It builds the tension. It shows that these guys are suspicious characters, that even the bartender sees it!"

"Don't yell," yelled Goldwyn. "Didn't we make up no yelling?"

"You'll drive me *crazy*, Sam," said Wyler, lighting a cigarette. "You're trying to ruin this picture."

"Sure," said Goldwyn. "I'm trying to ruin the picture because every goddam nickel in it is mine, so naturally I can hardly wait to lose my money."

"I don't want to hear about your money," said Wyler. "Let's get back to the cut."

"It's *out!*" shouted Goldwyn. "I don't want any of those arty, subtle jokes that nobody understands but a few of your friends."

"Arty?" said Wyler.

"Furthermore," said Goldwyn, "it wasn't even in the play. On the stage. Show me where it was in the play. On the stage."

"It wasn't in the play," said Wyler, "because that was a play and this is a movie and the play was written by Sidney Kingsley and the movie was written by Lillian Hellman and there are a *lot* of things in the movie that weren't in the play and that's no reason to cut them out."

"But this one," said Goldwyn, stubbornly, "is out."

Wyler changed tactics abruptly and said, pleadingly, "But why, Sam?"

"Because," said Goldwyn, "it's too complicated. Nobody will understand it."

"Don't be stubborn, Sam," said Wyler. "It's the simplest little piece of business you could imagine. A child can understand it. Any child."

At this moment, almost as though it had been planned, Samuel Goldwyn, Junior, appeared in the doorway, barefoot, holding a bottle of Coca-Cola. We all looked up.

"Come in, Sammy," said Goldwyn. "Come in. Sit down. I want to show you something." Sammy obeyed. The film was rolled back, the scene was run again. The buzzer. The film stopped. The lights came on. Goldwyn turned to his son. "Did you understand that?" he asked. "That bottle business?"

"Sure, Pop," said Sammy.

Goldwyn stared at him. "You did?"

"Sure."

"All right, then. Let me hear you explain it to me."

"Well," said Sammy, haltingly, "the guy puts down the—bottle—but then he sees—that these other two—guys are sort of like—gangsters so he doesn't—trust them so he makes a mark on the bottle so he'll know—how much they took."

The pause stretched out. Finally Goldwyn turned to Wyler. "Ah, what the hell does a child know?" he said.

I recall a day during the time when I was still indentured to this powerhouse. A few of us on the staff were having a drink with George Haight, a departing associate producer. (There seemed *always* to be a departing associate producer.)

George described his final, surreal meeting with Goldwyn. It had been vitriolic, sentimental, choleric, caustic, sarcastic, humorous, Kafkaesque, and totally inconclusive.

"But how did it actually end?" I asked. "Did you shake hands, finally?"

"No," said George. "We shook *fists.*"

16

In the days when the Players Club produced an annual all-star revival, they did one of Arthur Wing Pinero's bittersweet recall of theatre folk, *Trelawny of the Wells.*

The incomparable Laurette Taylor played Rose Trelawny in this 1925 production at the Knickerbocker Theatre. The supporting cast included John Drew, William Courtleigh, Charles Coburn, Violet Heming, Amelia Bingham, O. P. Heggie, and the beloved old Mrs. Thomas Whiffen.

Driving to her home on Riverside Drive after the dress rehearsal with her husband, Hartley Manners, Miss Taylor noticed that his praise was oddly reserved.

"Don't you like me in this part?" she asked.

"Not entirely," he replied.

"Why not? What is it?"

"Well, my dear," said Manners, "an essential characteristic of Rose Trelawny is that most important quality that theatre people must possess—to *love* the *players.* It matters not whether you are a dramatist or a director or a stagehand, an usher or even another player, the important thing is that you must *love* the *players."*

"I do," protested Laurette. "I do!"

"That may be," said Manners, "but your Rose Trelawny does not."

Laurette Taylor used to recount that she stayed awake throughout that night thinking of what she first considered an unjust, harsh criticism, but slowly recognizing that her husband was right. She corrected her error. The next night, she loved the players and triumphed.

My own experience leads me to believe that Hartley Manners knew what he was talking about. Usually, it is not difficult to love the players. Actors and actresses are a splendid breed apart. In the main, I have found them to be courageous, helpful, industrious, witty, imaginative, resourceful, unselfish, and the best company in the world. I love the players.

There are always exceptions. Charles Laughton was mine.

I could hardly have admired him more, having first seen him on the New York stage in a thriller called *Payment Deferred.* In Alexander Korda's film, his Henry VIII was a work of art. Even in the unsuccessful *Rembrandt,* there were unforgettable moments. His Hollywood films, *Ruggles of Red Gap, If I Had a Million, Mutiny on the Bounty,* left little to be desired. I thought Charles Laughton could do just about anything, which is why I cast him as Tony, the Napa Valley vintner in Sidney Howard's *They Knew What They Wanted.*

It was a daring piece of casting, but I needed only Laughton's assurance that he was willing to accept the challenge to make me feel it would all come out right. I knew he could look it, certainly could play it. Could he sound it? Why not? It would be no more than a technical question of acquiring an Italian-American accent.

When the point was raised by the front office, I reminded them that Charles Laughton had, a few years earlier, accepted an invitation from the Comédie Française, had gone to Paris, and played *Le Médecin malgré lui* by Molière in flawless, unaccented French. (To this day, productions of the piece at the Comédie contain elements known as *"la tradition Laughton."*)

Robert Ardrey had supplied a fine screenplay of the Sidney Howard work. Carole Lombard had agreed to play the mail-order bride, and I looked forward to the making of this film with greater anticipatory excitement than I had ever known.

The producer was to be Erich Pommer, the former head of UFA and now Laughton's partner. Pommer's English was sketchy, his grasp of American production methods weak, his manner brusque. In addition, he was in the process of giving up smoking, which increased his innate nervousness and caused

260

him to suck and puff constantly on a plastic prop cigarette. He was fiercely devoted to Laughton, who had been his savior for the past several years. He saw it as his present mission in life to get Laughton whatever he wanted no matter how difficult or unreasonable.

My first meeting with Laughton was a failure.

Reporting it to my father that evening, I said, "He doesn't like me. Why do you suppose that is? Why doesn't he like me?"

"Probably," replied my father from the depth of his wisdom, "because you don't like him."

"I do," I said.

"No," said my father. "You like his work. Not him. That's not the same thing."

What had put me off almost at once was his opening gambit, which conveyed clearly that he proposed to take charge. What troubled me even more was his patronizing attitude toward his co-star, Carole Lombard.

"A movie star," he said with undisguised scorn. "Well. Perhaps if she doesn't attempt to act she'll get by."

"She's better than that," I said. "She's a fine actress."

"Yes," said Laughton looking down at me from the heights. "I *so* admired her Hedda Gabler at the Old Vic."

I changed the subject.

"About Tony's speech pattern," I said. "It's strictly Italian-American. Bob and I have spent some time up there in the Napa Valley. St. Helena, Napa. The Italian-Americans there sound pretty much like the ones down here or in San Francisco or New York."

"Or London," he said. "We have Italians in London, too, you know."

"Yes," I said. "But that's not the sound."

It was in the next moment that I realized he did not like me.

"Suppose *you* do *your* job," he said, "and let *me* do *mine.*"

"Of course," I said, "but if there's anything I can do to help—"

"Yes. Actually, there *is one* thing," he interrupted. "One *very* important thing."

261

"Yes?"

"Leave me alone."

I left him alone.

A few days later, Erich Pommer burst into my office, waving his prop cigarette wildly and shouting, "I haf him here mit me. Outside. Tony. You vish to see him?"

"Of course," I said.

He stepped out and led Laughton into the room. Laughton had spent all morning in the makeup department. They had done an outstanding job. His skin was swarthy and glistening; his black mustache typically Italian. His wig, shiny and curly with the hair parted in the middle, was an unexpected, artful touch.

Wearing the cloak of his role, happily, confidently, Laughton began to gesture in a volatile way. He came toward me and said, "Howayoua doa mynama Tony Patucci glada mee tayoua!"

"Grand," I said. "They've done a fine job."

Tony became Laughton.

"They?" he said, in an ascending tone.

"The makeup boys."

"They simply did," said Laughton, haughtily, "what I told them to do."

"Vot he told them," said Pommer.

"Well," I said, cowed. "What's the difference, so long as it worked out so well?"

Laughton wheeled about and left abruptly. Pommer hung behind for a moment, looked at me, shook his head sadly, indicating sympathy for my clumsiness, and followed Laughton out.

Nothing is more important in a director's work than to stay in control of the over-all project. I could feel my grip on this one slipping and called a meeting for the following day. I made it clear that I wished to confer with Laughton privately.

"We seem to have a problem, Charles," I began.

"So?"

"Yes. I sense a testy, nervous beginning and I'm not accustomed to it."

262

"Don't fret," said Laughton. "You'll find, in time, that I'm really an awfully nice fella." (The last three words with an American accent as a concession to me). "You have an enormous burden—your youth—but I can assure you that it will pass in time. Be patient."

"The trouble is," I said, "that with a forty-two-day schedule I don't have *time* to be patient, so I think I ought to tell you now that I'm worried about your accent."

He looked at me as though I had spat in his face.

"What do you know about my accent?" he asked.

"Well, that sample I heard yesterday. It won't do."

"I was funning, you fool," he said, rising. "Do you suppose for a moment I was acting? Auditioning? Is *that* what you thought? That I was doing a test for you?"

"No," I said, "but I did get a feel and it worried me."

There was a two-minute pause during which each of us assessed strengths, his own and his adversary's. Finally Laughton spoke.

"What do you suggest?" he asked, too quietly.

"I have a friend," I said. "A young Italian named Paul Lepere. He speaks perfect English, of course, but he does an imitation of his father that's absolutely authentic, and perfect for Tony. I'd like him to work with you. Not on the part, you understand. He hasn't read the script and I don't want him to. But just listen to him talk. Maybe have him read the daily newspaper aloud. It's not an unusual way of doing it. Vivien Leigh, you know, worked with a young Southerner named Will Price. That's how she got that marvelous Southern accent for *Gone with the Wind*."

"Vivien Leigh," he muttered.

"Look, Chuck," I said. "I don't give a damn about method. All I care about is result."

"Chuck?" he asked.

"That's our familiar form for Charles. Do you mind?"

"I don't mind about the Chuck," he said. "I *do* mind you getting familiar."

We both laughed. The ice was not precisely broken but perhaps it had begun to melt a bit.

"I'm only trying to be of assistance, Charles," I continued. "If it doesn't work out, then—"

"Call me Chuck," he said.

"Unless, of course, you have your own method."

"My dear boy," he said, inventing a new, improved brand of superciliousness. "Of course I have a method. From now until the first day of shooting, I propose to study the paintings of Michelangelo, listen to nothing but Vivaldi, and read aloud, in the original, the epic poetry of Dante."

I was impressed. Nothing more was said about the accent.

I had prevailed upon the studio to allow me a two-week rehearsal period; unusual at that time, unprecedented at RKO. On the first day, the principals assembled. They sat around in a semicircle in the way of a theatrical production. We began to read through the script.

Laughton's turn.

"Eesasoma*ting*awannayou*bout!*" he spluttered. The cast looked at him, amazed. Others spoke two or three lines, then Laughton said, "Shu*bin*tagaldina."

"Hold it," I said. "Charles, I know we're still in the early stages, but I'm afraid the others are going to find it hard to recognize their cues."

"Fuckin' well right," said Carole Lombard.

"Charles," I said, "there is *no* Italian *anywhere* on the face of the *earth* who sounds like *that.*"

He was suddenly deflated, apprehensive, terrified. He had, after all, been working on the accent in his own way for seven weeks. He became a small boy before our eyes, as he whimpered, "There *must* be!"

He went on with the reading, but dropped any attempt at an accent and the effect of the play was strange indeed. On the lunch break, he approached me.

"This friend of yours," he said. "The Italian. Is he available?"

"He's right here," I said.

"Send him up to Curson Avenue tonight."

Paul Lepere began to work with Laughton, telling him stories about his father, an Italian restaurant owner in Norwalk, Connecticut, and reading newspapers aloud as he imagined his father would.

Laughton listened, absorbed, digested, and a few days later began to use an Italian accent in his part. Such was the excellence of his ear and the greatness of his talent that he sounded neither like Paul, nor like Paul's father, nor like Laughton. He sounded like Tony Patucci.

He continued to work with Paul daily. He had Paul record hour upon hour of speech. There was never a problem again about the accent.

A week or so before shooting was scheduled to end, an interviewer from *The New York Times* came to talk to Laughton on the set. We were back from the Napa Valley location and in the studio now. I went to get a drink of water from the cooler and could not help overhearing a part of the interview.

"—that terrific Italian accent?" asked the interviewer.

"Quite simple, really," said Laughton, grandly. "For several months I have studied the paintings of Michelangelo, listened exclusively to Vivaldi, and read Dante. In the original, of course."

The closest we ever came to becoming friends was one night during the location trip.

Laughton had stayed after the last shot to discuss some problems involving the next day's shooting. As sometimes happens, his difficult problem was swiftly and easily solved by a surprising idea that luckily occurred to me at the right moment.

"Grand," said Laughton. "That's simply grand. Why don't we go somewhere and have a drink?"

"Somewhere in town do you mean?" I asked.

"No, no. Come along. We'll find a place."

We drove out onto the main highway and rode along until we came upon a small ramshackle bar and grill.

We went in. It was virtually deserted, but it would not have mattered had the place been filled because no one there recognized Laughton, who was still in his Tony get-up.

In a corner booth we began to talk, not about *They Knew What They Wanted* but about beginnings. Suddenly he wanted to know all about me. Where I was born (Rochester, New York). What education I had had (very little). What other jobs I had had (a great many). He seemed genuinely interested and after his third drink, started to tell me about his beginnings.

I knew most of it, having made a study of his biography before starting the picture, but much of what he told me was new.

"I *hated* the success of *Henry the Eighth*. It was the wrong sort of success, don't you see? Showy. Flashy. All they cared about was Henry's table manners. And it troubled me in other ways as well. It was the kind of success that defies topping it and that's what the bastards always expect you to do. Each thing has to be better or more impressive than the one before. What sort of a life is that? I want another drink. Do you?"

"Not just yet."

"One more here!" Then to me. "Korda was furious, of course, but I told him I had to chuck it for a bit. 'You're a great star now,' he said. 'You've got to build on that.' I said, 'I'm not *interested* in being a great star. I want to be an *actor*. I haven't learned anything about my craft for too long.' He asked me what I was going to do and when I told him, he bloody almost died. I told him I'd called up Lilian Baylis at the Old Vic and said to her that I would like to come and do a season there. Twenty pounds a week, you know, is what they paid then. A hundred dollars. I said to Lilian Baylis, that extraordinary woman, 'I'll come if I can choose the plays.' She gave in at once because the Old Vic was on its uppers and she knew that with a film star she would have at least one profitable season. I decided after a long time to do *Henry the Eighth*. Shakespeare's, of course. And *The Tempest* and *The Importance of Being Earnest* and *Macbeth*. I threw in *Uncle Vanya,* too, for good measure. We opened with *Henry the Eighth* and it went off well enough, I suppose, but it was a disappointment. I was foolish to do it. They compared it with the film, don't you see? And we followed it with *Macbeth*. I'd been told that that was the Jonah part of all time, that it was ill-fated, that hardly anybody ever succeeded in it. There's a curse on that damned play and on that part. But my ego had been so overblown by that time that I thought I could do anything. I could, too, without the audience. That's been the bane of my existence. That damned thousand-headed monster sitting out there waiting to devour one. Rehearsals of *Macbeth* were electrifying. Even the dress rehearsal. You remember at the Old Vic, they only give you *one*. But it wasn't what they said. It was the looks on their faces. I knew I had that damned part down. The whole production was stupendous. Then came that opening night. We never made the slightest connection. At the end I came off and there's this great long stone passage that leads out to the dressing rooms. I was numb. But even so, hoping for some little word of encouragement, and there stood Lilian, and she looked at me and said, 'Well, Charles, you were a nice little Macbeth.' "

He laughed and added, "I think that was the most damning thing ever said to me. The rest of the season was all right. We even gave a few good performances of *Macbeth*. That was a fine year for me, playing every night, rehearsing, throwing up. I felt I was getting control of my instrument, don't you see? Oh, I did other things. At the Old Vic. *The Tempest* and *Measure for Measure*. I suppose if one does enough films, one can learn about film acting but I don't think it's possible to learn about acting. Acting is communication, don't you see? Communication of emotion. And you've got to have a human element to communicate *with*, damn it all. Shall we have another drink?"

"I don't think so, Charles. I think it's probably time for some food."

"No, no. No food. I'll have an apple later on. You know, you're not such a bad sort."

"Thank you, Charles."

I took him home. He talked all the way, loosely, happily.

The next morning, I walked up to him on the set, said, "Good morning, old fellow," cheerfully, and put my hand on his shoulder. He recoiled as though he had been touched by an electric prod. I moved away feeling precisely like Charlie Chaplin in *City Lights*. Befriended by the drunk every night, thrown out into the street every morning.

The Old Vic had the most loyal, enthusiastic, and loving audience in the history of the British theatre, especially the gallery gods. There was a custom at the end of the season to send gifts backstage to the favorites in the company. At the final call, these were presented on stage. All sorts of things. Little baskets of strawberries or knitted neckties, drawings and sketches, socks, jewelry, family heirlooms.

It became a matter of pride to see how many presents each one would get. Fourteen for this one. Thirty-five for that one. Seventy-five for the old character woman who had been there for years and years.

As the closing night of Laughton's season approached, his wife, Elsa Lanchester, began to fret. She worried about the embarrassment of the final call. She knew that everyone was bound to get more presents than Charles. Charles had not endeared himself to the audience. He never stopped to chat at the stage door. He never gave an autograph or a photograph. He never smiled at the curtain call. He never looked up into the gallery.

Elsa went out and bought seventeen little presents. Pots of jam, neckties, a hat, a funny little doll, a book, a map of old London, and so on. She prepared little messages for each one. "Oh Charles, we love you." "Algie sends affection." "You are my favorite, Charles"—and so on.

The closing night came. Twenty-one for Roger Livesey, twenty-three for Ursula Jeans, fifteen for So-And-So, twenty-nine for So-And-So, and for Charles Laughton, seventeen.

Laughton resented Carole Lombard. Perhaps it was because she worked so easily. She stayed relaxed, and had not only facility but joy in her work. For him, acting was torture.

He had difficulty learning lines. He was unable to absorb a change unless given ample time. The slightest adjustment in the text would throw him completely, and even the original text was something he seemed never to master. Carole, on the other hand, would look over the text once or twice; sometimes would have an assistant director read it aloud to her while she brushed her hair, and by the time she came before the camera, knew it perfectly.

Throughout the film, I do not recall that a single take was ever spoiled on her account. She did not make mistakes. Whatever she was asked to do, she was able to do.

Conversely, giving a direction to Charles was like offering him a cup of hemlock. He could not bear to accept it. He would agonize. He would frustrate himself and me. He would attempt to argue his way out of doing what I wanted him to do. He would analyze and rationalize and intellectualize until the air about us was thick with ideas.

He could not believe that Carole was good. How could she be? She did not seem to suffer. He began to patronize her. The crew resented him for that, as did I.

Under the circumstances, it is remarkable that the work went as smoothly as it did. There were several unfortunate explosions, each one caused by my inability to be unendingly patient.

Laughton would pretend to misunderstand any direction he did not like. When it had been repeated several times, he would say, "I don't understand what you mean."

I would explain it again.

"But what do you want me to do?" he would ask. "Just tell me what you want me to do. Show me."

I would tell him, show him. He would do it. Of course it was absolutely worthless. An actor must not do what he is told literally. He is meant to take a direction as no more than a stimulus. He is meant to make the idea his own, to put it through the crucible of his individual imagination and talent. But Laughton would always make a fool of the director momentarily, by trapping him with nonsense questions. "Well, what do you want me to do?" Or, "Tell me. Show me."

I have known a good many amateur actors who thought of themselves as professionals. Charles Laughton is the only professional I ever encountered who thought of himself as an amateur. He had a little set speech in which he proclaimed himself an amateur, said he was proud of it and never wanted to be anything else. There followed a discourse on the etymology of the word "amateur": one who loves; who does something for the love of it.

"A professional," he said, "is a whore."

Various players have various styles. The great permanent acting companies, such as the Comédie Française, the Moscow Art Theatre, the National Theatre of Great Britain, develop, in time, a uniform style. The difficulty of American acting companies, particularly in films, is that the director is faced on the first day with a motley group of players, each one of whom brings an individual approach, training, and style.

There are players who have to be cosseted. Others who must be bullied. There are some who thrive on praise. Others require the abrasiveness of criticism to bring out what is best in them.

With some stars it is necessary to use what is sometimes called the Charvet Method. This derives from the practice of the great Parisian haberdashery of sending merchandise to its customers on approval. Charvet will send over, say, a dozen neckties. You may choose one or two or none and return the rest. Thus, with some stars, the director submits on approval six or seven suggestions. The star then accepts one or two and returns the rest.

Other stars require the complex Boomerang Method. This calls for considerable skill since it involves discussion, hinting, obfuscating, until the star comes up with the idea that the director thought of in the first place. Whereupon the director says (or shouts), "Great! That's terrific. Let's do it that way. *Your way.*"

Then there are the privy players. Charles Laughton was the King of this category.

The privy player is one who goes home at night, closets himself, and figures out precisely how he is going to play what is planned for the following day. Having done so, he then does it, regardless of what the director says or what any of the other players do.

An important scene in *They Knew What They Wanted* had to do with the arrival of Amy, the mail-order bride. Tony, fearful that she might not come if he sent her his own photograph, sends instead a photograph of his handsome foreman. Amy arrives. A great feast has been prepared. She confronts Tony, who must now reveal the deception.

In the center of the large ranch room, a table had been set. Following the suggestion of the property man, who coincidentally came from the Napa Valley, the table held a large wooden bowl with a mound of freshly churned butter.

We rehearsed the scene and it was going beautifully until all at once Laughton, acting the nervous Tony, sat—right into the butter.

A difficult moment. Not only was the bowl of butter ruined, but wardrobe had to supply another pair of trousers. By the time all this had been rearranged, we were running late and I decided to attempt a take.

"All right to try one?" I asked.

Laughton nodded, briefly.

"Shit, yes," said Carole.

A bell rang.

"Settle down," from the assistant.

"Roll 'em."

"Speed," from the operator.

"Anytime," from me.

The scene began. It was even better than the rehearsal and was charged with the energy of drama. Then Laughton sat down into the butter again.

"Cut!"

A problem, since wardrobe was running out of trousers.

I approached the star. "Charles," I said, "you seem to be sitting down into the butter all the time."

"Yes," he said. "Why don't you move it?"

"I would," I said, "but I have a feeling you'd sit in it anyway."

"Why would I do that?" he asked.

"I don't know," I replied. "Maybe you like to sit in butter."

He ignored this thrust.

"Don't you realize *yet,* my dear boy," he said, "that I have prepared this scene and that *that* is where I sit?"

I moved the butter.

We made the scene. Laughton sat where the butter had been.

I told the butter story to a good many people, including our friend Tony Sanford. He was not at all surprised and told me of the time Laughton came to New York to do a radio broadcast for him. Tony was then the leading figure in radio drama and had prepared a program in which Laughton was to read a long poem called "The Hudson" by Carl Carmer.

"I went over to the Gotham," said Tony, "where Charles was staying. He'd been studying the poem. I don't think anyone in the world ever read verse better than Charles and up there in his suite, he sprawled in a big armchair, threw his leg over the arm, and read that damned thing so movingly that I was choked up. I timed it and said, 'That's all, Charles. Let's not spoil it by drilling it. It's going to be marvelous.' But the next day, at the studio, at the rehearsal, it was anything *but* marvelous. He seemed tight and tense and mechanical. And *he* must have known it, too, because he kept stopping and starting again. I could see him working himself up into an immobilizing rigidity and so I did what I could to calm him down. No luck. He got more and more tied into knots. I said to him, 'But Charles, you did it so beautifully yesterday. Just sitting there sprawled in that chair at the Gotham.'

" 'Yes,' he said, 'could we do it from there, do you suppose? I'd feel much better there.'

"Of course this was impossible and I told him so and then someone—I can't remember who, probably Elsa, although I'd like to think it was me—said, 'Let's get that chair from the Gotham.' This wasn't as simple as it sounds because we had to explain the whole thing to the management of the hotel and send an NBC truck over there and the guys had to load the chair on and bring it to the studio, and there were union problems. But they did it, finally, and we got the chair from the Gotham into Studio 8H and lowered the mike and got Charles into the chair and he sprawled and threw his leg over the arm and gave the most beautiful reading of that poem, of *any* poem, that I have ever heard."

Norman Corwin recalls: "I was doing a program in the series called *26 by Corwin,* over CBS, and Charles appeared in a trilogy based on three American writers—Sandburg, Whitman, and Wolfe. This was the Whitman show. I went out to Santa Monica to rehearse Charles's performance, and I found him busy copying the entire script into longhand. 'What are you doing?' I asked him. He told me. 'Why do you want to do that?' I pressed him. 'It seems like such a lot of work, and your longhand is of inferior legibility, compared to the crispness of L. C. Smith.' Charles then went into a quasi-occult explanation of his theory that, by *copying* a text as special as Whitman's language, the very transmission of the words from his eyes to his arm to his hand to his fingers and thence to the paper, would so deeply instill the material, that it would become a part of his *subconscious,* and hence would enable him to master the material. He had already done so much work, and was so earnest about his theory, that I did not try to disabuse him of it. I waited until he had finished transcribing thirty-six pages of script, and then we got to work."

Laughton enjoyed being difficult, not because it disconcerted others, but because being difficult made him special, the center of attention.

273

During the making of the location part of *They Knew What They Wanted,* in the Napa Valley, the company and crew were variously billeted. Laughton refused to accept his assigned house, the largest and most beautiful in the Valley, and insisted on staying at a small hotel some twenty miles away.

My own billet was a farm outside the town of Napa—an old hacienda, sitting in the midst of a succession of peach orchards. Paul Lepere was there with me, along with Jules Dassin (an apprentice), and Frank Fay. One warm evening, sitting out on the porch after dinner, we saw a small truck drive up.

Charles, looking disheveled and wild-eyed, jumped out wearing corduroy trousers, no shoes, and pajama top.

He walked up to me and said, "I must speak to you at once— it's imperative—about this idiotic scene we're going to try to do tomorrow morning."

"Which scene?" I asked.

He waved some manuscript pages in my face, and cried, "It's *impossible!*"

I invited him into the house. He declined, probably because he did not want Frank Fay to hear us. (The irrepressible Frank had taken to ragging Charles from time to time.) Charles and I walked off together into an orchard. We walked and walked, up one row and down another, Laughton acting the scene first one way and then another.

I could find nothing wrong with the scene or with Laughton's attack on it, but something was troubling him—something he could not verbalize. He had a highly developed sense of rhythm and it might have been that the over-all rhythm of the scene was throwing him. He asked if he could make a few adjustments in the lines, dropping a word here, adding a word there, transposing a phrase. None of the things he suggested seemed to make any difference, but apparently they did to him.

We continued to walk. He continued to struggle. It grew dark, darker. Finally, walking through the orchard became difficult. We were both stumbling, often bumping into trees, now and then tripping and falling against each other. My falling against him was negligible, but every time he fell against me, it was serious, since he outweighed me by a hundred and twenty pounds.

He was silent for a time as we moved carefully through the rows of trees. I had to take care to stay beside him. When he got in front of me, I had to deal with the added problem of snapped-back branches. He did not seem to want to talk. He was cerebrating. After a while, he began to mumble. I had been playing the scene with him, filling in the other parts, but now I could not make out any of the cues. He continued to mumble. Occasionally, I caught a word. All at once, the quality of his voice changed. Laughton disappeared. Tony replaced him. He began to act the scene.

We had stopped in a clearing. There was a certain amount of moonlight. Laughton's genius turned it into sunlight. Standing there that night, in the muddy orchard, I saw and heard and felt great acting.

The scene ended. He looked to me as though he were about to shout, exultantly, but what emanated was a quiet sound made up of passion and relief.

"I've got it," he said.

"Bet your ass!" I said.

"I've got it!" he repeated.

"And that's a pretty big bet," I added.

He looked at me disdainfully and walked off toward the house. I followed him, not quickly enough to avoid being snapped by two branches.

We reached the house. The boys were still on the porch. Laughton spoke to them.

"Forgive me," he said. "I'm sorry to have interrupted your evening, but I had a problem. We've solved it now," he went on, graciously, with a nod toward me. "I've got it," he added. "Goodnight."

We all said goodnight. Laughton got into the little truck. As it drove off, we heard him say to the driver, "I've got it."

The next morning I made it a point to be on location earlier than usual. I thought that for once, in his eagerness, Laughton might turn up on time. I was wrong. He was late as usual, and had found someone else to blame. It was always someone else. The wardrobe man. The hairdresser. Makeup. The driver. Or room service. Or a telephone call. Today, he was blaming the driver who, he said, had flatly refused to drive fast.

"I had the sumbitchin' 'celerator on the goddam floor," said the driver, miserably.

"Never mind," I said. "We're all here now. Let's take a crack at it."

" 'A crack'?" said Laughton, in his high-falutin tone. "And just what is ' a crack,' may I ask?"

"Come on, Cuddles," I said. "Don't start up first thing in the morning. We've got a big scene to do. At least *you* have. Let's get going. The light may change."

The other players were called. The scene was rehearsed quickly for the camera. Carole and Bill Gargan played as though we were shooting, but Laughton simply marked it, reading his lines in a flat, toneless, meaningless way. We had all become accustomed to this method and no longer minded it as much as we had in the beginning.

At length, at great length, everything was ready. We began.

"Roll 'em."

"Speed."

"Anytime."

The scene began and it was instantly apparent that it was dead. I cannot say that Laughton was not trying. In fact, he may have been trying too hard. He was forcing. As he became aware of this, he stopped pressing. The life went out of the scene. He began to trick it, to fake it—overgesturing and under-playing.

I knew it was no good and so did he, and so did everyone watching. But I let it go on, hoping that the effort would somehow prime his creative pump. It failed to do so. Halfway through the scene, he shrugged, shook his head, and gave up.

"Cut," I said. "All right, one more. Right away."

The scene was reassembled. We rolled again. The result was no better. In fact, worse.

"Cut. One more."

Laughton looked tense, seemed miserable. I walked up to him and put a hand on his shoulder.

"Relax, Charles," I said. "You'll get it. It's going to be terrific."

He looked at me. There were tears in his eyes.

"I've lost it," he said.

"You'll find it," I insisted.

"How?" he inquired, hopelessly.

"Just by doing it, Charles. You won't find it by worrying. Let's just keep doing it—looking for it. You had it once. You'll have it again."

Another take. Another failure. We had no more than begun again when he stopped, looked up and said dolefully, "It's no use. I've lost it."

Half irritated and half in jest, I said, "Where do you suppose you lost it?"

He took the joke literally, looked at me, and said, "In the orchard. I lost it in the orchard."

There are people who possess strange powers. Laughton was one of them. He had the power to draw one into the orbit of his pattern of thought, sense of feeling, and mode of behavior.

This explains why I heard myself say, in all seriousness, "Do you think we ought to go back there and look for it?"

Even the cast and crew were silent. They neither laughed nor smiled. Laughton had drawn us all into his mad fancy.

"Would you mind?" he asked. "Can you spare the time?"

"Well," I said, "I don't see what else we *can* do. We can stay here doing take after take, looking for it, but if it isn't here, if you lost it in the orchard, I suppose we'd better go back there and look for it."

A studio car was summoned. I got into it with Laughton, and we drove off. The orchard was over nine miles from the location and the roads none too good. It took us about fifteen minutes to make the trip.

He was delighted to see the orchard again. His spirits rose noticeably a short time after he had jumped out of the car and begun pacing up and down through the rows of trees. I followed, trying to keep up with him.

Unfortunately for me, this was the morning the trees were being sprayed and since my single but serious ailment is a chronic allergy, I was soon in deep trouble. I began to sneeze. This made it difficult for me to play the several parts I had played the night before. The fact that I was giving a sneezy rendition bothered Laughton, and he let me know it with grim frowns.

We continued, however, eventually reaching the point where he began to mumble, then recite, then play. He was no more than three or four lines into the scene when he stopped, said "I've got it!"—and headed back for the car.

"Fast," I said to the driver. "Fast as you can."

He nodded. I sat up front with him. Laughton sat on the back seat, his eyes closed, mumbling like a praying monk in the midst of strange incantations. We made the trip in about five minutes. There was no sound except that of my continuing sneezing.

Back on the set again, the scene was reconstituted. Even in my misery, I could not help but appreciate the thoughtful co-operation I was getting from everyone.

We began again. The scene was playing beautifully, so beautifully, in fact, that everyone, including me, forgave the silliness and star-nonsense we were putting up with. If an eighteen-mile trip and half an hour's time could achieve this result, it was worth it.

Then—I sneezed, ruining the take. I had been holding it back, pressing the cartilage under my nose until it hurt. But the scene was fairly long and I sneezed. Sneezed again. And again. Again.

I apologized profusely, blew my nose, and asked for another take. It began. I did not sneeze and Laughton did not act.

He stopped, looked up and said, "I've lost it."

"My fault," I said. "My fault entirely. Do you want to go back to the orchard?"

"Yes," he said, "but not with *you.*"

Adele, the script girl, got into the car with him. They drove off.

I went to my trailer and took a triple dose of Pyrabenzamine in an effort to abort the attack. Like all such drugs, it had the effect of making me drowsy.

Laughton and Adele returned, having been gone about half an hour. By this time, all my energies were focused on simply staying awake and I was not in a position to judge the quality of the work. We did three takes. Laughton said he would like to do another. I dozed through that one. He wanted to do still another. I slept through that one, but was awakened by a gentle nudge from Adele who whispered, "Cut."

"Cut!" I yelled. "Great. Print it. Print them all."

Laughton came over and offered his hand. I took it.

"Thank you," he said. "Thank you for your patience. Are you all right?"

"Fine, fine," I said, yawning in his face.

"You look ill," he said with some concern.

"That's only because I'm sick," I said.

"Are you going to be sick?" he said, stepping away quickly. Sick, in his British lexicon, meant only throwing up.

"No, no," I said. "Ill."

We went on working, shooting the other angles of the scene. Laughton had it locked up now and spent a happy day.

As for me, I drank Coca-Cola and coffee until I *did* throw up, and kept worrying about the scene I had been able to observe only through glazed eyes. Since we were on location, the dailies were always two days late, so it was not until forty-eight hours later, in the little town theatre, that I was able to see the result of that crazy day.

It was perhaps the best scene in the whole picture.

The shooting finally ended, to the great relief of all. Many times in the course of it I had had serious doubts as to whether it would ever be finished.

Elaborate end-of-shooting parties were the order of the day, but the atmosphere on *They Knew What They Wanted* was not conducive to celebration. Still, I sent out for a few bottles and most of us hung around after the final shot, having a drink.

An hour or so passed and then, to my astonishment, Laughton walked onto the set. For a moment, we all failed to recognize him because he had gone back to his dressing room, taken off his elaborate makeup, and changed into street clothes. Behind him came his driver carrying a case of champagne. Laughton opened the first bottle, poured himself a glass, offered a mixed-up toast to the company and went about shaking hands with each one.

The gesture failed to take. The cast and crew were still resentful and, although they did not show it openly, subtly made it clear.

Presently, I saw Charles standing alone, leaning against a grand piano, sipping champagne but looking forlorn.

I went over to him and said, "Well, that's that. And we're all still alive."

"Yes. We've done it."

"*You've* done it," I corrected. "Now starts the hard part, putting it all together. I wonder how many people in the audience realize that it isn't just one long piece of film they're watching, but a jigsaw made up of maybe three or four thousand little pieces of film."

"Is that so?" asked Laughton.

"And the difficulty," I said, "is that you have to get all the pieces in the right place and the right length to make a picture work."

"Yes."

"Incidentally, Charles," I said, "I want you to know that you're welcome at any time to come by and monkey around with us. I'd be grateful for any suggestions, especially about your own performance."

"Very good of you," he mumbled into his glass.

"That's the hell of film acting, I suppose," I said. "An actor gives a performance and only he knows the design he has in mind but then it's taken away from him and other people put it together and build it. Sometimes ruin it. That's why I say it would be helpful if you *could* drop around once in a while."

"I'm going away," he said.

"Yes, but you'll be back, won't you?"

"I don't know. Every time I finish one, I can't bear the thought of ever starting again."

"Well, we all feel that," I said. "But something'll come along and charge you up. You'll see."

Our conversation was running down, going nowhere. We were silent for a time.

He looked up and said, "What's so terribly, terribly sad about all this is that some day you'll come to know what a damned nice fella I really am."

I wanted to say something, but it stuck in my throat. He had shaken me. All at once, I believed it. That he was, at heart, a damned nice fellow and that it was the burden of his talent that made him behave oddly at times. I reached out and touched him. He laughed.

"Don't do that," he admonished. "There's enough talk about me now."

"But most of that talk," I said, "you're responsible for yourself."

"Is that so?" he asked, bristling.

"Like that crack of yours to McCarey on *The Ruggles of Red Gap* set."

He smiled his sweet smile and confessed, "I couldn't resist it."

During the shooting of *Ruggles of Red Gap,* Leo McCarey, anxious to finish a scene one night, insisted on working overtime. Some time after eighty-thirty, still shooting, he stopped a take and said to Laughton, "*Jesus,* Charles, do you *have* to be so nancy?"

And Laughton replied, "But, my dear fellow, after eight o'clock a bit of it is *bound* to show!"

Success is hard to handle, but failure is harder. Some years after our work together, Laughton's star began to fade. The offers came in less frequently. The public was apparently tiring of him. He began to play supporting parts. They became smaller and smaller.

It is difficult to be good in a bad part. I remember going to the Radio City Music Hall with Bob Sherwood to see a Deanna Durbin picture in which Charles played a supporting part. It was called *It Started with Eve*. Toward the end of the picture, Laughton had a long, sappy death scene. He did his best but just before he dies, it was given to him to say, "I'm—so—so—*happy!*" At which point, Bob leaned over to me and whispered, "For '*happy*,' read '*hammy*.' "

Many years after we had worked together, I was at a dinner party at the Samuel Goldwyns'. Laughton was seated on Mrs. Goldwyn's right. I was on her left. We were facing each other across the table.

Billy Wilder's delicious comedy *Some Like It Hot* was going to be screened by the Goldwyns and we were all looking forward to it. The picture had been shot at the Goldwyn studios, so Mrs. Goldwyn knew a great deal about the day-to-day problems that had been encountered, especially those involving Marilyn Monroe.

"Sam has solved just about every problem that the motion-picture business ever presented," she said, "but the one he never *has* been able to solve, and I don't suppose anyone ever has, or will, is what to do with difficult, sometimes impossible actors or actresses. I mean to say, it's so hard because once you're into the picture, then they've got you. What can you do?"

Two drinks before dinner and a glass of wine had affected me and I heard the pompous side of me take off.

"Well, Frances," I said. "You must be alert to the situation at the very beginning. When you start a picture and it turns out that you have someone in it that's difficult, I don't care who it is, or how that difficulty manifests itself, when you recognize it, the thing to do is to take a stand immediately. Take charge. Never lose control, not for a moment. Let them know that either they're going to do what they're supposed to do, or else get rid of them at once. That's the only way."

Charles looked up from his soup and said, "Why *didn't* you?"

When films dried up for him, he created a remarkable one-man show of readings. As always, he was nervous and uncertain, and before embarking on this project called my wife, his longtime friend, and asked if he could come out to the country, where we were then living, to do something for us. It turned out to be the one-man show he was planning.

After dinner, he stood up in the parlor and read for two hours. It was wonderful. The Bible. Shakespeare. Mark Twain. Edgar Allan Poe. Kipling. E. B. White.

Still later, he was to organize the First Drama Quartet with himself, Charles Boyer, Cedric Hardwicke, and Agnes Moorehead, for a staged reading of Shaw's *Don Juan in Hell* that became a Broadway triumph.

Back in California, he formed an acting group that met three or four times a week in the basement of his house on Curson Avenue to read and rehearse scenes from the classical repertory. He became a teacher, a coach. Later, a director.

He invited us to see a production of *The Cherry Orchard* in a tiny hall on the outskirts of Hollywood. He had assembled a company of unemployed and unemployable players, convinced Eugenie Leontovitch to play Madame Ranevskaya. He cast himself in the supporting part of Gaev, her brother, and directed the whole company as though he and they were truly Russian. It is a play I go to see performed at every opportunity, but I have never seen its quality as fully realized as in Laughton's production, not even by the Moscow Art Theatre.

Toward the end of his life, Laughton effected something of a comeback as a screen actor, appearing in *Salomé, Young Bess, Hobson's Choice, Witness for the Prosecution,* and others. Billy Wilder admired him and was planning to build up the part of the bartender, Moustache, in *Irma La Douce* for him, but Laughton fell ill. Billy knew the situation but pretended that all was going forward as planned. He conferred constantly with Laughton, sent him various versions of the script, and kept hope alive until Laughton succumbed to cancer.

I called on him a few weeks before his death. He was in New York at the St. Moritz Hotel. He had asked for rooms overlooking Central Park. He was a great lover of nature, of birds and animals and flowers, and was able, his wife told me, to sit looking out of the window at the park for hours on end.

He seemed to be wasting away before my eyes that day but he talked cheerfully enough, and joked. He recalled grand days in London with my wife, when she had gone there to the Old Vic, to play Margery Pinchwife in *The Country Wife,* and the Laughtons had acted as her guardians.

As we sat there in the fading light that late afternoon, pretending that the tea-bag tea was good and that the cookies were scones, I could not help but reflect upon the long and active and unique creative life this man had lived. I could scarcely find in that wan, translucent, bony figure on the bed the face of the fellow with whom I had worked. Only his blazing eyes seemed alive.

I thought of the fat boy from Scarborough, helping out after school in his father's small hotel, then being sent down as an apprentice to Claridge's, in London. He was put on as an assistant night clerk but did not last long. The guests complained. He did his work well enough, was courteous and polite, but they found that he *looked* too alarming. The management put him into several other jobs and finally had to sack him.

In London, he had been smitten by the theatre bug. He went to the theatre whenever he could. He began to read theatrical publications, books, and plays. He dreamed of going on the stage, unlikely as that prospect seemed. Somehow, he got into the Royal Academy of Dramatic Art. World War I. He went into the Army, and was a good soldier. Constantly attempting to improve himself, he used his service in France to learn the

French language, which he continued to use and to improve for the rest of his life.

After the war he returned and finished his courses at the Royal Academy, where he was most impressive in his graduation parts. After an inauspicious debut in *The Government Inspector,* he got a job in an Edgar Wallace play called *A Man with Red Hair* in which he made a success. He then went into Sean O'Casey's *The Silver Tassie.* After that, he was an actor in demand.

I thought of his great parts. *The Devil and the Deep. Payment Deferred.* Of his unforgettable classic bit in *If I Had a Million,* where he blew the most celebrated raspberry ever. *The Private Life of Henry VIII. The Barretts of Wimpole Street, Ruggles of Red Gap, Les Misérables, Mutiny on the Bounty,* one after the other. *Rembrandt, The Hunchback of Notre Dame. The Paradine Case.* On and on.

Now it was ending, but there was no reason for sadness. Here was a man fulfilled. Here was someone who had beaten the odds. Martha Graham has said, "The unique must be fulfilled." Charles Laughton was an example of this precept.

And, I thought, he will soon be dead. And how much longer for me?

What matters, then? The life he lived, the work he did. Film actors or directors leave something tangible in the way of a legacy. There they are, those films, to be run and rerun for whatever turns out to be forever. This is what matters to the living.

All our quarrels and bitterness, our clashes and spat words fall away to nothing, not even dignified by memory.

What matters, I thought, watching the fine actor as he lay dying, is what he did while he was doing it (to him), and what he has left behind as a record of his work (to us).

I wanted to ask his forgiveness, but he was too tired.

17

Every movie star is a leading character in a fairy tale. Once upon a time (July 16, 1911, in Independence, Missouri), a little girl was born. She was christened Virginia Katherine McMath. While she was still young, her mother and father were divorced. Her mother resumed her maiden name, Lela Rogers, and took little Virginia to Hollywood. Lela tried without success to break into the movie business as a scenario writer. Virginia, aged six, was offered an acting contract. Her mother turned it down.

They moved to Texas. Lela went to work for *The Fort Worth Star* as a reporter, later became its theatre critic. Virginia Katherine began to dance, sing, mimic, and act on the local amateur show-business scene. Before long, her first professional engagement materialized. She was signed as a substitute dancer by Eddie Foy, who was touring his act.

The Charleston struck, a dance craze such as had never before been known. The vitality of the dance suited Virginia's style perfectly. She became an expert. Charleston contests were being held everywhere. Virginia won them all, and minor fame as well. An enterprising vaudeville producer put together an act around her. "Ginger and Her Redheads." Virginia Katherine McMath was no more. She was obliterated, melted away by the sunlike spotlight of success. In her place stood, or rather, Charlestoned, Ginger Rogers. She Charlestoned her way across Texas, through Oklahoma, across the Mid-West and found herself, eventually, at the Oriental Theatre in Chicago.

Paul Ash, the local favorite, was a bandleader who produced

stage shows that supplemented the feature picture. Ginger, then sixteen years old, became the darling of Chicago, appearing week after week in the stage show at the Oriental with Paul Ash.

One week, a comedian named Jack Pepper was on the bill. His real name was John Edward Culpepper, but he thought Jack Pepper more suitable. He found Ginger Rogers pretty suitable, too. He kept her up late, night after night, selling her the idea that they were fated for each other. What could be a more telling sign from above than the fact that his name was Pepper and hers Ginger? How would that be for a name for the act? Pepper and Ginger. Ginger and Pepper? No. Pepper and Ginger. Sure. Sounds better.

In later years, Jack Pepper was to claim that he gave her the name Ginger for the purposes of billing. Ginger denies this, pointing out that she had already appeared in Texas with that act called "Ginger and Her Redheads." There is no argument however about the next name change. Both agree that in 1929 she became Mrs. Jack Pepper. The marriage lasted no more than two years.

She did a musical short with Rudy Vallee called *Campus Sweethearts*, but no one seemed to take notice. She went to New York and worked constantly in clubs, in vaudeville. Out on the road. Fairs. People who remember her in those days say that she was the hardest working, most professional and determined young performer of them all.

She landed a small part in a Broadway musical called *Top Speed*, and made an impression. This led to her first feature picture, a Paramount film shot in the East, *Young Man of Manhattan*. She played a supporting part opposite Charlie Ruggles, sang a song called "I've Got *It* but *It* Don't Do Me No Good," and spoke that unforgettable line—"Cigarette me, big boy!" It was echoed through the 1930s.

Her next show was *Queen High* with Charlie Ruggles and Frank Morgan. Movies again: *The Sap from Syracuse* with Jack Oakie, *Follow the Leader* with Jack Oakie and Ethel Merman. Broadway again: George Gershwin's *Girl Crazy*. In this, at long last, she made an enormous hit. Her career was under way. For Pathé, she made *The Tip-Off*. Then came *The Suicide Fleet, Carnival Boat, The Tenderfoot, Hat Check Girl*. She went from studio to studio.

"I did anything in those days," Ginger recalls. "I just wanted to stay an actress. I did second leads and third leads and straight pictures and musicals and mysteries. The truth is I don't even remember all the pictures I made. They'd just say, 'Go to Stage Eleven,' and hand you some script and you'd learn it and go on and do it and a lot of the time I didn't even known the *name* of the picture. Of course, I *do* remember *Gold Diggers of 1933* and *Forty-second Street*—both at Warner's. I *think*. Then it happened. Finally. That great, wonderful, unbelievable accident —getting together with Fred Astaire. I was under some kind of a nothing contract to RKO, and Thornton Freeland was going to do a musical."

"When was this?"

"About nineteen thirty-three, I think. Or thirty-four. Gene Raymond was the leading man and Dolores Del Rio was the leading lady. And there were these two small parts. They didn't really tie in as I remember but they knew we could do a number. The idea in those days was to get an idea for a dance, say like the Charleston, and then they'd have somebody write a song for it. Well, in this picture—*Flying Down to Rio*—it was 'The Carioca,' by Vincent Youmans, and what a song that was!

"Fred hadn't been having too great a time in pictures either. Of course, he was a star on Broadway teamed up with his sister, Adele, but even though he had done these tremendous shows on Broadway, they didn't cotton to him out here. They made a test and Fred once told me that the report on his test read, 'Can't act. Slightly bald. Dances a little.' But because they were think- ing of doing musicals, RKO signed him and right away loaned him to M-G-M to do one little number in *Dancing Lady* with Joan Crawford. Then *Flying Down to Rio*—'The Carioca'—hit for both of us."

"I'll say," I said. "I'll never forget it. It tore up the screen. Nobody'd ever seen a dance team like that. Not on the screen, anyway."

"And we were off," she said. "They saw right away what they had and Pan Berman bought one of Fred's big hits, *The Gay Divorce,* with that Cole Porter score. 'Night and Day.' My God, was *that* something! You remember how they had to change the title of the picture because the Hays Office wouldn't let them call it *The Gay Divorce?* So it had to be *The Gay Divorcée.* Anyway, that was a real hit for us, and the dance they stuck in that one was called 'The Continental.' We did *Don't Let It Bother You* and *Let's Not Leave.* Then we did *Roberta,* and after that Irving Berlin wrote *Top Hat* for us. Those were some days. I don't think I ever worked so hard in my whole life. That Fred. He never stopped till he dropped. And that's how he made you feel, too. A lot of wonderful things've happened to me, but that was the greatest. All we thought about was the work and making each picture better than the one we'd done before."

The films, the teaming, the style, were a landmark. Mark Sandrich directed most of them, and he once said to me, "Isn't it curious how difficult it is sometimes to learn the simplest thing? Take an Astaire-Rogers dance. Now, most of them were worked out by Fred with Hermes Pan, and they were, in their way, living works of art. But do you know it took us well into the fourth picture before we found out how to cut an Astaire-Rogers dance number?"

"How *do* you?" I asked, always anxious to learn.

"The trick is," said Mark, "never to cut away from it. Now, for the first three Astaire-Rogers pictures we did what we'd always done. Keep the story going, cut away from the numbers to keep it alive. Who would dare have nothing but a dance going on on the screen for, say, five minutes? We'd always believed that you had to keep the yarn moving and keep the jokes going, so while they were dancing, we'd cut to Helen Broderick coming in, and do a take at her guy with another woman and then cut back to the dance. And then we'd cut to someone else coming in and sitting down to do something, or do a joke. Then back to the dance, then cut back to the plot where they're whispering about should they call the cops if the heroine doesn't show up by midnight, or whatever the hell. And all the time we'd cut back and forth from these bits of story to the dance. Now the dances always did very well, but nobody thought they were really going through the top of the roof. So instinctively we began cutting a little bit less, then less, and still less. And somewhere, working on the fourth picture, I said, 'Why not shoot the dance and just stay with it? Never mind all the rest.'

"Well, this got a lot of objection, especially from the people who'd been around a long time and knew exactly how everything should be done. You know the types. And there were plenty of hot arguments. Tell you the truth, even Fred and Hermes weren't too sure they wanted to risk it, but I insisted and pointed out that cutting away from the dance was like interrupting somebody's number on the stage. I said to Fred, 'When you did "Night and Day" on the stage in *The Gay Divorce* no one cut away to anything.' Well, that sold him I think, and we tried it and after that we never did it any other way."

The Astaire-Rogers output was carefully marshaled. They made a picture a year for a time. No more. In between, Ginger made other pictures, usually straight, while Fred and Hermes brooded about numbers for the next Astaire-Rogers.

Ginger was ever ambitious and courageous.

John Ford was on the RKO lot preparing to make *Mary of Scotland* with Katharine Hepburn and Fredric March. The studio had bought the successful Maxwell Anderson play and was planning it as one of its most important productions of the year.

In Anderson's version of the story, there is a small but showy part—Queen Elizabeth. Anderson had taken the dramatic license of giving Mary and Elizabeth a great scene together, although history has no record of their meeting. Anderson's point was that they *should* have met.

Ginger had seen the play in New York. Perhaps because she envisioned herself stealing the picture with a comparatively small part, she went to Pandro Berman and announced that she wanted to play Queen Elizabeth.

He said no, but Ginger did not get where she was by taking no for an answer. She persisted. He argued against it, saying he had no intention of putting one of his big stars into a small part.

"There are no small parts," said Ginger loftily. "Only small actors."

Pandro had never heard this old theatre chestnut and was momentarily impressed.

"I'll tell you what I'm willing to do, Pan," she said, "and you can't turn me down on this because I'm asking it as a personal favor and one of these days you're going to be asking *me* for a favor. So what I'm asking is this. Let me make a test for it. Okay?"

"Okay," said Berman wearily.

Ginger did not insist upon making the test immediately. She wanted time to prepare. She engaged Constance Collier to coach her. She asked Mel Berns, head of the RKO makeup department, to work with her.

Berns went all the way. He shaved part of her head, painted an Elizabethan face on her, and shot some makeup tests secretly on a weekend without letting anyone know he was doing it.

On another weekend, the test itself was made, with full makeup and costume and other players. The story is that they put a phony name on the slate. Constance Elliot. When the test came on in the projection room, everyone went wild.

"Sign that girl!"

Later, they found that the object of their enthusiasm was their own Ginger Rogers.

It was left to Berman to talk her out of the idea.

"Ginger," he said, "we just can't have this picture with

Ginger Rogers as Queen Elizabeth. It sounds ridiculous. It *is* ridiculous. Jack Ford says he'll quit and Kate says—"

"Yes?" asked Ginger briskly.

"Kate didn't say anything. She hasn't even seen the test."

"Why not?"

"I mean she hasn't seen it yet."

"Oh."

"Anyway Jack's the one in charge. So let me put it this way. If you can convince him, I won't stand in the way."

"Where is he?" asked Ginger, her eyes ablaze.

But John Ford agreed that Ginger Rogers as Queen Elizabeth was not a good idea. Ginger begged, pleaded, cajoled, and threatened, but this was one battle she lost.

Some thirty years later, remembering the old days at RKO, we reviewed the Queen Elizabeth test.

"They should have given me that part," said Ginger. "I would have been sensational."

One of Ginger's successes was *Stage Door,* in which she finally did appear with Katharine Hepburn.

George S. Kaufman and Edna Ferber had written the play, and following its Broadway run the film rights were acquired by RKO. By the time Gregory LaCava, the director, and Morrie Ryskind, the screenwriter, had finished, the result was something like a distant cousin to the original *Stage Door.* A rough cut was shown to Kaufman.

"Have you any suggestions?" he was asked.

"Only one," he replied. "I think under the circumstances you ought to call it 'Screen Door.' "

Another Kaufman title idea comes to mind. Howard Hughes was spending a part of his fortune in an attempt to make a star of Jane Russell. He succeeded to the extent that she was well known to the public even before she made her first film. Each publicity still revealed more of her capacious major endowment. When at last the film was ready for release, it seemed that every twenty-four sheet in New York bore that famous, reclining

292

figure and its beckoning bosom over the title *The Outlaw*.

Walking down Broadway, George and I counted five such billboards.

"They've got the wrong title on that picture," he said.

Ever the straight man for him, I asked, "And what is the *right* title, George?"

"They ought to call it," he replied, " 'A Sale of Two Titties.' "

How do you do, my partner?
How do you do today?
Let us dance in a circle.
I will show you the way!

Ginger Rogers and I used to perform this kindergarten jingle (with appropriate gestures and steps). The place was RKO; the time, about 9:00 A.M.; the occasion, the beginning of every shooting day of the two films in which I directed her: *Bachelor Mother* and *Tom, Dick, and Harry*.

Our act began accidentally. I greeted her on the first morning with the first line (nervous, I suppose). She astonished me by replying with the second. We finished together.

The following morning, we did it again. From then on, it was a standard routine. It survived because it epitomized the theme of our relationship. "I will show you the way!" we sang at each other—and proceeded to do so.

We had a large roster of stock players on the lot at that time, handsome boys and pretty girls. They all had sponsors who would bring them around to the various sets each day, hoping to find a bit or a part or a line. Directors were expected to use as many of the stock players as possible.

There was a soda-fountain scene in *Tom, Dick, and Harry*, involving Ginger on a date with a young man played by Burgess Meredith, and in it we were able to use a good many of the stock players. The scene consisted of an argument between

293

Ginger and Burgess. I thought it might be interesting as a counterpoint to see a couple in the booth just beyond them having a warm, loving exchange.

One of the stock boys on the lot was named Jack Briggs. He was extremely attractive and said to be talented. The casting department had recommended him many times. As we were lining up the shot he happened to turn up, and I asked if he would like to play the silent bit.

"You bet," he said.

"Mind you, Jack, there's not much to do. It's just background."

"Never mind," he said. "I want to be in this picture."

I rehearsed him and a girl. A short time afterward we began to shoot the scene. I had worked on the Ginger-Burgess exchange, so my attention went to the background. Jack Briggs was indeed talented. He conveyed perfectly the ice-cream parlor intimacy I had asked for.

In the middle of the first take, Ginger stopped and said, "Sorry." She left her seat, came over to me and asked, "Is that what he's going to do?"

"Who's going to do?"

"That kid in the background. You don't think it's distracting?"

I looked over at Briggs who seemed about to leave this life. Here was his whole career going down the drain and he had not yet said a line.

"I'll take care of it, Ginger."

She returned to her seat.

"Maybe a little less, Jack," I said.

"Right," he whispered.

On the next take, he did not only a little less, he did nothing. The effect was ruined. I went over to Ginger and tried to explain what I was getting at.

"Oh, sure," she said. "I think it would be great, but you know, without all that bouncing around."

"Don't bounce around, Jack," I said, "but do what I told you."

This time he nodded, apparently unable to speak.

"Who is that?" asked Ginger.

"Jack Briggs," I said. "One of the stock boys."

"Well," she said. "Okay."

With each succeeding shot I gave Briggs further encouragement and finally had one that pleased me and did not upset Ginger.

I was drafted by the Army before the picture was finished, and completed the editing on twenty-four-hour leaves.

About two years later, overseas, I read some news from Hollywood in *Stars and Stripes*. Ginger Rogers had been married. The groom was a young actor named Jack Briggs. It took me a minute or so to remember where I'd heard that name before. Of course. Jack Briggs. The guy she was ready to have me fire. I wondered if the whole thing could be a practical joke on me. No, it was true. She married Jack Briggs and stayed married to him for six years. How they got from the ice-cream parlor to the altar I have never yet learned.

In Ginger's day, stars had power. She had been at RKO as one of their most important contract stars for seven years.

Some time after she left RKO, she went to Paramount to do *Lady in the Dark*. Although not particularly suited to the role of the magazine editor in Moss Hart and Kurt Weill's dazzling show, she was the outstanding musical performer in films at that time and the compromise was made.

Paramount and RKO were neighboring studios but since each lot involved several acres, distances were considerable. At RKO, Ginger had always had her own suite of dressing rooms, improved and refurbished and enlarged each year to keep her happy. Finally, it was a large establishment with a kitchen, bedroom, sitting room, hairdressing and makeup room, wardrobe and fitting room, and so on. At Paramount they tried to outdo RKO and furnished her with a spacious bungalow in addition to an impressive trailer to use as a portable dressing room, and a special rig for location days.

One day, the director, Mitch Leisen, was shooting a fantasy sequence, with a cloud effect. The floor would never be seen. The dance number was going to be done in and around the mist.

The special-effects men were in charge. They are among the Hollywood elite, difficult to replace: technicians with mysterious secrets. This time, even they were having their problems. The area was huge, three connected sound stages. The special-effects men had never attempted to cloud as large an area as this and apparently did not have sufficient equipment. By the time they had finished clouding the last part, the first part had begun to disappear.

"Hold the lights."

"Hold it! Don't move around so much."

"Close the doors."

"Stand still."

Someone would come through the door and a breeze would ruin the effect. It was one of those hell days. The cloud effect, produced by using a kind of oil, began to get all over the costumes and camera and makeups.

Work continued all morning. Miss Rogers was ready, made up, and rehearsed, the playback track was ready, as was the chorus, but the clouds were not. Finally, Leisen broke for lunch. The special-effects men stayed and tried to figure out new ways to proceed.

After lunch, the routine began again. Everyone ready but the clouds not.

"Standing by."

"Not yet. Just a little more in the middle."

"Tell everybody stand by. It'll be any minute now." A little after three in the afternoon—the company dispirited at not having made a shot all day—the special-effects men and the cameramen pronounced it ready.

Ginger started for the set but stopped and said to Leisen, "I'll be right back."

"What're you *talking* about?"

She leaned closer to him and said, "I'm sorry, Mitch, but I've got to go."

"Jesus, Ginger!" said Leisen. "We've been working for seven hours. It's all set. It's delicate. Critical. Couldn't you just do it once?"

"I *have* to *go* to the *bathroom,* Mitch," said Ginger tightly. "Do you want me to announce it to the whole company, for heaven's sake? I *have* to *go* to the *bathroom.*"

"Couldn't you—couldn't we just make the one shot, honey? Just one?"

"Mitch, I've got to *dance* in it and everything. I've got to go."

"All right, Ginger. But listen, for God's sake, will you hurry up? We'll try to hold the effect."

She flounced off the set followed by her hairdresser, her maid, her wardrobe girl, and her press agent.

Leisen informed the special-effects men that they would have to hold the effect for a few minutes. They were lying all over the sound stage with gas masks on and slowly pumping the clouds in.

"Keep pumping it in. Don't let it go. Keep it even."

Every few minutes the camera operator had to wipe the oil off the lens. The extras were ready and standing by.

"Nobody leave the set, now!" shouted Leisen. "We're going to shoot this in about one minute, one minute and a half."

The minute did indeed get to be a minute and a half. Then five. Ten. Fifteen. Twenty minutes later it was hopeless.

"All right. Kill 'em."

"Hold the arcs."

"Effects out."

The effort had gone for nothing. The company and the crew sat and waited. About forty-five minutes later Ginger came sailing onto the set looking lovely and ready to go.

Mitch Leisen, who had aged several years in the forty-five minutes, looked at her and said, "Where the hell have you been?"

"Don't talk to me like that," said Ginger. "I have a perfect right to go to the bathroom."

"It took you forty-five minutes to go to the bathroom?" he

asked outraged. "Where the hell did you go?"

"Why, to RKO," she said logically.

Mitch Leisen began to laugh uncontrollably.

When he told me about it he said, "We never did get the shot that day. In fact, we didn't get it for another two or three days. But that thing with Ginger, it was sort of a Pavlovian thing. They'd given her this beautiful dressing room at Paramount and she had a sensational portable, but she was accustomed to her own pot, that's all. She'd been seven years in that dressing room at RKO, and we found out later that she wasn't using the Paramount accommodations at all. First thing in the morning, she'd go to her own old rooms at RKO and get made up and dressed and then she'd drive through the gate from one lot onto the other lot, and that's how she worked it. So naturally when she had to go to the bathroom, she went back to her old studio. I mean, she was a *star* when she was a star."

The first time I saw Ginger was in 1928, when she was doing songs and dances and snappers in front of Paul Ash's band at the Paramount Theatre. I see her often now. The impressions are interchangeable, because Ginger is a genuine movie star and, therefore, a permanent presence. People grow older, but stars remain. A movie star is a creation that, like a painting or a statue or a symphony, does not age.

In 1938, many in Hollywood made fun of *Alexander's Ragtime Band* because, while it spanned fifty years or so, Tyrone Power and Alice Faye did not grow older. Perhaps the makers of that film knew best, after all. Who would have wanted to see a white-haired Ty or a shapeless Alice? Better by far to leave the ideal intact. What the hell. A movie is a dream and anything can happen in a dream.

In 1967, when a festival of Ginger Rogers films was being planned, the young man in charge told me that the job of selecting a representative dozen or so was "utterly nonplusing." Since *Young Man of Manhattan* Ginger had appeared in some seventy-five feature pictures. Which of her films could best demonstrate her unique comic gifts: *Vivacious Lady*? *The Major and the Minor*? *Tom, Dick, and Harry*? Which of her dramatic roles would be most compelling: *Kitty Foyle*? *The Primrose Path*? *Stage Door*? As to the musicals, which of the ten in which she co-starred with Fred Astaire should be shown? *Top Hat*? *Roberta*? *Shall We Dance*? *Carefree*? *The Story of Vernon and Irene Castle*? *The Gay Divorcée*? Faced with so many choices, the festival's planners wisely decided to put together a compilation of her musical work.

The magic of Astaire-Rogers (and of Hermes Pan, their dance director) cannot be explained, it can only be felt. Around the studio it was rumored that their off-screen relationship was strained. No matter. On the screen, where it counts, they created a style, a mood, a happening.

Making a film is hard work. For a leading actress it involves rising at 6:00 A.M. or 5:30 A.M. Studio. Makeup. Hairdressing. Wardrobe. Lines. Rehearsals. Changes. Hit those marks. Watch those lights. Act, feel, be charming but don't move your chin. Hold it, she's sweating again. Makeup! Quiet, please! Quiet, please! Hold it down! Roll 'em! Take six! Speed! Go! And so on. A full day of tense, exacting work seldom nets more than three or four minutes of screen time.

We talk easily of Ginger's seventy-five feature pictures, but is there any imagination that can total the sum of human effort and strain and stress that went into their making? In a lifetime of work, of striving for excellence, of seeking ephemera, of pondering imponderables—only the result matters.

Robert Burns, in his day, yearned:

O wad some Power the giftie gie us
To see oursels as ithers see us!

He did not foresee the screen.

I attended several of the festival's programs with Ginger. I watched her as—by means of this "Power the giftie gie" her—

she saw herself as the rest of us see her.

"What do you think?" I asked after one of the screenings.

"I don't know," she replied, her attention on the past. "It was a lot of hard work, that I *do* know."

"But it doesn't look it, Ginger. That's why it's magic."

"Okay," she said, and smiled for the first time that afternoon.

August 1954. I was involved in planning the first theatre production of *The Diary of Anne Frank*. The dramatists—Frances Goodrich and Albert Hackett—and I journeyed to Amsterdam to consult with Otto Frank, Anne's father, and others in the story. We wanted to cover the ground and to absorb the atmosphere as completely as possible. This involved visiting Anne's school and playground; the Franks' apartment; the route by which they traveled to their hiding place; and, finally, the hiding place itself. Prinsengracht 263. We moved through the still active enterprise on the lower floors—packaging pectin for jelly-making—and made our way to the attic area. Talk ended. We moved about quietly. At one moment, I was possessed by the shuddering notion that we, not the missing ones, were the ghosts. Alone, I wandered into a tiny space that I recognized at once, from Anne's description, as her room. Table (for homework), chair (for dressing), cot (for lying awake). The only decor was the mass of pin-ups on the wall: the Royal Family, two or three boys (friends?), a number of Dutch film stars (male, grinning professionally), Winston Churchill, and—Ginger Rogers in a *Tom, Dick, and Harry* still, smiling her celebrated smile.

How had the still found its way to this place? What had Anne Frank seen in that face? Mr. Frank told me afterward that Ginger Rogers was one of Anne's favorites.

18

The story was Sam Goldwyn's obsession always. Perhaps it is this factor that explains not only his success, but the length of his career.

Shortly after the formation of the Goldwyn company, he organized in 1919 an autonomous unit within the company called Eminent Authors Pictures, Incorporated. He began by signing Gertrude Atherton, Mary Roberts Rinehart, Rupert Hughes, Gouverneur Morris, Basil King, LeRoy Scott, and Rex Beach.

It was Goldwyn's idea that the writers should prepare original material, adapt the work of others, and be involved with the production throughout its various stages.

In at least one instance the theory paid off. Rupert Hughes, in 1921, wrote and produced *The Old Nest.* This was a screen adaptation of a story he had written for the *Saturday Evening Post* eight years earlier. It was an ambitious family epic, moving over a long period of time, and earned for the Goldwyn company a profit of well over $1 million. This translates into something like a $10-million profit on a film today.

Although the Eminent Authors Pictures plan did not work out to Goldwyn's complete satisfaction, he did not abandon his theory and continued to engage the finest, most successful writers he could get.

When I came to work for him in 1937, the name plates on the doors in the Writers' Building read: Dorothy Parker and Alan Campbell, Donald Ogden Stewart, Lillian Hellman, Sidney Howard, Anita Loos and John Emerson, Sam and Bella Spewack, Dudley Nichols, Robert E. Sherwood.

At one time or another, Goldwyn employed Thornton Wilder, Edna Ferber, Francis Marion, Montague Glass, Joseph Hergesheimer, Elmer Rice, Ben Hecht and Charles MacArthur, Morrie Ryskind, Howard Estabrook, Moss Hart, George S. Kaufman, William Anthony McGuire, Nunnally Johnson, Willard Mack, Harry Wagstaff Gribble, Preston Sturges, Maxwell Anderson, Mordaunt Shairp, Rachel Crothers, John L. Balderston, Rose Franken, S. N. Behrman, Sonya Levien, Jo Swerling, John Howard Lawson, John Van Druten, Niven Busch, Arthur Kober, Billy Wilder, Charles Brackett, Herman J. Mankiewicz, Joseph L. Mankiewicz, Paul Gallico, Harry Kurnitz, Leo Rosten, James Thurber, John Patrick, John Collier, Irwin Shaw, and Damon Runyon.

"They think I'm crazy," said Goldwyn. "I tell them the story is the most important thing and they think I'm crazy."

"You're not crazy, Mr. Goldwyn," I said.

"They tell me stars and spectacles. They tell me Technicolor and production values and gimmicks and some of them, f'Chrissake, they think sex . . . You're damn right I'm not crazy. The story."

"Certainly. Everyone loves a story."

"A *good* story," he said, correcting me.

"Yes. A *good* story. It's one of the ways we get a sense of form out of the chaos we live in."

"Chaos. You said it."

"It's probably one of the first things everyone remembers. A story being told. A bedtime story."

"Nobody ever told *me* a bedtime story," he said absently.

"But most people," I said. "And isn't it interesting that when we're kids, little kids, we sometimes want to hear the same story over and over again so that we can react in the right way at the right places, laugh or be scared or excited or applaud? And then pretty soon we want to make up our own stories and tell them—imagination begins to be important. And sometimes, if we can't invent a story, we tell about something. What happened in school today or about a trip or an accident we saw. And hardly anyone ever tells it exactly as it was. We all like to embellish it with a few little touches of our own—it's a way of making the story ours. Listen, when you come right down to it, life itself is a story."

He regarded me gently and said, "That's very good, my boy. Very nice. Very well said. I tell you what. Go and write that down for me."

"Write what down?"

"What you just said."

"I don't know if I can remember it exactly, Mr. Goldwyn. I was just talking."

Suddenly he was on his feet. "God damn it!" he thundered. "If I tell you write it down, write it down! Who said anything about exactly? What do you mean you were just talking? What the hell good is that? That's all you do around here f'Chrissake is talking. Is that what I pay you for? You think? For nothing? For talking? You know your trouble? You talk too much. Talk, f'Chrissake. What can you do with it? Can you release it? Would the exhibitors buy it? Now I'll tell you what to do. You go to your office and you write it down. Like I told you."

I went back to my office and wrote it down. Like he told me.

Monday morning. A letter from my friend Robert Ardrey. He is in despair. The failure of his play, *How to Get Tough About It* has hit him hard. He and Helen had hoped to marry shortly after the opening. Now the plan has been indefinitely postponed. Helen has returned to Ardmore, Oklahoma, to teach school. Bob has remained in New York, at loose ends. He appears to be running out of confidence.

He is one of the best writers I know, and it seems monumentally unjust that he should be having such a hard time while glib hacks here in Hollywood are earning thousands per week for adapting, trimming, revising, polishing, and borrowing.

What can be done? Goldwyn needs a writer for *The Cowboy and the Lady*. It is right up Bob's alley. Do I dare suggest it?

Monday afternoon. I have behaved impulsively and, as is usually the case when this happens, committed a blunder.

I asked for an appointment with Mr. Goldwyn. Granted.

"Mr. Goldwyn, have you decided yet on a new writer for *The Cowboy and the Lady*?"

"No. They're all lousy."

"Who?"

"All the ones that goddam Sam Marx keeps bringing up. I've had them all. I know them. I can tell what they're going to write before they write it even."

"Maybe you ought to get someone *new*. You know what I mean? Fresh. Somebody who hasn't been around so much."

"That's what *I* say," said Goldwyn. "But who knows where to find people like that?"

"Well, listen, Mr. Goldwyn. There's this marvelous young playwright from Chicago. He's a protégé of Thornton Wilder's and . . ."

"Thornton Wilder would be very good. He's a good writer. Find out if he's available."

"All right," I said, deflated. "But in case he's *not,* I think you ought to consider this boy."

"What's he done?" asked Goldwyn nervously.

"Well, he wrote a play called *House on Fire* and practically every producer and director in New York went wild about it and finally it was produced and directed by Arthur Hopkins and . . ." I hesitated for a split second trying to decide whether to lie, to exaggerate, or to obfuscate.

". . . and it flopped," said Goldwyn.

"Not completely," I said. "It wasn't a smash but— Anyway, then he wrote another play called *How to Get Tough About It* and Guthrie McClintic bought that."

"I've heard of him," said Goldwyn. "Guthrie McClintic."

"Yes. Well, he bought it."

"And what happened?" Goldwyn asked.

"It hasn't opened yet," I lied at once. "But this fellow's marvelous—and listen, what can you lose? Give him a chance. Bring him out and let him work on the material for a few weeks. I'm sure you could get him for—I don't know—maybe three or four hundred a week."

Goldwyn looked at me as though I had uttered an obscenity in the presence of his wife.

"This is the writer you're recommending me?" he asked. "A three-hundred-dollar-a-week writer?"

"Well, he's—maybe he'd want—"

Goldwyn's voice went into a key one tone higher. "Do you know this is a picture is going to cost maybe two million, maybe two million three by the time we're finished?"

"Yes, I heard that."

"You heard that and you want me to put on a two-hundred-dollar-a-week writer on a picture's going to cost—"

"I said three or *four* hundred, Mr. Goldwyn. Not two."

He looked at me again, this time with pity, then waved the back of his hand at me four times. I counted.

"Go away," he said.

I went away.

Tuesday afternoon. I told my Ardrey story to Sam Marx. No sympathy.

"Why didn't you take it up with *me,* for God's sake? I'd have told you how to handle it."

"Impulsive," I said.

"You didn't know beforehand you'd strike out with a proposition like that?"

"I suppose I should have. Do you think there's anything I can do?"

"No," said Sam. "It's too late now. You've mentioned the guy's name and that's it."

"Wait a second," I said. "I didn't. I don't think I did."

"You *didn't* mention his name?"

"No. I'm *sure* I didn't. In the first place, I knew it would mean nothing to Goldwyn, and in the second place— I don't know. I know I just didn't."

"In that case," Sam advised, "wait a few days and make him sound like somebody else."

"Why a few days?" I asked.

"Because," said Sam. "I would judge your stock with Goldwyn now is selling at about one and a half."

Friday afternoon. I can hardly believe it. This morning Goldwyn asked me to join him at lunch. Moss Hart is coming in to discuss a story. He knows that Moss and I are friends.

Lunch began gaily but ended badly. Goldwyn did not respond to Moss's story. Afterward we sat around the table, awkwardly trying to find a way to end the meeting. All at once I muttered, "God damn!"

"What did you say?" asked Goldwyn.

"Nothing."

"You're upset about something. What is it?"

"Well," I said, "I had a call this morning from Robert Ardrey and he tells me he's probably coming out here to do a picture at Metro, and I'm *furious* with myself."

"Why?"

"Because, God damn it, he's the *perfect* writer for *The Cowboy and the Lady* and I know him and why the hell I didn't think of him in time I can't imagine. I'm just *sick* about it."

"Who is Robert Ardrey?" asked Goldwyn blankly.

"Robert Ardrey," I said impressively. "He's a fantastic writer. Isn't he, Moss?" I looked at Moss significantly.

He looked at Goldwyn and said, "Fantastic."

"And perfect for *The Cowboy and the Lady,*" I said. "Wouldn't you say, Moss?"

"Perfect," said Moss.

Goldwyn looked at Moss Hart and said, *"You* couldn't write *The Cowboy and the Lady.* It's not your kind of picture at all. Not your cup of tea."

"You're right," said Moss. "It's not right for me. It's right for Robert Ardrey."

Goldwyn finished his coffee, looked at me, and said, "Have you got his telephone number?"

"Ardrey's?" I asked.

"Yes."

"No, I don't think so."

"Well, *get* it, God damn it!" said Goldwyn. "You hardly ever do anything around here f'Chrissake. You haven't even got this man's *telephone* number."

"Well, maybe I can get it from Metro," I suggested.

"Metro!" yelled Goldwyn. "You're going to call up f'Chrissake Metro? What's a matter with you?" He looked at Moss helplessly. "This kid's supposed to be a smart kid and every day he says something stupid."

"I think you could get his telephone number from the Dramatists Guild," said Moss sagely.

"Did you hear that?" asked Goldwyn. "Call up those dramatists and get that man."

"It may be too late," I said.

"Sure, it'll be too late," said Goldwyn, "if you sit there f'Chrissake on your ass and don't get to work. Get him on the phone. Tell him it's a great picture. He'll get lost at Metro. It's a factory. Tell him. And he can get twelve-fifty a week here."

"And a ten-week guarantee?" I asked.

"Certainly."

I moved around to the other side of the table, embraced Moss, and was on my way.

I phoned Ardrey.

"Bob, I've got a job for you."

"I don't believe you."

"It's right here at Goldwyn's."

"Doing what?" asked Bob.

"Writing. What the hell did you think?"

"Writing a movie?" asked Bob.

"Jesus, Bob," I said. "You sound real dumb. I hope you improve your dialogue by the time you get here, otherwise you won't last twenty minutes. As it is, I've got you a ten-week guarantee."

"Oh, God," he said.

"Plus your fare out here. I think you ought to fly."

"No," said Bob. "The way my luck's been going I'm sure to crash."

"Fly," I said. "By the way, how does three hundred a week strike you?"

"Really?" he asked, unbelieving.

"Or six hundred?"

"Come on, kid."

"Would you settle for a thousand?"

Silence.

"Bob, listen. Your contract with Samuel Goldwyn is for ten weeks at twelve-fifty a week. . . . Bob? . . . . Bob, are you there?"

Finally, in a new voice, I heard Bob say, "Praise God from whom all blessings flow."

Robert Ardrey came to Goldwyn's. On the first weekend we went together to Tucson, Arizona, where we met Helen, who had traveled there from Oklahoma. We stood together in a small desert church and they were married.

Back at Goldwyn's, Ardrey made good (although not on *The Cowboy and the Lady*) and went on to a long and distinguished career as a Hollywood screenwriter. Having achieved Hollywood fame and fortune, he was now in a position to return to his first love, anthropology, and has since contributed *African Genesis, The Territorial Imperative,* and *The Social Contract.*

"What did you think about the Edna Ferber book?" Goldwyn asked one day as I was telling him the story of Robert E. Sherwood's *Abe Lincoln in Illinois,* upon which he had asked me to report.

"Crazy about it," I said.

"So is Frances," he said, "but you two are the only two, Talboig. Everybody else thinks it's old-fashioned."

"What do *you* think, Mr. Goldwyn?"

"Me? Well, I'll tell you," he said. "I've given it a lot of thought and I believe I have come to the conclusion that the trouble with that Edna Ferber story is—it's old-fashioned."

"That doesn't make it bad," I said. "Wouldn't you say *Romeo and Juliet* is old-fashioned? And what about *Peter Pan*? Or Beethoven's Fifth?"

Goldwyn shook his head sadly. "Classics," he said. "Classics don't mean a God damn thing. Not in the present market. There's new people all the time and they want new things. Do you read a lot?" he asked suddenly.

"Well, not as much as I should, I suppose."

"Frances reads *everything.*"

"Is that so?"

"I'm talking about every damn book that's *published* she reads."

"That's a lot of reading," I said.

"She's brilliant, you know," he said. "I don't mean from reading. She's brilliant anyway. She would be brilliant if she never read anything, but she reads everything. You want me to tell you how brilliant she is? When I broke away from the M-G-M thing because I can't stand partners—never have partners, that's my advice to you—I decided to go on my own so I formed a company. *This* company. And they drew up all the papers—the lawyers—all the papers for the incorporation and they kept asking me, 'What's the *name* of your company?' And I had to say, 'Just leave it blank for the present.' And we started in to think of a name for the company. *I* thought and the *sales* people thought and the public *relations.* Of course by that time a lot of good ones were used up already. Like Universal and Paramount and so on. So there wasn't much left. But we all kept on thinking—but *nothing clicked.* Somebody said, 'Apex Productions.' But it didn't *click.* Neither did 'Prudential' click. I told them. I said, 'It sounds like an insurance company.' And finally, I'll tell you what I did. I called in all the writers I had working for me at the time. Big-name writers. Stars. And I said to them, 'Gentlemen, I want you all to take a few days off from whatever you're doing, whatever you're writing, and help me out with a problem.' And I told them about how I needed a name for my company. And I told them the ones we had thought of so far and how they didn't *click*. And they all went back to their offices and this was costing me thousands a day every day and they all sent in their suggestions and would you believe it? *Nothing clicked!* I went home that night. I was so depressed, I can't tell you. And while we were having dinner, Frances looked at me and she said, 'Why are you so depressed, Sam?' I said to her, 'What makes you think I'm depressed?' And she said, 'Because you *look* depressed.' I said to her, 'Well, Frances, I'll tell you. I *am* depressed.' Then I told her everything I had gone through. About not having a name for the company and how nothing clicked, and the date was coming up to file the papers and we couldn't wait any more. And Frances looked at me and she said, 'Why don't you call it "Samuel Goldwyn Productions?" ' And it *clicked!* You see what I mean when I tell you about Frances brilliant?"

"Yes," I replied.

In *The New York Times* I read a review of an English novel titled *Late and Soon* by E. M. Delafield. It sounded interesting. I bought a copy and read it. It was a bizarre romance, the story of a mother and daughter who fall in love with the same man. It struck me as having distinct film possibilities. I took it into Mr. Goldwyn.

"Tell it to me in one paragraph," he ordered.

"I can't," I said.

"Then it's no good."

"It is," I insisted. "It's a *remarkable* story."

"If you can't tell it in one paragraph it's no good."

I told it in one paragraph.

"It's no good," he said.

"Why not?"

"What is it?" he thundered. "A middle-age love story f'Chrissake! You can't sell a middle-age love story. Who the hell cares about a middle-age love story? Nobody. Not even middle-age people are interested in a middle-age love story."

I should have known by then to avoid debate but I was annoyed at having been pushed into an untenable position.

"Oh, I don't know," I said. "You've done pretty well with a middle-age love story."

"Me? Never."

"What about *Dodsworth*? Wouldn't you call that a middle-age love story?"

"*Dodsworth*—f'Chrissake. Don't talk to me about *Dodsworth*. I lost my goddam shirt. I told them. All of them. I told that Willie Wyler. He can be *so* stubborn. And Sidney Howard, too. And everybody. I told them. 'You haven't got a *chance* with a middle-age love story.' But they talked me into it and I went ahead. Walter Huston and Ruth Chatterton and Mary Astor and I lost my shirt. I'm not saying it wasn't a fine picture. It was a *great* picture but nobody wanted to see it. In *droves*. You know why?"

"No. Why?"

"Because, God damn it, why don't you *listen* to me? I just *told* you why. Because nobody wants to see a middle-age love story like that. Like *Dodsworth*. I lost my shirt."

Some months later, in the course of a casting conference, various important character actors were being discussed.

"Listen!" Goldwyn shouted suddenly. "I got it! I'll do it personally. I'll call him up and ask him to do it for me. All right, so it *isn't* such a great part. But he will be great *in* it. I'll ask him as a personal favor. I'll tell him. He'll do it for me, won't he?"

"Who are you talking about, Sam?" asked Willie Wyler.

"Why, Walter Huston," said Goldwyn.

"Oh, sure," said Willie. "He'd be great. But I thought you wanted someone with more box office."

"More box office?" shouted Goldwyn. "Who's got more box office f'Chrissake than Walter Huston? Didn't I have him here in *Dodsworth*? You should remember *Dodsworth,* f'Chrissake. You *directed* it. One of the biggest hits I ever had. It made a *fortune!*"

This, too, exemplified Goldwyn's strength. A never-ending resilience, a way of suiting the argument to the circumstances.

As Walt Whitman said, "Do I contradict myself? Very well then I contradict myself, I am large, I contain multitudes."

In late December 1924, Samuel Goldwyn left aboard the *Majestic* on his annual trip to Europe. He announced to the press that he was going to spend Christmas in Paris and that soon afterward, he was going to Vienna to meet with Dr. Sigmund Freud, because he felt that Freud's ideas might be useful for the screen. Therefore, he was going to try to get Dr. Freud to write a scenario or, failing that, sign him to come to Hollywood as an adviser.

To a shipboard interviewer for *The New York Times,* Goldwyn said that 70 per cent of the moviegoers in the United States were young people, that they appreciated the opportunity to sit together in the dark, watching love on the screen.

"There is nothing really so entertaining on the screen as a really great love story," he said. "So you see, I thought I would go and see Freud and at least have a talk with the greatest love specialist in the world. When I say that most of the young people who go to see pictures want a love story, I feel that I am right. Some time ago I remember going to see 'Twenty Leagues under the Sea,' an unusual production, made by J. E. Williamson. It was a remarkable film but two girls behind me got tired of it long before it was finished, and suggested going to the New York Theatre 'where they have lots of love in the picture.'

"Of course young people don't want to see a man of forty-three and a woman of thirty-eight in love, any more than they wish to be introduced to a couple who have been married ten years. That kind of theme holds no romance for them. They want to see young people of their own age, sweetly in love with each other. The screen has caused many a young couple to be married. It has put the courage into the young man to ask the girl. So I am going to see Freud. . . .

"Scenario writers, actors, and directors can learn much by a really deep study of everyday life. How much more forceful will be their creation if they know how to express genuine emotional motivation and suppressed desires? And the finished pictures produced with Professor Freud and his collaborator will have audience appeal far greater than any productions made today, because these love revelations and psychological truths will strike fire with the deepest thoughts and feelings of the people who unquestionably react more strongly to the genuine in pictures."

"Whatever happened with Freud and you?" I asked Goldwyn one day.

"Who?"

"Dr. Freud. Sigmund Freud. I read somewhere that you went to Vienna to see him."

Goldwyn was insulted.

"There's never been anything wrong with me," he said. "I wouldn't go in for that stuff where you tell everything about yourself to somebody who writes it down."

"No, no. I didn't mean as a patient," I said. "I read that you went to Vienna to try to get him to *work* for you."

"Listen, f'Chrissake!" said Goldwyn. "In those days, in 1924, nobody ever even *heard* of Freud. In America, hardly anybody. In 1924 had *you* heard of him?"

"In 1924, Mr. Goldwyn, I was twelve years old, and I'd heard of Babe Ruth and Lou Gehrig and Jake Ruppert and Eugene V. Debs."

"What the hell has *Debs* got to do with it, f'Chrissake?"

"Nothing. What about Freud?"

"He didn't want to do it," said Goldwyn, fearfully. "He claimed he was too busy, that he couldn't get away. But that was a good idea I had, just the same. Because look what happened in the advertising business, years and years later, when they started in to hire all kinds of scientists and psychiatrists and psychologists. That's how they made it into a great business. The advertising business. Albert Lasker told me about the whole thing. He said the advertising business learned how to use mass psychology, and that's what *we* got to learn because that's our only chance to appeal to the masses. For a picture to be successful, *millions* of people have to like it. That's very hard. To make something that *millions* of people are going to like. Isn't that so?

"I want to tell you something. Freud was very foolish not to come. But you know how it is. There are some people, you can't tell them a goddam thing. Like him. Freud. Or Abe Lastfogel. Your agent."

19

In a business as complex, as diversified as the film business, agents and agencies are frequently important as catalysts, go-betweens, and matchmakers. Looking back on it all, I find that there are a larger number of agents I admire than there are producers. Agents have frequently been helpful and creative, even imaginative.

I am convinced that we would never have known the joy of Marilyn Monroe had it not been for an extraordinary agent named Johnny Hyde. He was a diminutive man, packed with surprising power.

He had what used to be called "a roving eye." When finally it lit on an obscure, unemployed, struggling film actress named Marilyn Monroe, the roving stopped. Johnny Hyde, at that time a senior partner in the William Morris Agency, and a multimillionaire, was about fifty. He fell in love with Marilyn, and she fell in love with him.

His belief in her future as a screen personality was every bit as passionate as his love for her.

I was subjected to a barrage of pressures and arguments having to do with her suitability for the leading role of Billie Dawn in *Born Yesterday,* which I had sold to Columbia Pictures. With great craft, Johnny had convinced Columbia Pictures to sign Marilyn Monroe to a stock contract. He reasoned that if she were on the lot, there was always a chance that she might be the dark horse (blonde horse?) who could make it.

Finally, after a month of scheming, Marilyn Monroe did make a test for the part. Those who saw it thought it was excellent. But Harry Cohn, the head of the studio, did not trouble to take the six steps from his desk to his projection room to look at her.

Despite Cohn's indifference, and Johnny's failure to get anyone in a key position to see Marilyn through his eyes, he persisted. It was with no little embarrassment that I once said to him, "Johnny, you're a darling fellow and a wonderful agent, but you certainly are a bore on the subject of Marilyn. Give it a rest, will you?"

"You'll see," said Johnny, pointing up at me. "You'll *see*! They'll *all* see. This kid has really got it. It's not just her looks, although everybody admits she's a knockout, but she's got the spirit. And she's funny. And a hell of an actress. And what's more important, she wants to do it. She wants to get there and be somebody. And people who have that kind of drive, nobody can put them down. Nobody."

"All right, Johnny," I said. "All *right*."

Johnny went so far as to discuss the setting up of a syndicate to buy the film rights to *Born Yesterday* and making it with Marilyn Monroe. For a short time, Max Gordon and I considered this proposition, not because we liked it, but because there were no other offers.

It was curious. The play was a success on Broadway and went well with audiences night after night, but the film companies were cool. They saw it as censorable material that could easily be ruined when hammered into a shape that would be approved by the Production Code. There were questions of sexual morality involved, but, more important, political morality. The film companies had too many axes to grind on the Washington grindstone to consider putting a venal senator on the screen.

Still, there were a few producers who thought it might work. One of them was at M-G-M. Clark Gable and Lana Turner were Metro's biggest box-office stars. The producer saw *Born Yesterday* as a double vehicle. He made his proposal. It was tentatively approved by the Hollywood front office. Tickets for the play were arranged for Nicholas Schenck, at that time chairman of the board of Loew's, Inc. The final decision would be his.

His nephew, Marvin, was a friend of mine. A few days later, he showed me a copy of the interoffice memo that Nicholas Schenck had sent back to the coast. It read: "At your suggestion I have last night seen *Born Yesterday*. It is the worst play I have ever seen. The idea of making it with Clark Gable or with Lana Turner or with anyone is ridiculous. N. S."

It was shortly after this blow that Johnny came up with his Marilyn Monroe idea, but nothing came of that either.

Johnny Hyde prevailed upon his friend John Huston to let Marilyn test for the part of Louis Calhern's mistress in *The Asphalt Jungle*. Huston responded to her, spotted her beautifully in the film, and she made an impression.

Johnny acquired a print of her scenes in this picture and, for months, carried it around in his car. He would screen it for anyone who was willing to watch it. He became, for a time, a familiar sight, walking around the various lots with a can of film under his arm.

It was Marilyn's luck, and his, and ours, that Joseph L. Mankiewicz was also a client of the William Morris Agency. At Twentieth Century-Fox he was preparing *All About Eve*. Johnny read the script and found a small but effective part that he thought would be right for Marilyn. He badgered Mankiewicz until Mankiewicz agreed. Then the Twentieth Century-Fox front office vetoed the idea.

"We've had her," said Lou Schreiber, the head of the talent department. "We had her here under contract for a hundred and a quarter a week. We had her in *Scudda Hoo! Scudda Hay!* and we had to cut her out. And then she was in something else here, a horrible abortion, *Dangerous Years*. We had to get rid of her. So why do we want her back?"

Johnny did not give up, took it to the top, which at that time, meant Darryl F. Zanuck. Again luck. Zanuck owed Johnny a favor and Johnny called his note. Marilyn got the part in *All About Eve* as George Sanders' girl friend, a minor actress described in the picture as "a graduate of the Copacabana School of Dramatic Art."

"It wouldn't have happened, any of it," she once said to me, "if not for Johnny. When I did *The Asphalt Jungle*, it was like that was some kind of a discovery. But Jesus, I'd been knocking around, and I mean knocking around, for about six years before that, modeling and everything. And finally Howard Hughes got interested. That was nothing. And then Twentieth and getting kicked out. And then Columbia, and that turned out another nothing. And did you see me in *Love Happy* with the Marx Brothers? I was good in that, but nobody knew it. And *A Ticket to Tomahawk*. I swear I was getting ready to give up and maybe learn to be a negative cutter like my mother or something—at least make a living. And that's when Johnny Hyde happened. Look, I had plenty of friends and acquaintances —you know what I mean, acquaintances? And, sure, I played the game the way everyone else was playing it. But not one of them, not one of those big shots, ever did a damn thing for me, not one, except Johnny. Because he believed in me."

"He loved you," I said.

"I know it. And I loved him."

Those luminous eyes moistened as she continued. "You know what a creep town this is and, naturally, when I was living with Johnny, it was like I was doing it because he could do me some good. He was the first kind man I ever met in my whole life. I've known a few since, but he was the first. And smart. Remember how fast he used to talk and how high?" She smiled in fond recollection. "Once he got an idea or some kind of a strategy, he would just stay on it, and he wouldn't stop. He would pace around, or walk up and down, for hours, sometimes till two or three in the morning, figuring out all the angles. He was certainly a wonderful man. When he died like that, all of a sudden, I really thought maybe my whole life was over, too. But just before he died, he got me this contract with Twentieth, a second one. And without him around to promote me— It's something I don't know how to do. I mean, I know how to put my body over, but I don't know how to put *myself* over. Does that make sense?"

"Sure."

She laughed suddenly, that celebrated little-girl laugh of hers, and said, "Did you ever hear what Constance Bennett said about me? We were in something together, I think the name of it was *As Young as You Feel* or something like that. And I hardly had anything to do, just kind of walk-throughs. So naturally, I tried to make the most of that. And one day, Connie said to somebody, 'There's a broad with a future behind her.' "

She laughed again, and was suddenly serious. I was always troubled by this swift change in mood that was one of her characteristics.

She went on. "So after then, it was practically nothing but loan-outs and cheesecake. And I don't know what would've happened if it hadn't of been for that whole thing with the bare-ass calendar."

"What whole thing?" I asked. I knew the story, but I wanted to hear it from her.

"You never heard about that?" she asked.

"Vaguely," I said.

"Well, somebody in the modeling business told me they were going to make some art calendars. And it was for a lot of money, which I needed at the time. And when I got there, they wanted me to pose in the nude. So I said, 'Nothing doing!' So they upped the ante, and finally I took a drink and thought, What the hell. This guy, the photographer, he told me that for a calendar in color, they were going to do it with a lot of silk screen and a lot of retouching and he said, 'Listen, nobody's ever going to know it's you by the time we get finished. After all, you look like a lot of other bimbos and *they* look like *you,* so if the subject ever comes up, you can just say it's *not* you.' Well, anyway, we did it. And he was right, it hardly *did* look like me. And I guess nothing would've happened about it, except when I got to be a little well known, these bastards who owned the rights to the calendar started putting it out by the millions. And, of course, said it was me. My new agent, I thought he was going to drop dead, and, of course, the studio was upset. And then my press agent came up with that great line, you know, when they ask me if, during the posing, I had anything on. And I said, 'Yes, the radio.' And all of a sudden, even those dumbheads at the studio began to see that it wasn't such bad publicity. It was sort of good publicity because it was kind of sassy. So that's when they stuck me right across the top of that whole *Niagara* billboard and, I don't know, things sort of got going from there. But I tell you again, it wouldn't have happened without my Johnny Hyde. None of it."

Marilyn Monroe was starring in *How to Marry a Millionaire*. The screenplay had been written by Nunnally Johnson, who, in self-defense, was also producing the picture. Marilyn had a short, but complicated scene to shoot, involving breakfast in bed and a simultaneous phone call. The director, Jean Negulesco, explained the routine patiently. Marilyn listened patiently. They rehearsed for about an hour, but she appeared to be getting more and more confused.

Negulesco decided to shoot the scene and pray. Maybe something would happen. They made ready to shoot, a complex matter involving the wardrobe woman, the hairdresser, the makeup man, and the property man. When everyone was ready, and the lights, and the camera, they began the scene. Again, Marilyn became hopelessly confused, answering the phone before it rang, drinking out of the coffee cup before she had filled it and so on.

"Cut!"

"One more."

Preparations again.

The one more became six more, sixteen more, twenty-six more, and still the shot had not been made. Something went wrong each time. It was approaching six o'clock and Negulesco could already hear the production office explosions when they saw on the sheet that not a foot of film had been produced all afternoon. He was desperately anxious to make this one shot at least. He kept trying. No success. He sent for Nunnally Johnson and asked if perhaps something could be done to simplify the scene. Johnson simplified it. They tried two more takes, then decided to give up. It was six o'clock. Time had run out.

"Okay," shouted the assistant director. "That's it. Wrap it up."

The tired day had ended.

Negulesco sank down in his chair and put his head into his hands.

Marilyn sat up in bed, looking bemused. Nunnally Johnson, a warm and benign figure, went up to Marilyn, took her hand, and said, "We'll do it in the morning, honey. Don't worry about it."

"Don't worry about *what?*" asked Marilyn.

Nunnally reports that he dropped her hand in astonishment.

The power of agents and agencies in Hollywood derives from the fact that most artists are unequipped for business. The temperament required to write a story, to act a scene, or to make a film is, as a rule, diametrically opposed to the temperament required to make a deal, to negotiate effectively, to read and understand the fine print.

Moreover, in Hollywood's great, productive days about 700 feature films a year were made. It was impossible for an individual to cover the ground, to know what was going on at each studio, to have access to the producers and the directors. Thus, the agent fulfilled an important need.

Leland Hayward, who represented Edna Ferber, struggled with the financial aspects of the deal he was about to make for her successful novel *Saratoga Trunk*. Miss Ferber had spent some three years writing the book, and now it appeared that she would be taxed on what she made from the book in a single year. This seemed blatantly unfair, but nothing could be done.

Hayward came up with an idea that has been copied many

321

times since. Instead of selling the property outright to Warner Brothers, he decided to *lease* them the rights for a period of ten years, at so much a year. It was a brilliant idea and has worked well ever since.

Irving Paul Lazar is another of the superior brains in representation.

He operates alone, has a small but select list of clients, mainly writers and directors. It was he who conceived the audacious idea of collecting a commission from the buyer rather than from the seller.

James Jones's novel *From Here to Eternity* was being bid for competitively by virtually every studio in Hollywood. The price kept going up and up and, as it did, Lazar's spirits went down and down. It depressed him that he did not represent this plum. Brooding about it early one morning, he hit upon an idea, jumped out of bed, and called Harry Cohn at his home.

"Listen," said Irving, "you want that book don't you? *From Here to Eternity?*"

"What do you mean, want it?" said Cohn. "I've got it."

"No, you haven't," said Lazar. "Don't bull me, nobody's got it. Yet."

"Well, I'm *going* to get it," said Cohn.

"Not if you're outbid, you're not."

"What the hell have *you* got to do with it?" asked Cohn. "You don't represent that book, do you?"

"Never mind that," said Lazar. "Let me ask you something. If I can get it for you, will you pay me my commission?"

Cohn was flabbergasted and saw the whole business collapsing about him.

"I should pay you for *buying* it?"

"That's it," said Lazar. "What do you care? You're not paying the ten per cent that Jones is going to pay his agent. And if I can guarantee to get it for you, and if I *do* get it for you, I think it's worth it."

"Ten per cent of what I pay for it plus?"

"That's it exactly," said Lazar.

Cohn could not understand this concept. It was probably for that reason that he agreed.

Lazar then went to Jones and his agent, explained that he was representing Harry Cohn and Columbia Pictures, and that they were prepared to top any offer made by anyone else.

"Besides," Lazar argued, "it's not only the money, it's the setup. Cohn sees this as his big one for the year. He'll probably put Fred Zinnemann on it. He knows how to do this kind of a picture and how to sell it. You guys're nuts to take it anywhere else."

The property was acquired by Columbia and commissions were paid at both ends. It was a great day for agents. With one stroke, they had doubled their take.

One of the functions of an agent, by no means the most important, is to sell. Selling requires force of personality, subliminal communication, imagery, fantasy, persuasion, and an occasional fact. The great salesmen also add timing.

Irving Paul Lazar was once anxious to sell Jack L. Warner a play.

"I had a long meeting with him today," Lazar explained, "but I didn't mention it, I didn't even bring it up."

"Why not?" I asked.

"Because I'm going to wait until the weekend after next, when I go to Palm Springs."

"I don't understand."

"You don't? I go to Palm Springs every weekend, but Warner isn't going this weekend. He's got a preview or something. So he's not coming down till the *next* weekend, so that's when I'm going to bring it up."

"Irving, I'm more and more confused."

"Look," said Irving impatiently, "I know what I'm doing. I know how to sell Warner. This is a type of material that he's uneasy with, so I have to hit him with it hard and suddenly to get an okay."

"But why Palm Springs?"

"Because in Palm Springs, every day he goes to the baths at The Spa. And that's where I'm going to be when he's there. Now there's a thing about Jack, he's eighty, you know, and he's very vain, and he doesn't like people to see him naked. So when I walk up to him naked at The Spa—I mean *he's* naked— well, I'm naked too, but I don't care who sees me. *He does.* And I walk up to him naked, and I start to talk to him about this thing, he'll be very embarrassed. And he'll want to get away from me, and the easiest way is to say, 'Yes,' because he knows if he says, 'No,' then I'm going to stick with him, and stay right on it, and not give up. So to get rid of me, he'll probably say, 'Yes.' "

Two weeks later, I read of the acquisition of this particular property by Warner Brothers. I phoned Lazar and asked how it had been accomplished.

"How do you think?" he said. "In the buff, that's how. In the altogether, just the way I told you it was going to work. Well, that's the way it worked."

20

Edward J. Mannix of Metro-Goldwyn-Mayer was an executive who reached his position in an unusual way. When the Schenck Brothers owned Palisades Amusement Park they were plagued by gangs of toughs who lived in the surrounding New Jersey area and would come into the park— swiping, stealing, or often simply disrupting the place for the hell of it. One of the ringleaders was a stocky little pug-nosed Irishman, named Eddie Mannix. The Schencks attempted to buy him off, without success. They tried to discipline him, but to no avail. When they threatened him, he made things hotter for them.

They decided to hire him, and gave him a job at the Palisades Amusement Park, where he became a security officer, charged with keeping the peace. He went from this job to others and, after a few years, became the manager of the whole enterprise.

Later, the Schencks went into the film business. Still later, they went to Hollywood, and Mannix came along with them as one of their strong and able people.

When I first met him, he was a solid, immovable fixture in the M-G-M front office. I liked him. He was extremely tough but eminently fair. He said what he thought to everyone, including Nicholas Schenck and L. B. Mayer.

He once expressed himself as troubled about the human situation. "You know," he said to me, "I went around the world last year. And you want to know something? It *hates* each other!"

On another occasion, he said, "It's no good. The whole everything. There's somethin' wrong with the way things've

325

turned out. See, everything's too *easy* for people. When I was a kid, if I wanted a baseball bat, or a glove, I had to sweat for it. I had to work for it."

"I heard sometimes you used to steal it," I said.

"Sure. An' you think *that* was easy? That was hard. But what I was sayin' was things just didn't come to me. *Now* the trouble is people are all soft; they're soft because things're too easy. Lemme give you a for instance. I'm ridin' along in my car the other day, one of my cars. The Cadillac, and it starts in to knock. And I thought to myself, Well, when I get to the studio, I'll have the secretary call up the garage. They'll come and get it and see what's a matter. And then I started in to think. What the hell? A car starts to knock, it's like somebody starts to get sick. From that time on, it's all downhill. I'll fix the knock and somethin' else'll go on the blink, so I thought what the hell? The thing to do is trade it in, get a new one. Y'know what I mean? Start from scratch. So when I got in, I called up the Cadillac place and I said to the guy, 'I need a new car. How soon can I get it?' He said, 'What color you want?' I said, 'The same color I got.' He said, 'What color is that?' I said, 'Maroon.' He said, 'You're in luck. I happen to have a maroon right here.' I said, 'When can I get it?' He said, 'Where's your old car right now, Mr. Mannix?' I said, 'It's in my parking spot, at Metro, where do you think?' He says, 'I'll take care of the whole thing.' An' you know that at the end of the day, when I went downstairs, my old car was gone, and the new car was there, and that's the way I drove home. Y'understand now, what I mean when I say things are too easy for people? That *that's* what's makin' 'em soft?"

Writers were not often invited to the M-G-M executive dining room, nor were directors, except important directors on special occasions.

Since my wife and I were not part of the studio setup, or of the community, we came under the heading of "Special Visitors" and frequently, when we were working at M-G-M, we were taken by Dore Schary or Lawrence Weingarten or L. B. Mayer to lunch in the executive dining room. It was located on the top floor of the Thalberg Building; one long table, set with fine linen and beautiful silver, china, and crystal. The food was excellent, but the conversation erratic.

Each executive had his own seat. In front of each place was a collection of pill bottles. No executive had less than a dozen. Some had as many as twenty or thirty. Various pills and capsules and drops to be taken with various types of foods, for all sorts of ailments, some real and some imagined. Whenever a new bottle appeared on the table, it was subject to scrutiny, sometimes caused envy. The owner of the new bottle would explain its contents, generally a new and expensive wonder drug.

One day, Benny Thau, a vice-president, took his seat, swept all his pill bottles and boxes into a manila envelope and said, grandly, to one of the waitresses, "Throw all this way, Amelia. I'm not going to need it any more."

His announcement caused a stir.

"What happened, Benny?"

"You all right?"

"You're not allowed to take medicine any more?"

"You sure you know what you're doing, Ben?"

"Oh, yes," he said, and ordered knockwurst and sauerkraut. When he had finished his lunch, he took his watch from his wrist, put it on the table, and studied it carefully. Then, in the middle of someone's analysis of the current political situation in France, Thau said, "Excuse me, please."

He unbuttoned his vest, leaned back in his chair. Conversation continued. Thau took no part in it. He remained in his strange, withdrawn position for five minutes, then sat up brightly, and said, "I swear to God, it works."

"What works?"

"This new short-wave radio treatment I'm on. There's this doctor and I'm on a short-wave with him. After every meal, he sends out these short-waves and they completely digest my food."

All at once I realized that my wife and I were the only ones in the room laughing. The others took it in dead earnest.

We were to learn later that it was so meant. There was, indeed, such a doctor and such a treatment. In the months to come, Benny Thau was not the only executive who unbuttoned his vest, leaned back, and had his food digested by short-wave.

Joe Pasternak is an energetic, enthusiastic, laughing Hungarian who, in the 1930s, produced films in Budapest. Later, he went to Germany and encountered a bright young director named Hermann Kosterlitz. They made a number of arresting pictures and were brought to Hollywood by Universal. Joe continued to call himself Pasternak, but Hermann Kosterlitz became Henry Koster.

At Universal, they began with a remake of one of their German pictures, *Three Smart Girls*. The following year, they made *One Hundred Men and a Girl,* one of the outstanding successes of the year.

It was an idea that met its time and triumphed. A Depression story. Adolphe Menjou played an unemployed violinist who was growing more shabby by the minute. He organizes an orchestra of unemployed musicians. They play beautifully but cannot manage a livelihood. Here comes Deanna Durbin as Adolphe Menjou's young daughter. She breaks in on Leopold Stokowski. With youthful fervor and charm she convinces him to do something about it. She leads him to the ragged musicians in the rehearsal hall. They begin to play. Stokowski sits and listens. Then—the *magic moment*! One hand comes up, then his other hand. Now he is on his feet and begins to conduct. A dissolve, and they are playing in Carnegie Hall, conducted by Stokowski. They are a smash. Fade-out. The end.

Pasternak and Koster were in business. They were offered everything on the lot.

One day in a story conference, Pasternak began to outline an idea. The writer said, "I don't know. It's just another Cinderella story."

Pasternak said, "Just a moment. It seems to me I hear that word over and over again here. And how do you say? 'Cinderella'?"

"Yes. Cinderella."

"Spell it," said Pasternak. It was spelled. He wrote it down.

"But what does it mean?" asked Pasternak.

The writer told him the story of Cinderella. The wicked sisters, the fairy godmother, Cinderella at the ball, the glass slipper, the search, the prince, the pumpkin coach, the happy ending.

When he finished he looked over at Joe Pasternak who sat behind his desk, tears streaming out of his eyes.

"Why, that's the greatest goddam story I ever heard in my whole life," said Joe. "My *God,* what a story! Why don't we make *that?*"

Everyone in the room was astounded.

"Why don't we make that?" repeated the writer. "It's been made a hundred times."

"I've never even *heard* of it," said Joe. "And I've certainly never seen it. Have you?"

The writer had to admit that he had not, not in the original form.

"We'll make it," said Pasternak. "With Deanna. My God, it will be *fantastic!*"

They began to prepare it. Alas for them, Walt Disney decided to do it in animation, and in those days, no one tangled with Disney.

Joe Pasternak regretted it always and would frequently bring it up in conversation. Cinderella—the plain, unadulterated Cinderella—was a dream of his life that went unrealized.

The literary appreciation of the executive mind often gave me pause.

329

In 1937, along with millions of other Americans, I had a profound literary experience. A friend of mine who worked as an editor at The Viking Press in New York sent me an advance copy of *The Grapes of Wrath* by John Steinbeck. I read it through the night in a single sitting. I was moved, shaken, overwhelmed. I could think of nothing else for days.

At the end of that week, I was spending an evening at the home of Pandro Berman, the head of RKO.

"Pan," I said, "there's a book you must read. I don't consider myself a literary expert, but I'm willing to say that it is, without question, the greatest American novel I've ever read. I'm sure it will live forever."

"Send it to me," said Berman.

"I can't," I said. "I've loaned my copy to a friend."

"All right then," said Pan. "Write down the title and I'll get it." I did so. He glanced at it. "Oh," he said. *"The Grapes of Wrath.* Steinbeck. Sure, I've heard about that. I hear it's great." He crumpled the piece of paper I had given him and dropped it into an ashtray.

"Aren't you going to get it?" I asked.

"No," he replied, sadly. "And damn it, I wanted to *read* that book. From what I hear it's the kind of book I'd go for, so I *wanted* to read it and then—damn it—Twentieth *bought* it!"

Darryl Francis Zanuck, former head of Twentieth Century-Fox, is the very definition of the word executive. He was, and as far as I know, still is, a dynamo. A small man who thinks big. If there is such a thing as the Napoleonic complex, Zanuck possesses it in full measure.

Energy is the key to his progress and to his success. He has suffered many reverses, any *one* of which could have sunk a lesser man; but Zanuck, in addition to everything else, possesses resilience.

He came to California in the early 1920s, a young and ambitious writer. He wrote anything and everything. Articles, stories, plays, novels, and scripts for Rin-Tin-Tin. He worked his way into production and in 1931, at the age of twenty-nine, became head of production for Warner Brothers. This job lasted only two years. He was not meant to be an employee. He was meant to be a boss. With Joseph M. Schenck, he founded Twentieth Century Productions. Two years later, when it merged with Fox, he became vice-president in charge of production for Twentieth Century-Fox.

No one who ever ran a studio was as completely involved as Darryl F. Zanuck. No detail of any one of the many productions made at the studio escaped his notice. The purchase of stories, the development of treatments, the writing of the screenplay. Casting. Designing. Direction. Cutting. Scoring. Dubbing. Advertising and promotion. He had his hand in everything.

He has always had passionately loyal advocates and bitter detractors. Clearly, when a man works in contact with so many others, on so many different projects, there is going to be a fluctuation of efficiency.

I worked with him, or, rather, for him on several occasions, never with much joy. Still, I could appreciate the energy, the enthusiasm, and the driving force he represented.

I once tried to sell him an original screenplay. A comedy.

"I've read it," he said. "I like it. But I don't know much about comedy. Comedy's not what I do best. So you'll have to give me a couple, three days to let a few people around here read it who know about comedy. Because frankly, I don't. I want to tell you I've had strange experiences with comedy. I've read comedy scripts, been crazy about them, watched the rushes every day. Loved them. Taken the picture out and previewed it and laughed. And heard the audience laugh. Brought it back here to the studio. Recut it, fixed it, scored it, sent it out, and you know, in many cases—they've turned out to be my *worst successes!*"

Stories were told about his idiosyncrasies and eccentricities. He was an able polo player. Frequently, he would stride up and down his spacious office, swinging a polo mallet as he talked, improvised, invented.

A member of his staff was the former flyweight champion of

the world, Fidel La Barba. He was called a production assistant, but in fact acted mainly as Zanuck's trainer. He would exercise with Zanuck, box with him, give him rubdowns, and generally help keep Zanuck in shape. He would also sit in on production meetings.

One evening, as Zanuck was striding up and down the office, swinging his polo mallet, Fidel took an olive from a plate on the buffet table (late-conference food had been brought in), and tossed it in Zanuck's direction. Zanuck swung his mallet, caught the olive neatly. It went sailing across the room. Fidel repeated the action, time and time again. The other conferees found it necessary to duck, to shield themselves, and to be alert at every moment as the olives went careening around the room, ricocheting off the walls.

A friend dropped into Fidel La Barba's office one morning and was surprised to find him packing his things.

"I'm through," said La Barba.

"What happened?" asked his friend.

"I struck him out," said La Barba.

Darryl Zanuck bought an original screenplay from me, called *Come What May*. It had to do with a meeting at the New York Foundling Hospital, eighty or ninety years ago, in which there are three sets of applicants, each of whom wants to adopt a baby girl. The film was to consist of a projection of what her life might be in each of the cases. In one, she dies in her early twenties. In the second, she lives to be a great old lady. In the third she ends badly in middle age.

Before buying the screenplay, Zanuck insisted I come to California to confer with him, if only for an hour. He had one element he thought the story needed. If I agreed, he would buy it at a handsome figure. If I did not agree, he did not want the story and no harm done. I went out. He told me his idea. I have hardly ever, in a long working life, been more stunned. It was the one idea that, in my view, ruined the story completely.

"My idea is this," he said. "I like what you've done. It's got a lot of heart and she's a great character. Hell, she's *three* great characters! Isn't she? And that's the whole point. I get your drift. You're talking about environment being what molds characters, and I agree with all that. You're right. And it's really a sensational script. The only thing is you've got three stories and two of the endings are downbeat. That's no good. The thing I want you to do is give me three happy endings. I mean, you've been around the business long enough to know that that's what they want. You can't sell a picture with a downbeat ending, with an unhappy finish. It's not worth a damn. There's never been a hit picture with a downbeat ending. So here you have a terrific opportunity. Because you've got not only *one* story. You've got *three* stories. So instead of *one* happy ending, you've got a chance to have *three* happy endings! It makes the whole thing better and it doesn't change anything, really. It's still the same baby who grows up to be three different people. So what's the difference?"

I stared at him. I could scarcely believe what I was hearing. I was even more stunned and surprised to hear myself say, "Terrific, Darryl. I'll do it."

"Great," he said, "Listen, I'll work it out with Lastfogel and we'll be in touch. But start thinking about it, will you? I've got to go see the dailies. Thanks for coming up."

"Not at all," I said.

He left the office. I was still sitting there, alone, trying to understand the moment. I had an excuse for my reprehensible behavior. I was broke. I needed the money to fulfill pressing obligations. I tried to convince myself that I had done the practical thing.

I returned to New York and directed a play. When it failed, I returned to Hollywood and wrote the three happy endings. George Cukor was assigned to direct, and Susan Hayward was cast to play the girl. Everything was going forward to Zanuck's satisfaction and to my dismay. I could see nothing but disaster ahead. Four days before the first day of shooting, the production was canceled because the board of directors in New York failed to approve the budget, and neither Zanuck nor Cukor, nor the production department could see any way of making the picture much more cheaply.

I felt rescued.

Three years later, Zanuck was riding high, having produced a string of commercial successes.

He sent for me and said, "Listen. We're going to make that sensational picture of yours now. What was the name of it?"

"Come What May," I said.

"Well, we'll change that. That's not a good title. Too soft. But we'll get a title. Don't worry about it. And listen. I really have got a sensational idea for that picture. I went over it a few nights ago. I read it over fast, just to refresh my memory, and I want to tell you I've got an idea for it that's perfect. In a way, I'm glad those clowns wouldn't let us do it last year."

"It was *three* years ago," I said.

"Was it? Well, whenever. But I've got them by the balls now, and they're going to do things *my* way. I'm getting a lot of my own back right now. This is one of them. Sons of bitches. Pulling the picture out from under us at the last minute. That was a terrible thing to do. I felt so bad for you."

"Yes," I said.

"But we're going to make it now, boy. We're going to make it great."

"What's your idea?" I asked, and thought that since he had already suggested the worst possible one, I had no fear. Nothing could be worse than that notion of the three happy endings. I was wrong. His new idea topped even that.

"We're going to make it," he said, "with three *different* girls!"

"What do you mean?" I said. "How could that be?"

"Three stars," he said. "See, the way things are going now, there's not one big star, girl star, who could carry the picture. No matter who she is. But two stars, or three stars, that's always box office. So we'll get the three best girls we can snow, and see, in each story, she grows up to be a different girl. A different actress. Is that great?"

I was not broke this time and said, "Darryl, that's the worst bloody idea anybody could *possibly* think of for this picture, and I hope you're kidding me. I hope this is some kind of a monumental tease."

"What are you talking about, kidding?" he said. "I've got no sense of humor. You know that."

"Darryl," I said. "You own this material. That means you can do any damn thing you want with it. But I couldn't, in good faith, even be around to see it murdered. And while we're at it, let me tell you that those three happy endings are lousy, too. There's only one way to do this picture, and that's to do it pretty much the way I wrote it. That's my opinion."

He looked at me and shook his head sadly. "Jesus Christ," he said, "I thought you were different. But you're not. You're just a *writer!*"

Sam Spiegel, the celebrated independent producer, was known for a time as S. P. Eagle. It was hard for those of us who had known him as Sam Spiegel to make the adjustment. Even now, I wonder why. It should have been easy. In temperament, mien, method, and looks he certainly resembled a predatory bird.

The wags went to work almost at once, signing letters and scripts K. U. Rnitz, or K. R. Asna, and addressing letters to Z. A. Nuck, Twentieth Century-Fox Studios, T. Racy, M-G-M Studios—and so on.

Prior to "Eagle" or "Spiegel," he had been known as "Joe Schenck's man," the one who produced and directed the finest New Year's Eve parties ever known in Beverly Hills. Other than his work on this annual spectacular, his duties and functions were not clear. Was he an assistant? An associate? A major-domo? A mastermind? Or simply a hanger-on? Joseph M. Schenck was a power, the head of Twentieth Century-Fox, and as such had a large and active staff surrounding him. He was a large and colorful man who came to the United States in 1900 at the age of twenty-two, became a pharmacist, then a fairground operator, built Palisades Amusement Park across the Hudson from New York City, became chairman of United Artists and organized its national chain of theatres, married Norma Talmadge, headed Twentieth Century Productions, merged it with Fox Films and in later life took a French lesson every day.

The fact that his younger brother, Nicholas, was head of M-G-M gave him reserve power which he did not hesitate to use when needed. Example: getting Spencer Tracy to star in *Stanley and Livingstone* by means of an unprecedented loan-out.

The daily complexities of his professional and personal life required much assistance. Thus there were many associates, and for a time Sam Spiegel was one of them. A large, florid, charming Pole, Spiegel was colorful in his own right. He was never less than perfectly dressed and groomed, was an accomplished linguist, and suggested a mysterious background.

A year or so after his arrival in Hollywood, he co-produced *Tales of Manhattan*—a complex episodic film directed by Julien Duvivier. Like most such grab-bag works, it was uneven —a Mulligan stew of good and bad, with a few delicious bits. No matter. Eagle/Spiegel had achieved identity. He was now a producer. Still, three years were to pass before his next film, *The Stranger*. When it failed he followed it with a plural title, *We Were Strangers*. More jokes. Further speculation. Three years more and then—*The African Queen*. The C. S. Forester novel had been around, admired, and considered by many for some time, but was generally thought to be too difficult to film. By 1950, back-lot production was proving to be increasingly unacceptable to the new, informed audience and *The African Queen* presented seemingly insurmountable location problems. Hollywood had not forgotten the hell of *Trader Horn*.

Sam Spiegel, confidently readopting his name, was undeterred.

He engaged James Agee (virtually unknown to Hollywood) to write the screenplay, John Huston to direct, and negotiated brilliant percentage deals with both Humphrey Bogart and

Katharine Hepburn in order to facilitate financing. He knew that an exceptional cameraman was required and hired Jack Cardiff.

The result, after a year of near-killing work on the part of all concerned, has a permanent place in the library of outstanding films. Spiegel's reputation was made. All at once he was a power himself, with assistants and associates of his own.

He did not rush into his next production, in an attempt to cash in. What he now wanted was to top *The African Queen.*

To the industry's astonishment, he did precisely that three years later with *On the Waterfront.*

This time, he dealt with one of the riskiest of ventures—an original screenplay. It means beginning from scratch with nothing pretested or presold. Budd Schulberg provided the electrifying screenplay, Elia Kazan, at the peak of his considerable powers, directed, and Marlon Brando proved to be a continuing revelation. The picture was a triumph.

The jokes and cracks faded into silence as Sam Spiegel went on to produce *The Bridge on the River Kwai* and *Lawrence of Arabia.*

To illuminate the idea of Sam Spiegel's style—the class, the panache, the approach that have made him the superior figure he is, I offer the following:

1955. I am directing the original production of *The Diary of Anne Frank.* We are trying out in Philadelphia, at the Walnut Street Theatre.

All is going well at last, but it has been an extremely difficult production to mount, mainly because of financing. Kermit Bloomgarden, the producer of the play, had found his usual backers unwilling to risk capital on what they thought a depressing subject. Who would go to see it? Some who admired the play did not admire it enough to invest money in it.

As one put it, "Look, there's a difference between an investment and a contribution. If Kermit asks me for a contribution —well, maybe. That's different. I'll think about it. But an investment? What kind of investment is *that*?"

A few days before rehearsals were to begin, prospects were bleak. And then—Doris Vidor came through. The play would go on. Hallelujah.

Mrs. Vidor was the daughter of Harry Warner of Warner Brothers. She had been married to Mervyn LeRoy and was now the wife of Charles Vidor. She had long expressed her interest in the theatre in the most charming, tangible way—by putting money into it. She always backed what she liked or admired or thought worthy. Moneymaking was secondary, even tertiary.

Fortunately, she responded to *The Diary of Anne Frank,* or it might not have gone on at all.

The morning after the opening, she phoned me.

"How did it go?" she asked.

"I wish you'd been here," I said. "Everything worked. Maybe it'll never work again, but it worked last night."

"I'm thrilled."

"Doris, I can hardly believe it myself. By the way, I finally got Pepi Schildkraut to shave his head. It made all the difference. Turned him from an actor into a person."

"Great."

"Anyway, it was the worst possible night. Hot as a son of a bitch and no air-conditioning in the theatre. So they had to open all the doors to keep the audience from suffocating. And the street noises. Trolley cars go right by. People walking by stopped and watched for a while. It was—I mean could have been—a nightmare. But that thing on the stage—those people, characters—the situation, the story—God damn. It held them like hypnosis."

"And it's not depressing? Not that I ever thought it would be."

"Not a bit. It's exalting, for Christ's sake. Listen. Come down and see it. Come soon."

"No. I'll wait for New York. I get nervous at tryouts."

"Nervous is good for you," I urged.

"No. Packing and hotels and all."

"Come to a matinee. Come Wednesday. Take a morning train. We'll have lunch here at the Barclay. See the matinee, have a drink, and you'll be back in New York in time for dinner."

"I'll have to be," she said, weakening. "I'm having dinner with Sam Spiegel."

"Bring him down," I suggested. "Then you're sure."

"Well," she said. "I'll ask him. If he can make it, all right, I will."

"You owe it to yourself," I said. "A lot of this show is yours. It might not have got on without you."

"Don't be silly," she said. "Anyway, I'll let you know."

An hour later, Spiegel called me.

"I know what tryouts are," he said, "and I'm not coming unless I hear from you personally that you don't mind."

Class, I thought.

"Sam, you're more than welcome. In fact, I'd like your eye."

"I'll bring it," he said.

Lunch was joyful. The play was going better with each performance. The small cuts were improving the pace. The cast was gaining confidence, playing it like a hit. The audiences were responding more and more as they were meant to.

The performance was to begin at 2:40 P.M. At 2:00, I called for the check.

"What's the rush?" asked Sam.

"Well, you know, at this hour—taxis—"

"What taxis?" he asked, astonished. "We have a car."

"We have?"

"The car we drove down in. How else?"

"Fine, but I'll get the check anyway."

"It's all done," said Sam. "Let's go."

My protests were useless. Sam Spiegel was in charge.

In the lobby, Doris began looking about.

"Where's the ladies' room?" she asked. "Do you know? I won't be a minute."

"It's right there past the elevator," I said. "You turn—"

"Just a moment," said Sam. "What do you think you're doing?"

"Me?" I asked.

"Wait here," he commanded Doris.

He stepped over to the reception desk.

"I'm Sam Spiegel," he said. "Have you got a nice suite available?"

"For how long, Mr. Spiegel?"

"Just for today," said Sam.

"Let me see. Yes, we have 19D available, facing the Square. The rate on that is—"

"Please," said Sam, wincing. "Just give me the key."

As Sam signed the register, the clerk asked, "Can I have a boy show you up?"

"The key," said Sam.

The key passed from the clerk to Sam.

As he put Doris into the elevator he said, "Nineteen" to the operator, handed him the key, and added, "Open the door for Mrs. Vidor." Then, to Doris, "We'll be on the sidewalk."

Outside, we strolled down the street. Sam was delighted to find the Curtis Institute of Music on the corner.

"Zimbalist," he said. "What a virtuoso! And now a teacher. Teachers and doctors. They are the best in the world."

We returned to the Barclay. Doris came down. We went to the theatre.

I found it hard to concentrate on the performance. I kept thinking of the event back at the hotel. What had it cost? Perhaps $50 or $60. But that was not the point. What was? The notion. Who but a grandiose, highly imaginative man would have so much as thought of such an idea?

I began to understand something more about the phenomenon of men like Sam Spiegel who think in different categories, larger than life.

21

Although Samuel Goldwyn clung to his belief that it was the material, the subject matter, the story, that mattered most, he was equally interested in supporting the telling in every possible way. To that end, his art department was always the best in the business.

So what? the detractors say. So he was buying taste. Anybody with dough can do that.

There were many with money in Hollywood, but Goldwyn knew best how to use it. Yes, anyone *could* have hired Chanel, but Goldwyn *did*.

A young songwriter was once putting down Irving Berlin as overrated.

"Hell," he said. " 'All alone, By the telephone—' what's *that*? *Anybody* could write *that*."

"Yes," said Oscar Hammerstein, "anybody *could*, but Irving *did*."

Groucho Marx claims that for many years every time he ran into Samuel Goldwyn anywhere, Goldwyn would look at him, sometimes shake his hand, and invariably inquire with great solicitude, "How's Harpo?"

"Fine," Groucho would say, and go on to other things. A few weeks later (or a month, or a year) they would meet again somewhere; in New York, Chicago, London, or Paris.

Again Goldwyn would ask, "How's Harpo?"

This went on for years. Groucho got fed up.

The next time they met and Goldwyn asked, "How's Harpo?" Groucho said, "Listen, Sam, every time we meet— every time for *years*—you always ask, 'How's Harpo?' You never ask me anything else, and to tell you the truth, I'm getting goddam sick and tired of it. Why don't you ever ask me how *I* am?"

"How are you?" Goldwyn asked.

"I'm fine," said Groucho.

"And how's Harpo?" asked Goldwyn.

Did Goldwyn make Goldwynisms famous or was it the other way about?

A rich and famous and powerful executive who speaks convoluted, accented English is certainly an entertaining character. Credit (or blame) for the creation of this character has been variously attributed.

Without doubt Sam Goldwyn often expressed himself colorfully, oddly. The more comical remarks were repeated and it soon became apparent to someone—some say it was Pete Smith, then Goldwyn's press agent—that there was mileage in this. He collected the funniest of the cracks and began planting them with columnists. He considered that it was his job to publicize the name of Samuel Goldwyn.

When he ran out of reported remarks, he began to invent them. Why not? Malapropisms are easy.

Goldwyn was, at first, happy to be getting all this attention. In the early part of a career it is pleasing to see one's name in print or hear it mentioned. The greatest publicist of them all, Phineas T. Barnum, once said, "I don't care *what* they say about me as long as they spell my name right."

Later on, when some of the more idiotic cracks began to be pinned on him, Goldwyn became troubled. He told his publicity people to cut it out. It was too late. The idea had boomeranged. In the way of joke telling and repeated wit, for a time every such crack was tagged with Goldwyn's name. It generally got a better laugh.

There have been thousands, far too many for Goldwyn to have created personally. Some of us who knew him have become expert in detecting the genuine, the phony, and the professionally created.

"Goldwynisms!" Goldwyn said to me one day in a temper. "Don't talk to me about Goldwynisms, f'Chrissake. You want to hear some Goldwynisms go talk to Jesse Lasky!"

There it was. A pure Goldwynism, created as he was attempting to deny the existence of such a thing.

There are some I can vouch for:

One evening, after dinner at his house, I admired a new painting on his wall.

"Where did you get this beautiful new Picasso?" I asked.

Goldwyn peered at it and said, "I don't remember. In Paris. Somewhere over there on the Left Wing."

Arthur Hornblow, Jr., came to work for Goldwyn. Goldwyn persisted in calling him "Hornbloom." Hornblow corrected him several times throughout the first few months of their association.

When Goldwyn called him "Hornbloom" again, Arthur said, "Not Hornbloom. *Hornblow.* Not Bloom. Blow. Here, look." He picked up a sheet of paper, printed his name in large letters and handed it to Goldwyn.

"Show me later," said Goldwyn, waving it away.

Names were apparently always difficult for Goldwyn. Danny Kaye swears that for the first three years of his Goldwyn contract, Goldwyn called him "Eddie." It may have been that Goldwyn associated him with Eddie Cantor who had previously been Goldwyn's male musical star.

When Goldwyn was trying to get Louis Bromfield to do a picture for him, he said, "You should work in pictures, Louis. Sure, you're a great novelist but how many people have heard of you? If you write two or three successful pictures, the name of Bloomfield will be known all over the world!"

It was once reported that Goldwyn said to Anita Loos, "Anita, you've got to cohabit with the director more." (Obviously a phony.)

Compare that with an authentic one. Playing bridge, he chides his partner, Constance Bennett, for overbidding.
"But how did I know you had nothing?" she protests.
"Didn't you hear me keeping still?" asks Goldwyn.

Harpo Marx told of playing golf with Goldwyn.
Just before he putted, Harpo kicked a stone out of the ball's path.
Goldwyn (shouting): "You can't do that! It's not allowed."
Harpo: "But *you* just did. I *saw* you."
Goldwyn: "But didn't you hear my caddy say I *shouldn't?*"

I suspect that Goldwyn's most widely repeated remark— "Gentlemen, include me out"—is an invention, as is, "We can get all the Indians we need at the reservoir."
Also: "He worked his way up from nothing, that kid. In fact, he was born in an orphan asylum." (This sounds more like Pete Smith than Goldwyn.)
Or: "I had this terrible thing happen at the track. My horse was winning and then his caddy fell off."
Or: "I've been laid up with intentional flu."
Or: "He treats me like the dirt under my feet."
Or: "I would be sticking my head in a moose."
Or: "Somebody should do a picture about the Russian Secret Police. You know, the GOP."
Or: A director tells Goldwyn that a story he is considering is too caustic. Goldwyn: "The hell with the cost. If it's a good picture we'll make it."
Don't believe a word of these.

Goldwyn himself categorically denied ever having said, "I

can answer you in two words. Im possible."

I was later to learn from Charlie Chaplin that Goldwyn's denial was justified.

"It was an old gag from a sketch they used to do in the halls," he said, "and I thought it would be fun to pin it on Sam."

At M-G-M one morning, Arthur Freed said to me about a screenplay, "I read part of it all the way through."

Two days later, someone told it to me as a Goldwynism.

Goldwyn walking in a garden.
"What's that?"
The gardener: "A sundial."
Goldwyn: "What's it for?"
The gardener: "It tells time by the sun."
Goldwyn: "My God, what'll they think of next?"
Does *anyone* believe that?

It is time for a real one. During a conference on *The Goldwyn Follies,* we were discussing possible choreographers. Martha Graham is suggested.

"I think I've heard of her," he says, "but just what kind of dancing does she do?"

"Well, you know. Modern dancing."

"No, no," said Goldwyn. "I don't want it."

"Why not?"

Goldwyn: "Because. Modern dancing is so *old-fashioned!*"

At the time, he was dead right.

There is at least one I know is false because I invented it myself at the request of Goldwyn's press agent.

"Anything that man says you've got to take with a dose of salts."

I would like to think that Goldwyn said, "A verbal agreement isn't worth the paper it's written on." I doubt that he did.

Lillian Hellman invented: "Anybody who goes to a psychiatrist ought to have his head examined."

He *did* say, one bright morning at the beach, "What a wonderful day to spend Sunday!"

Goldwyn, ever the seductive wooer, was working on Preston Sturges. "Will you give me your word of honor," he asked, "that you will come over here to me when you finish your Paramount picture?"

"No," said Sturges. "I won't."

"All right," said Goldwyn. "If you won't give me your word of honor, will you give me your *promise*?"

After a game of golf, he and Danny Kaye are dressing in the locker room.

Goldwyn notices Danny's drawers, moves to them, examines them, admires them.

"They're beautiful" he says. "Where did you get them?"

"At Jerry Rothschild's."

"I'm going to get some," said Goldwyn. "Call me up tomorrow morning and remind me."

No matter how oddly he expressed himself, his intention was always clear, although it sometimes took an awkward minute to get the full meaning.

Irving Thalberg and Norma Shearer invited the Goldwyns to a preview of *The Barretts of Wimpole Street*. A party of ten drove to Glendale, had dinner, and went on to the theatre.

The Barretts of Wimpole Street was one of M-G-M's most ambitious productions that year. It co-starred Miss Shearer, Charles Laughton, and Fredric March. It had been personally produced by Thalberg and directed by Sidney Franklin.

The Goldwyns sat directly behind the Thalbergs during the screening. When it ended, there was a great rush toward the spot. Everyone connected with Metro was anxious to express acclaim. Miss Shearer was, after all, the boss's wife. She was praised and extolled until the whole party was knee-deep in compliments.

At this point, Goldwyn leaned over, touched her shoulder, and topped them all.

"Norma," he said. "I swear to God, the way you play that part—f'Chrissake—you should never make another picture!"

Whereupon he kissed her and left.

Billy Wilder has an account of a Goldwyn adventure:

"It was when Charlie and I were doing *Ball of Fire* for him. Gary Cooper, Stanwyck—wasn't she a dream? We came into his office one morning for a meeting. He'd sent for us but when we got there he was sitting around with that great cutter Danny Mandel, and a few other guys, and they were working on the picture Sam had previewed the night before. He looked up when we walked in and kind of scowled the way he did as if to say, 'What the hell do *you* want?' But we'd gotten used to his cuckoo ways by then so we just walked in and sat down. All of a sudden he seemed to remember we were connected with a different picture and he smiled and he said, 'Gentlemen, I must tell you this. I know how happy you'll be. This preview I had last night? You know about it. I told you. I was going to take the picture out? Well, this preview was the *greatest*—I've been in this business *forty years*—and this preview last night—I've made over a hundred pictures—and this preview last night— let me tell you I've seen *plenty* of previews, not only my own but *other* people's previews. Thousands. But this preview last night—I want to tell you—was the *greatest,* the *greatest* preview I was ever at. I want to tell you when that picture was over last night—that whole audience stood up—' With this," Billy continued, "he stood up himself to make it more clear, and he said, 'That whole audience stood up and they cheered— listen to me—for *thirty minutes!*' Charlie and I looked at each other. I mean the whole idea was so ridiculous. If an audience cheers for a *minute,* it makes history. Goldwyn must've suspected that we didn't believe him so he came out from behind his desk and he went on. 'Did you hear what I said? They cheered for *thirty minutes*. Without stopping.' Then he turned to Danny Mandel and he said, 'Isn't that something?' And Danny said, 'I was *there,* Mr. Goldwyn.'

" 'We can *fix* it!' Goldwyn yelled."

I was surprised when I found that Goldwyn possessed the rare and valuable gift of laughing at himself.

"You know what I did last week?" he once asked me. "In Chicago? I did something funny. It'll make you laugh. F'Chrissake, it made *me* laugh. Let me tell you what I did. I went into my room in my hotel. The Ambassador East. I was in a hurry and I picked up the phone and I said to the operator, 'Get me my office.' And she said, 'What?' And I said, 'What do you mean, what? Get me my office, God damn it!' And she said, 'Who is this?' So I said, 'Who is this? This is Samuel Goldwyn.' So she said, 'I never heard of you. Where's your office?' 'In California,' I said. 'In Hollywood. You never heard of me? Samuel Goldwyn?' 'No,' she said. 'What's your number out there?' And I said, 'I don't know. Look it up!' And she said to me, 'You must be crazy,' and she hung up."

He laughed until his pink face turned red.

"**C**an I see you a minute? A *half* a minute, Grouch?"
Groucho Marx put down his cards (he didn't have anything anyway), picked up his cigar, and got up from the table.

There were few who could achieve this instant response. Harry Ruby was one of them. He was perhaps Groucho's oldest friend. With Bert Kalmar, he had written some of Groucho's most memorable material:

CHORUS
Three Cheers for Captain Spalding!
The African Explorer!

GROUCHO
Did someone call me Schnorrer?

CHORUS
"Hooray! Hooray! Hooray!

As well as the immortal:

Show me a rose
And I'll show you a girl named Sam.
Show me a rose
Or leave me alone!

Groucho followed Harry out onto a secluded terrace of the Hillcrest Country Club.

Harry looked to his right, his left, then over his shoulder.

"Get goin'," said Groucho, in his celebrated nasal monotone. "You're beginning to look like George M. Cohan in *The Tavern.*"

Harry stepped closer to Groucho.

"Shall we dance?" asked Groucho. He took Harry into his arms and began a waltz.

Harry disengaged himself roughly and said, "Cut the comedy, Grouch, this is serious."

"What is?"

"I'm in a situation, and you've got to do me a favor."

"Sure, Harry, if I can."

"Look, it's a quarter to twelve. At three o'clock, I've got two girls coming to the bungalow."

(The bungalow was Harry's "studio" in South Beverly Hills; ostensibly a workplace, actually an assignation point.)

Groucho regarded him. "You're sure it isn't three girls at two o'clock?"

"I mean it, Grouch. It was a misunderstanding and now I can't get out of it without a whole lot of trouble. What am I going to do with two girls?"

"Search me," replied Groucho. "What do you *usually* do with them?"

"You don't want to be even a little serious, huh? Not even for a second, huh? The great Russian actor—Neveroff!"

"Harry, what do you want from me? Let me go back to the game, will you? I'm a loser."

"The hell with that game!" shouted Harry. "I'm offering you a better game. A matinee. A foursome."

"Harry, let me ask you something. Do you know how old I am?"

"Not exactly, no." Groucho looked right, left, and behind him, in imitation of Harry's earlier moves. Then he said softly, "Fifty-nine."

"So what? I'm two years older."

"Three."

"Two."

"Three!"

"Two!"

"Four."

"Three."

"All right."

"So?"

"So I'm through, Harry. I'm finished with that foolishness. You know that's hard to say? Finishedwiththatfoolishness? No, it isn't. Not so hard."

"You should be at your peak," said Harry.

"That's about all I *can* do," said Groucho, "is peek. Don't get me wrong, Harry. I'm not bitter. I've had my share, nice while it lasted. Now I'm interested in other things. Books, and so on."

Harry looked at him with compassion and said, "Listen, my old friend, you're just like *I* was about two and a half years ago. Then, thank God, my doctor sent me to this doctor."

"A doctor's doctor?"

"A specialist."

"In what?" asked Groucho.

"In power. He gave me this shot, and the same day—*the same day,* mind you—"

"Yes?"

"I *functioned.* And, since then, I take a shot a week, sometimes two, and I live. And I want *you* to live too, Grouch. Hear me out. This is my plan. Let me call the doctor, this doctor. I'll make an appointment. Then we'll have a bite, you and me, and we'll drive down. He'll give you the shot. And three o'clock, you'll see."

"Harry, for God's sake, you're embarrassing me."

But Harry Ruby, a persistent man, persisted. He continued to talk, to sell. In time he had hypnotized Groucho and had him in his car, speeding down Wilshire Boulevard to the Wilshire Medical Building.

In the parking lot, Groucho hesitated again. But Harry, artfully describing the joys that lay immediately ahead, led him into the building and propelled him into the big elevator, peopled with wheel-chair cases, the very old, babes in arms, bandaged heads, and one trembling victim of Parkinson's disease.

Harry, troubled that Groucho might bolt at any moment, held on to his arm tightly. When the elevator was full, the operator closed the doors and the gate and called out, "Floors, please. Speak up."

"I can't get a hard-on!" shouted Groucho. "What floor is that?"

Harry Ruby swears that the elevator went up fourteen floors without stopping, then came down, one floor at a time, bouncing.

Hollywood was a raunchy, hip, swinging community. Can it be that its wild private life was a revolt against its overcensored public life?

American whorehouses are not, by and large, as interesting as the French, Japanese, or Scandinavian varieties. However, I found one in Hollywood when I went there to live and work that was *more* than interesting. It was, in fact, enthralling. It contained elements of the best and the worst of Hollywood—glamour, vulgarity; aesthetics, commercialism; originality, imitation; heady eroticism, covert pornography; art, industry; industry, art. It had charm, wit, color, imagination, talent, a sense of professionalism, and offered—above all—Stars.

Cut the word "whorehouse," an unsatisfactory label for what it is meant to describe. It is a hollow word, in any case, and fails to serve its purpose either descriptively or onomatopoetically. Is there another, a better word? Brothel? Worse. Bordello? No. Callhouse, hookshop, house of ill-repute, disorderly house (*disorderly*?), house of assignation, house of prostitution, bagnio, bawdyhouse, seraglio? No, none of these suggests any such establishment I have ever known, and certainly not that alluring oasis high in the Hollywood Hills.

My wife once brightly observed that the residential architecture of the movie capital is composed of a series of replicas of the finest homes in each of a thousand cities and towns.

"It stands to reason," she said. "When you make good, you want to live in a house exactly like the one that impressed you early in life. The best one in town: Dayton, Ohio. Or Providence. Or Prague. Look around. See what I mean?"

If this is true, then Mae's house was built by a Southerner who made good. It was a spacious Greek-revival structure with stately columns and wide porches and even a porte-cochere. A rolling, well-tended lawn in front; in back, a topiary garden.

Inside, there were a surprising number of rooms. I suspected, when I first entered the house, a considerable amount of alteration and remodeling.

Johnny Hyde introduced me to Mae and her pleasure palace during my first week in Wonderland. He and his nephew-assistant took me and Rita Johnson (another new client) to a preview of *The Awful Truth* at Pantages on Hollywood Boulevard.

The evening began with cocktails at the Beverly-Wilshire. From there we were driven in an agency limousine to The Brown Derby on Vine Street. Endless hellos and wavings and table-hoppings went on as I ate what had been ordered for me: enchiladas (my first), Cobb salad (finely chopped raw vegetables, designed to spare the bustling Hollywood crowd the time and trouble of mastication), draught beer, Cranshaw melon, and coffee.

At one point in the course of the frenetic activity, I found myself sitting and eating all alone. My agent had taken Rita across the room to present her to Darryl F. Zanuck. (Why not *me*?) His nephew had been summoned to a nearby booth by a single imperious gesture of Adolphe Menjou's head.

I looked around the room, feeling light-headed. Could it be the alcohol, to which I was then unaccustomed? Hardly. One martini and half a glass of beer could not produce the euphoria I was experiencing. No. The cause of my inebriation was the near-presence of all these film celebrities in the flesh. Barbara

Stanwyck. Gary Cooper, for God's sake! Jimmy Durante and Bing Crosby and Joan Crawford. I stared and stared. In similar circumstances I *still* stare.

Ernst Lubitsch once explained why. "You see a shadow up there on a screen, yes? It is black and white, maybe. And it is a head, yes?—maybe Garbo's?—sixty times as big as a real head, yes? All right. You believe it is something real but you don't. There *is* no black-and-white head sixty times bigger. But you believe it. You try. Because you want to. Then comes one day—in the street, in a restaurant, a theatre. You see that head. Real. Regular size. In color. So. The shadow has come to life. Unreal into real. The dream, true. So why shouldn't that be excitement, godammit? Yes?"

The Vine Street Brown Derby was the place for this sort of showcasing and it never disappointed me. Jimmy Cagney. Frank Capra ("I'd rather be Capra than God," I had once said. "If there *is* a Capra"). Jean Arthur. Look! Irene Dunne. Edward G. Robinson.

The nephew returned.

"Sorry," he said. "That Menjou! Jesus."

"Is he a client?" I asked.

"Not yet," the nephew replied, and bounced his eyebrows meaningfully.

"I'm glad you're back," I said. "I was beginning to feel like the guy in the Lifebuoy ad."

"Who?"

"You know. The one with the B.O."

The nephew, his mind on Menjou, did not get it, but laughed a fill-in laugh. Sensing correctly that I was miffed, he attempted to entertain me.

"Some of these booths," he said. "You've got to be careful as a son of a bitch."

"What do you mean?"

"I think this is one of them. Yuh. Watch this."

He scurried to the other side of the room, a distance of about a hundred feet, and slid into the booth opposite the one I was occupying. He waved to me, then turned to the wall and spoke.

"Can you hear me?" he said. "Can you hear me?"

I could, clearly. He went on. "That's why you've got to watch it in here. Good-by."

He returned.

"Well, I'll be damned," I said.

"It's some kind of a crazy acoustical thing. And boy! The things that've happened on account of it! Like there was this guy supposed to be up for V.P. in charge of production at Warner's? So what happened? He was sitting talking to J. L. Like here. Where *we* are. Then he went over to there—where *I* just was—and sat with his lawyer and started in to tell him what a jerk J. L. was and all that. So of course J. L. heard it all plain, but instead of blasting off, he didn't let on, didn't say a thing. That's how he is, J. L. But what he put that poor guy through! He just kept him on the string and negotiated and negotiated and kept changing and it went on for a year almost, and every time the guy agreed, J. L.'d make another change and finally he negotiated the poor son of a bitch into a nervous breakdown. He's out of the business, now, I think. The guy. And all on account of sitting in a wrong booth one night. The one right across over there."

I was fascinated.

The others returned. We finished dinner in a gulp and joined the sudden exodus. It was almost as though a cue had been given for everyone to leave.

We all streamed half a block to the theatre.

There again, myriad contacts—spoken and pantomimed.

At last, the film. A hit for everyone. Irene Dunne, Cary Grant, Leo McCarey.

Sidewalk talk. The limousine parade.

We are at Ciro's. Another drink. Scotch, this time. I dance with Rita, comforted by the touch of reality in the illusory razzle-dazzle of the evening.

We stay less than half an hour. I wonder why we came in the first place. I learn later that Ciro's after a preview is *de rigueur.*

We go to The Clover Club, a posh gambling house. Roulette, *chemin de fer,* blackjack.

Rita is given some chips. She plays and loses. I decline, explaining that I do not know how to play. The nephew loses.

It is getting late. Rita has an early interview. The nephew takes her home, sends the car back.

Johnny Hyde is a big winner at the roulette wheel. His delight is contagious. We drink some more. I am beginning to feel the effects.

Johnny Hyde had turned into my buddy.

He looked at his watch and said, "I don't think it's too late. Do you?"

"For what?"

"To go on up to Mae's. Come on. It's only like a quarter to twelve."

"What's Mae's?"

"You don't know Mae's?" he exclaimed, making me feel like a bumpkin.

"No."

"Oh, baby!" he said, and began to laugh. "Have *you* got something coming! This is one of those you-won't-believe-its. Nobody does. Not the first time. You mean to tell me you've never even *heard* of Mae's?"

"I've heard of it *now,*" I said. "But I still don't know what it is. A club?"

"A *club?*" He laughed again. "Well, yeah. I guess you could call it that. You sure in hell can't get in unless they *know* you. In fact, she doesn't go for drop-ins, not even the ones she knows, but once in a while I get away with it. I tell you what. Order us another round. I'll go take a leak and also give her a buzz." He started off, turned and came back. "Who's your favorite movie star? Female, I mean."

"Several," I said.

"Name *one,*" he insisted. "Come on. There's got to be *one* comes to mind."

"Barbara Stanwyck," I said.

"Right," he said. "Barbara Stanwyck. I'll see what I can do for you. I mean, what *Mae* can."

He moved off, giggling excitedly.

I ordered a whisky sour for him, plain Perrier for myself. Something told me I was going to need my wits about me in the hours to come. It was becoming difficult enough as it was to marshal my vagrant thoughts.

Should I decline and go home? Of course. That would be sensible. But this did not seem to be the night for sensible. What did he mean about Barbara Stanwyck? ("I'll see what I can do for you. I mean, what *Mae* can.") Was all this really happening? And if so, was it happening to *me*?

The waiter brought the order. As he served it, Fred Astaire came in with his beautiful wife and a young man who resembled him. (I learned later that this was Hermes Pan, his brilliant choreographer.) They sat at a nearby table. I watched them, agape. The impeccable Astaire was an idol. Since I was roughly his size and shape, I wanted to acquire the effortless tact of his dress, the grace of his movement, and his sophisticated air.

He glanced over at me and found me studying his shoes. I looked up, could not look away.

He nodded and said, "How are you?"

"You bet," I replied.

I tore my look away, picked up my Perrier, and wondered what the hell I had said that for.

From the corner of my eye, I saw Astaire lean toward his companions. A moment later, they laughed, all three. At me, I decided. At my dumb remark. Maybe at my stupid pre-tied bow tie? (I would certainly never wear it again!) At my Perrier?

Johnny returned, but stopped at Fred Astaire's table for a bit of backslapping, wife-kissing, and shoulder-rubbing. I prayed he would not introduce me. It would be, at this moment, mortifying. My prayer was answered.

Johnny rejoined me, took a sip of his drink, grinned, and said, "We're all set."

"You bet," I said. Was my needle stuck? Would I ever say anything else again?

"She wasn't sure about Barbara, though. She's going to try, though. But just in case—I mean in case not—who's your second favorite?"

"Greta Garbo," I said.

"Not a chance."

"Why not?" I asked, by now emboldened.

"Because she's not there, you cluck, that's why not. She never *has* been. Not so far as *I* know, anyway."

"Katharine Hepburn," I said.

"Come *on!*" he said, irritated and impatient.

"What's a matter?"

"Katharine Hepburn," he said as though pronouncing the name of a deity. "What're *you, nuts?*"

"You asked me favorites," I said stubbornly. "So I told you. So don't yap at me."

"Favorites, sure," he said loudly. Fred Astaire looked over. I touched Johnny's arm in an attempt to turn down his volume. I failed. "Favorites, for Chrissake. But *possibles.* Don't be unreasonable. *Jesus!"*

I became reasonable. We went on to Mae's. Winding up through the Hollywood Hills—up up up through the thinning, rarefied air—I wondered what awaited me at the top. Who? Barbara Stanwyck? Bette Davis? Carole Lombard?

I could hardly wait.

My buddy-agent-mentor-sponsor whistled all the way.

We drove through the impressive entrance gate, up a winding driveway, under the porte-cochere, and stopped.

"Nice place," I said.

"About an hour and a half, Eddie. Go get a bite if you want."

"Yes, sir," said Eddie, impassive.

The driver's extraordinary good looks suddenly troubled me, because they made me aware of my *lack* of good looks. Just before he drove off, he winked at me. Twice.

We stood before the imposing main door. Johnny rang the doorbell. I heard chimes sound from within. The door was opened by a stunning, coffee-colored maid, wearing a black uniform and a lace apron and cap.

"Good evening," she said.

"Good morning, Della," said Johnny. He laughed. She nodded politely, marking his attempted joke, but not responding.

Class, I thought.

"Miss West is in the library," she said. "Would you join her there, please?"

Miss West. Mae's! My head snapped around to Johnny on a delayed take. My obvious astonishment delighted him.

Miss West! What the hell *was* this? What was going on? Where *was* I? What *time* is it? What *year*?

As we moved through the ante-bellum atmosphere, my sense of disorientation was sharpened.

Greater astonishments lay ahead.

We moved into the formal, paneled library, its shelves replete with fine bindings.

My experienced theatre eye indicated to me that the room had been lighted by an expert. David Belasco himself could hardly have improved upon the soft glows and the strategically placed spills. It did not occur to me until much later that the entire establishment was arranged in half-light, and that this was essential to the success of the fantastic enterprise.

Near a gently burning flame in the fireplace, in a large armchair with a matching footstool, sat a vision of Mae West, wearing, I could have sworn, the gown she had worn five years earlier in the nightclub scene of *Night after Night* when the innocent ingenue, wide-eyed at the spectacle of Mae West's dripping jewels, exclaimed, "Goodness!" And Mae said, "Goodness . . . had *nothin'* tuh do with it!"

On a board before her, she was playing what appeared to be a complex form of solitaire. Beside her, on a small end table, stood the largest brandy snifter I had ever seen, about one-third full. Could she lift it?

Had I not been in wine, and overexcited; had the makeup been less skillful and the lights brighter, I suppose I would have seen at once that the woman in the chair was not actually Mae West, but a remarkable facsimile, a *pasticheuse.*

However, the surrounding mood was such that it was impossible not to play the game. The necessary suspension of disbelief was instantaneous. I was thrilled to be in the presence of —and about to be presented to—"Miss Mae West," the great Paramount star and, obviously, the Madam of this establishment.

"Hullo, 'Chollie,' " said her nose. "Glad t'see yuh. *Real* glad."

Johnny went to her, leaned over and, of all things, kissed her hand.

" 'Miss West,' " he said. "I'd like you to meet my friend 'John Smith.' "

I came forward.

"This is a great honor, 'Miss West,' " I said, sounding like someone else.

She offered her hand. I took it.

She squinted at me, and asked, "Y'wouldn' be, I s'pose, *'Captain* John Smith'?"

"No," I said. "I'm sorry. He was my great-great-grandfather."

"Mmm," she said. "I knew 'im well. He was great-great, all right."

So. It was going to be one of *those* nights. Trading toppers. I wished that I was less fatigued.

"What can I offer you genimen t'drink?" she asked.

"Scotch soda," said Johnny.

"Just soda," I said.

"Sorry," she said. "We don't happen t'have any of that."

"Water?"

"That neither."

"Nothing?"

"That's what we've got the *least* of, sonny." (Was she annoyed?) "Have a drink," she commanded.

"All right, 'Miss West.' Same as him."

"Fine. Call me 'Mae.' " She turned to the hovering Della. "Got that?"

"Yes, ma'am."

Della left.

"The first rule of the house," said "Mae," "is no lushes and no teetotalers. I don' know which is the worse."

"A lush teetotaler!" cried "Charlie."

"Y'got it!" purred "Mae."

Della was back (already?) with the drinks on a tray. She served "Charlie," then me.

"Mae" picked up her brandy glass—she *could* lift it!—and raised it.

"Your health 'n'strength, men."

We drank. The Scotch was superb. How could I find out what brand it was?

"I'm sorry, 'Chollie,' but 'Irene' isn't in tonight. She had to go to her preview."

"I know," he said. "We were there."

"How was it?" asked "Mae."

"Smash," said "Charlie."

"Great," I said.

She looked at me, critically, and inquired, "Y'mean great, or *Hollywood* great?"

"Well," I said, deflated, "*you* know."

"Sure," she said. "I don' mean t'be a pain about it—but I'm a writer, don't y'know, and words are important t'me. I write all my own stuff. That's why it's so good."

Was this a whorehouse I was in, I wondered? As I was wondering, "Alice Faye" came into the room.

I had unaccountably finished my drink and been served another. This time I was not so sure it was *not* Alice Faye.

"Hi, 'Alice,' " said "Charlie."

"Hello, sugar," she said.

They kissed, lightly and politely.

"Mae" spoke. "This is 'Mr. Smith,' 'Alice.' 'Miss Faye,' 'Mr. Smith.' "

"How do you do?" she said.

"How do you do," I echoed.

We touched hands.

I said, "I'm really delighted to meet you, 'Miss Faye.' I saw some stuff the other night on *Alexander's Ragtime Band*. The cutter's a friend of mine. You were marvelous. Better than ever."

"Thank you," she said demurely. "That 'Blue Skies.' Isn't that some *wonderful* song?"

"Wonderful," I said.

I was now living an inch or two off the ground and the entrance of "Barbara Stanwyck" did not reduce my elevation.

Greetings. Another introduction. Another drink.

We are in the long, impressive living room. A grand piano at one end. A pianist who, in the circumstances, looks to me like Teddy Wilson.

"Alice" sings. "Night and Day" from *The Gay Divorce*.

I am alone in the room with "Barbara." We talk of the theatre, of her hit in the play *Burlesque* with Hal Skelly. I did not see it, but pretend that I did and hope she does not suspect I am lying.

Later, in her room, I study the stills all around. She is with Neil Hamilton in *The Bitter Tea of General Yen,* with John Boles in *Stella Dallas,* with Preston Foster in *The Plough and the Stars,* and alone in *So Big,* the Warner movie in which she first captivated me.

The five of us are in the library again. Elegant little sandwiches and champagne. Tender goodnights. Promises to meet soon.

Eddie is waiting in the driveway with the car. "Charlie" or Johnny or whatever the hell his name is talks all the way home. I do not listen. I am fully occupied in digesting the experience.

At the very last moment, I remember to say, "Thank you."

I never became a regular at "Mae's." The fees were far beyond my means. But from time to time, "Charlie"/Johnny would take me up there, and I found that there were others who were acquainted with "Mae" and with "Mae's."

More often than not, I went along only as a nonparticipating hanger-on. "Mae" and the girls did not seem to mind. I was young and eager to please, and full of conversation.

The girls. In addition to "Barbara Stanwyck" and "Alice Faye," I met "Irene Dunne," "Joan Crawford," "Janet Gaynor," "Claudette Colbert" (speaking beautiful French), "Carole Lombard," "Marlene Dietrich," "Luise Rainer," "Myrna Loy," and "Ginger Rogers." But *never,* as had been earlier indicated, "Greta Garbo" or "Katharine Hepburn."

There were, needless to say, cast changes from time to time. Stars faded and fell away. New stars appeared. Novas. A stage star, say Margaret Sullavan, would come out, make a success and settle down. Before long, "she" could be seen at "Mae's."

I came to know a good deal about "Mae's" unique institution as the months went by. The large house contained fourteen suites. There were four maids. The excellent food was prepared by Marcel, a French chef, assisted by his Dutch wife. The pianist played on weekends only. The basement contained the makeup, hairdressing, and wardrobe departments.

The wardrobe mistress turned out to be a dear Jewish lady from the Boyle Heights section, the mother of an assistant director who was, later, to work with me. She had spent years in the wardrobe departments of Metro, and Twentieth, as well as Western Costume, and had many valuable contacts. Often she would buy clothes from the studios, then remodel them to fit the girls at "Mae's."

On other occasions, she would watch current films with a sketch pad on her lap and draw what she saw. Her reproductions of the work of Adrian, Orry-Kelly, Irene, Howard Greer, and other leaders of the Hollywood fashion world were excellent. It was not uncommon to see a dress on Myrna Loy in one of the *Thin Man* pictures and later the same night, see it on "Myrna Loy" at "Mae's."

Two beautiful young men—a couple—were, respectively, the house hairdresser and makeup man. They quarreled often and acrimoniously, but did superlative work. It was this team that was mainly responsible for the amazingly accurate likenesses upstairs.

"Mae" had, in the manner of the Hollywood upper crust, a projection room. Here were shown old films (by request), previews ("Mae's" contacts were solid), and often break-up reels and tests.

One of these was Paulette Goddard's test for *Gone with the Wind*. "Paulette" arranged the screening. The girls, along with the rest of us, were most impressed. (Only "Margaret Sullavan" seemed, understandably, less than enthusiastic. After all, *"she"* was up for the part, too.) When, eventually, Vivien Leigh was signed to play Scarlett, the girls were stunned, said nothing, and "Paulette" was unavailable for a week.

This was not in itself unusual. There were frequent absences. The most common reply to the question, "Where's 'Myrna' tonight?" (Or "Claudette"? or "Jean"?) was: "Oh, she's on location." Often the information would jibe with items in *The Hollywood Reporter* or in *Daily Variety*—those morning harbingers (one green, one red) that started every movie person's day.

The "trades," as they are known, were much in evidence at "Mae's." Her girls were trained to read them daily and carefully, in order that they might be able to converse convincingly with the clients.

And they did. The house was invariably filled with gossip, rumors, innuendoes, reports, inside info on movies or the people who made them, and on the homes some of them owned. A surprising amount of the information at "Mae's" was accurate.

There was the intriguing case of the husband of a Big Name who shall be nameless. He had to deal with a difficult marital problem, because Big Name was convinced that during those periods of time when she was shooting, she had to abstain absolutely from all sexual activity. She was not getting any younger, she pointed out, and those close-up lenses could be cruel—no matter how soft the focus or how kind the diffusion.

One Monday morning, following a splendidly wild Sunday night, she had overheard the cameraman, Joe Ruttenberg, mutter to his gaffer, "Jesus! I think the only way to shoot her today is through an Indian blanket!"

That did it.

She made her resolution of abstinence and held to it from then on. She was disciplined, as are all long-lasting stars, and although she loved her husband, she loved her career equally.

The trouble was that she was under contract to one of the major studios, which meant that she averaged about three pictures a year, each of which shot for approximately seven weeks. This meant that for some twenty-one weeks each year her husband was—so to speak—on his own.

He told me all this late one night in the bar at "Mae's," and added, "I'm telling you—I swear to God—if I hadn't wandered into this place one afternoon—Gene Fowler told me about it, but I thought he was giving me a heart-to-heart—you know how he is—full of pranks. Anyway, I dropped up and—God Almighty!—when 'she' walked in, I damn near keeled over. I mean, I thought it was *her*! And three martinis later, I *knew* it was. So my problem got solved. I mean to say, I'm not like some of these town tomcats around this town. I'm a one-woman man, and that's it. And as far as I'm concerned, I've never cheated on my wife, not once, not in eleven years. That's how I am."

That's how he was.

A single experience of my own was equally weird. I was directing *They Knew What They Wanted,* starring Carole Lombard and Charles Laughton.

I was a young Hollywood bachelor, and like everyone else who ever came into contact with Carole Lombard, I fell. The fact that she was married to Clark Gable did not seem to deter my fantasies. She was everything I had always wanted a girl to be: beautiful, funny, talented, imaginative, able, warm, dear, and no-nonsense.

I found myself touching her at every possible opportunity, and when those opportunities did not arise, I invented some. I was, to put it mildly, bedazzled by this golden girl—although I knew I was in a hopeless situation.

Then my brother married. His friends gave the customary prenuptial stag dinner. When it ended, part of the group, by prearrangement, repaired to "Mae's."

And in came "Carole." I took her aside and we talked for a long time. We discussed the stuff we had shot that day, and I explained what we were going to do on the following day. She *loved* my ideas. We panned Laughton. She told me she was thinking of leaving Clark. A clash of careers. I told her I thought she was doing the wise—the *only* thing. She asked me if I was hungry. I said yes. She suggested we have supper up in her suite. I told her I thought that was a great idea. The rest is a Glorious Technicolor, out-of-focus, slow-motion dream.

The next morning, I was the star of our little on-the-set ritual. Carole Lombard and Frank Fay and I had fallen into the habit of meeting in my trailer every morning right after the first shot for coffee and conversation. Our meetings soon developed a theme of sorts. We agreed that we would each tell—in precise, unsparing detail—what we had done the night before. Often, there was little to tell; more often, I suspected Frank of soaring invention; Carole and I usually played it straight.

I told of my visit to "Mae's," of my encounter with "Carole," leaving out nothing.

My account was punctuated by Carole screaming with laughter, "I'll die! I'll die. Wait till I tell Clark! Jesus, no, I better not. He'll *go* there! I'll die! I'll die!"

A friend from the East came to visit. He was a journalist, a columnist, and interested, of course, in Hollywood put-down material. He did not get it from me. I was, by then, a Hollywood patriot.

One night, at the Trocadero, my friend began to expatiate

upon the dull and colorless nightlife my new town had to offer. I disagreed. We began to argue.

When it became clear I was losing, I said, "Excuse me."

I went to the phone and called "Mae."

Within half an hour, we were sitting around the bar up there with "Myrna," "Claudette," "Ginger," and "Paulette."

My friend looked as though he had been issued a mouth that wouldn't shut.

Later, much later, we were having a sandwich and nightcap with "Mae." I could hear the wheels of my friend's writing machinery clicking fitfully in his head. He was frowning. I could guess the problem that occupied him. What a story! But if he wrote it, who would (in 1938) publish it? And say it did in some way manage to get published, who would believe it?

Still, his newspaperman's drive could not be braked. He began to ask questions; small, large; discreet, indiscreet. "Mae" answered them all in kind.

Finally, there was a pause. Information was being digested along with the superlative club sandwiches and beer.

My friend took a breath and plunged back in.

" 'Miss West'—" he began.

"Call me 'Mae,' " said "Mae."

"Really?" he asked.

" 'Fcawss," she said. "I'm *pahsh'*l to genimen of the press."

My friend blinked. "I know y'," "Mae" continued. "Seen y'pitcha many times. Read y'stuff sometimes."

"Oh," he said.

"Did y'think I bullieved you're 'Jay Gatsby,' f'cryin' out loud? Anyway, I happen t'know *he's dead.*"

She looked at me reproachfully. I had indeed introduced my friend as Fitzgerald's hapless hero.

"Go ahead, Jimmy," she said, now on a new footing.

"Well, what I was going to ask—'Mae'—was just—"

He hesitated, feeling less free now that his anonymity had been shattered.

"Go ahead, fella," she urged. "We're all friends here."

367

"Well," he said, "do all your girls—I mean every one—do they all do—well, *everything?*"

In the circumstances, his blush seemed out of place.

"Whaddaya mean *everything?*" asked "Mae" as if she didn't know.

"I mean, you know, right down the line?" He winced at his own clumsy locution. "I mean—"

"Mae" rescued him.

"Okay," she said, "I know what y'mean. Y'got no business askin' such a thing. It's—y'know—pretty innamit after all. But now that y've ast . . . Every one of my girls here does *everything.*" She paused, looked off. "Except, of course, that stuck-up little 'Janet Gaynor'!"

Jimmy never did write about "Mae." It would have seemed a betrayal of sorts. Even now, several wars later, I wonder if *I* should be doing so. No matter. "Mae's" is no more. A condominium stands on the site and what good is that?

"Mae's" was most certainly the most memorable—well, I suppose "whorehouse" *is* the word, but somehow it did not then, and does not now, seem to fit "Mae's."

"And the winner is—"

We all waited for the voice on the radio to continue. Suddenly Einstein's incomprehensible theory of relativity became crystal clear. It was taking only a few seconds for Brod Crawford to open the envelope. He would then read the name of the winner. Those few seconds seemed like an hour to some and like a year to others, depending upon their involvement in the results.

It was 1951, and the annual ritual sponsored by the Academy of Motion Picture Arts and Sciences had not yet become the present-day television spectacular which is viewed world-wide, they say, by over 600 million people. The event had progressed from the first modest hotel banquet to a ceremony that was being broadcast for only the tenth time.

As it happened, many of the nominees as well as other interested parties were in New York. Among them José Ferrer, nominated for his performance in *Cyrano*; Gloria Swanson for *Sunset Boulevard*; Judy Holliday for *Born Yesterday*.

Ferrer and Miss Swanson were acting together on Broadway in a revival of *Twentieth Century*. Other nominees who were in New York were Celeste Holm, Sam Jaffe, Thelma Ritter, and George Cukor. José Ferrer decided to give an after-theatre party in New York at La Zambra Café. Most of his fellow nominees attended.

In Hollywood the presentations were being made at the RKO Pantages Theatre. In New York about 300 people were gathered listening to the results on an amplified radio. When

José Ferrer was announced as the winner, the little crowd went wild. The ABC radio network cut in from Hollywood to pick up his acceptance speech. It was packed with emotion, since Ferrer had been under a cloud of suspicion as a result of having been subpoenaed by the House Un-American Activities Committee.

He said, "This means more to me than an honor to an actor. I consider it a vote of confidence and an act of faith and, believe me, I'll not let you down."

In Hollywood, Helen Hayes officially accepted the Oscar for him.

. . . *"And the winner is—"*

The words were frozen in the smoky air.

During the pause, I looked across the room and watched Judy. She appeared to be remarkably calm. Did she care? Beside her sat Gloria Swanson, smiling a professional smile. Was it confidence or merely nerves? She leaned toward Judy and whispered something in her ear. Judy nodded.

Later, I asked Judy about that whisper. She told me that Miss Swanson had said, softly, "One of us is about to be very happy."

As the pause stretched out, I reflected upon the curious set of circumstances that had brought Judy to this time and place.

I had written *Born Yesterday* in London during the war for my friend Jean Arthur. When eventually she read it, she was not enthusiastic about the play, and even less enthusiastic about the idea of herself in the leading role.

I made the mistake of talking her into it. Rehearsals were almost immediately fraught with difficulties and compromise. Jean had been a movie star for some years and had become accustomed to playing carefully tailored roles. She had become highly adept at projecting her enormously attractive personality, but less skilled in creating a character. It was soon clear that we were going to get, not Jean Arthur as "Billie Dawn," but "Billie Dawn" as Jean Arthur.

I decided, under pressure from the management, to settle for this condition. Commercial considerations outweighed artistic ones. But Jean grew increasingly restive. An actress playing a part for which she does not feel suited is as uncomfortable as one wearing a badly fitted dress. Still, we struggled our way through rehearsals, hoping—as theatre people are wont to do—that it would all come right on the night.

It almost did. The first tryout performance in New Haven was half-triumphant. It looked as if there was a show in there somewhere. I expected that Jean would be, along with the rest of us, sufficiently encouraged to work toward the fulfillment of the promise.

Instead, she wrote me a note asking to be replaced as soon as possible and insisting that five important lines and two vital scenes be omitted from the next performance. Trouble.

The producer was Max Gordon, a strong manager of the old school, who was not prepared to give it all up without a fight. He used all of his considerable wiles to keep Jean Arthur from resigning. Changes were made. Some for the better, some not. By the time we opened in Boston, we had neither gained nor lost ground.

The on-stage and off-stage tensions began to affect Jean's health. She missed performances.

Friends came up to see the play in Boston and agreed that it was that most tantalizing of theatre products—a Could-Be.

After two rocky weeks, we moved to Philadelphia for a scheduled Tuesday-night opening. Jean did not appear at the Monday rehearsal and on Tuesday morning, Max Gordon and I were summoned to her suite at the Hotel Warwick and were told by Dr. Barborka, who had flown in from Chicago, that in his considered medical opinion Jean Arthur could neither open that night nor play the Philadelphia engagement.

"What's the matter with her?" asked Max.

"Nervous exhaustion," said the doctor.

"Me, too," said Max. "Have you got something you can give me for it?"

The doctor explained that Jean was under sedation and that he planned to take her back to Chicago, where he would have her admitted to the Passavant Hospital for an indefinite period of time. Clearly, there was nothing more to say. We left.

The question: was there anything to *do*?

. . . *"And the winner is—"*

From the time Jean asked to be replaced, I had begun to consider other actresses. Three prospects turned me down without consideration. Two others had come to New Haven, and one to Boston, and all had declined.

Max Gordon sent for his general manager, Ben Boyar, and began to discuss the agonizing details of closing.

"Don't worry," Max said to me. "We'll put it together again and we'll do it. Don't worry."

The more he said, "Don't worry," the more I worried. Shows that close out of town seldom reopen.

I began again going over the list of possibilities, wondering if any of them were worth a second try. I recalled that during a rehearsal in New Haven, I had mentioned something about my difficulties to Mainbocher, who had designed Jean's clothes. He was anxious to change one of the dresses and I had to inform him that there was a possibility Jean would not continue.

"Do you know Judy Holliday?" asked Main.

"From The Revuers?" I asked. "Sure, she's very good."

"What about *her*?" he asked.

"Well, she's terrific, Main, but not for *this*."

"Oh," he said. "I saw her in a bit last season in *Kiss Them for Me*. One scene. She played a little San Francisco tart. Superlative."

"I didn't see that," I said.

"Pity," said Main.

I had long respected Mainbocher's theatre acumen. So, on the way from Boston to Philadelphia, I had stopped in New York and met with Judy Holliday and her agent, Belle Chodorov.

Judy, teamed with Betty Comden and Adolph Green and Alvin Hammer (and sometimes Leonard Bernstein at the piano), had made an impact on the New York cabaret scene. Judy was a standout; pert, versatile, comical, talented. But as we talked that Sunday afternoon in New York, she did not look anything like the girl I had in mind. Rattled and dispirited, I was making the common mistake of looking for a type rather than an actress.

Max and Ben were still discussing the closing. The economics of storing the scenery as against abandoning it was the topic.

"Listen," I said suddenly. "Let's try Judy Holliday."

"Who?" asked Max.

"Judy Holliday," I said.

"What are you talking about?" said Max, impatiently. "Who? That fat Jewish girl from The Revuers? No. Like Dick Rodgers said one time at an audition, 'This show is *by* Jews and *for* Jews, but it can't be *with* Jews!' "

"She's not so fat," I said. "And, come to think of it, not so Jewish. But she's funny and a hell of a good actress."

"How do you know? She's never done anything in the theatre."

I repeated Mainbocher's account. Max had seen her in that play.

He nodded and said, "She was damn good. But I don't know. For this, a big part like this, a star part?"

Economics again. Ben Boyar sagely pointed out that it would, in fact, cost no more to play out the Philadelphia stand than it would to close.

. . . *"And the winner is—"*

Judy Holliday came down to Philadelphia late that afternoon. We had arranged for a room for her at the hotel. She had neither seen the play nor read it. I gave her a copy of the script and she went up to her room to read it. Two hours later, we met. She nodded her head, tentatively.

"The only thing is," she said, "when?"

"Whenever you're ready," I said.

"Saturday night," said Max.

Judy looked thunderstruck.

"I *couldn't!*" she said.

"Saturday night," said Max.

Judy shook her head in terror.

"Let's go to work," I said, "and then we'll see."

"Saturday night," said Max.

I hustled Judy out of the room, took her upstairs to her room, and said, "Leave it to me. First, the words. That's the main thing. Learn the words. If there's anything we can do to help—a stage manager or anything like that, let me know."

"Okay," said Judy. "By the way. It's a good play."

The next three days were unreal. We hardly ever left the Locust Street Theatre. The rest of the company was all that one could hope for: helpful, cooperative, and warm. Mainbocher arrived and redid the clothes. Paul Schmidt of Elizabeth Arden's came down and, late one night, in Judy's bathroom, changed her hair from what it was to the unique reddish-blonde that was to remain her trademark for years to come.

From the first day, almost the first hour, it was plain that we were in luck. Judy was creating the character before our eyes.

There were, however, two disconcerting matters. First, Judy kept insisting that she could not possibly open on Saturday night. Second, there was no way to avoid seeing the long, long queue lined up at the box office. Generally this is a joyous sight but in this case it was not. The action was topsy-turvy, upside down, a nightmare. The tickets were being handed *in* and the money was being handed *back*!

I was appalled, but Max said, "Don't worry. We've got a great show. We're going to have. I wish that kid would lose some weight."

"Don't worry," I said. "She's losing about a pound an hour."

"Good," said Max.

"And I'm losing about *two* pounds an hour."

"Don't worry," said Max.

He was not being merely willful about insisting upon opening Saturday night. He knew that in the circumstances a Monday-night opening would draw a small house. Free passes would prove nothing. People who get in for nothing generally believe that that is what it is worth. Max knew that on Saturday night we could get a full house, that the play would go better, look better, and, in fact, *be* better.

We opened on Saturday night. Judy had rehearsed less than

four days, as opposed to the customary four weeks. She gave a near-perfect performance. The show was an instantaneous success and was not to play to an empty seat for the next three years.

Harry Cohn, that hard-headed, single-minded original, responded to the show personally (I wonder if he ever realized that the leading male role, Harry Brock, had been named after him?) and he wanted it.

The trouble was, he and I were not speaking at the time. I had informed his New York representative that although the play was for sale, it was not for sale to Harry Cohn.

"You mean that?" he asked.

"I certainly do," I said, and added gratuitously, "Not for a million bucks."

This conversation was duly reported to Harry Cohn. Two months later he acquired the film rights to *Born Yesterday*— for a million bucks.

He is reported to have said to his staff, "I'll show you how we'll make a bum outa this guy!"

When the time came to make the picture, he accepted my suggestion of George Cukor as director, but that was all. He wanted me to write the screenplay "as a labor of love." When I refused, he engaged other screenwriters to do the job, paying them twice what I had asked, but winning his point. I was later to work out the screenplay with George Cukor for nothing. Or was it "a labor of love"?

My suggestion that he do the picture with the excellent New York company, or at least with Judy Holliday and Paul Douglas, was ridiculed.

"What's a matter with you?" said Cohn. "I've got Broderick Crawford here under contract. He just got an Oscar for *All the King's Men*. And he's perfect for the part."

"Yes, but not as good as Paul Douglas."

"No? Then how come you offered it first to Crawford and he turned you down?"

He had me there.

"And the girl. Yours? For the stage, all right, but for the

screen, I've got Rita Hayworth under contract. I've got Lucille Ball. Maybe I'll go for Alice Faye or Stanwyck. I mean, Jesus, this is no B picture here. I paid a lot of money for it. In fact, *too* much."

No amount of persuasion was effective.

We began the long and complex strategy of building up a part in *Adam's Rib,* which my wife and I were writing for Tracy and Hepburn at Metro. The idea was to have Judy play it as a sort of screen test which Cohn had refused to make for *Born Yesterday.*

The strategy succeeded with the help of Katharine Hepburn, Spencer Tracy, and George Cukor.

Judy scored decisively in *Adam's Rib.* Cohn, to his credit, recognized her quality and signed her to repeat her stage role in the film.

. . . *"And the winner is*—Judy Holliday for *Born Yesterday!"*

Gloria Swanson blanched, recovered at once, leaned over, embraced Judy Holliday, and kissed her.

Judy was truly astonished. She had not expected to win.

In Hollywood Ethel Barrymore accepted Judy's Oscar. At La Zambra Café in New York the excitement was so intense that the ABC crew failed to make the necessary connections and although Judy made a touching little speech, it was neither broadcast nor heard by more than a few people at her table.

Thus through the quiet defection of one star and the fading brilliance of another, a new star was indeed born. Judy Holliday went on to make a string of successes: *The Marrying Kind, It Should Happen to You, The Solid Gold Cadillac* (in which she was at last reunited with Paul Douglas), and *Bells Are Ringing.*

She was an unlikely type for movie stardom but made it by dedicated use of extraordinary talent. Her death in 1965 at the age of forty-two deprived the screen of one of its most uniquely gifted artists.

"Many Hollywood producers were called, or called themselves, "independent," but Samuel Goldwyn was the only truly independent producer I ever knew. He purchased this independence expensively by putting up his own money to produce his films.

Other so-called independent producers, and even the majors, borrowed money from banks, from institutions or from private lending sources, at high interest rates, giving up, of course, pieces of the finished product. Goldwyn used his own money, often losing it. But when he made a success the profits were all his.

He fought the distributors and exhibitors, believing them to be largely parasitic, and at one time undertook the complicated method of hiring a theatre and exhibiting the picture on his own.

Once, I heard him talking to the house manager of a theatre in Chicago which he was using for the release of *The Best Years of Our Lives.* He was giving all sorts of instructions, many of which I did not understand. I heard him say, "Well, then, the only thing you got to do is put a chaser on. Get some kind of a chaser. Or I'll have somebody here get you one. You know, like a two-reel travelogue about Denmark or something like that. And you see that you use it. If we don't get a turnover, we're not going to get a gross." He hung up.

"Did you say 'a chaser'?" I asked.

"Certainly. Chaser. What's wrong with that?"

"What's 'a chaser'?"

Goldwyn laughed. "My God," he said, "you're taking me

back. You know, you wouldn't believe it, but there was a time when the whole movie business practically was chasers. You see, they had these vaudeville houses and on rainy nights, or cold nights, or sometimes if they happened to have a couple of good acts, somebody would buy a ticket and go in, and maybe stay for two or three shows sometimes. Say, listen. I remember not so long ago, M-G-M, they were telling me what they were going to do at the Capitol. In New York City. They had this movie, *Babes In Arms*. Remember that? Dick Rodgers and Hart?"

"Of course."

"Well, it turned out good and they wanted to break all the box-office records in the history of the Capitol Theatre. They thought this would be a good exploitation thing for later, if they could say to the exhibitors, 'This picture broke every record in the history of the Capitol Theatre.' So Arthur Freed was at my house one night and he was telling me about what they were going to do, to break all the records of the Capitol Theatre. He said that Mickey Rooney and Judy Garland—they were the two stars of the picture—and they were great. Well, say, those young people are great. And Arthur said to me, 'We're going to send Mickey and Judy to make personal appearances at the Capitol. We're going to play six shows a day and seven on weekends, and we're going to have Mickey and Judy make a personal appearance at every single show. Not long. Maybe they'll just come on for, say, ten minutes, and maybe do a couple of numbers and talk to the audience, but we'll be able to say: 'In person Mickey Rooney and Judy Garland,' and what the hell? They're so young, they can *do* seven shows a day. They'll just stay in the theatre and go on.' And I said to him, 'Arthur, you're making a big mistake. This is a strong picture, and if you play enough shows at the Capitol you will break the records. This personal-appearance thing is not so good, and anyway, it'll take up too much time. You could put in an extra show without the personal appearance. And there's another reason.' But Arthur wouldn't listen to me and he said, 'No, no. It's all been decided.' And they went ahead and they did it? Do you know what happened? The first two days not only they didn't break any records, but they had practically the lowest gross the Capitol had had in years, for those first two days."

I was puzzled. "But how could that be?"

"I'm telling you. Trying to. If you'll stop interrupting me, f'Chrissake. You're like Arthur Freed. He wouldn't listen either. This is what happened. This is what I wanted to tell him was going to happen. This was such a great attraction, this fine picture and this personal appearance, that what happened was that people bought a ticket and they went in and stayed for two, three shows. Like if they went in two or three of them together, one of them would go out and buy some candy or popcorn or food, or go to the bathroom, and the other ones would save his seat, and then they would come back and they would sit through a second show and sometimes these kids sat through a third show. So instead of each seat being sold several times, during the morning, it was only sold once."

"Well, I'll be damned!"

"What they should have done—what I wanted to tell Arthur to do—was to run this on a schedule basis. One show, then you clear the house. Then another show. Nowadays you can do that. In the old vaudeville days, the ones I was telling you about, they didn't know how to do that. And it was too complicated. So what they used to do was, they used to buy a movie from us—like a two-reeler, sometimes a one-reeler—usually terrible, and at the end of the last vaudeville act, they would put this movie on. And people hated it so much they would leave the theatre. That's why they got to call them 'chasers.' You still have them. All those shorts and those travelogues, and that junk they put on between the shows. To get people out of the theatre. So that's what I was just now telling him in Chicago he has to do. You never heard of that, huh? You didn't know what a chaser was. My God. Some people."

Long careers are interesting careers, especially in the film business. The life-span of a movie star is comparatively short.

"We're something like the common housefly," Spencer Tracy once said, although the length of his own career belies his crack. Directors and writers, too, come and go, lose their touch or use up their bag of tricks or begin to repeat themselves or fall out of fashion.

Samuel Goldwyn's span was the more extraordinary because it encompassed the full story of American film-making from its virtual beginning until the present day. He was producing feature films with great stars and important directors long before the word "Hollywood" was known to the general public.

In one of the most recent manifestations of film activity—the leasing of libraries for television viewing—Goldwyn, in his eighties, proved to be the most brilliant negotiator of them all.

The value of old films for television exhibition was wildly undercalculated by most of the owners of the vaults. Great blocs of films were leased, sometimes sold, for television for a few hundred thousand dollars, when their actual worth turned out to be in the millions. The revenue was considered at first to be something of a windfall. Found money. And, of course, there exists, in the hard-hitting business community, an element of greed.

In the first years of this new development, Goldwyn sat tight, refusing to make any of his films available for television.

"They're gonna *kill* it!" he said passionately. "They're gonna kill the whole damn *business*. You think people are going to go out and pay for something they can get home free and a bottle of beer and their shoes off? All right, sure, those television wiseguys will pay a few dollars but that won't go far, and these bastards here, they're gonna kill the whole business. I'll tell you what the box is. The box is just a different kind of a distribution business. That's all. We're going to have to figure out some way to use it, but to use it like a *distribution* business. Not to sell some goddam toothpaste, f'Chrissake."

René Clair is not only one of the three or four greatest of film directors; he is also a philosopher and theoretician of the medium.

380

When he visited Hollywood in the mid-1950s, I thought Goldwyn would be interested in hearing Clair's ideas and arranged a meeting. It lasted three hours. Goldwyn appeared to be greatly impressed, but he was habitually so cagey, undemonstrative, and careful, that I could not be certain.

Goldwyn phoned me the next morning and said, "Listen, all that stuff he was saying. That Mr. Renéclair. Tell him I would appreciate it very much for him to write it down and send it over here."

"I can't do that, Mr. Goldwyn."

"Why not? I thought this Renéclair was a friend of yours."

"Well, yes, he is. But I can't ask him to sit down and write a whole article just for you to read."

"It's not just for me, f'Chrissake! I want to show it to a lot of people. And who's talking about an article? Did I say article? Just tell him to write me a letter."

"I'm sorry, Mr. Goldwyn. I don't see how I could do that. Why don't you ask him yourself?"

"*Myself*? Because he's not a friend of mine. He's a friend of *yours.*"

"Even so—"

"All right, God damn it, if you don't want to do me a favor, don't." There was an awkward pause. Then he continued, brightly, "Say, *you* were there. *You* heard it. Why don't *you* write it down and send it over here?"

"For how much?" I asked.

"What?" The sound he made was the very definition of outrage.

"I'm a professional writer, Mr. Goldwyn," I said. "I live by my pen. So I don't think it's right for you to ask me to do something like that as a favor. You don't ask actors to act for you as a favor, or directors to direct for you."

"I don't know what's happened to you," he said sadly. "When I first met you, you were a nice quiet kid with a lot of ambitions and you were interested in pictures. I remember how you used to come back to the studio every night and run my pictures to learn the business. You cost me a goddam fortune, f'Chrissake! And *now* look what's happened to you! All you think about is money. That will get you no place."

I said nothing.

"All right," he continued. *"Don't* write it down. You think I don't remember what he said? I remember. I remember it better than you do."

"All right, then," I said. "Why don't *you* write it down and send it to *me*?"

"Wisecracks," he said. "I've told you how many—a thousand times maybe—there's no money in wisecracks."

"But I'm not interested in money, Mr. Goldwyn. *You* know that."

"Listen," he said. "I want to tell you something."

"Yes?"

"I want to thank you very much for bringing over that Mr. Renéclair. He's very intelligent and I like his ideas and I appreciate it very much that you brought him over, and gave me an opportunity to hear his views. Good-by."

Actually, Goldwyn's second suggestion would have been simple to carry out. I had been so struck by René's thesis that I had already written it all down.

René had said: "We are not yet thinking of this television business in the right relation to the 'mauvaise.'" (Although René's English is splendid, there are a few words he sticks on and this is one of them. To him the "movies" were always the "mauvaise." Freudian?) "I see a screen. For me, it is no different if the screen is a large one in a theatre, or a small one in my room at the Beverly Hills Hotel. A screen is a screen, *n'est-ce pas*? Now. What is the job? The job is to tell a story, to hold the interest, foot by foot, on that screen, with scenery and actors and dialogue and music and the most important thing always—the cutting. So. For me the television is a form of the mauvaise. Now everyone I meet here in the business and in France, too, everyone considers the television to be an enemy. A competition. I say not. I say it is another form. An extension. To look at the situation as it is today only, that is the mistake. That causes the disaster in the thinking. One must think back, back in time to the time of Lumière and Edison. Then one must think forward so far as possible. Then looking at the whole story, the whole history, one can begin to perceive what is the true situation. I wish to pose something to you— upon the subject of inventions. Let us say, let us imagine that for all our lives there has been such a thing as television, that when all of us were children there was, in every home in France and in America, such a box. This box, which had the capability of receiving, through the airwaves, images of football games, Le Tour de France, a performance from the Comédie Fran- çaise, or the Ziegfeld Follies, or a speech by a politician. So. All our lives we have known this. We have seen this. And used it. Lived with it. Now!" He had jumped up excitedly and had begun pacing about as he reached the penultimate point of his imagining. "Suppose now, this year, in 1958, some brilliant inventor, somewhere, invents such a thing as film. We have never heard the word 'film.' We are not sure what is celluloid, but now he invents it. And it becomes possible to put all these things, the politicians, Le Tour de France, the Follies, onto this film and the film onto reels and this can be put onto some machine and shown on the television. The television we have always known. And this film can even be sent from place to place and stored and put on whenever it is wanted or needed. Now, would not this thing, would not the invention of film be the most profound, the most greatest thing that has ever hap- pened in the history of television? And not such a bad thing for this new film idea, either. And if we could be, any of us, in either business, in the television business or in the film busi- ness, which would we choose? I do not know of you—but me? I prefer the film business because the film is, after all, the prod- uct, and the television, the box, is only, after all, the means of distribution, n'est-ce pas? If we can think of it in such historic terms, then we can recognize that the invention of television is *not* the enemy of film-making but maybe its best friend."

This is, in essence, the argument Goldwyn found attractive. I often heard him repeat it. I never heard him credit "Mr. Renéclair" with the idea, and at times he presented it in a maddeningly garbled state. Still, as always, Samuel Goldwyn was able to communicate what was in his heart and mind.

"Say, you want to hear another mistake of mine? I'll tell you. Gary Cooper. That was some mistake. I always liked Westerns. I liked to watch them, to see them, but I never made one. Maybe because I didn't think I knew how. But then we got ahold of this book by Harold Bell Wright. A great book. Very popular. The name of it was *The Winning of Barbara Worth* and it appealed to me. And Henry King—a very fine director—loved it. And this woman, this Frances Marion, she did the screenplay. And we were starting in to cast and somebody brought in this fellow. He was very tall and he looked a little on the dumb side. Dumb but nice. And he didn't talk much. There was a nice part in this picture. Not the lead. That was Ronnie Colman. But there was this part, a kind of a cowboy part, and I can't tell you why, but this big, tall fellow appealed to me. So we tried him out and took a chance and he made it. He was in it. *The Winning of Barbara Worth*. Vilma Banky. Beautiful. The picture did very well and I had this fellow, Cooper, under contract. But I tell you the truth, this Western was very hard to make, with all the locations and the outdoor stuff and the weather. And I thought, what the hell? I'm not going to make a lot of Westerns. And this guy? What am I going to do with him in the kind of pictures I make? So what did I do? I went ahead and I sold his contract to Paramount. You know, looking back, I still see why I did what I did, but it turned out to be, I would have to say—I would have to admit it—it was a mistake. See? Even *I* make a mistake. Once in a great while, I mean."

One tends to think of the Goldwyn output as being the best of the Hollywood product, and to some extent, it generally was. "A Goldwyn Picture" came to mean a quality product.

The fact is that Samuel Goldwyn, like everyone else in the

384

business, had more failures than successes. Perhaps, over-all, six failures for every success.

But workers in the arts are, thank fortune, remembered for their successes and not for their failures.

No producer was ever more courageous or more daring than Goldwyn. All the more credit to him that he continued to work and to produce well into his eighties. Even then, he was vigorous and ambitious and driving.

A good part of this remarkable condition stemmed from the fact that he took great care of himself. He respected himself as a being and attended to his body as he would to any other possession.

He always presented himself as a careful, successful arrangement of elegant details. I am not certain how all this was accomplished but I suspect that Frances Goldwyn had a good deal to do with it. Since she was *Mrs.* Goldwyn, she took pride in *Mr.* Goldwyn. One noticed his shirts and ties and socks. His manicure.

The last time I saw him, he was nearing ninety and his health had quite suddenly broken down. He was irritated and irritable, impatient and outraged—yet there was not a single wrinkle on his cherubic face. Mrs. Goldwyn once told me that Sam believed in facial massage and arranged to have one virtually every day of his life.

"In his case, at least," she said, "it seems to have worked, doesn't it?"

I cannot believe it was that alone.

There was the matter of diet. He was always a careful, sensible eater.

One evening I was dining with him at Le Pavillon in New York. The famous dessert wagon was rolled by, bearing confections and pastries and delectable creations.

Goldwyn watched it, sighed, and said, "Every time I see that, it's like they're wheeling away the body of an old friend of mine!"

He drank moderately, sensibly.

As to smoking, he had a nerve-testing custom. He smoked

one cigarette each day. No more, no less. The cigarette would be produced after dinner, ceremoniously lit, carefully smoked, and enjoyed, and that was it until the following evening. How many are capable of a similar discipline?

Throughout the years, he made a point of taking various forms of exercise, usually combining them with business activity.

Back in the days when I worked for him, he would sometimes send for me at six o'clock, as the studio was closing, and say, "Get in the car and ride home with me. There are a few things."

The first time I did so, and the chauffeur took off, I wondered how I was going to get back to the studio. The thought never occurred to Goldwyn. From his point of view, I was being honored, favored in some way.

He asked me about the daily doings around the studio, ever avid for any scrap of information. What did I think about the day's rushes? Why was Willie so slow? Was there some way to force those goddam actors to learn their lines before they came on the set? Did I know anyone in New York who would be good for the part of the press agent? He was getting sick and tired of these same old Hollywood faces in every picture.

All at once, to my horror, the car pulled up to the curb. The chauffeur got out, came around, and opened the door. Goldwyn got out. I followed. We were at the top of The Strip, where Sunset Boulevard divides.

Goldwyn strode off and I was soon making every effort to keep pace with him. He continued his questioning. My mind was only half on the answers. I was trying to calculate the distance I was being asked to walk. I was not overly familiar with the geography of Beverly Hills at that time, but I figured it out to be about a mile from his home at 1200 Laurel Lane. A mile! And some of it uphill. Should I protest? Impossible. My estimate was off. It turned out to be two and a half miles, precisely. Goldwyn had measured it and by walking from his house to this spot every morning and back again every evening, he put in his five miles.

Goldwyn was much taller than I am, with longer legs and a

386

greater stride. I had a hard time keeping up with him and often felt as though I were running.

Forty minutes later, we reached the house. I was exhausted, he was exhilarated.

He thanked me, said goodnight, and disappeared into the house.

I stood for a moment, regaining my breath and wondering what to do next, when my second-hand Buick came through the gate, driven by my secretary, Jean.

"Pretty good," I said. "But how did you—?"

"Al, the driver. He phoned me and told me. He says Mr. Goldwyn does it all the time. So Al always calls, either somebody with the guy's car or a cab or something."

Tycoons do not concern themselves with unnecessary details —such as how is someone else going to get home.

That was 1937. Years passed. A war or two came and went. I returned to Hollywood for a short stay.

Driving to the Beverly Hills Hotel early one evening, I saw him. The same erect figure, the same long stride, and beside him a small young man bouncing along in an awkward attempt to keep apace. Was it still me, I wondered? Some leftover form of me?

For Samuel Goldwyn, not much had changed across the years. He had found a practical plan of life and work, and there was no need to deviate from it.

About that beautiful home on Laurel Lane. Mrs. Goldwyn recalls:

"For a long time we thought of building a house of our own. Sam had never really had one. But of course it's a project, isn't it? And there never seemed to be time. Then one day we had lunch with Joe Schenck at his place and afterward, sitting out on the patio—they hadn't begun calling them lanais yet, thank God—Sam suddenly looked up at this hill and said, 'That's a nice hill up there. That would be a nice place to have a house.' It was a casual, throwaway remark, nothing more. So I was

387

good and surprised when we left at Sam insisting I drive up to this hill. Well, you know what Beverly Hills is, especially in this area and it took me what seemed like hours to find a way to it— but I did, eventually. And we padded around in the underbrush and I ruined my shoes and stockings but Sam was like Balboa discovering the Pacific. Something about the spot drew him to it and he couldn't rest until we'd taken title to it. And the day *that* happened, he said to me, 'Now, darling, I want you to go ahead and build our house. That's your job. You go ahead and you do it and I don't want to mix in because I don't know how to build a house.' And I said, 'Neither do I, Sam.' And he said, 'Sure you do.' That was all. He never discussed architects with me, or plans or specifications or costs. As a matter of fact, I soon learned that he didn't want to discuss it at all. He was afraid it would distract him from his work at the studio. So in the year that the house was in progress, the subject hardly ever. came up. Oh, he was aware, of course, that it was going on— but that was about it. Well, if you've ever built and furnished a house, I don't need to tell you. It was a full-time effort, what with the house and grounds and landscaping. Pool. Tennis court. And then the carpeting and drapes and furniture. Mind you, this was all from scratch. Well. Finally, finally, finally. It was ready. As ready as I could make it. And staffed. And full of flowers. And ready. So one evening, I picked Sam up at the studio. The driver knew my plan, so nothing more needed to be said. We drove off. It had been a rough day at the studio, I gathered. Sam looked absolutely harassed. Anyway, we drove along and when we reached Coldwater Canyon, the driver turned right and Sam began to yell, 'Where're you going? Where's he going?' And I said, 'Take it easy, Sam. It's all right.' But he didn't like it and said, 'I don't want to go for any joy rides to-night. I'm tired. I want to go home.' And I took his hand and got his eyes and said, 'That's exactly where we *are* going, Sam. Home.' Well, he began to get the idea—that at last at last, after all this time and this long wait and tremendous expenditure of time and money and energy—our home was finished, ready. He looked as though he couldn't believe it was happening, and he held onto my hand tightly, tightly. We drove up the hill to Laurel Lane and into the driveway and there it was. I thought it was the most beautiful house in Beverly Hills—in fact, I still think so. And we sat for a moment and I said, 'We're home, darling.' Now from this point on, Sam behaved like a man in a dream—and in a way that's what it was. We went to the door and the maid opened it and curtsied. Sam offered his hand and they shook hands. He went in and began floating about—looking, looking. I don't know what he was thinking— but as I watched him, I was all choked up—and I was thinking of that penniless little orphan boy of thirteen coming to this strange country, wondering what would happen to him, going to Gloversville and working, then later New York and the struggles and the disappointments—and that awful disaster of the first picture—and the near-bankruptcies—and now here he was on top of the world—and the master of this beautiful home. And I began to follow him around. He didn't say a word. He went through every room, looked into the closets, saw the projection room and the paintings on the walls, the dining room —we'd set the table with the best silver and china and linen— the grand kitchen and finally he started up the stairs and I let him go by himself—because it was the upstairs part I was really proud of. It had been conceived and designed and executed out of my understanding of him. And I was confident he'd be pleased with his bedroom and bathroom and dressing room, study, gym—all his things that were and always would be the heart of the house. I wanted him to take it all in by himself. So I waited downstairs, knowing full well that what he would find up there would thrill him. Then I heard his voice—excited— shouting 'Frances! *Frances!*' And I rushed into the front hall just knowing he was going to have trouble expressing his joy— and there he stood at the top of the stairs and I looked up and he yelled again, 'Frances!' And I said, 'Yes, darling. What is it?' And he said, 'There's no soap in my soap dish!' "

Mrs. Goldwyn tells this affectionately and it always gets the expected laugh, but it is more than simply anecdotal to me.

It expresses perfectly the characteristics that went into the making of the man Samuel Goldwyn.

As he moved about his remarkable new home he must have appreciated it, but basically, he was not looking for what was right, but for what was possibly wrong, and in time, he found it.

No soap in the soap dish. There are some who see in the account a petty ingrate. Others make the valid point that when a man has invested a million and a half dollars in a residence he is entitled to soap in the soap dish.

By the mid-1960s, Samuel Goldwyn had become set in his ways and in his tastes. He had, after all, been producing pictures for over forty years and was frozen into certain attitudes. He had little artistic resilience, and could not accept the opening up of the screen to the new sense of morality and behavior and expression.

It made him angry. One night, at his home, in the middle of a screening, a nude turned up on the screen for no more than a fleeting moment. Goldwyn rushed to the front of his projection room and began shaking his fist at the screen.

"Get off!" he said. "Get off! Stop the picture. I don't allow such filth in my house. Stop the picture!"

Mrs. Goldwyn calmed him down, got him back into his seat. The picture did not stop.

The incident, however, provided Goldwyn with a theme for a discourse when the movie had come to an end.

"They'll go on their ass, f'Chrissake, with that kind of dirty filth. People don't want dirty filth. Not real people. Not most people. Sure, maybe here or there a few degenerates. And pimps. *They* like to see filth. Filth likes filth—but who makes more money than Disney? Nobody. Walt Disney. Clean family pictures. People go into filth—into the filth business—they go on their ass. I've seen it happen a thousand times. They think they can get away with this and with that and for a couple of minutes, all right, so maybe they do. You think we'd have had to have the goddam Hays Office—Will Hays—and all that non-sense, all that trouble and expenses, if not for these dirty bas-tards with their goddam filth? I can't stand it. Nobody can stand it. Only a few degenerates and pimps. I don't believe in dirty pictures. Not for the motion-picture business. You want to be in the dirty-picture business, you make stag reels or you go to Paris—to the whorehouses there—but not for a big business, the way we're supposed to be. These goddam dirty pictures. They'll go on their ass. . . . We've had them before. Naked women and sex things and even fairies. We've had fairies. But people don't like that. Only *fairies* like that. Fairies like fairies, but people don't. These goddam filthy pictures. They're going to ruin the whole goddam business."

Some months later, in New York, I went to see a highly praised Czechoslovakian film called *Closely Watched Trains,* directed by Jiri Menzel.

It struck me at once as being a small masterpiece—if there can be such a thing as a small masterpiece. Perhaps all master-pieces are large.

A few weeks later I had a meeting in Hollywood with Sam Goldwyn and told him about *Closely Watched Trains.*

"You'll be absolutely bowled over by it, Sam," I said. "You especially. I don't know why. I think maybe because of its marvelous European color and that spirit. I've noticed that you always tend to respond to that."

"Yes, I am," said Goldwyn.

"And this picture, *Closely Watched Trains,* is so delicate, so all-of-a-piece, and it's funny, yes, but also very, very moving."

"Funny and moving," said Goldwyn, "is a great combination. When Charlie was good. Charlie Chaplin. That's what he had more than anybody. Funny and moving. I'll get this picture. Write it down for me. I'll screen it at the house. I'll have Frances call you."

Three days later, at eight o'clock in the morning, my tele-phone rang.

"Mr. Goldwyn calling."

"Sure."

"Is that you?" said Goldwyn.

"Good morning, Sam."

"What the hell's the matter with you?" he asked. "That goddam filthy picture. Were you kidding me, or what?"

"I don't know what you're talking about yet."

"That goddam Hungarian picture, or whatever the hell it was."

"Oh," I said, understanding. "Czechoslovakian."

"Czechoslovakian, Rumanian, what the hell's the difference? It's nothing but a goddam dirty picture. What's a matter with you? You know better than that. I had people in, ladies and gentlemen in, and I put this picture on—in black-and-white—and this dirty picture with this girl showing her bare ass. I was shocked. I don't know what's happening to you, f'Chrissake. You're not making any sense lately."

"For your information, Sam," I said, "that picture has had the best reviews of any picture this year. Sensational reviews, and it's doing terrific business and—"

"Sensational reviews. They're probably all *degenerates* those reviewers. Don't ever recommend a picture to me any more. You've lost your whole taste. That's your trouble."

"I'm sorry, Sam."

What else was there to say?

Samuel Goldwyn was always sensitive to changing trends and methods and fashion—whether he approved of them or not.

Those who deal with the mass audience tend to become cynical as they search for the lowest common denominator of appeal.

At one time there was general agreement in the Hollywood front offices that the average filmgoer had a twelve-year-old mind. But what is average? It has been truly observed, "The average man is unusual." And has not this mind aged across the years, along with everything and everyone else?

In any case, the collective mind of an audience is something else again. Whatever the shortcomings of individuals may be, when they are bound together in the shoulder-to-shoulder theatre experience they become one, great, sensitive supermind.

In this important matter Goldwyn did not run with the pack. Having long been himself a member of the mass, he had respect and admiration for it.

He retained much of his innocence, which may well have been the principal reason for his lasting success. Whatever his shortcomings—intellectual, moral, or emotional—his love affair with people as a whole flourished until his death at ninety-two.

His philosophy was expressed in my presence one evening.

Harold Mirisch had invited a group of friends to a private preview at his home. The film was *The Thomas Crown Affair,* starring Steve McQueen and Faye Dunaway.

After dinner, we gathered in the projection room. Mirisch, a nervous man, rose, faced the small audience, and began a complex introductory speech. He explained that what we were about to see was a rough-cut, that the opening of the film was still in the cutting room being assembled by the director, Norman Jewison.

"But let me explain it to you the best I can," said Harold, and began a long, involved dissertation on the subject of the preparations for a bank robbery.

Billy Wilder interrupted. "But it sounds like a lot of boring exposition, Harold. You really think you need all that? On the front of the picture?"

"Yes," said Harold, tightly. "I'm *sure* we do."

"Why?"

"Because it's a very complicated plot with a lot of characters and we're worried the public won't understand it."

"Sit down, Harold," said Samuel Goldwyn. "And stop worrying. The public is f'Chrissake smarter than *we* are!"